PENGUIN BOOKS

ASPECTS OF AFRICA

With the advent of the 1990s, South Africa helped to complete a cycle in Africa's long history: the continent was freed of the 'rigours if not the scars' of European domination. Suddenly, borders were opened and all of Africa became accessible to South Africans — as if they had at last been released into their broader home.

Aspects of Africa is South African travel writer David Robbins' account of visits he made to Namibia, Zimbabwe, Zambia, Malawi, Zaire, Tanzania (including Zanzibar), Kenya, Rwanda and Uganda. It is a vivid evocation of people, places and themes, from Namibia's relaxed capital city of Windhoek to the tragedy of Rwanda; from the tensions of Kinshasa to the heat and silence of Olduvai.

Robbins does not claim to provide a definitive overview. His approach is intentionally narrower and deeper and his penetrating yet sensitive writing uncovers the often startling images inherent in a continent whose vastness and complexities continue to fascinate and perplex. Here is an essentially African writer involved in some of the realities of his 'broader home'.

David Robbins was born in East London in the Eastern Cape in 1940. *Aspects of Africa* is his seventh book. *The 29th Parallel*, first published in 1986 and reprinted by Penguin Books in 1990, earned him South Africa's prestigious CNA Literary Award, confirming his reputation as the country's most respected travel writer.

GW00482843

ASPECTS OF AFRICA

David Robbins

PENGUIN BOOKS

PENGUIN BOOKS

Published by the Penguin Group
27 Wrights Lane, London W8 5TZ, England
Viking Penguin, a division of Penguin Books USA Inc, 375 Hudson
Street, New York, New York 10014, USA
Penguin Books Australia Ltd, Ringwood, Victoria, Australia
Penguin Books Canada Ltd, 10 Alcorn Avenue, Toronto, Ontario,
Canada M4V 3B2
Penguin Books (NZ) Ltd, 182-190 Wairau Road, Auckland 10, New
Zealand
Penguin Books South Africa (Pty) Ltd, Pallinghurst Road, Parktown,
South Africa 2193

Penguin Books South Africa (Pty) Ltd, Registered Offices: 20 Wood-
lands Drive, Woodmead, Sandton 2128

First published by Viking 1995
Published in Penguin Books 1996

ISBN 0 140 26281 4

Typeset by Iskova Image Setting in 10.5 on 12 point Times Roman
Cover design and map by Hadaway Illustration & Design
Cover photograph taken at Benaco Refugee Camp, Rwanda, by David
Gilkey (South Light Photo Agency & Library)
Printed and bound by Interpak, Natal

For Kathy,
friend and inspiration

Contents

Acknowledgements

Much of the material for this book was collected while the author was being sponsored by the Henry J Kaiser Family Foundation (USA) to write on African health issues for *The Star* newspaper in Johannesburg. The Foundation's contribution to the considerable amount of travel involved is gratefully acknowledged. Others who assisted in this regard were Sabena Belgian World Airlines, Barlow Rand Limited and Free Spirit Adventures.

1

Finding the Cause

The cardinal object of his (General Smuts's) policy was the creation of 'a British confederation of African states'. The response of the Nationalist leaders... was to denounce Smuts as 'the apostle of a black Kaffir state... extending from the Cape to Egypt'.

— Professor Bruce Murray, *A New Illustrated History of South Africa,* 1986.

There had never been very much to the south of us down there in the frozen places. These words — their exact intent — I had carried with me from my childhood in South Africa, when maps had shown that the world was all too clearly far away to the north. The irony in later years, sojourning in this northern world, was that the reverse became true. So I went down to the bottom edge of Europe one lengthy summer to catch a glimpse of the old continent. Difficult to acknowledge such whimsy; but as difficult to ignore the pull of a place which had begun to assume the essential characteristics of home.

Perhaps the heat and hues of Barcelona had brought me to this ebb. The extravagant sunlight striking through narrow streets, the dipping lines of washing enlivening the grime of venerable walls, windows behind wrought-iron balconies, crooked shutters flung wide open, doorways with dirty children, warm evenings and warm shouts, men talking loudly of the genius of Catalan. 'Bull fighting, hah! Go to Andalusia for that. We know nothing about el torros here. Remember that we in Catalan belong to Europe; Andalusia is to the south, it is poor, it belongs to Africa.' Even these Spanish prejudices lured me.

Yet the lure had been everywhere in Europe. Earlier that summer and much further north, someone with slightly blue hair and a cigarette holder had said to me: 'Take Paris. It is terrible there now. I am so angry about it. I have been there just now — the first time in eleven years — and there was Arabic or something scribbled all over a sign needed by tourists. I could not read it. It is a disgrace. All the West Africans and Algerians. Paris is so dirty, and it is sitting on a time bomb. So is England. England is full of blacks now. Brussels also. These places are sitting on time bombs.'

In Brussels, I drove with a man named Claude into that wedge of city in the vicinity of the railway station called du Midi which Belgians speak of as the Sahara. Claude had been anxious enough to show me the sights, but he had not wanted to take me into the Sahara. 'There is not much to see,' he said in his formal way, 'and sometimes it is quite rough.'

We drove for half an afternoon in other directions in Claude's stylish car. His pride in the vehicle had been immediately apparent. 'My luxury,' he called it. He demonstrated the quality of the sound system; he told me about the power steering; he toyed with the electrically operated windows and sun-roof; he smoked thin brown cigarettes, and frequently wiped, like a gesture of obsession, flecks of ash from the moulded dashboard.

He began to point out various landmarks: the Belgian parliament; the King's city palace, a large building with long rows of identical windows marking each floor; and here a statue of a bearded man on a horse, Leopold II, the 19th-century monarch who had been obsessed with Africa and the idea of empire.

We drove through expensive shopping in the Sablon and later stopped on a wide square before the monumental architecture of the city's Palace of Justice. From the low parapet on the western side of the square, we were able to look out over a wide section of the city, the occasional high-rise and church spire punctuating the general sprawl. Claude described a wedge of this view with his arms and said with a faint grimness: 'It's in there.'

As we drove towards it, I wondered suddenly whether my host felt at all nervous, but Claude's manner and expression seemed more determined than unsure, as if he had resigned himself to doing something faintly unpleasant. Perhaps the truth was simply a conviction in Claude that the Sahara ought not to be the concern of a tourist to his beautiful and historic city.

'Typical Arab women,' Claude said now, pointing to figures in black robes, faces covered but for the eyes. The streets had become more populated, the faces and limbs revealing the browns and deep olive hues of North Africa. 'Moroccans and Algerians, mostly,' he added.

Children played in the narrower streets, while their elders sat in doorways, watching. I saw a black youth lying on the ledge of a shop window, his slightly hostile eyes turned to mine. The sign above the shop was in Arabic. A group of men in fezzes stood at a street corner, tassels swaying as they talked. In some places, litter lay strewn across pavements and piled up in the gutters. The houses rose hard against the edges of narrow streets to three or four storeys. I noticed a few boarded-up windows and doors, some broken panes of glass; otherwise the buildings seemed in reasonable repair.

'No, they aren't,' Claude said, shaking his head. 'You should see at the back and inside. They're falling down.'

'Can we stop and walk around a bit?'

Claude ignored the request, saying suddenly instead: 'There's a stolen car.' He pointed to a vehicle with the boot and bonnet open, a policeman, notebook in hand, standing nearby. Claude slowed his car to walking pace, and signalled a greeting to the policeman when he looked up.

'It can be very dangerous to walk here at night,' he said. 'Youths of fourteen to seventeen, they form gangs and make robberies and muggings. The police go on horseback here, in pairs, for safety.'

Something rolled smoking into a gutter ahead of the car. There was a loud bang, then a scream of laughter. Claude's small eyes were inscrutable as he drove past some men in tattered shirts and hands in their pockets. Others drank and played cards at a rough table outside a shop with dirty windows.

'Do you think someone deliberately threw that cracker at your car?'

Claude snorted. 'They must not touch my car.' Then, after a moment: 'Is this enough? Can we go back to Europe? I would like to take you for a drink.' And as he drove in this new direction, Claude's mood lightened. 'See how clean,' he commented, 'where the Belgians live?'

That evening, in these cleaner parts, I saw a woman wrapped entirely in black cloth with only her eyes and hands revealed, a North African with gnarled and begging hands, her plight written on a piece of cardboard propped up on the pavement beside her.

Outside Brussels, on the far side of a forest and expanses of rich grass studded with daisies, I came upon a large building set in elaborate gardens: the Royal Museum of Central Africa. Strange, the juxtaposition of Africa's rough and earthy things with the high spaces — and extravagance and sense of immutability — of Europe's early 20th-century architecture. In the central circular hall I found marble columns and a domed ceiling which soared away to end in a skylight at least ten metres in diameter; and at ground level an exhibition from a development project in Zaire showed exuberant child art, models of motor vehicles made from tin and wood and wire, a row of modern-day clay fetishes with feathers in heads and beads pressed in for eyes.

In one of the display halls hung the Panorama du Congo, a large triptych painted in 1911. The first panel depicted primitive people fishing with open-weave baskets in the rapids of a big river; in the centre panel a crowd of Africans stood listening to a white man in pith helmet and leggings; and the final painting showed a railway being constructed by crowds of lifting, carrying, crouching black men.

The museum had been thoughtfully laid out. The various halls — there were around twenty of them — each showed a specific aspect of the African continent: its geological formation, its volcanoes, its scenery, its flora, its insects and fish and snakes, its birds and mammals, and of course its people. Skeletons in glass cases illustrated the shift from primate to early man, a process which had probably occurred in Africa several million years ago. There were early stone-age relics, while other cases showed the middle stone age, as well as the neolithic and iron age in Africa. Copper crosses from Katanga, the currency of an old civilisation; details of smelting kilns; a skeleton laid out, bangles on its wrists and ankles, and pots of food for the long journey to the place of the ancestors; intricate carving from the 12th and 13th centuries.

And here were sprites and charms, and icons for graves, and clay and grass-work figures, all crowding the glass cases in the silent halls. I stood silently, listening for a faint echo of drums.

There were other moments as compelling. In Paris, I rented a room on the second floor of a hotel in a street called le Goff. A North African woman in a Western-style blouse and ankle-length skirt had carried up my luggage and unlocked the door for me. She had great reservoirs of unhappiness etched into her face. On the narrow stairs one night I came upon her sitting on the landing which gave access to my room, surrounded by crumpled tissues and cigarettes she had tried to light. She looked up at me with glazed and red-rimmed eyes, sightless eyes almost. In the morning, the tissues and the broken cigarettes had all been cleared away. No trace at all, except perhaps a few spill marks on the carpet, of what she had been through.

This consciousness of Africa became a minor irritant to me during my time in Europe, emerging at unexpected moments and demanding to be assuaged. More so in Barcelona where the weather was hot and the light harsh and familiar, and where men boasted that they were not like the Andalusians who were regrettably of Africa. I went south.

Poppies grew in profusion by the side of the railway, and later I saw orange plantations, huge fields of maize, and occasional towns, but dilapidated, houses subsiding into dusty ground, broken balconies, collapsed roofs; empty towns, everyone gone to the cities. Through high country then — jagged rocks flung upwards in wild configurations, grasses blowing on steep hillsides, ravines of dense green bush — and down into the wide plain of the Guadalquivir, with endless olive groves on the hills, sudden flourishings of aloes, of prickly pears, of gum trees, reminiscent of South Africa, real Kaffir country as southern Spain has sometimes been described, with the train smelling powerfully of garlic and urine by the time we got to Seville in a sunlit evening filled with the hubbub of arrival and greeting and all those demonstrative embraces.

On the bus in the morning we travelled a highway which reached through flat fields of sunflowers stretching away on either side, and then a long avenue of gum trees outside Jerez, and beyond this avenue the bus turned left and drove into hills. A man on horseback watched as we passed; enormous dandelions grew by the roadside; ploughed fields covered whole hillsides; and white flowers as big as plates swarmed in a damp depression. The road climbed now through hills scattered with darker bush, rock outcrops at the summits, and set against their lower slopes stood farmsteads, clustered buildings with white walls beneath terracotta tiles, a gathering of horses with tails swishing, an old man in pursuit of two donkeys; and now a hedge of prickly pears filled with yellow flowers, and beyond it a field of grass shining in a purple sheen. The verges of the road were like long strips of vivid garden in the morning sun.

Then a sudden town in the hills where the bus stopped for a few moments: old men under orange trees; a collection of pale houses sloping steeply upwards from the road. Then on into bush country, black-trunked trees crowding the hills, with slabs and mounds of sheer rock thrusting out at the top, big bald faces of grey rock dominating the landscape now, until the bus came round a corner and there we saw in the distance the biggest rock of all, jutting out into the sea, white high-rise buildings bristling about its base.

Closer at hand, a Spanish coastal town, rubbish blowing in the gutters, neon signs and a conglomeration of white and pale brown people under a deep veranda where the bus stopped. Narrow streets descended steeply to the harbour. On the far side of a wide bay, the outline of Gibraltar looked cool and massive in a slight haze. On the quays of the Spanish town I found dark faces, close-set eyes, narrow shoulders jostling past. A great fluttering of gulls adorned the sterns of fishing boats. On the seaward side, the vessels were bigger; and white horses scurried on the surface of water coloured deep blue, almost cobalt in its intensity. A few freighters were passing through the Strait, while pleasure cruisers rode the swell closer to the shore.

And here was a ferry coming in from Africa, white water at its bows, a smudge of black from its funnel. And beyond the vessel, in the haze on the far side of the Strait, lay a range of grey mountains. That was all.

But it reminded me of the southern end, and those other mountains of harsh grey rock. These mountains were the extremities of a continent. Always in my boyhood it had lain piled to the north. Now it lay to the south. I could see the outline of Africa clearly in my mind, and my position in relation to it, first at the southern end, now here, as the ferry turned sideways and subsided against the quay. But what lay between the two extremities? What existed in the void?

I watched the passengers coming off the ferry in a long line: men with close-set eyes, poor people with mounds of luggage, faces bristling with black stubble, faces the colour of teak, women in flowing black costumes with only their eyes visible. Slowly they filed off the ferry, passing groups of policemen and other officials who stood with their boots on tables or chairs, elbows on knees. Once or twice, the policemen drew someone from the line, looked at papers, asked questions, opened bags. Some of the passengers seemed bewildered. A small man — black-spotted cloth wrapped loosely about his head and mouth, a cardboard suitcase gripped in his hand — looked wildly about him in the terminal building as if searching for help. A man from the desert perhaps, at the beginning of his first foray into Europe. And those women in black head-dress, were they destined to beg for their survival one day in the streets of Brussels, or to sit with their sadness and broken cigarettes on the stairs of shabby French hotels?

I saw them again at the railway station, these North Africans waiting for trains to take them to the opulent cities of Western Europe. They sat in groups or lay on the floor of the dank and unswept station hall. Their luggage was sometimes no more than cloth bundles and bulging plastic bags. These Berbers from the Maghreb, what reality did they represent? Through such questions I began to look into the African void, that space between the two extremities.

It was there, the tumultuous continent, just across the blue water with the small white horses dancing in the sunlight. It was here, in the station, personified in these Berbers looking like migrant workers at the end of a South African weekend, coming along the platform in droves, desert men in their robes with hoods down, eyes searching. An old woman struggling with luggage, the little wheels of her suitcase grinding sideways against the platform; young men laughing under the weight of bags and rucksacks, forcing through crowds on to the train.

And as the train moved, a great cheer went up. Arms thrust bristling through windows; people surged forward to touch hands, to clasp; and then the waving began, like an urgent fluttering of disturbed birds, as the train moved out into the muddle of the town. On one of the curves I had a last glimpse of the Strait and of those harsh grey mountains on the farther shore.

I heard singing on the train. It seemed like a sense of momentous times, at once joyous and a lament. But it was the void beyond the song, and beyond the mountains, which engaged my mind. I sat on the migrant workers' train as it wound up and away from the coast, and searched back through my memory for the beginning point once more.

There was never very much to the south of us, except the end of our country and of course the increasingly cold oceans beyond. Easy enough to see, poring over atlases, that the world lay to the north. Since the cartographer's convention was to place north at the top, the world was inevitably piled above us. Below, there seemed only to be a foundation of emptiness and ice; above, the full weight of a bulky continent rested on the rocks of our southernmost shores. But could these rocks by themselves hold so much geography in place? When I heard what the French had done at Suez, cutting the whole of Africa so dangerously adrift, I expected that the sheer mass of the western bulge would pull the continent over, and as it fell it would crash into Brazil, snapping South America off at its umbilical cord, and then the world would never be the same again.

These youthful excesses were tempered somewhat by my first sight of Pangaea, earth's early continent, with the clear shape of Africa in the centre. When 175 million years ago this huge land mass began to drift, giving rise to northern Laurasia and southern Gondwana, Africa had given the impression of staying more or less in the same place, while South America, Madagascar, Antarctica and Australia slowly drifted away. This African constancy was reassuring. Our continent had stood upright, balancing on those most southerly rocks, for millions of millennia.

But was it our continent? Naturally enough, as white South Africans, we had lived in that double isolation so characteristic of the colonial experience. There was the isolation from cultural precedents, that sense of being remote from a central anchoring point; and also the deeper isolation from the land on which we lived.

Since the first isolation had been the easier to deal with, we tended to look initially towards Europe. The outline of Africa during those days served largely to delineate the distance between our own remoteness and our supposed metropole. While we sailed around it or flew over it, the great continent itself lay in another reality, waiting to claim us. And in the end, after our linkages with Europe had been explored and in a sense assuaged, and after I had looked at the harsh mountains on the other side of the cobalt-coloured straits, this simpler claiming began.

But it was not as simple as it might have been. A perception widely held in our country was that Africa was essentially somewhere else, not actually underneath our feet; or that, yes, technically, it was beneath our feet, but that above it we had somehow managed to establish like a low mist down here at the bottom of the edifice, at the balancing point, something that was not African at all. We were, so the cliché attempted to persuade, a bastion of Western civilisation in need of protection in a continent inimical to any civilisation at all.

As colonialism collapsed, so the need for protection increased. South Africans watched without too much alarm the countries of the western bulge slide into independence. These places were far away. So was the Belgian Congo. Yet the events in central Africa in 1960 were promenaded as horrifying confirmation of what white people in our country already knew. The savagery of Africa must be held at bay; our Western values must be protected. The danger was primarily one of being overwhelmed.

But for how long could the quiescence within the bastion remain immune to the clamour rushing down from the north? In truth, not long. However tightly our borders were sealed with soldiers and wire, something of the northern reality came across in a vague quality of light, or sailed in the air like the smell of dust at evening, under which the rigid fences seemed irrelevant. African nationalism raised its fist in our midst. Yet in practical terms such merging was like a one-way street. We in the bastion could not easily go into Africa because most of the continent, in retaliation against our arrogance, now held us at bay.

Time enough and to spare, then, to attempt an understanding of this huge shape above us on the map. Beyond the smell of dust and the high red light of evening which, in our imaginations at any rate, was not quite like our own dust and light, there predominated two popular theories. Firstly, that beyond the Limpopo only muddle and corruption, and sometimes bloody chaos, reigned. This was a refinement of the theory concerning the dangers of the huge black tide. And secondly, that Africa would have been altogether idyllic had it not been for the great scourges of slavery and colonial partition and, more latterly, the economic imperatives and greed of neo-colonialism and its many allies in the African ruling classes. This was a reaction to the theory of the savage black tide, and by itself as unsatisfying.

Despite our self-inflicted isolation, the outline of Africa had slowly begun to fill up for me. For centuries the continent had been a blank of darkness to Western eyes, even its geography uncharted. Well into the 20th century, Africa had habitually been described as an area of barbarism without history through which, at last, that broad red British pathway had led from Cape to Cairo, promising a railway if nothing else, and then disappearing even more rapidly than it had appeared, as had the colours of the French and other colonial powers as well. These last events, the independence of country after country, had invaded my teens and early twenties. But an essential part of the filling up was at another level entirely.

I saw the artefacts from Tutankhamun's tomb in London: those golden treasures which had been crafted in the north-east corner of our continent well over a thousand years before the birth of Christ. Certainly, I heard the claims of those who urged that ancient Egypt belonged more surely to the Middle East than to Africa. Whatever Egypt's pedigree, however, its influence seeped steadily south. When the knowledge of iron came to Egypt via its defeat by Assyria nearly seven hundred years before Christ, it was perhaps along the Nile, spreading south through the succession of cataracts, that this knowledge was transmitted first to Nubia and Axum, ancient kingdoms in present-day Sudan and Ethiopia, and thence west across the grasslands of the Sahel to emerge at Nok in central Nigeria three or four centuries later.

Or had it come across the Sahara from places like Carthage, around two hundred years earlier? Perhaps the ancient caravans had carried such dynamic technology. The caravans might have stopped at the Tigidit Escarpment, a thousand kilometres to the north of Nok, where people had smelted copper and then iron when the Sahara was still grassland. Or could the vital technology have developed in sub-Saharan Africa itself, at Katuruka on the western shores of Lake Victoria?

There seemed to be no direct answers, much less simple ones. Yet it appeared probable, from what I read, that as the Sahara gradually dried, people were forced down into the Sahel, carrying or encountering as they went the technology of iron and the attendant concept of farming. Large population movements ensued.

It was certainly from these quarters in West Africa, not long before the birth of Christ, that the great migrations of the iron-age Bantu had begun. They descended into the Central African forests, and out on to the open country to the south and east, defeating or circumventing or assimilating the stone-age Pygmies and Khoisan as they went. By the year AD 750, iron-age farming communities were established deep inside the territory later to be called South Africa, especially along the eastern and southern seaboard; and it was here, after another one thousand years, that these farming communities encountered the vanguard of European settlement as it gradually expanded from the halfway station which the Dutch had established at the Cape of Good Hope in 1652.

These were enthralling continuities, but there were others. The most ancient included the Olduvai Gorge and other places in the Great Rift Valley, sites for that slow emergence of humanity at last: the hunter-gatherers becoming herders, the herders learning cultivation; great empires emerging in the Sahel in the first millennium AD: Ghana, Songhay, Kanem, and Mali. And then the trans-Saharan intercourse; the impact of Islam on both sides of the desert, and later (from about AD 1000) down the east coast where Muslim traders established a series of settlements from Mogadishu in the north to Zanzibar and Kilwa in the south. Only later did Europe appear in the form of Portuguese mariners, to be followed by traders, and then soldiers. By the end of the 16th century, Portugal dominated sizeable areas on the east and west coasts of central and southern Africa. Although they suffered severe defeats in many areas, they were to stay a long time, leaving only in the mid-1970s after their increasingly expensive and wasteful adventures in Africa had brought revolution to their European home.

From approximately this time (that of the Portuguese retreat) radical changes began to overtake South Africa. Through the nearly two decades of upheaval and repression and renewed upheaval which followed the outburst at Soweto in 1976, there emerged an inescapable sense that Africa was drawing near. Old assumptions about the essential differences between our continent and our country, between the bastion and the huge black tide, began to wither away.

All through the 1980s, the departures boards at South African airports showed few African destinations. This was the manifestation of our dogged assertion, and the African reaction to it, that we were not of the continent. But this perception, and the names on the boards, changed with the advent of the 1990s. South Africa could afford to live the lie no longer; and at last it turned its bloodied face towards the risks and plentiful euphorias which would mark its first clumsy embrace of democracy.

Of course, in pursuing this new direction, South Africa helped to complete a cycle in the continent's long history: Africa had now everywhere shrugged off the rigours if not the scars of European domination. At the same time, as in some joyous rite, the old barriers were lowered and all Africa was suddenly accessible. It was as if we had at last been released into our broader home.

In this way, that presence to the north, the light and dust and ancient continuity of it, became my neighbourhood. What at first had been a largely forbidden region over which I flew and about which I read, now took on a different hue. Travel in Africa seemed inevitable. I went to various parts of it then to take the tactile experience of being there; and in this way, I climbed up into the continent which had always loomed above me on those boyhood maps.

2

Legacies

We say, down with colonialism and down with the
notorious Berlin Conference and all their stinking legacies
in Namibia.

— Theo-Ben Gurirab, Namibian Minister of Foreign
Affairs. Quoted in the *Namib Times* in February 1994.

A vigorous storm marked my first afternoon in Namibia's
capital city. At first some dust and rubbish were
whipped up, and then the rain lashed down, turning the roads
on which we drove to mud. People told me there had been a
great deal of rain that summer, in Windhoek and generally
throughout the country. This normally arid place, held in by
deserts to the east and west, lay in a luxury of growth. And
later I was to see diminutive grass growing like a miracle in
the crystal sand of the Namib for the first time in a decade,
sprung up simply because the air was more moist than usual.

But to begin with, from the aircraft, I had watched the
grey-brown Kalahari spread forward into pale green tints;
and then as we landed, the pilot said: 'Look to the right.
There's still water in that river from the downpour last night.'
An unusual sight, the shining serpent between those sandy
banks and verdant bushes all around. Verdant hills, too,
cradling the capital city, and the piling up of those clouds,
with sunlight slanting through to catch the faces of buildings
and make them brilliant sometimes, especially when the

clouds beyond went black and thundered as the storm developed.

I had been to the country before, when blue-clad United Nations soldiers had filled the streets and the future was on everyone's lips. I had driven in without the use of a passport then, merely crossing an invisible line which had demarcated South Africa from what for many years had been considered no more than a fifth South African province. Now I was coming to an independent country. People wanted to talk to me about the independence celebrations of 1990 and events since then. The name of Windhoek's main thoroughfare, for example, had been changed from Kaiserstrasse to Independence Avenue; and while I was there the first Namibian currency appeared, symbol of the fledgling state's increasing economic independence.

On the surface, though, not much had changed. The old colonial statuary remained, in particular Kurt von Francois, a dapper man with moustache and a wide hat, the right-side brim raised and attached quite jauntily to the crown, and he leaned with a slight swagger on his sword.

According to the inscription, Von Francois had founded Windhoek in 1890. Of course, the site had been inhabited by others before him, at first Hereros and their cattle, and then a group of well-armed Nama people. The Namas' most famous leader, Hendrik Witbooi, had found his way on to the new Namibian dollar note, while for the moment his first white adversary remained on his plinth.

I discovered what looked like a hornets' nest built behind Von Francois' left ear. This addition to the statue possessed a certain historical veracity, especially in view of what the Germans unsuspectingly stirred up in this apparently empty territory, even though Von Francois himself did not bear the brunt of it. Resistance to the German colonisation by both Herero and Nama had been unexpectedly fierce, ending for the Hereros in terrible genocide, and for the Namas finally only through heavy military defeat and incarceration.

In spite of the disappearance of some original street names, the atmosphere of this small city remained quite determinedly German. In Independence Avenue itself, a few ornate façades, steep roofs and dormer windows testified to this. More recent additions continued the Teutonic tradition. A smart new shopping precinct had been erected since my last visit, its flavour depending on paved and cobbled walkways, some evidence of dark imitation timber built into plaster façades, the arrangement of roofing over windows, and the way upper storeys overhung the ground floor sometimes. Even in Katutura I came across a newly built police station with a roof pitched steeply enough to shed the heaviest snowstorms.

Katutura lay sprawled away to the north west of Windhoek's central parts. In pre-independence parlance, these dusty places would have been the black townships, for Namibia was a country which had inherited South Africa's obsession with race, and Windhoek had been planned as an apartheid city: whites here, coloureds there, blacks in Katutura.

A missionary doctor named Eric, who would be my host while I was in Windhoek, took me to one place in Katutura where the doors of houses still bore the marks of ethnic classification. Crudely painted Os for Ovambos, Ds for Damaras, goal-posts for Hereros, and so on. There were twelve ethnic divisions in Namibia, thirteen including a category marked 'other', all adding up to a feast of anxiety for the engulfed white mind.

'But of course,' Eric said, 'most apartheid legislation fell away in 1976, and attempts to divide living areas along ethnic lines were scrapped. The South Africans were trying to ease international pressure regarding their mandate over South West. An interesting thing about 1976 — which of course was the year of the Soweto uprising in South Africa — was that Sowetos sprang up all over the country. There's a Soweto in Katutura. It was a way of indicating that Namibian blacks shared the aspirations of their South African counterparts.'

Extraneous involvement in what had been a German colony since 1884 began in 1915 when South Africa, encouraged by Great Britain, overwhelmed the colonial forces stationed there. After the war, the League of Nations entrusted South Africa with the administration of the country. Other German colonies were disposed of in the same way: with Tanganyika handed to Britain, Rwanda and Burundi to Belgium, Cameroon to France, and Togoland divided between France and Britain.

After World War II, the newly formed United Nations turned down a South African request to annex the territory. South Africa nevertheless proceeded in this direction. By 1949 the whites of the old German colony were granted direct representation in the South African legislative system. By 1966, however, internal resistance among the territory's indigenous people had developed into armed struggle. But the South Africans were obduracy itself, turning ruthlessly on any opposition to their designs and ignoring an International Court of Justice ruling (in 1971) that they should immediately withdraw from South West Africa, or Namibia as it was by then called.

So another war had escalated in southern Africa, to go with the wars being fought in Angola, Rhodesia and Mozambique. The 1960s and 1970s were stark with war, as the European hold on the subcontinent, appearing reasonably firm for a few meagre decades, was broken: first in the Portuguese colonies, then in Rhodesia, and finally in Namibia. Other wars followed, particularly the civil conflicts in Mozambique and Angola which tore at the entrails of communities already exhausted by tumult and danger. Now, only Angola was embroiled in fighting, while to the south, in my own country, the dense clouds of violence seemed about to part for the miracle of a new beginning. Our part of the world was nearly at peace at last. And in the Katutura streets people waved sometimes.

Eric smiled as he returned these greetings. 'I must tell you that our independence celebrations were remarkable. I still think of them. People were dancing in the streets for days afterwards. In many ways, the mood still persists four years later.'

He was a man in his late forties, a South African who had been living in Windhoek for the past decade. But he seemed mercifully free of the notion that black people needed to be assisted out of some unsatisfactory state. Eric seemed too human a man for such censoriousness. The fine lines which splayed on to his temples when he smiled, and the warmth and expressiveness of eyes which looked slightly tired behind the lenses of his spectacles, expressed a deeper and more complex engagement with Africa than simply as a place which needed saving from itself. But perhaps this was because he had been born here.

We drove from point to point in Katutura, with Eric showing and explaining the settings of the various stages of urbanisation. Here were the site-and-service areas, then the suburbs of basic housing, which all lay on the northern perimeters of the urban sprawl. Shacks proliferated; women talked at communal taps; men sat in the shade of low trees. And above this whole untidy vision of people living in close proximity − the stones and pumpkins holding down roofs, taxis bouncing through the potholes in the road, children shouting out as we passed − the southern sky went black and seemed to fly towards us, and we could see it raining in the hills which ringed the town.

Eric said: 'The whole process − urbanisation, I mean − is out in the open. That's the important thing now. Yes, there's quite a bit of foreign investment in the housing. Also shacks are springing up everywhere. But they're officially recognised. There's guidance now from the state, rather than the censure and prohibition of pre-independence days. The effect of this is that the whole urbanisation process has been taken out of the hands of criminals. You know the sort of thing. Exorbitant prices to settle in this or that area; and then the extraction of regular protection money for the right to continue living there . . .'

And here was Single Quarters, he said, a low shanty town where people from the north, particularly from Ovamboland near the Angolan border, lived when they first came in search of work. Now the narrow roadways and the open spaces grew suddenly thick with dust blowing through and men holding down tarpaulins in the wind. A figure disengaged from this activity and ran towards the car, calling out a greeting with a flash of congenial teeth. Eric laughed and clasped a big black hand while dust billowed in through the open window of the car.

Then the rain burst down into the dust of Katutura, reducing it in seconds to glistening mud. Streams of water surged in the ruts and runnels of the roads. Figures bent low as they ran for cover between the sagging shacks of the Single Quarters. We sat looking out at this frantic view which blurred and cleared repeatedly in the swing of the windscreen wipers. For a few moments the noise of the rain was too great for talking.

I awoke the following morning to the sound of steady rain on corrugated iron, and to the peal of bells which reached me thinly through wet air. 'The Dutch Reformed Church,' Eric told me later.

It struck me as a mark of some tenacity, that these bells still pealed. I had encountered some Afrikaner Namibians on the aircraft. One of them had a flaring ginger beard and a black ribbon tied around his head; another man, considerably younger, wore a yellow golfing cap; the third had pale blue eyes and a head so shorn that it was almost bereft of hair. They were, with cans of beer in their hands, completely unabashed. They spoke to everyone. They began to make a nuisance of themselves, especially with the long-suffering air hostesses. They stood drinking in the aisle, looking about them with slightly bloodshot smiles. They addressed as 'the Arab' a stout Indian who tried to pass. 'This Arab wants to get through,' they said among themselves in Afrikaans. And to the Indian: 'If you pull in your stomach slightly, it will be much easier.'

Were these men part of the Afrikaner generation which would take their language, their religion, their whole apparatus of Western civilisation, to irrelevance and obscurity in Namibia? The answer was clearly provided by the undertones of defiance in the men's behaviour. It seemed that they stood almost the whole distance between Johannesburg and Windhoek, mainly so that they could be seen and their implicit statement heard: we are still here, we are not yet defeated.

Of course, their language had immediately been rejected by an independent Namibia and English chosen as the official medium, even though English had never been spoken by any but a minority. Nor had England or the British Empire ever had much to do with Namibia, except the small enclave called Walvis Bay, the country's only deep water port. As part of the absurdities of the European partition of Africa, Walvis Bay had remained British (and later South African) while the rest of the territory had become German. Even after Namibian independence, South Africa had somewhat perversely retained Walvis Bay. But not for ever. Now the harbour town and the small piece of desert surrounding it was to be incorporated — or reincorporated, as many Namibians styled it — into the territory which it had in any case served for so long.

Eric's view of the language issue he expressed in this way: 'I think there can be no doubt that Afrikaans is seen as the language of the oppressor. Yes, everyone speaks Afrikaans, not only white Afrikaners. Surely, German colonialism was brutal. But my feeling is that Africans have an amazing ability to forgive. They see the experience of the German yoke as something in the past. More difficult to forget are the long-term manipulations of the Afrikaners. There's been a fairly widespread rejection of Afrikaans since independence, even by people who own it as their home language.'

Ironically, though, the church service to which I accompanied Eric in Katutura later during that sodden morning was conducted entirely in Afrikaans.

The Evangelical Bible Church, built as a cluster of three hexagons, filled with the light of the slowly breaking weather, and with the scraping of metal chairs on brick flooring as the congregation settled. The singing was characterised by a definite slurring between the notes, as if the instinctive African musicality could never altogether accept the rigours and logicality of Western music. Rock of Ages was sung in this way in Afrikaans, with elaborately dressed children sitting on the steps to one side of the pulpit. One of the suits of the small boys had been adorned with a carnation, another with the neatly protruding corner of a handkerchief; and close by the chiffon extravagance of a small girl with white socks pulled just below small brown knees.

The congregation stood as they sang. They were (as Eric had informed me would be the case) for the most part dark-skinned Herero people, a few of lighter hue, and a few Europeans as well. I noticed the hair of women who occupied the pews in front of mine: long thick strands tied with ribbons, scraped back with headbands, or teased out in a dark and tightly curled mop.

Beyond a window, sunlight had broken through upon unmown grass, small Katutura houses in pastel shades, and a group of women in the distinctive Herero dress, Victorian in style, the making of which they had learned from the wives of early missionaries. Africans in bustle skirts with plentiful petticoats underneath, embroidered bodices above, and wrapped fabric headgear: they looked graceful and anachronistic, and also they constituted an unconscious acknowledgement of the power of European ideas in Africa. Within the church as well: the dogmatic tones of Christian theology — along with more general Western perceptions like individualism, work ethics, career paths and material possessions — still reverberated long after the European flags had disappeared.

After the service, groups of people stood talking in the church or in the newly emerged sunshine outside.

Eric introduced me to an elderly white woman, a lifelong missionary, who said: 'I was here at independence. It really was a good feeling. We were in Nigeria during their independence in 1960. We were in the bush, and I think most people weren't aware that it was happening. Mind you, I suppose in the remoter parts here, some people weren't aware either. Life has probably gone on very much as before.'

Nevertheless, the process of independence seemed still close to the surface of people's minds. Eban, a young Herero, reprimanded me gently when I asked who he had voted for in the elections. 'Look, it was a secret ballot,' he said, but with a friendly smile. 'All I can tell you is that I didn't vote Swapo. I'm part of the opposition: we are a multiparty democracy here. Now the opposition is criticising the Swapo government. Promises have not been kept. There is also a lot of waste.'

His face shone with intelligence and good humour. I asked him what he thought of Walvis Bay now becoming part of Namibia. His expression grew suddenly more serious. 'Look, it's good. It's right. But I hope there'll be no trouble. Friends in Swakopmund tell me there are gangs of Swapo people waiting to rob the whites in Walvis and then chase them out when the day comes.'

'Where would they chase them to?'

'Look, it's just what I've heard,' Eban said.

Someone else said: 'Yes, there is a lot of waste. There's over-spending now. There's also corruption. What is one to think when the president gets a jet aircraft worth more than fifty million? How long can the spending spree last? The honeymoon will have to end.'

Eban laughed, spreading out his arms to imitate an aeroplane.

'As missionaries, of course, we are against ancestor worship,' an Englishwoman with red hair told me. 'There is a vast difference between respect for the dead and the actual worship of them. This is what we try to teach. A minority deal with the difference intellectually. But the traditions are strong. Most people end up with a merging of African and Christian ideas.'

'Forty-one to Swapo; twenty-one to the opposition. That was in the 1989 elections. But the opposition has lost a lot of its force. Maybe we are drifting towards a one-party state. Maybe multiparty democracy is just too much trouble to sustain.'

I caught Eric's gaze upon me. He smiled apologetically, as if he held himself responsible, at least to some extent, for what everyone was saying. As we walked to his car, he pointed out a small aircraft flying well below the scattering clouds in its approach to Windhoek's Eros Airport.

'The Mission Aviation Fellowship,' he said. 'They've been flying supplies in and sometimes missionaries out of those Angolan areas worst hit by the upsurge in the civil war.'

Gert Hanekom had a round, heavy-jowled face, and fair hair combed back from his forehead. He told me he was 63. He lit cigarettes one after the other as we talked, and his smile was pleasant.

He said: 'I was here during the independence struggle. Of course, South West could not afford the border war. But then, after it was over, I began to wonder whether we could afford the peace. The northern parts of the country had been kept alive for years by the war. Millions of rands put in each day by the South African army up there. The peace affected our economy tremendously. After the war, there was a small benefit from the presence of all those United Nations people. But it didn't last long. Now these extra sources of income have gone, and we've had to learn to live without them.'

We sat on easy chairs in one corner of Hanekom's large office. His secretary brought in coffee. He looked across at me in his pleasant way, his eyes slightly narrowed in a haze of smoke.

'Now, after some lean years, we expect good growth into the foreseeable future. Nothing spectacular — unless of course we find oil. Prospectors are drilling off shore. Meanwhile, the general recovery of the world economy means a good market again for our diamonds and other raw materials. The rains mean that news from the agricultural sector will be good. And our manufacturing efforts will certainly be enhanced by the acquisition of Walvis Bay.

'The plan now,' he went on, 'is for a free trade zone in Walvis to encourage manufacturing and export. Walvis will become the major development region in Namibia, and a real boost to our manufacturing capacity.'

He spoke about foreign debt, pointing out that as a percentage of gross domestic product Namibia had less than half the debt which South Africa had. And if it wasn't for considerable pre-independence borrowing with which the new regime had been saddled, Namibia's debt would be minimal.

I said this made an interesting change for an African country.

'Oh, yes,' Hanekom responded with a certain energy. 'Some lessons have been learned. People are very conscious here of that African syndrome: the collapse. I think we are all working to avoid it. For that reason, our policy is not to borrow at all.'

And what about wasting the money that was available? I said I had heard stories about corruption and some lavish spending.

Hanekom laughed. 'Ag, the president's aeroplane.' Then he said more seriously: 'I agree there are definitely areas where money is being wasted. My job is to minimise it as much as possible. Percentage-wise, it's no worse than it was before independence. But we're more conscious of it now, with everyone waiting for the collapse.

'Take, for example, the misuse of government cars. This is a favourite topic in newspapers here.' He shrugged his shoulders. 'I agree it happens. We're doing our best to stop it. But have you thought? In a lot of countries you wouldn't know about any misuse because the cars carry ordinary number-plates. In Namibia, the plates are green, unmistakable. A good way of stopping the complaints would be to change the number-plates,' he added with a crooked smile as he held his lighter to a new cigarette.

'There are officials, even ministers, who are not as cost-conscious as I'd like them to be. But we are transparent at least, certainly with the number-plates. Before independence, let me tell you, corruption was rife. I could take you right now and show you a palace here in Windhoek, built by a farmer with a four per cent government loan.'

I asked why such a loan had been arranged.

Hanekom laughed, but offered no explanation. He said instead: 'I'm not saying things don't go wrong. But it's no worse than it was. That's my contention. Perhaps it's even better.'

He took a mouthful of coffee in a momentary silence.

I asked: 'What's it like being an Afrikaner in the cabinet of a black African government?'

He eyed me with a keen, half-amused expression. 'You know, I wasn't even a member of Swapo when I was first appointed. I was minister of agriculture, fisheries, water and rural development. I was one of two whites. Then about two years ago I was brought into finance. I'm now the only white minister in the cabinet.

'Now let me be honest with you. During the first two years there was a little bit of mistrust. The situation has changed though: now there is one hundred per cent trust and confidence. But it took time for them to accept me and for me to accept them. When I talk to these people now, I don't talk to black men, I talk to men.'

He leaned towards me, turning his head only to exhale. 'Last year I had the biggest fight of my life, and my adversaries were all fellow whites. They tried to destroy me politically, to get me kicked out as Finance Minister.

'The trouble started when I did a complete reform of our tax system. My mistake was to do too much in one year: I closed all the loopholes. I knew where they were because I had worked for years on the other side of the fence. Someone said in parliament, "it takes a thief to catch a thief", but afterwards he apologised.

'The farmers especially were enraged by what I had done. They staged a protest, driving their tractors into town with banners demanding my resignation. The President called me in. He said: "It's their democratic right to protest, but I'm standing right behind you." That afternoon, I got out of town. I went hunting with a few friends,' he said with a smile. 'To relax, you know. In the evening, the protest was on the television. The President phoned my wife and spoke to her for over forty minutes.

'He just kept reassuring her,' he added, and it was easy to see how this act of thoughtfulness had moved Hanekom at the time, and how it had changed something hitherto immutable at the centre of his life.

German tourists were plentiful, frequently ageing, and inevitably strung about with expensive-looking photographic equipment. Those who travelled in groups spoke in loud voices, and I often saw their dough-coloured faces behind the tinted windows of luxury buses, or descending steep steps from these vehicles into the searing sunlight and frequent rain of Windhoek at this time.

Tourists were plentiful in the historic Alte Feste fort. Originally built by Kurt von Francois, that dapper man still standing on his plinth in the centre of town, the fort now housed a museum, a curio shop and a restaurant of sorts where people liked to drink at tables set out on the deep veranda.

My attention was caught by the most recent exhibits: the pale blue berets worn by the United Nations personnel who had supervised the 1989 elections, and some of the political posters from that time. There were photographs of the first cabinet, including Gert Hanekom; and one of Prime Minister Geingob in an elaborate robe (a gift from Nigeria to mark Namibian independence, it appeared) and holding an ornamented staff which suddenly reminded me of Von

Francois' sword, and not dissimilarly held with the base resting on the ground. I had heard it said in Windhoek — but such things were not loudly uttered — that the easiest way of achieving a statue of Geingob, whose Ovambo name seemed close enough to the German for 'no head', was simply to decapitate the slightly swaggering Von Francois. But it struck me, as I looked at the proud artefacts (the coat of arms and the presidential seal) of the fledgling Namibian Republic, that the joke possessed a distinctly unpleasant flavour. It was a white man's joke, with undertones of carelessness, as if nothing mattered any more, as if some battle had been lost, leaving only the fatalistic expectation that Africa would start to break things soon enough. People were waiting for the collapse.

'Where is the service here?' said a loud voice in German. 'We have ordered beer but it has not come.' This from a man leaning back at the head of a table on the veranda, short-cropped hair, eyes like opaque blue glass; and then he lifted his video camera to capture the young blonde woman with a tray who hurried towards them.

But I went also to places where few tourists had any interest in going. In Windhoek's state hospital I met a quiet-spoken Afrikaner in a white coat with an assortment of pens protruding from the pocket. He spoke to me of the high birth rate in Namibia, the lowering death rate, the population increasing at three per cent each year. He looked tired. 'It's too high,' he said, swinging his stethoscope, 'the population growth. It's the same all over Africa. What are we saving these people for? So they can die later of starvation?' But he said it without emotion, as if his emotions had long ago been drained away.

I spoke to an attractive secretary in a government office. She wore a white trouser suit and her dark hair spilled down sumptuously over her shoulders. She told me she had been born in Rehoboth, south of Windhoek. Then her family had moved to Swakopmund, a coastal town just to the north of the Walvis Bay enclave, where she had gone to school.

'My family is still there. Now at the end of the month I am going home. I am going for the Walvis Bay celebrations. Oh, it's going to be a very big party.'

The winsome smile; the dark eyes and accentuated eyebrows. Then she spoke on the telephone, running her fingers absently through her hair. She was a Rehoboth Baster, baster being Afrikaans for bastard or half-caste. Yet she was a young woman whose ancestry seemed hardly to matter any more.

Upstairs, a black bureaucrat shook his head, saying there was no definite Africanisation policy in Namibia, although one of affirmative action was being pursued. 'Most of the directors in this department are now women,' he said. He had slow-moving eyes, which he sometimes closed to gather his thoughts before he spoke.

He explained that the civil service had been dominated by Afrikaner males. It was wise to learn from them, and then to replace them when they left 'of their own accord', he added scrupulously.

'Yes, there were some problems at the beginning,' he said. 'There seemed to be a definite sense of resistance. It was a subtle type of thing. There was a gut feeling that some white civil servants were not wanting change, and that they were wanting the new dispensation to fail. We had to be very vigilant on this issue, especially in outlying areas where people are still sometimes living in the style and with the ideologies of the 1950s. But we have tried to be fair. We have promoted some white civil servants on merit since independence. But at the same time let me admit freely that more affirmative action is needed,' he added, his slow eyes moving across my face.

I went to lunch with one of those white civil servants who had been promoted since independence. He told me that more than fifty per cent of the administration was now black. Yet he had doubts about the future.

He said with considerable candour: 'It's a strange animal at the moment, the Namibian civil service. There are whites who are undermining the system, or are perceived to be doing so.

There are blacks who are in the administration as a reward for services rendered to the independence struggle, and through affirmative action, who are quite clearly duds. It's secure employment with no incentive for excellence.

'The result is a certain stagnation which is driving the good white technocrats away. They're going into the private sector. And it sometimes seems to me that the government wants it this way. They don't really want whites in the civil service, in spite of what they say. But all this is beginning to add up to poor government. You can't walk into administration without experience and do it well. But it's what Africans think can be done.

'So what will happen?' He shrugged his shoulders and then answered his own question. 'More whites will leave; things will get worse; and then colonialism and the disloyalty of the whites will be blamed for the collapse − if it gets to that. Then they'll ask people from the international community to come and sort out the mess, but these people won't have the local knowledge that the original civil service had, and everything will just grind along, misfiring and spluttering like so much of the continent. For newly independent countries in Africa, the honeymoon usually lasts no longer than four or five years. We're not far off that now...'

While I waited for an appointment with an important politician, I got into conversation with his personal assistant, a woman named Petronella Coetzee. For a while we chatted about the Walvis Bay party. I told her I would be going to the coast soon. I would also be driving north towards Oshakati and the Angolan border.

Petronella listened with half an ear, asking polite questions, and telling of a game lodge on the way up north, not far from Etosha Pan. 'Make a note of the name,' she told me. 'It's a superb place. The best in Namibia. I had there such a sense of tranquillity and peace...'

She had several telephones on her large desk which from time to time she was obliged to answer. I sat on the far side, examining her face in greater detail than would have been possible if the telephones had not rung.

I guessed her to be in her middle thirties. She was pale skinned, pale eyed behind an ornate pair of spectacles; her jaw seemed set with habitual resolve, and a slight white scar ran at an angle through both lips. When she smiled, these lips went thin, an expression encouraged by what I imagined to be her image of herself as efficient, clipped, not to be trifled with. I noticed that she referred to her callers as 'comrade'. I wondered what had happened in her past to leave her with that scar across the mouth.

She said to me after one call: 'I'm afraid your appointment is delayed. Will you come back? You're welcome to wait here.'

I chose the latter option, and it was in this way that we got into a more serious conversation.

I asked if she would mind telling me how she had come to occupy the position she did. It was an important and responsible position, I conjectured. I asked her, in effect, to talk about herself. She sat before me with her curly hair teased out, with smallish silver pendants dangling from her ears, and with her eyes self-assured and pleasant.

'I was born in Mariental in the south of the country. You want to know my race? I am a so-called coloured. My father was a Nama, a farm labourer on a white farm. My mother was a coloured washerwoman who never saw a school from the inside. I was one of six children. We went mostly to Catholic schools. Then I went to a bigger town, Keetmanshoop, to matriculate. After that I went to the University of the Western Cape in Cape Town. You know, the coloured university there. I did a four-year degree in social work. I was there from 1984 to 1987.'

One of the telephones rang. I gathered the caller wanted to establish a private hospital in Walvis Bay now that it was being incorporated into Namibia. 'These are the procedures,' Petronella said. She sat at the big desk, looking slight, and even slighter under the almost life-size portrait of the President, Sam Nujoma, which hung on the wall behind her.

Presently she replaced the receiver and returned her attention to me.

I asked whether it was at university that her political education had begun.

She shook her head. 'My mother started it. She had no ideology, only a strong sense of what was right and wrong. But of course things developed at university. Do you remember the troubles in Cape Town, at Crossroads especially, in early 1985? I was in charge of the students' relief effort. We used to try to get women and children away from the chaos, the burning shacks.'

She looked suddenly strong to me, with determination in her eyes, and resolve in the angle of her jaw and the slight scarring across her mouth. She was a person with a definite mission.

'No, I wouldn't call myself a feminist,' Petronella said with a smile, 'certainly not a burn-the-bra feminist. But I am a woman, and I'm conscious of the position women occupy in society and in terms of their relationships. It's a very repressed position, even in a democratic country like ours.'

Now comrade so-and-so was on the line, and Petronella spoke about some visitors from Eritrea for whom a tour needed to be organised. She gave precise and accurate-sounding instructions.

To me she said: 'After university, I came back and started working with the people in the south. They're my people. I was a community worker for the Catholic Church. Then in October of 1990, I came here — but only after a lot of soul searching.'

She looked at me from across the large desk, which I then noticed had an embossed leather inlay. It seemed she waited for me to ask a question, but I remained silent, providing her only with my attention.

'Deep down in my heart,' she said, her pale eyes unflinching behind the lenses of her spectacles, 'I felt that I may have been making a little bit of a difference down there in the south as a social worker. It was something I had started, and I didn't want to leave it. But my friends told me: the country needs people with knowledge, with energy, with the will to work hard in the crucial first five years. And my friends told me I had the necessary qualifications. Yes, I did have a desire to contribute something at a national level as well. So here I am.'

I asked her if she was married. She shook her head. Then, unexpectedly, she laughed.

'But I have plenty of children. Three of my own. Four adopted. My mother is still alive. We live here in Windhoek now and she looks after the younger ones. The boys I have put into boarding school. You know what teenagers are like. In a household of two women they can really drive you mad.' Again she laughed.

It was a remarkable glimpse which she had offered me. I imagined the illiterate old washerwoman living in a Windhoek suburb now, her daughter working in government, children rushing headlong through the rooms and passages and garden beds towards their place in the young democracy.

And Petronella in her spacious office saying: 'Ag, I miss the old work. It was quite a shift to come from being a community activist to being a petty bureaucrat in the office of the second most important ministry in the country.'

I asked if she considered herself to be an African.

'First and foremost,' she replied, 'I am an African and a woman. For closer identification, I am a Namibian woman.'

What difficulties, humiliations, subserviences and triumphs had gone into the making of this slight figure whose eyes were so calm and friendly behind her ornate spectacles, and whose lips were slightly scarred? In spite of the clues, it was impossible to tell. The result, this toughness of spirit and engagement with the world, was plainly manifest, however.

She said, when I finally prepared to go: 'Thanks for the chat. And don't forget my favourite game lodge when you go north.' She shook my hand at the door, looking up at me with proud yet smiling eyes, and then turned back towards a telephone ringing on her desk.

To get to the Namib of the publicity posters, those voluptuous and untouched dunes, there is a broader belt of
great natural aridity to be traversed. I entered these blasted
places a few hundred kilometres to the north of Windhoek
and drove jolting on rough roads on the way to the sea. The
day was hot and the country — I was in Damaraland —
spread out in a searing panorama of stones and twisted
growth. Hills were plentiful, some of them made of red sand
and sparse growth, with my road of dust and jagged rocks
turning through them. The earth looked hard as steel, and it
was suddenly difficult to believe that the highland places
around Windhoek had been so lavishly blessed with rain that
summer; and yet, like constant surprises, the flooding of
yellow daisies filled up the roadside glades sometimes.

I passed a small collection of corrugated-iron shacks
erected at a place where thorn trees had grown through
scalding stones cascading down a slope. I saw no people, not
even any goats, while the sun was high. At the diminished
watering places, crowds of raptors clustered and strutted, or
circled in ominous spirals high above. They were the only sign
of life, and I had a sense of being close to the infernos which
must have raged and erupted when the earth was young.

Yet I came across two youths walking by the roadside,
alone in all that shadeless terrain. They carried a single plastic
holdall between them. They motioned for me to stop. One of
them wore a balaclava cap rolled above the ears; the other
walked bare headed. I could see dust adhering to their faces
below their eyes and on their upper lips. I asked them where
they were going.

They looked at me with slight incredulity, as if it could
only be delirium that had intimated a multiplicity of
destinations in a landscape which clearly denied such choice.
'We are going home,' they said.

Yet this reply, in turn, roused a certain incredulity in me.
This landscape here, this isolation in hills of red and black,
and huge boulders simmering in heat and sometimes clasped
by claw-like roots, this miracle of gnarled grey life supporting

a few leaves which glimmered green, could this contain a human home?

The youths sat in the back of the car, the holdall between them, perspiration running on their faces. We spoke Afrikaans together in a desultory fashion. Yes, they were Damaras. They had finished school last year. Now they were looking for work. No, they had found nothing so far. Their home was down the road. They would tell me when to stop.

When they did, it was opposite a few iron dwellings, fewer still of brick, and some pepper trees softening the scene. This was Houmoed, they said, which was Afrikaans for keep courage. They stood outside the car, both hands raised in gestures of thanks and farewell. Then they turned and walked in burning sand towards particular destinies of their own. I wondered, as I drove on, what the independence of Namibia had meant to them at the time, or meant to them now, engrossed as they seemed to be in their individual attempts to survive.

Ahead of me now lay the Brandberg, an abrupt mountain which looks as if some parts had been blackened in an ancient blaze. It seemed more a gigantic rock outcrop than a mountain, and reared without vegetation from an increasingly level plain. Although the road on which I travelled brought me no closer than 25 kilometres to the first slopes, for nearly an hour the sight of the seared rock slopes and faces of this formidable massif dominated the horizon ahead and then drifted slowly on my right as I headed out into the desert. Close enough, those colossal buttresses and the steep ravines between, to draw the Brandberg into the web of preoccupations which enmeshed my mind as I drove interminable Namibian distances through great heat and even greater solitude.

Walvis Bay, that colonial enclave, a pawn in the games the European powers played in Africa during the 19th century. At first British, then South African; now there was to be a party to mark its return to its rightful owners; the first time that any colonial boundary in Africa had been annulled. Into these thoughts the Brandberg found an easy passage. For the mountain contained the White Lady, 'probably the most famous rock painting in SWA/Namibia', according to one travel brochure I saw.

In a cave among the burnt rocks of the Brandberg is a frieze of painted images at the centre of which stands the White Lady, a half-metre representation of a definite human form. Some early interpretations claimed the image was modelled from a European woman who had survived shipwreck off the treacherous Namibian coast and was later claimed as queen by the local stone-age San. Others thought the White Lady had been fashioned by Cretans sailing down the west coast of Africa. She was a white lady from Knossos. People saw pearls adorning her breasts and hips; they saw anklets and armlets; and they saw a cup in her right hand. Still others saw that she held a lotus flower.

Strange to think, as I drove towards the desert now, of this idea of a white queen worshipped by the people of Africa. From Rider Haggard's romantic legend in his novel *She*, to the White Lady of the Brandberg, painted long before the arrival of Europeans, but seen (certainly by Europeans) as the image of the white queen-god for which all Africa waited in quite breathless anticipation. This notion had grown up alongside colonialism, and appeared to be little more than another manifestation of the European sense that their intrusion into Africa was a civilising and uplifting gift from God to a continent otherwise steeped in frightening barbarism.

Laurens van der Post has referred to the great hush which fell over Africa with the arrival of Europeans, 'a calm and tense air of expectation of growing wonders to come, and as a result there was also the most moving and wonderful readiness of the African to serve, to imitate and to follow the European, and finally an unqualified preparedness to love and be loved'. Van der Post's point, however, is that such a climate did not last for long; that the European superiority and greed (including, I thought, the arbitrary drawing of those invisible lines to demarcate the Walvis Bay enclave) soon darkened the willing African eye.

Queen Victoria, Kaiser Wilhelm, King Ferdinand and Queen Isabella — these historic figures had been singled out as 'tormentors and usurpers of our rights and dignity' by Namibia's Foreign Minister (according to a newspaper I had seen that morning) as he attacked those white parliamentarians who had dared to oppose the incorporation of Walvis Bay into the country as a whole. There were others of similar ilk who could not escape the Minister's invective: Albert Schweitzer, organist and surgeon; David Livingstone, missionary and explorer; Cecil Rhodes, imperialist; Heinrich Vedder, historian; Hendrik Verwoerd, South Africa's apartheid supremo; Ian Smith, architect of Rhodesia's ill-fated independence. This diverse band was dismissed by a single contemptuous sweep. 'They neither really cared nor understood the aspirations of the indigenous peoples of Africa because they could not allow themselves to become Africans. They kept on listening to the drumbeat of a forlorn European ghost which is nowhere.' The forlorn ghost of the White Lady, the European queen, is also nowhere.

Many of the paintings in the Brandberg, this huge bulge of rock and heat which lay behind me now, were made a thousand years before Christ, and there are no white women depicted there. This is the opinion of the scientists now. How quickly the legends crack and the ghosts lie dead in sunlight.

'The celebrations on the occasion of the reintegration of Walvis Bay are to be the main event of the year,' the Foreign Minister said with an obvious and defiant satisfaction. 'We say, down with colonialism and down with the Berlin Conference and all their stinking legacies in Namibia.'

But by now the desert had forced itself upon me, and the anger of these words faded on the slightly rumpled sheets of white-hot emptiness upon which my road was faintly etched. The extent, the final desolation of this ancient landscape, invaded my consciousness like the trickling of an hour-glass. Sand the texture of coarse salt; a terrain without vegetation; a road which dipped slowly and rose again but which made no turnings to the right or left for a hundred kilometres and longer.

There were mirages in the desert. You could see what you desired because in reality there was nothing to see. The flat plain reached forward to meet the pale white sky in a hardly distinguishable line. The steady sound of rushing air filled the car, perspiration gathered and occasionally dripped, and the illusion of shining water stretched frequently across the way ahead. And then at last a grey cloud billowed before me.

Once inside it, the air became markedly cooler and the desert was littered with mounds of white sand surmounted by coarse low-growing coastal bush. Telephone poles marched across the empty spaces. And then in the distance a flat grey sea appeared as anticlimax under overcast skies.

The road between Swakopmund and Walvis Bay hugged an often rocky coast. Powerful four-wheel-drive vehicles roared past with fishing rods attached upright to front bumpers, or the vehicles stood parked on the beach, adjuncts to the frequent sight of fishermen on spray-soaked rocks. On the landward side, the dunes came right down to spill across the dark blue tarmac of the road. The four-wheel-drive vehicles had left their marks here too, all over the closest dunes, and doubtless on the dunes beyond.

Highest structures in Walvis Bay were the cranes which lined the wharf of the only deep water port along the full 1 500 kilometres of Namibia's coastline. The town itself — streets of low houses and a few shops, a few warehouses, some fuel storage tanks — seemed in danger of being swamped by sand. The desert stood hard against the eastern perimeters, and when the wind blew, it invariably did so from the desert side and brought sand sifting into the streets and interiors of the isolated town. But they had the natural bay, a precious asset which harboured many thousands of flamingos in the shallows and allowed big ships right into town. Their superstructures formed a backdrop to the clashing of railway wagons in the station yard. These manifestations of transport formed the core of the reason for Walvis Bay's existence so far.

Absurd to think of another country controlling this link with the world, yet this is what had happened for the four years since independence. Understandable, the plans of which Gert Hanekom had spoken which would make this minor port into the major development region of an independent country, with factories reaching up and down the coast and out into the desert. Equally understandable, the enthusiasm with which people in Windhoek had spoken to me of the pending Walvis celebrations.

The ships tied to the wharf came from the Cape, from Europe and the East; and more vessels waited in the roadstead beyond the bar. The wharf was filled with the cries of seagulls and working men. Jibs with attached bundles swung over lorries and railway lines set into the concrete between the big rusting sides of ships close on one side and the blank walls of sheds on the other. The smell of oil and stale galleys wafted on the breeze, and the peculiar smell also of fishing trawlers.

I came across two white men in blue overalls who worked on a pump which would help suck pilchards from a vessel due to dock in a few hours' time. They spoke to me congenially in Afrikaans. They shrugged their shoulders in the face of the coming of independence to their town. One of the men had been born there, had lived nowhere else. The other was from Cape Town, but had no intention of going back. 'Once you live in this world, you can't leave it,' he said, shifting a thick shock of ginger hair away from his forehead.

'We are worried most about theft,' the other one said. 'Everywhere in Namibia theft is now very high. That's what happens when the police are your friends. The police don't even try to solve crimes any longer. They just give a number for the insurance claim. My sister lives in Windhoek. She has been robbed three times in two months.'

'Here it will be even worse,' the ginger-headed man said. 'You have heard of the celebration party they will have here? They are bringing in tens of thousands of people to drink and sing in the streets. Then they'll leave them here to settle permanently. That's the rumour. But where are the jobs? They'll have to steal to survive.' Again a hand was lifted to remove the matted forelock from above blue and foolish-looking eyes.

I said I found such a rumour faintly ridiculous.

Both men were adamant, however, both expressing a sense of vague foreboding, that foreknowledge of deterioration which had become the stock-in-trade of so many whites in Africa.

Would they join in the celebration party?

'Ag, maybe we can buy some beer and watch it on TV,' the ginger man said with a sudden laugh.

Swakopmund, 35 kilometres to the north of Walvis Bay, possessed a gentility of sorts, the tourists saw to that. Few tourists in the dull streets of Walvis, but they strolled everywhere in Swakopmund, a picturesque town wedged between the searing hostility of the desert and the cold hostility of the sea.

The curio shops in Swakopmund's Kaiser Wilhelmstrasse were filled with African things of widely varying quality and from places as far away as Zaire; tours into the desert, or shorter dune trips and gem-stone tours, could be arranged at a price; and at least a score of restaurants beckoned after dark, many of them offering venison in various forms. The sea front was often shrouded in fog. Nevertheless, hotels and *pensions* did good business. Luxury buses came and went, and confident German voices punctuated the brisk coastal air.

Whole streets of turn-of-the-century buildings — turrets and steep roofs and ornate façades — had been carefully preserved; and in general the town seemed well preserved and well drilled. Tourists spent their money in an orderly fashion. The sea beat like an army against steep beaches, and smashed in a perpetual wreath of spray against the rocks and concrete at the end of the mole which the Germans had built in an unsuccessful attempt to provide anchorage for deep-water ships.

Every evening that I walked on the mole, a bearded man in a worker's cap sat at the end, staring out to sea as the sun drowned in the lavishly golden waters of the south Atlantic. He sat always in the same place, and always alone, as if some peculiar magnetism existed for him in the heaving waters as the light ebbed slowly from them and from the sky beyond.

But it was the architecture, nearly always immaculately maintained, which reclaimed my attention. These distinctly central European buildings, although often crowned with the incongruity of corrugated iron, gave a sense not simply of the state of German architecture at around the beginning of the 20th century, but also an inkling of much earlier times. Especially the public buildings possessed what one writer accurately describes as an 'air of ancient breeding'.

I remarked to a retired doctor that Swakopmund sometimes felt like a starkly misplaced imitation of a Germany much older than the late 19th-century one which had colonised this corner of Africa.

'Yes,' he replied, 'that is true. I believe the settlers had a yen for transporting the highlights of their culture and their past. They remained absolutely loyal to Germany, but they were determined to make the best of things here. They wanted to re-create the Germany they remembered. And never forget they were Germans: they built everything to last. They worked for permanence of tenure in the belief that German control would never falter.'

Undoubtedly it was this belief which brought a peculiar ruthlessness to German colonialism. Not far from Swakopmund's lighthouse, a bright red and white structure surrounded by palm trees, stood a monument to the German soldiers who died in the war against the Hereros in 1904/5. On two plaques, about a hundred names were listed, as well as fifteen battle sites. I noticed a line of ants marching across a bottom corner of one of the plaques and disappearing into a hole. The monument showed a bronze soldier advancing over stony ground, his rifle at the ready, his eyes filled with a mixture of fear and resolve. But there was another soldier too, this one lying on the rocks, his rifle still clutched in his fists, but limply now because he is mortally wounded.

The Hereros had rebelled against the colonial presence, against the hardship inflicted by drought and disease among their cattle, and especially against the loss to white settlers of land used for generations as grazing for their animals. Well-armed German forces left the Hereros only an eastward passage for retreat, and in this way forced them into the northern Kalahari. When they were safely in this arid trap, the Germans sealed the last of the waterholes and erected a line of guard posts along a 250 kilometre front. The Hereros were then left to die of thirst and starvation in the Kalahari, or they were shot in great numbers when they attempted to reopen the waterholes.

'Yes, there was appalling cruelty,' the retired doctor said. 'Also in the south, against the Nama. At over 80, old Hendrik Witbooi took up arms for the last time against the colonists. Finally there were more than 15 000 German troops against less than 1 500 Namas. Witbooi had been influenced by a prophet from the Cape who said that God was on his way to help Africans rid themselves of the white intruders. But towards the end of 1905, the old man was killed and his followers soon capitulated to the Germans. It was a terrible time for the indigenous people.'

The Nama fighters were placed in labour camps, where survival was almost impossible. Further north, only a few thousand Hereros succeeded in crossing the Kalahari to sanctuary in what is now Botswana. But the real extent of the devastation inflicted on these people, in ruthless military campaigns and brutal camps, was only revealed in the 1911 census. More than half the Nama population and three-quarters of the Hereros, in total more than 75 000 people, had perished at the command of a Kaiser whose name is still remembered in the main street of Swakopmund.

One historian I read quotes a Herero as saying to a German settler: 'The missionary says that we are the children of God like our white brothers ... but look at us. Dogs, slaves, worse than baboons on the rocks ... that is how you treat us.' This outrage and bitterness remains, and not least in the determination to celebrate in Walvis Bay the passing of another colonial folly.

M y retired doctor friend, a pleasant and talkative man named Martin, took me into the desert one afternoon to show me the grass. We travelled north for some time, with a sluggish-looking ocean on our left making small waves which rolled themselves into oblivion on huge sweeps of flat grey beaches. Then we turned inland and drove in among the mounds and depressions of the desert.

Martin had gone out of his way to help me; and as my stay in Swakopmund lengthened he revealed, in his pleasant and cheerful way, many facets of the country he loved and of his life in relation to it.

He had only recently retired. He told me in a jocular way: 'Take some advice. Get done everything you want to get done before you retire. Afterwards, there simply isn't time.' He looked fit; his grey hair was neatly combed; his clothes were fashionable and confidently worn; and his pale eyes showed frequent sparks of liveliness and interest. 'Yes, I'm an Afrikaner. I was born in the Cape. Yes, I speak German, but my ancestry is French.'

He told of his great grandfather, a young man of a wealthy family near Versailles, who had disgraced himself by entering into a liaison with a chambermaid. His father had sent him to South Africa. Further disgrace had followed. He had married a Dutch woman, produced three children, and then, telling her he had urgent business in France, had disappeared for ever.

'I keep telling my own wife to be careful,' Martin said. 'Next week, for example, I am going to Cape Town for a reunion of my unit in the South African navy. But all my wife says to that is: you're too old for adventures now; you'll be back. The predictabilities of growing old, hey?'

Martin had stopped the car in a depression and we got out. The silence of the desert, even here on its periphery, was so thick and absolute that the clash of one pebble against another as we walked on the roadway came to the ears as a loud affront.

'Yes, the navy. I finished my training in 1945, just after the war ended. I wept my heart out.' He looked at me with amusement sparking in his eyes. 'The folly of youth, hey? I had thought all through my training: what fun to fight in a war.'

Only when Martin kneeled in the depression and placed his open hand, palm upward, against the sand did I see what he had brought me into the desert to see. Protruding through his fingers now were tiny yellow blades of grass, already in seed. And then I saw the grass everywhere, hardly ten centimetres high but shuddering in a thin cloak of yellow life all through the depression and beyond.

'Miraculous,' he said. 'We have good rains on the plateau hundreds of miles to the east, and the grasslands visit our desert. This is the first time in the last ten years. In between times, the seed just lies and waits.'

I saw something, during that moment, of the profound attachments which could be made between the desert places of Namibia and the people of European descent who ventured there: this ageing doctor kneeling in the sand, showing me the tiny seeds which had already formed at the head of the grass. He had spent most of his adult life doctoring in rural Namibia. The country had taken hold of him. He read its history with something like a passion. He restored its old furniture. He had also become attuned to its new reality.

'On the day the election results were announced,' he had told me, his pale eyes alive with the memory, 'I was in my surgery, here in Swakopmund. I heard a roar. Through the window I could see thousands of black people in the street — there are many Ovambos from up north here. Do you know what I thought? I thought: this is the end. Everything is going to be destroyed. That is the African way. They will set everything alight when darkness comes.

'But do you know, then I really looked at these people cheering outside in the streets. I mean, I looked into their faces. And all I saw was joy and elation. Yes. And their response to me did not change. They continued to greet me with respect. And I thought: we have walked here in this country all these years with our blinkers on. The warmth of these people. They have a joy in living from which we can learn a lot, especially the Afrikaner with all his rigidity and suspicion...'

And yet there was a darker side.

I thought immediately of the woman, Petronella Coetzee, the woman I had met in Windhoek, when Martin spoke to me about a locum he had once undertaken in the southern parts of the country. The southern parts had been Petronella's stamping ground. She had been born in Mariental. And as a social worker she had worked among the defeated and decimated Namas, her absent father's people.

'Down there on this locum,' Martin told me, 'I had a view of hell.'

He paused for a moment, looking away across the pale white space of the desert. 'In Mariental. Also in Gibeon, Hendrik Wibooi's old capital. I wonder if I exaggerate if I say that ninety per cent of the Namas are alcoholics. I'd certainly never seen alcoholism on this scale. Men, women and children. Malnourished and drunk. On a Saturday morning, I couldn't believe it. Sitting on the pavements and drinking. Drunk by ten o'clock. In Gibeon, that ugly town, wine bottles and rubbish everywhere; and people lying in the dirt where they had fallen.'

This view of hell, and the steady eyes of Petronella regarding me from the far side of her large desk. I remembered how, as we spoke, she had looked suddenly strong to me, this self-styled community activist working inside what the Namibian Foreign Minister would undoubtedly call another 'stinking legacy' of colonialism. I remembered the clarity of her proud eyes and that slight scarring which she carried, as if something at an earlier time had torn to bloody tatters both her lips.

When my time in Swakopmund had ended, I turned north towards newer battlefields, stopping en route at Petronella's favourite game lodge near Etosha Pan. But as I travelled my thoughts lingered for some time at the coast, especially with the pending celebrations which promised to transform the mundane streets of Walvis Bay into thoroughfares of triumph and a form of joy perhaps similar to that which Martin had seen from the windows of his surgery.

The expectation in Swakopmund had been everywhere apparent. One afternoon while I admired some of the town's architecture, I came upon the railway station, itself an ornate structure with a Gothic-looking tower and plentiful façades. The building seemed in need of some repair, and I entered it on the assumption that it would be empty.

Almost immediately, a man in a railway uniform emerged from an office and asked, but not unpleasantly, the nature of my business.

I asked him about passenger trains to Windhoek. He said there were three a week. I asked about fares. He told me, adding that the journey took eleven hours. Then he said that I might be interested to know that a special train was leaving Windhoek at noon next Friday, and would arrive in Walvis Bay at ten that night. 'This is faster than usual. It's for people wanting to join the party.' He could not help smiling in a slightly self-conscious way as he told me this.

The Walvis Bay celebration was again mentioned by a garage attendant who filled my car on the morning that I left Swakopmund. He told me he would definitely be going. 'It's a big victory,' he said.

I told him what I had heard from the white workmen in Walvis Bay: that ten thousand people would be left to settle permanently after the party was over. He laughed in amusement. 'Where can so many people stay? They will have to go home.'

One of his eyes had been damaged, remaining closed while he spoke; but the other seemed lively enough. He leaned against the car as he listened with some relish to what I had heard from that young Herero, Eban, outside the church in Katutura. Gangs of Swapo supporters waiting to rob the whites and then chase them away. He laughed uproariously. 'The white people will not be chased away,' he said, regarding me quite impudently with his one eye, 'they will run away by themselves.' As I drove off, I heard him repeating like gossip the gist of our conversation to people lingering on the garage forecourt. He waved, providing me with a flash of white teeth and a final burst of his boisterous laughter.

Once beyond the aridity of the desert, the drive to the north took me through the great open spaces which dominated Namibia's central spine. The country was ripe now in the latter parts of a bountiful summer. Late flowers still bloomed in the high grass of the road preserve, hawks and falcons rose suddenly from the tarmac as the car approached, and the empty country rolled away in a sea of grey-green bush which provided horizons on every side which were nearly as flat as distant water. The car charged forward, devouring the kilometres. I was going to the border which for at least two decades had been the battleground between Swapo and the South Africans.

A whole generation of young men in my own country had grown up with the prospect of being conscripted and of 'going to the border', which meant doing duty in northern South West Africa. Huge camps had grown up in Grootfontein, and another at Ondangwa. But thousands of black Namibians had fought alongside the South Africans, trying to curb the infiltration of Swapo insurgents who had their bases in Angola. The task was rendered more difficult by the natural sympathies prevailing in the Ovambo villages. In consequence, villages were often laid waste; and South

African involvement in Angola itself increased. And then Cuban troops were brought in, and the entanglements became more complex, and much blood was spilled, and only after many years could the South Africans be persuaded to withdraw. They did so under the eyes of a strong United Nations presence, those blue-uniformed soldiers who then turned their attention to the elections which preceded the independence celebrations of 1990.

For many miles, the railway ran beside the road as it drove through endless green bush and beneath a sky which during the afternoon grew heavy with flat-bottomed cumulus promising but yielding no rain. A train rumbled past on this same railway which not so long ago would have carried troop trains up to Grootfontein.

At a town called Otjiwarongo I stopped for some refreshment. Here were wide streets, single-storey buildings, a café called Carstensen's, and behind the counter a large blonde girl with bedraggled ringlets. Slouching black youths came and went. A few whites sat at the tables, talking in German or Afrikaans. Pictures of wild animals decorated one wall: elephants, giraffes, kudu with birds on their backs. Etosha Pan was less than 200 kilometres away now. I pressed on into the deepening afternoon.

Then at last the high thatch and dark poles of the evening time. The fine glass and cutlery. The ease and tiredness seeping through. A young waiter, his dark face set in a constant smile, spoke of the Angolans coming across the border looking for a haven. Even Zaireans, breaking out of the hunger and collapse in their own country and emerging into war and a thousand kilometres of Angola, and then at last reaching Africa's haven. 'Namibia is the best,' the waiter said through his fixed smile. 'You are going tomorrow to see the animals? There are many.'

The animals of Etosha. My room, as all the rooms of the lodge, had been built on stilts with a small veranda looking out at the setting sun. The rooms occupied a hillside which provided sufficient high ground for a shallow valley to be visible in its full extent, right to the low hills which formed a slightly lumpy horizon now in silhouette against the dying of the day. The sun was a fire of low rays which came through the branches of gnarled trees and into my room and across the rich fabric of the bedspread and on to a far wall in an intricacy of shadows and ochre light. The animals of Etosha in great herds, more animals than could ever be depicted on the walls of Carstensen's café. But this valley before me now at Petronella's lodge, it lay apparently empty and in deep shadow while the horizon seemed to pull down the sun so that its fire turned to amber behind the trees. I heard a sudden cry from the bush, then silence. And when the sun had gone, some thin clouds caught the hues of its extinguishment, holding them a moment as if in memory, and then allowing them to slide to grey.

Later, as if in final salute, the sky flared crimson again out there towards the west, and was glowing still when all else had submitted to the warmth and aroma of the night.

B eyond Etosha lay the densely populated far north, yet it took an hour and a long straight road to get there. The landscape flattened, meanwhile, into an immense plain which had no visible edges, no hills or ridges, on any side. Here was featureless country, upon which the soil changed to sand, and the bush thinned, giving way sometimes to tall palm trees, some of them no more than dead trunks bereft of fronds.

First signs of habitation came in the increasing sight of muddy minibuses bouncing on subsidiary roads; then came millet planted in small fields, and cattle standing inside bleached and thorny branches drawn together in rough rectangles; then children on bare white sand between the low structures in which they presumably lived, and young boys tending herds of goats. I caught sight of a single ox dragging a plough across a ragged-edged field: this ancient emblem of settled existence, this acknowledgement of dependency on the earth's bounty, which continued everywhere, an irrepressible human activity, even when the fields and farmers had been rent by war. Anthills flourished everywhere, looking like monuments.

Many of the houses consisted of corrugated iron, others had been built with grey concrete blocks. But also there were structures the colour of the earth, and crooked poles collected from the bush, and grass and reeds, and rough thatching clutched together at the apex. Puddles of rain-water had appeared; on the flat country drainage was impossible, and the water lay in sheets sometimes, reflecting palm trees, and also the shapes of wrecked cars which crouched at random among the increasing settlements. Now pedestrians thronged roadside market stalls filled with the colour of fruit and fabrics.

The road had become crowded, and rickety shop-fronts intimated that I had reached the town of Ondangwa. Hundreds of vehicles stood on the sandy verges of the road, many undergoing black and oily repairs. And scores of bars and bottle stores beckoned: System Beer Garden, Water is Life Bottle Store, Old Black Disco, We Like Bar. Men in flowery shirts shouted to each other; engines revved; and children laughed while they played in rain-water pools.

And then, unexpectedly, the unmistakable remains of war: a military base with barbed wire fences, pillboxes on stilts, the sight of derelict bungalows behind a long mound of weed-filled earth, and the sandbagged roofs of subterranean arsenals.

A man at the gate said: 'There is no army here any more. Now it is a training school.' I said I wished to speak with the principal. He offered a notebook in which I wrote my name, and then he raised the boom and let me pass.

I drove on broken roadways through a profusion of weeds and neglect, bungalows with broken windows, concrete breaking away from incomprehensible installations, a crowd of men sitting in the windows of an old building, looking inwards as if they might be listening to a lecture.

In an office of sorts (the man at the gate had directed me) I surprised a young Ovambo woman lounging behind a littered desk.

'The principal is busy,' she said, pulling herself upright. She had full lips, painted red, and she regarded me with an unabashed and nonchalant boldness.

She responded lazily to my questions. 'Six hundred students. Men and women. Living in the bungalows. Ex-fighters from the war. Yes, from both sides. Carpentry, bricklaying, electrical, typing. I am not allowed to answer questions. I do not know when the principal can see you.'

I drove on to Oshakati. There, in a government office, a man said: 'The development brigade offers retraining, sometimes the first civilian training they've been exposed to, for former fighters who are now unemployed. Our transition to peace has been often traumatic, with widespread vandalism and theft. Thousands of Ovambos fought for the South Africans against the Ovambos fighting for Swapo.' He smiled at this irony.

Then he told me he had been active in Swapo since the early 1970s. He had been harassed, arrested and imprisoned, had even survived an assassination attempt. He had a chiselled face, which seemed to be made up of distinct planes with no softening where the planes met, and with a jutting jaw and white teeth when he smiled. His peppercorn hair was beginning to turn grey.

'I left in April 1978,' he said. 'And I spent most of my time in Angola. I worked in the Swapo headquarters in Luanda, and then I came down to the front line. We had a tough time. South Africa was making incursions into Angola. You know, hot pursuit. Once I got a bullet in the leg, but luckily no bone was hit.'

He pulled up one trouser leg to show me a pale pink scar disfiguring his calf. He was smiling again, his chiselled face turned to mine. 'But this is all in the past. Now we are working hard to make Namibia a success. It's our country. We fought for it for more than twenty years.'

Oshakati was the capital of the north, an untidy conglomeration of litter and people and animals, with wide streets made even more spacious by generous verges, the buildings set far back beyond them: petrol stations, a few banks and supermarkets, and again the proliferation of drinking places with names like Zambezi Nights, Face to Face Bar, and a small structure hardly two metres square called the Hot Box. Water lay everywhere in wide sheets, often with grass growing out of it.

'Malaria,' a nursing sister at the hospital said. 'It's going to be very difficult this year. That's the bad news when the rains are good. People plough and plant and then they get malaria.'

A lot of the hospital consisted of prefabricated bungalows set down in long rows on the sand of Oshakati. I sat on a plastic chair in one of the bungalows given over to administration. The secretary had told me to wait. She was an unsmiling young woman with a large engagement ring and not much to do except absently turn it round and round on her finger. The room seemed over-furnished with dented metal desks; on the secretary's stood an electric typewriter and a telephone which from time to time disturbed her reverie. A radio somewhere played tinny jazz. The heat was oppressive. A poster on one of the walls proclaimed: 'the Namibia Dollar: our money, our pride'; and there, depicted on the new notes, was the gaunt face of Hendrik Witbooi, the Nama leader who had made his headquarters at Gibeon where later his people were to lie drunk in the gutters. Another poster warned of the danger of AIDS. People came and went with the aloof secretary doing as little as she could; the door creaked noisily each time it was used; and outside I heard chattering voices and the occasional wailing of children.

At last a busy man beckoned me into his office. He wore an open-necked shirt and gold-rimmed spectacles. He was the senior superintendent of the hospital, a Dr Naftali Hamata, who in his obliging way answered my questions about the Angolans coming across the border in search of medical attention.

'Health services in southern Angola have collapsed due to the civil war. It's been like this for many years. Of course the South African military presence stopped, or at least partially stopped, the flow of people into Namibia. The border was very tightly controlled. Since the South African withdrawal, a fence has been built, but it's more to keep the animals out. The people come and go at will. Yes, of course we treat them.'

Dr Naftali Hamata sat before me in his pleasant way, telling his secretary to hold his calls, and then turning to me again.

'Oshakati is the referral hospital for the whole northern region. Even so, at least ten per cent of our patients here are Angolans. Closer to the border the percentage is much higher, of course. Go to the hospital at Engela, less than ten kilometres from the border. There the percentage is around eighty,' Dr Hamata said. Then he added: 'Look, I will be most willing to send someone with you tomorrow, so you do not lose your way. Come to my office after breakfast.'

It rained fiercely that evening. I sat in the dining-room of an Oshakati hotel and watched the storm send flashes of cold blue light into a garden made turbulent by wind. Thunder rattled the windows. Then the rain fell in a frenzy, as if it had burst out of a thundering sky which could no longer restrain it. It came shooting down under pressure. A waiter hurried to close the sliding doors. The clatter on iron roofs drowned out all other sounds. Then I saw it streaming on one wall of the dining-room, and a passage leading to the public conveniences was soon awash. Some hail hit sharply against the glass of the sliding doors. Guests talked loudly to be heard above the dinning of the storm. The waiters had wet shoes, even the bottoms of their trousers showed dark with moisture, but they came and went without obvious concern. It was simply another evening in the rainy season.

But the morning proved fine enough — blue skies and hundreds of children playing in a shallow rain-water lake — even though the air felt burdened with humidity. I drove north towards the border in the company of a white-clad nursing sister who told me her name was Limey. That at any rate was how she pronounced it. She sat with her elbow protruding through the open window, obviously enjoying some time away from the hospital. She was a short woman, beginning to reveal some signs of age now, but with a face finely marked by that mixture of resolve and patience born of hard experience. She struck me as a woman who would not be easily cowed.

'Yes, I was born here. My parents' home was not far from Engela. We lived almost on the border,' Limey said, gazing out of the window as we skimmed through a flat landscape clothed with clumps of palms and an endlessness of marula trees between. At regular intervals, fields of millet surrounded low homesteads, thatched roofs reaching hardly higher than the crop sometimes; and schoolchildren and plump cattle straggling on the verges of the road.

I asked Limey if she had trained as a nurse at the Oshakati hospital.

She shook her head. 'South Africa. At Baragwanath, you know the big hospital in Soweto. I was so far from home,' she said with a smile. 'And there I was working in Baragwanath in 1976, when the children made the riots. I saw the injured children coming to the casualty departments. I was afraid, shoo! I wanted to come home. But at home here, at the same time, my parents were being moved out of no man's land on the border. I cried. I said: now you are a nurse in the middle of a war. This is my life, I thought; this is how I must serve.'

She sat silent a moment. We passed a group of women with baskets by the roadside. Limey acknowledged their greeting, then she remarked, and clearly for her it was a continuation of what she had been saying: 'But, shoo! These people suffered more. Sometimes we would just see the smoke when the soldiers burned their houses. Or neighbours would say: we only heard the shooting, and now here are the dead ready to be buried. These families, many of them, had some sons with Swapo and other sons with the South Africans.'

The homesteads which we passed seemed so peaceful now, surrounded by palisades of bleached branches within the tall ripe millet. But then there had been columns of smoke rising into the clear air, and flies on the corpses flung out in the sandy yards.

'Turn here,' Limey said. We drove in among the homesteads on bad roads, with anthills thrust upwards like gnarled and warning fingers, and children watching as we bounced through dongas hardly five kilometres from the Angolan border.

'Engela was the only health facility here that remained open during all the years of the war,' Limey said. 'The nurses had tough times. But they will tell you.'

The hospital had first been built by Finnish missionaries in the 1920s, a low building which seemed to have sunk with time at a slight angle into the earth. A few prefabricated offices now stood to one side, and many of the wards were rondavels topped with coarse reed thatch. People sat against the walls of the buildings to escape the sun, and chickens roamed in the sandy spaces between.

Limey moved easily among the people, calling out greetings to the nurses she encountered, and then directing me to the office of the matron − hardly more than a large packing case, but equipped with a noisy air-conditioner and a 1922 photograph of a stern-looking Finnish woman.

The matron herself seemed younger than Limey; she had a dark rounded face and searching eyes which burned brightly behind the lenses of her spectacles. Her English was poor, and she spoke it with a Portuguese accent. Yet she said, in some surprise, that she had never been to Angola, not even one step across the border.

She answered my questions about the number of Angolan patients in the hospital, confirming what Dr Hamata in Oshakati had said; she also spoke to me about the staff shortages with which the hospital was plagued, even now when they were so busy. Her voice possessed an earnestness which accorded with the brightness of her eyes. She sat leaning slightly forward, her gaze never leaving my face.

'But the hospital is not so full as in the war.'

She looked at me expectantly, waiting for another question. Limey said: 'Tell about the war.'

The matron clasped her hands together. Her epaulettes were crowded with bars denoting her qualifications.

'We worked in darkness here,' she said in her Portuguese accent. 'Candles and torches. There was no electricity. We were always frightened. They would come at night, asking for information.'

The air-conditioner clattered on, yet I noticed beads of perspiration on the matron's upper lip. I asked who had come at night.

'They all come,' the matron said, and now for some reason a flicker of amusement crossed her expression. 'South Africans. Swapo. Once some Unita people got blown up in a land-mine. We treated them here. Then their enemies, men from the MPLA, stood in the black doorways making threats against us.

'It was terrible,' she went on in her earnest way, her eyes fixed to mine. 'We could hear the firing and explosions nearly every night. There was a curfew. We could not move. We lived here in the hospital often.'

Her eyes seemed wide open behind the lenses of her spectacles. I asked why, with her qualifications, she had not found work in a safer place.

She replied without hesitation: 'I stayed here for my job, for my family, and for my country.'

'You are brave, shoo!' Limey said.

'Yes, brave,' the matron said with some vehemence, and then she and Limey laughed quietly together.

When the interview had been concluded, Limey and I drove back to the tarred road and turned towards the border. No inkling, in the flat country, the fields of millet, the bush, the vehicles on the road, that we were driving through what had once been a zone of war. No inkling even that the road was about to pass from one country to another, except that once we saw a dilapidated shack which proclaimed itself to be the Luanda Bar.

Limey was telling me that the hardest part for all nurses, whether at Oshakati, where Limey herself had worked through the worst of the war years, or at Engela, was to receive and stabilise the wounded when they were brought in.

'You keep wondering when you'll see a face you know. Or one that you love.'

She sat beside me in her white uniform with the purple epaulettes and the face which experience had marked with a combination of patience and resolve. Experiences like bomb blasts, a bad one in a bank in Oshakati one morning. Twenty-four dead. The mutilated ferried to the hospital where the blood had flowed on the floor and Limey had worked non-stop for nearly thirty-six hours. Tough times.

'It was strange that then, really for the first time, I realised what I was doing. There were South African army doctors working in the hospital. I worked beside these men, some of them so young, but in my heart...'

She left the sentence unfinished. I prompted her. She glanced at me with a slight smile.

'In my heart I knew they were the enemy.'

The border was marked by not much more than a barricade across the road, a tent and flag-pole on the Namibian side, and a crumbling building in Angola. A few vehicles waited to cross, a few pedestrians with bundles. Nevertheless we got out and stood on the verge of the road. Limey drew my attention to a nearby look-out tower which reared out of an enclosure surrounded by rolls of barbed wire. Inside the enclosure stood the shell of a low and roofless building, windows and doors ripped out. The gate to the enclosure stood open, but a warning sign with skull and crossbones rendered the prospect of entry uninviting. 'There are still land-mines in the ground in there,' Limey remarked.

I looked at the tower, this relic of war rearing from the flat earth of this remote and bloodied part of the continent. I thought of soldiers crouching on top of the tower, ready to blaze away at anything that moved too close to the border: this arbitrary line, meaning little to the people who lived on either side. I stood next to my Namibian nursing sister who was looking up at me as she spoke. But for a moment I hardly heard her words. I found myself caught in the strange coils of the aftermath of violence. There was heat and sunshine and blue sky and a few palm trees, one or two without fronds, and yet this unmistakable sense of violence and travail pervaded the very sand and stones on which we stood.

'It was like a dream, when the soldiers left.'

Words remembered when I read of the Walvis Bay celebrations a week or so later. Words, also, which I thought I could begin to understand. Thousands of Namibians lining the streets of that dismal sand-strewn harbour town. I wondered if those white workmen I had met at the fishing boats had watched all this on television. All those jubilant people in the stadium where 'the South African flag was taken down in the port town for the last time at midnight, replaced by Namibia's flag, as thousands of Namibians cheered . . . and sections of the crowd shouted "down, down" while the flag was lowered'. Down, down, I thought, away with this final stinking legacy of colonialism. That was the joy. The twenty-one-gun salute, the fireworks in the desert sky, the singing, the lifting of arms and faces to the gods of independence.

'It was like a dream,' Limey said as we stood on the Angolan border together.

She stood looking up at me, her expression seeming at once wise and calm from experience, yet caught in the illumination of this particular memory.

'I kept saying to myself: is it really true? You know how it is when you are too happy, and you want to cry. That is what I felt when the South Africans withdrew. We sang when the soldiers left, shoo! It was like a dream.'

The fireworks and the firing of celebratory guns and the exultant shouts − down, down − and a ramshackle vehicle jolting under the raised barrier and across a thin line dividing civil war from peace, states which perhaps the gods of independence could not yet tell apart. We stood watching for a moment longer, and then we turned back, driving slowly south through marula trees and fields of laden millet.

3

The Past Obscured

Since the war and the advent of independence, white artists have continued to paint the Zimbabwean landscape as if it was hardly inhabited by man. In many of these paintings there is a sense of the emptiness of the landscape, of vast tracts of space, of a feeling that nothing has happened and that nothing ever will happen.

— Celia Winter-Irving, *Stone Sculpture in Zimbabwe*, 1991.

The road, as we drove, descended gently and without curves towards the river. On either side, wide reaches of mopane trees had begun to succumb to the demands of autumn, and the bare earth between the trunks wore a russet mantle. A few fever trees reared in their ghostly way above the general level of the bush. Although the wheels of the truck were silent on the sandy surface, a flock of guinea-fowl raced suddenly from our approach. Then to the right, the eastern side, a high fence marched out between the trees and followed the direction of the road.

We were driving, a few days before I visited Zimbabwe, in the farthest north-east corner of South Africa. Beyond the fence lay Mozambique, a tangle of lala palms and climbers entwining the larger trees; and beyond the river, when we reached it, lay the country I would soon encounter.

'The fence is elephant-proof, that's what is said,' my companion told me. 'But it helps to an extent with people as well. It's supposed to encourage them to points which are then more controllable.'

Nevertheless, in the early morning, among the scuffs and markings of wild animals, we had seen the footprints in the dust of the road, two humans passing in the night, one barefooted, the other shod. We had conjectured on the excitements of traversing a teeming game reserve when the moon was dark. What impelled them? Almost certainly they were people from the neighbouring countries, crossing illegally, braving the night terrors in search of survival and peace, or perhaps more starkly simply in search of the faces of remembered ones who might still be among the living. The footprints we saw had wavered uncertainly in the roadway sometimes.

The river presented little more than a wide expanse of sand with a slow-flowing channel on the nearer side. The sun burned in a remorseless glare while dark-winged vultures circled silently overhead. We stood at the confluence of the Lavubu and the Limpopo. We stood at a place called Crooks Corner, thus named in the final years of the 19th century, when poaching was an industry and when adventurers had used the proximity of the wild parts of two other countries to recruit — or coerce — young black men from the bush villages to work on the mines in Johannesburg over 500 kilometres to the south.

My companion, a rugged-looking man named Sid, had shown me photographs: groups of black men in the company of their white recruiting agents. These agents would receive a quite handsome sum for each able-bodied man delivered to the labour-hungry Witwatersrand gold industry.

The wild parts of the two other countries were represented only by that tangled growth beyond the fence, and by the wall of bush on the far side of the Limpopo River, wisps of smoke still rising from between the crowded trunks.

We had seen the previous day, from the vantage point of the hill on which Sid worked in the middle of the game reserve, a pale grey smudge billowing from a specific point in the huge rolling away of the bush country. We could see for tens of kilometres into Zimbabwe from the hill. But at that moment our attention had been focused on the slightly drifting column of smoke.

Sid told me: 'They burn the grass on the islands in the river, and on the farther bank. The hope is that animals will be enticed across by the fresh green grass which appears after burning. They set traps. A buffalo was caught in this way recently.' He shrugged his burly shoulders. 'Yes, certainly, for the meat.'

Those many tens of kilometres of Zimbabwean emptiness, inhabited by people who, when they were hungry or otherwise in need, enticed game across the sandy river from the Kruger National Park. But the people were unseen, giving the illusion of emptiness. Even from a vantage point, the emptiness was as pervasive as the silence, certainly evoking a sense that nothing had ever happened there. Yet what a thriving of life there had always been to the north, and for that matter to all the compass points, of Crooks Corner. Sid stood with his hand raised above his eyes as he gazed in among the wisps of smoke and blackened grass. He carried a large revolver thrust a trifle carelessly beneath the shoulder strap of his rucksack.

That inkling of the thriving of life had come forcibly to me when I had the previous day walked with Sid in the wild bush, looking at the tracks of animals, hearing the bark of baboons and seeing them sometimes, the males the epitome of arrogant power, the skittish loping and leaping of the younger ones, or how they sat in loose gatherings and watched us passing from a distance.

We had come to slightly sloping ground at the foot of a hill and Sid pointed with the staff he always carried. At first I saw only chunks of slightly darker earth half buried in the sand, but then he turned one over with the point of his staff.

'Material from the impacted floors of huts. And look at this pottery.' He jabbed gently at a few terracotta shards, some blackened by the smoke of ancient fires. 'Look at the ornamentation. We're probably standing on the remains of an Iron Age settlement. How long ago? To judge by the pottery, about thirteen hundred years ago. But come and look at this.'

He moved forward, his eyes on the ground. After a brief search, he showed me a strip of rusted metal — almost certainly (he suggested) from the wheel of a European pioneer's wagon — and hardly a metre away the unmistakable shape and chiselled surfaces of a Stone Age tool.

'An archaeologist's dream. But at the moment I simply don't have the time.'

Sid's primary preoccupation was a Shona site, a late provincial outpost of the civilisation which had flourished at Great Zimbabwe across the river. He had already found gold beads. Perhaps more gold artefacts were waiting to be unearthed. He would soon excavate; meanwhile he was engaged in rebuilding some of the extensive stonework which covered the top of a rugged hill. The idea was to offer the site, called Thulamela, as an added attraction to visitors to the park. Thulamela meant the place of giving birth, and Sid had shown me pictures of clay smelting ovens built in a stylised female shape to enhance the sense that the production of metal from stones was a form of birth. Thulamela had almost certainly been linked by trade to the East Coast, probably Sofala on the Mozambique coast, and thence to the wider world. Glass beads from India and porcelain from China had yielded dates in the 1460 to 1640 bracket.

'Look down there,' Sid instructed one day as we stood on the edge of Thulamela's fortress hill. 'See the natural pathway. That was an elephant path. It still is. It was also the way used by the traders who came for the gold, the ivory, the skins.'

It was a wild and haunting sight, looking north from Thulamela: uninterrupted views as the massive golden country climbed out of the Limpopo basin to the hilly escarpment beyond. The Thulamela hill itself presented a spectacle of a different hue: this blending of natural feature with human endeavour from centuries past. On the level places near the summit, enormous baobab trees, growing still, had been admitted into the design of walls which at once barred the way yet allowed for limited access and secret pathways until the rocky high places were reached. Here the ruler would have lived. From his vantage point, he would have been able to see the escarpment hills in Zimbabwe to the north, and beyond them, in his inner eye at any rate, to the supreme authority and inspiration of Great Zimbabwe itself.

The Thulamela hilltop possessed such a grace and reassurance, I thought, as Sid told me of these things. The rivers also, graceful and reassuring, as we stood at the unhurried confluence of them, and at the joining of the three countries in the silence and sunlight with vultures circling in the blue above. This unconscious grace of ages and of being, however intricately the old was jumbled with the new: the artefacts everywhere in the sand, and the fires of late 20th-century poachers burning away only one summer's undergrowth. Everything seemed subdued by the grace and silence and vastness of the land itself.

During the afternoon, Sid drove me down to the locked border post in the fence between South Africa and Mozambique. A police station stood on the South African side, low buildings and a few dwellings surrounded by powerful lights which cast a ghostly yellow illumination far into the bush at night. On the other side stood the scattered structures, some of them in ruin, of the Mozambican settlement of Pafuri. And between was a heavy gate, closed and in chains.

A policeman wearing shorts and a T-shirt came out of his garden to greet us. He had splashes of mud on his bare feet. He squinted at us in the glare of the midday sun. He said we were welcome to go down to the gate. He said the

Mozambicans had taken it into their heads to start singing today.

'Well, it's a better noise than gunfire,' Sid remarked.

As we walked towards the gate, we saw that rolls of barbed wire and sandbagged positions characterised the South African side. A small square building — presumably passport control — stood empty and unused. We saw the fence come out of the bush, and pass across the rough road in front of us. The gate was padlocked several times, although presumably it was opened on occasion for pedestrians. During my time with Sid, I had sometimes seen lorries churning down the dusty roads through the game reserve with refugees returning home now that the Mozambican civil war had ended. Strange to think that while some returned in this way, others braved the animals of an unprotected night to walk in the opposite direction — this ceaseless coming and going of Africans across essentially artificial boundaries.

A crowd began to sing on the far side of the wire. People had congregated under a rusting iron roof which offered some protection against the midday sun. They were sufficiently close to the fence for me to discern individual faces and expressions, and I could see that hands were folded sometimes, eyes raised, or heads bent in the unmistakable attitude of worship. They were singing a Christian hymn. Later, they kneeled in the dust and stones to pray. Their voices welled up in a vaguely sad unison which found no echo in the absorbent silence of the bush.

I remarked on the extent of the hold which the religion of colonialism had established over so many Africans. Sid nodded but remained silent. I alluded to the power of Islam in the building of states and nations which had occurred in Africa, but much further to the north. The power manifested in Christianity seemed of a different calibre. It promised salvation from self, and also from that particular darkness of having no past. In this sense, I suggested, it seemed to be another form of the self-denial which colonialism had taught so many Africans to espouse.

'It also offers comfort,' Sid replied, 'especially in times of turmoil. These people have been through nearly thirty years of war, remember.'

Difficult, then, not to enumerate all the conflicts which had beset those people beyond the fence. First, the one between the liberation forces and the Portuguese. Then, when independence came quite suddenly in 1975, between the new government and a South African backed resistance movement. And overlaying these hostilities, complicating an often desperate situation for ordinary citizens, had been the Rhodesian war. Ian Smith's soldiers in hot pursuit, blazing away as the insurgents ran for sanctuary. Rhodesian refugees had fled into Mozambique, while Mozambican refugees had stumbled through the night dangers of the Kruger National Park to South Africa. Memories of such tumults lingered with me as I stood with Sid at the padlocked gate, listening to the singing, and later as we sat outside his cottage at sunset.

While Sid prepared a fire, I looked with a pair of binoculars at the village of Pafuri on the Mozambican side of the border: a few buildings embedded in the greyish bush, that was all; and one of them, once a trading store perhaps, now had its roof caved in and rusting, and the walls pock-marked by what looked like clusters of machine-gun bullets.

'Certainly they are,' Sid replied. 'During the bush war, the Rhodesians would raid frequently into Mozambique at this point.' He indicated the site on which his cottage and a few other structures stood. 'This used to be a mine labour recruiting station. It was ideally situated for this purpose, so close to Crooks Corner. During the bush war, the white staff used to sit on their verandas — much as we're sitting here now — and watch the action.'

In front of Sid's cottage the bush swept away in a grey uniformity, a wide sweep of country ending only at a low ridge several kilometres to the east. I tried to imagine what it must have been like: sipping sundowners to the sporadic crash and rattle of battles fought running through the intervening bush which seemed so peaceful now.

On the small ledge which formed his front garden, Sid was lighting the fire; and to one side, a large carving of a face stood among foliage. It was little more than a hollow log, with eyes and nostrils and open mouth cut through one side. With a candle inside, it might have looked like a Hallowe'en mask; as it was it seemed a sombre object, not menacing so much as exuding a sense of sightless weariness. Sid had purchased it in Zimbabwe, he told me. 'At a market by the roadside. I don't think it's anything special. But you know what it's like: you see something and you have to have it.'

A flame flared through artfully arranged sticks and small branches, and the eyes in the carved face went immediately dark.

'The Rhodesians blasting away with rockets from their aircraft,' Sid was saying. 'Flame and smoke spurting out of the bush. Or they'd come in on foot, and from the verandas the mine recruiting people could hear the rifle fire. It's a bizarre thought. Drinking gin and watching a war being fought not much more than a kilometre over there. And then in the morning they'd send another shipment of foreign labour to sweat it out underground.'

He stood before me with a quizzical expression on his rugged and unshaven face. He half snorted, then turned away, disappearing into the cottage to fetch himself another drink. I sat alone on the narrow ledge of garden. The bush stretched away in the last faint rays of a sun which was sinking at my back. Closer at hand, in the garden, the carved face stared darkly out. The eyes and mouth were black and open, as if in a half mocking representation of death. I felt suddenly chilled. Would this carving remain for me the most potent symbol of the country I was to visit?

On the morning that I went to see the ruins at Great Zimbabwe, the young waiter who attended to my breakfast seemed eager to talk. He had bright eyes and a smiling face. He told me that the ruins had originally been built in 1934. 'Anyway, that is what I have heard,' he said in his engaging way, his expression slightly unsure as he watched for my response. Then he added with some bravado: 'And I have also heard that there is now a plan to build more ruins soon.'

The ruins already there stood unavoidable in the harsh light of morning. Zimbabwe seemed to be a country of the most durable blues and browns and greens; and into this landscape had been inserted the stone-built walls of the Great Enclosure on flat ground to one side, and to the other the formidable fortifications of the so-called Acropolis (although this name had fallen into disrepute), structures which had been set among huge granite boulders on a steep-sided hill. These were the dominant remains of what, between the 13th and the 15th centuries, had been a thriving city, metropole to the site which Sid was restoring over 200 kilometres to the south, and to dozens of similar provincial or regional sites scattered about an extensive empire.

Was it strange that the young waiter at breakfast, who was himself a Shona, should appear so ignorant concerning these things? Perhaps not, I thought as I climbed the steep pathway which led me under the south wall — built as an extension of natural cliffs at the summit of the hill once called Acropolis. After all, when Great Zimbabwe was first discovered by a European — a man named Carl Mauch did so in 1871 — it had immediately been assumed to have been built not by Africans at all, but by men from Lebanon on orders from the Queen of Sheba. Later theories attributed the architecture to Arabs or, as favoured by Cecil Rhodes, Phoenicians.

The European position was simply that Africans, in this case the Shona who inhabited large tracts of the country when Rhodes's settlers had arrived, could not have been responsible for such imposing ruins. Had it been admitted that a past superior to mere barbarism might be a possibility, how could the partition and subjugation of an entire continent have been justified? Prevailing European views regarding the absence of African history, as well as the general inferiority of Africans who were marooned at a lower evolutionary level, supported quite admirably the notion of the civilising mission inherent in colonialism.

The civilising mission: was this the mechanism which had taught the young waiter to decipher menus and to believe quite cheerfully that he had no past? I had watched him, one evening, striking a hide drum outside the dining-room to call the guests to dinner; those deep and repetitive rhythms which developed under his hands and then fled reverberating into the heaviness of night. His dark face had offered a flash of white teeth as he caught my gaze upon him.

With these thoughts I climbed the ancient path, perspiring and encircled by flies, with the south wall rearing above me now, and the view unfolding into a distance which already shimmered. I could see tourists amid the ruins below, in the Great Enclosure and down there where the ground fell away into a steepening valley. All the country I could see was elegantly wooded. Someone below blew a few blasts on what sounded like an animal horn, the slightly baleful sound fading through the broken country. Then the pathway turned and levelled, and I stooped to enter a lintelled doorway giving access through the base of a stone wall built around eight hundred years ago.

The architecture on the hill comprised a skilful marriage of built walls and the sheer faces of the huge granite boulders which littered the summit. Areas were specifically delineated. Here were courtyards large and small, and labyrinths of passageways between. A sense of secrecy pervaded some of the areas — hidden entrances, high balconies — as if these corridors of Zimbabwean power had not been immune to intrigue and certainly not to ritual.

The hill would have been the place of the kings, a kind of castle, with important people of state and trade and religion coming and going, indicative of a complexity of hierarchy and organisation. This medieval palace in the middle of Africa, with even now the sudden suggestion of human figures, as though emerging from the rocks. And what embellishments these spaces, crumbling and empty now, must originally have had.

In an eastern-facing courtyard on the hill, the view was once more of the Great Enclosure, lying far below and with a wide sweep of country beyond. With its high walls and walls within walls, the Great Enclosure was thought by some archaeologists to have been an initiation school for the daughters of the ruling class.

Pleasant enough to view these interpretations from this eastern-facing courtyard on the hill. At the back of the courtyard huge natural rocks reared fifteen metres above the floor. This must have formed an impressive backdrop to the rituals enacted here, and to a display of birds, long since removed, which had been carved from dull green soapstone, each on its own pedestal.

I had seen these birds in the small museum below, floodlit and carefully preserved. On the plinth of one of them, a small crocodile was depicted, crawling upwards. The birds were not large; all were recognisable as birds of prey; but some had toes instead of claws, and a few of the faces seemed quite human. I had read that the Shona belief was that birds, especially eagles, fulfilled the function of messengers between the world of men and the complex spiritual sphere beyond. The ancestral spirits of past kings, in whom the well-being of the living resided, must be constantly propitiated.

So the rituals in the eastern-facing courtyard were enacted. The soapstone birds were worshipped, but not only as messengers; they were also the personification of those old king-spirits to whom the specific messages were directed; the carvings were for this reason part bird, part human. Send the rain. Cause crops to be abundant. Protect the cattle. Bring prosperity and peace to the whole Zimbabwe kingdom, including even those outposts down south of the Limpopo River where Sid was working now. In this way, a profoundly human need was assuaged: this desire for a sense of not being alone in a hostile world, and for divine aid to guide one successfully through it.

I asked a man in the museum if I might take a photograph of the birds. He shook his head. 'No photographs allowed.' Yet he lingered with me, his eyes glancing slowly across my own, his jaws engaged in a constant chewing. In a moment, he said that as a favour I could take one snapshot. When I declined, sensing the beginnings of a bribe, he seemed slightly disconcerted, slightly offended, and left me to peruse the exhibits on my own.

I looked at some of the artefacts which archaeologists had unearthed at Great Zimbabwe over the years. The iron technology was much in evidence: needles, axe and adze heads, the points of arrows, ceremonial spearheads. Also the objects of trade which had come to Great Zimbabwe via the East Coast: glass beads from India, copper ingots, bangles, glazed Chinese pottery, and much more. Arab traders had operated at the Islamic city of Kilwa on the southern Tanzanian coast since the 12th century. Then, aware of the rise of this new African kingdom, they established Sofala, a coastal outpost situated just south of present-day Beira and directly east of Great Zimbabwe. Considerable quantities of Zimbabwe gold and ivory had passed through this port en route to destinations in the Middle and Far East.

If Great Zimbabwe had been a solitary phenomenon, a sudden flowering of more complex ways of life which had as suddenly withered, it would have made the history in this region worthy of careful study. But of course it was not a solitary phenomenon.

I remembered again the young waiter at the hotel, an African with no idea of the past and with no conception of what had formed his own life. If only he knew this barest outline: that before the close of the first millennium AD farmers on the edges of the Kalahari, especially in the Limpopo-Shashi basin over 200 kilometres west of where Sid was working, had begun to form themselves into more complex societies and at about the same time to build in stone. The complexity came in the progression of production from subsistence to surplus, the commencement of trade, and the coming to power of a ruling élite which regulated the affairs of these fledgling states. The leaders lived in an elevated position, normally on an inaccessible hill, as at Mapungubwe in the Limpopo-Shasi basin. Here, they were separated even from their most important subjects by sheer cliffs; and stone walls were erected primarily to limit access to the high places.

Mapungubwe, itself the result of evolution, was the prototype of Great Zimbabwe. Mapungubwe controlled a kingdom of considerable size; and it traded quite vigorously with the East Coast. In later times, Great Zimbabwe grew rich on this trade. But at the start of the 16th century its Islamic trading partners at Sofala and Kilwa were destroyed by the Portuguese, and in any case the importance of Great Zimbabwe had begun to wane. Political power passed to new states emerging nearby, notably Mutapa and Torwa and Rozvi further to the north and west.

For another four centuries, these independent Shona states existed between the Limpopo and Zambezi rivers. They traded more or less successfully with the Portuguese. During the first half of the 19th century, the Shonas were disturbed by the appearance of the Ndebele, a powerful people who had been displaced from more southerly positions by the expansionism of the Zulu ruler Shaka, and then again by the effects of the Great Trek in South Africa. After considerable fighting, the Ndebele established their own kingdom at Bulawayo in the south west of present-day Zimbabwe.

By the end of the century, however, the full force of colonialism arrived in the form of Cecil Rhodes's British South Africa Company, including land-hungry settlers and an army of five hundred armed men. They came to exploit the gold which they believed, though erroneously, to be abundant here. In the process the Ndebele rebelled and were crushed with the aid of machine guns. Their cattle were confiscated, their land was divided among the settlers, and the Ndebele themselves restricted to relatively small reserves. The subjugation of the Shona followed. Thus was Rhodesia born.

Meanwhile, the Great Zimbabwe and numerous other ruins were being ripped apart by European fortune hunters. At least one commercial company had been established to exploit the riches of the ruins.

All this opportunism and conquest had brought into existence a short-lived country, Rhodesia, and at the same time had obliterated thousands of years of human development. What white people in their ignorance believed — that Africa had no past — was to become a widespread black reality. Africans had been left with a void, and not even with any conscious idea of themselves as truncated and bereft. They'll be building more ruins soon, my waiter had said with slight bravado and genuine friendliness. This, at one level at any rate, was the real legacy of colonialism.

I drove in magical landscapes that afternoon, heading by a circuitous route in the direction of Zimbabwe's capital city. The country was everywhere peppered with those abrupt outcrops of rock and stone, not dissimilar to the Acropolis hill at Great Zimbabwe, which provided large tracts of landscape with its distinctive quality. Some of the boulders were as big as houses and piled precariously one on top of the other. The sudden green of acacias and the straw yellow of ripe grass brought a richness of colour as the sunlight began to slant and fade. Children and groups of docile animals stood at the water pumps, and through the open window of the car I could hear their calls.

A while later, as euphorbias stood in dark silhouette against the setting sun, I turned in at a garage. In the dusk, while my car was being filled, I watched two laughing men at the next pump. The one was tall, quite thin, with legs which bounced slightly like rubber. He was well dressed in sports jacket and tie, and he was joviality personified. He smiled at me, his legs bouncing slightly at the knees.

He said: 'I'm living according to my culture, man.'

His companion came towards me, grinning and pointing at his nostrils, saying that the tall man's culture was to sniff. I must have looked nonplussed, for the second man drew from his pocket a small sachet of white powder. I asked what it was. The second man did not reply, but held the base of his thumb against his nostrils, and then laughed.

As I drove on, I passed them on the road. They had pulled their vehicle on to the verge to talk with acquaintances, perhaps to share a sniff or two. They waved generously as I passed, an indication of the lavish camaraderie engendered by cocaine, and also by the grace of Africa's evenings.

O n the way to Harare, I turned off towards a place called Serima Mission. The dusty road went deep into a rural remoteness. People walked on the verges, raising hands in greeting as I passed. Animals grazed on veld where grass was already thin. Some soil erosion showed, and low hillsides were studded with huts and homesteads. Then a sign indicated that Serima was over there.

I drove slowly over potholes. At the end of a long roadway with mature cypress trees growing on either side, I saw the shape of a church coloured grey from the raw plaster with which it had been finished. Getting closer, I could make out the belfry, decorated by figures and surmounted by a simple metal cross. Then I passed into the churchyard and parked the car.

To one side I found a single grave adorned with pieces of local quartz. Flowers grew on the raised surface of the grave, especially succulents with yellow and purple blooms. The grave had been surrounded by a crude mesh fence attached to timber stakes − presumably to keep out goats.

This was the grave of Father John Groeber, born in Switzerland in 1903, ordained in 1936, who had served as a missionary at Serima from 1948 to 1967, and dying at last in Africa in 1972. He was the architect of the Serima church, and a man who, at least in the visual sense, strove for synthesis between Christian concepts and an authentic African vision.

This was the essence of what I read later about this remarkable man and the monument he had left behind. For the moment, though, I stood by his simple grave and looked up at his big grey church rising from the bare earth of the yard.

The mission also contained a school, and I was reminded of this when a ragged line of boys in khaki came panting past. I guessed they might be involved in a cross-country race. We exchanged waves; a few of the boys smiled at me as they laboured across the churchyard and out into the hot and thorny bush beyond.

Father Groeber had started this school in the late 1940s, and he took a personal interest in the art classes which he delivered himself. Before becoming a priest, he had studied architecture and art in Europe; and it is clear that African art made a major impression on him. Once in Rhodesia, he spent a lot of his energy encouraging African boys to draw and carve. At the mission he founded here in the Serima Native Reserve, this energy and the talent it stimulated soon found full outlet.

The boys, his pupils, were taken through a process which developed from drawing to modelling in clay and finally to wood carving. The subject was always a face, the models most often illustrations of Central and West African masks. Stimulated by this approach, some beautiful masks had been carved at the Serima school. But Father Groeber's primary concern was the teaching of Christianity. The making of the masks had the effect of liberating the creativity of his students, a creativity which he then deliberately turned to the illustration of Christian themes and Christian personalities. Here is the story, he would say; now make the image, now carve the wood. And all the resulting images he had crammed into his beloved church.

Intimations in the portico: a pair of richly decorated doors set into the pale plastered walls, and between the doors a peaceful-looking wood representation presumably of Peter, a large key held in both his square hands. The detail seemed multi-layered, luring my gaze first to the pictorial panels in the doors themselves, then to the darker figures and faces in the elaborate surrounds.

But the portico could offer little to prepare one for the interior of the Serima church. Perhaps the effect was enhanced by the denser silence within, the limited sunlight falling in slanting bars in the hot afternoon, the feeling of controlled space inside which the carved treasures lived. Here was a great sense of thriving human life; and beyond that sense, as one stood in the special silence and light, the dawning of the reality of an attempt at synthesis.

At one level, certainly, there was a distinct sense of pleasing juxtaposition rather than fusion. It was like a celebration: all those African things fitted inside the unmistakably European proportions of the building itself. The high ceilings, the open arches, the twin naves converging upon the altar, the narrow windows flaring with light. And Africa's invasion of this: the uncut timber poles, many of them patterned with chevrons, which supported the roof; the reed ceilings beyond; the clay pottery which acted as legs for tables; and everywhere the carving in wood both dark and pale, ornamental and utilitarian. Faces and figures, sometimes crowding together as at the rear of the altar, or carved into poles like totems; the size of the hands nearly always exaggerated; the faces reduced to simple planes, sharply defined, yet with a depth of feeling everywhere, a sense of the crowding together of eyes and life which the European spaces could not cow.

At a deeper level, though, the idea of Christianity sat awkwardly on these images which seemed to flow backwards into ritual of another sort. The masks of Zaire and Nigeria had liberated the talents of these young artists, masks that served the purposes of rites and organic preoccupations which Christianity seemed for the most part at pains to repudiate. Yet, in the fervour of creativity which had guided the chisels of Father Groeber's schoolboys, such differences seemed hardly to matter. Here in the Serima church small sprites peered out among the sacred figures, and upon some rich gathering of reverence and worship the mysterious shadows of the ancestors sometimes fleetingly alighted.

These were my thoughts as I lingered in the church, sitting on a low bench and seeing how the walls had been discoloured at the height of hands, and how smooth was the concrete floor from the passage of the feet of countless congregations. And I heard the corrugated-iron roof noising as it expanded and contracted with the sunlight and shade outside. Clouds had suddenly arrived. And then a sudden shower clattered down, slightly raucous, and the smell of it — that stench of dust and dung and rain and warmth which is so special to the dry places in Africa — wafted through the narrow windows left ajar.

I tried to imagine Father Groeber, a thin man dressed in a black habit and crude leather sandals perhaps, striding about during the building and decoration of his church. It was a fitting memorial to his life's work: these lofty spaces filled with images of his God wrought by Africa's hand. Yet the slight sense of incongruity had become part of the eloquence for me now. Just as Europe had changed Africa's view of the world and of itself, so as surely had Africa placed veils upon the eyes of Father Groeber. And in both directions, these views would not focus sometimes.

When the rain stopped, the sun blazed down once more and the earth steamed. I left the church by a side door and went quietly on my way.

H arare, the modern city. Many structures of glass which flashed and glittered, and the frequent sight of those slender construction cranes in attendance as the shells of new buildings reached into the vivid blue of the sky. Like the flags fluttering up there, horizontal bands of colour with a representation of one of the soapstone Zimbabwe birds superimposed on a star. The same bird repeated on the coinage. The past recorded in this way, but the post-colonial present claiming precedence.

The Zimbabwe dollar had recently been devalued as part of the country's economic structural adjustment programme, an exercise in belt-tightening suggested by foreign banks to which African countries owed billions. For many thousands of Zimbabweans times were hard, yet the centre of Harare had a prosperous feel. The shopping spread over many blocks, street after street of specialist shops, a lot of curio outlets for the tourists, and the prices of imported electrical goods seemed extremely high, those of vehicles prohibitive.

Nevertheless, the stores and banks and hotel foyers were full enough, and people appeared well dressed and purposeful. Several times I saw a typical London taxi bearing the name of a famous local hotel whose foyer, in turn, bore the sumptuous stamp of colonial times. Jackets and ties after seven, and definitely no sandals or jeans.

But Africa pervaded the pavements and the open spaces. In spite of the glittering glass edifices which reared above, the evidence at street level pointed unambiguously to African realities, as did the exhaust fumes which thickened the air as high-loaded lorries trundled through the central streets. Palm trees adorned the island which ran the length of Julius Nyerere Way. I walked on Africa Unity Square, thus named in 1988 to commemorate the twenty-fifth anniversary of the founding of the Organisation of African Unity. A plaque said that the square had been opened by Comrade Robert Gabriel Mugabe, Zimbabwe's president. But someone had taken pains to scratch over Mugabe's name, a slight defacing. Above the plaque a grimy Zimbabwe flag, complete with soapstone bird, hung limp against its pole. The square was filled with cobbled walkways, gardens, and modern-looking fountains, water dancing everywhere. People sat in gatherings on the shady lawns, or on benches along an avenue of jacarandas. Other people were trying to sell wood carvings which stood in tiered and staring crowds on the paving near the walkways. And then, with some incongruity, the sudden sound of typical Westminster chimes came from a belfry located somewhere across the street.

Strange, the way the city contained so many small conflicts. But not so surprising perhaps. From Salisbury the capital of Southern Rhodesia to Salisbury after the unilateral declaration of independence in 1965. Ian Smith's stronghold. Now Harare, where the tension between colonial and African icons caused a small snap, as of electric energy, in the very air.

At the National Gallery this tension seemed to find its most eloquent expression. Here, in this modern building, the battleground was defined in stone. Stone sculpture abounded, but I forced my attention to begin with on a collection of paintings hung on the mezzanine, many of them depicting stone in its natural state, piled up and balancing sometimes like those brooding collections I had seen at Great Zimbabwe and many other places in the country.

The artist was an Englishman, Robert Paul, who had died in 1980, the year that Zimbabwe, after much travail, had gained its independence. Paul had originally come to Rhodesia in 1927 as a mounted trooper in the British South Africa Police. His sketchbook became an essential part of his field equipment, but he only began to paint after his retirement in the early 1950s. He possessed an instinctive sympathy with the rhythms and forces of landscape; and his style 'reaches beneath the cosmetic face to capture the spirit'. This much I learned from a neatly printed card mounted among the paintings.

But to me, as I stood before them, they seemed above all to emanate heat and loneliness. Was this the spirit beneath the cosmetic face? The rocks glared with stored sunlight, and the bigger boulders, commanding the tops of empty hills and mountains and dwarfing the trees below, were painted on the same plane as the sky. This had the effect of forcing them closer, with hardly any space beyond, so that they brooded inescapably against the gaze of the viewer, and at the same time seemed capable of reflecting the heat and emptiness of the landscapes beyond the confines of the frames.

The hidden themes of colonialism returned transmuted to my mind. This primitive force of landscape as Paul had seen it, a relentless solidity, a vision of rocks in their unutterably harsh and brutal reality. Rocks with immense force, but without history. Immutable stones which had no voice. This was the colonial vision.

But the gallery offered another besides, a vision much less monolithic and infinitely more plastic.

In the foyer I read the following paragraph in a book by Celia Winter-Irving: 'It is significant that stone plays a major role in the two most famous examples of Zimbabwe's visual culture, the rock art (of the Stone-Age San) and the ruins of Great Zimbabwe.' And now, the Shona sculpture which had suddenly flowered in 1956 should be seen as 'the Renaissance of the stone of Zimbabwe'.

Everywhere in the National Gallery this coaxed and sometimes polished stone stared out at me. It drew the eye, especially in the garden behind the gallery where many of the larger pieces were displayed. It seemed to represent some sort of transformation: natural stone giving birth to wrought images sometimes. Here was metamorphosis, something coming through in the greens or browns or blacks of the raw material. And even where the material was completely worked, the sense of metamorphism remained. Rocks changing under heat or pressure. Something new emerging, unlike the old, although still connected to it.

I had heard that some of the exponents of this new sculpture, hardly a generation in extent and sprung from nowhere, had been trained or associated in various ways with Serima and Father John Groeber, but the pieces on display seemed too rounded, too sympathetic to the raw material, to follow naturally from the strident, almost defiantly African flavour of Serima's feast. The comparison seemed to me like the difference between reaction, a process of conscious assimilation, and here in the museum a more subliminal response.

Some of the pieces allowed the natural shape of the stone to enfold a face or other characteristic of life, encasing the characteristic like a kernel. These evoked for me the image of the boulders on the hill at Great Zimbabwe, and how the walls of human design had fitted between. People living among rocks: that had been the Shona way. There was this unmistakable mixing of the natural with the shaped artefact. But there was more besides.

I stood in the garden as the sun set and the glass of the high buildings of Harare glittered in the dying of the light. Around me stood this thriving collection of living forms emerging from the rock. Human forms, in grief or supplication, some of them almost Eastern in their pose and serenity, but unmistakably African in their rounded simplicity and bulk. Here in the shadows were some figures which clung together, growing out of each other with gestures of dependency and support, a sort of collectivity without question or burden. I moved among them as darkness came, as the trees turned black, and as the high sky above the buildings blazed more redly.

They looked at me from an intangible level of history, these beings from the centre of the rocks, these crowding images from a single continuum, concrete and abstract worlds entwined, men and animals and birds, the living and the dead, and God drawing men from animals, half human faces raised, serpents encircling graceful necks, generous loins, children at breasts, eyes closed sometimes in a thrall of certitude and oneness.

Those moments in the garden were like a leap backwards for me. Here was a striking evocation of African spirituality, a sense of the place of man in his universe. But was there a certain sadness here as well? Were there soft voices in the shadows? This is what we once possessed, the voices said, and this is what we have lost without even knowing conscious loss, only an indefinable anger. The heat and pressure of guns and modernisation had caused this cry. Here was the hiatus; but where the reconnection, where the leap forward?

I had supper in Harare one evening with a youngish man named Steve. Already overweight in his early thirties, he had a pleasant enough face, adorned with a trimmed beard and spectacles, and the right shoulder of his shirt was stitched and quilted to take the butt of a rifle. We were talking about white Zimbabwean women.

'It's difficult to compete,' Steve complained. 'The girls tend to go overseas where they're soon snapped up. Rhodesian girls: they're in great demand. But for us here, the odds are against us, unless of course you happen to be rich.' He shrugged his shoulders a trifle absently. 'That's why I'm still a bachelor.'

Yet he seemed to make a good enough living. He had told me during our afternoon together that he erected telecommunications dishes, largely for well-off white families who wished for a larger selection of television channels than was provided inside the country. So far he had installed around two thousand. They were often visible, I had noticed, in the suburbs, these cage-like dishes three or four metres in diameter which pointed somewhat forlornly, all at the same angle, into space. I asked why he thought they were so popular in Harare.

He shrugged in that offhand way of his. 'Local TV is pretty poor, and apart from television what is there to do? There's not much entertainment here.'

By these observations, he suggested a post-colonial isolation which I had only vaguely caught in the city before. But now this picture of slightly bored white families clustered around the cathode ray sharpened my grasp of the city as a whole. I was reminded of the all-white cricket match I had encountered (although I noticed an Indian batsman), and the deckchairs arranged around the boundary and the desultory clapping through which black waiters carried their glass-laden trays. All this represented the slightly bitter aftermath of colonialism, like the licking of wounds, in this physically gorgeous country where not many more than 100 000 whites remained within a total population of around ten million. Did they feel trapped here as they watched the next load of electronic amusement garnered by their dish?

Another picture of isolation offered by Steve was simply the restaurant he had chosen for our meal, a Greek place of sorts with bright lights and inexpensive ornaments attached to a decorative brick wall. Most tables were occupied, and all the diners were white. A few of the male faces were sullen, vaguely aggressive, eyes searching for others to outstare, as if it would not have taken much for a fight to break out — one of those scuffles which so often characterise a general sense of humiliation. I ordered kleftiko, but it was unavailable. Steve settled for a steak.

'You shouldn't worry about my father,' he said. 'He's a bit of a racist. He won't change.'

His father, that afternoon, had raised his voice so that his wife looked uneasy, airing views which seemed bizarre rather than out-dated, his tanned face as bloated as the rest of him, his simple hatreds distorting the expression in his dark and smallish eyes.

I had asked Steve's father why he thought, as he insisted, that there had been so many deteriorations during the years since independence. He grinned angrily at me, shoving a finger upwards against his cheek. 'Because every time they pick their noses they get rid of more of their brains.'

'Mind you,' Steve said, looking at me across the table in the Greek restaurant, 'my father was one of the first to see the writing on the wall. I remember — I was only a youngster — my father coming in with a map one evening. Pointing at Mozambique and Zambia. Saying: we're surrounded; we're going to lose this war. His friends had shouted him down, but he was right.'

I asked what he, Steve, had thought about the war.

He shrugged. 'I was only a kid, really. I was in my last year at school when it finished.' He chewed steadily, glancing about him with calm but minimally interested eyes, then regarding me again.

'When I look back, I think we were manipulated quite a lot. By Smith. By censorship. People believed they were fighting against communism, fighting to save their wives from being raped. Then in the elections Mugabe got in. Everybody was expecting Abel Muzorewa, the moderate, to win. That was a real shock. People walked around in a shocked silence. All of a sudden they were living in a socialist-stroke-communist country.'

It seemed inevitable that I should repeat the question I had asked his father: how had conditions changed since independence?

Again the shrug. 'Everything has gone down. Except prices. Services have definitely become worse. The telephones...' He declined to describe them. 'Electricity: there are usually four or five cuts a month. There's permanent water rationing. The streets are full of unmown grass and weeds. Mind you, the roads themselves have been repaired a bit recently − but this is because a white is now in charge of them again.'

Had anything − anything at all − improved?

He glanced at me, and then his eyes were suddenly quiet and thoughtful. 'Look,' he said, 'there's peace.'

Here was some honesty, but he struck me most enduringly as a lonely man, but in a vague sort of way; he seemed already bleached and somewhat faded by the brilliance of the sky he perpetually pointed his electronic dishes towards; no urgent longings here, rather the slight tediums of post-colonial life and bachelorhood − and the occasional bitterness embedded in his post-colonial ideas.

He slipped easily enough into these ideas over coffee, telling me of Africans' inability to plan ahead, how the men who worked for him would always ask why the dishes should be greased and painted when they had not yet started to rust.

'They just can't understand the purpose of maintenance programmes. How do you explain prevention and conservation in a continent of such waste?'

'Would you have liked to fight in the war?' I asked, glancing at the quilted patch on his shoulder.

'Of course not.' The reply was immediate. He looked more carefully at me, as if he might find a hidden meaning in my sudden changing of the subject. 'I believe our security forces behaved well most of the time. It was only at the end, when they were morally if not militarily defeated. Then there was a ruthlessness...'

He shrugged, and the gesture seemed laced with a trace of petulance. 'We should have been given a chance to rule ourselves, to sort out some sort of gradual transition,' he went on. 'Look at the mess in Zambia, in Malawi. Britain rushed us into it. Couldn't we have been given the chance to work it out for ourselves?'

The question was plaintive. I offered no reply. We parted on the pavement outside the restaurant. The Bush War, the Second Chimurenga as it was called by black Zimbabweans (the first being the fight against Rhodes's settlers almost exactly a century before), lingered with me like the smell of old smoke: sixteen years of fighting and upheaval, 150 000 refugees and nearly 30 000 lives lost.

I remembered Sid telling me about the Rhodesians who would come clattering over the border at Pafuri while people sat on their verandas in South Africa and watched. I had asked several people in Harare if any of the graves of white Rhodesian soldiers had been preserved or their sacrifice in any way publicly honoured. They did not know. They seemed vaguely ill at ease with the question.

For the other side, of course, there were the memorials at Heroes' Acre.

For some time, though, I avoided the Acre. I was not sure why, except that my reluctance had something to do with a mild dread of having inevitabilities confirmed.

One afternoon though I drove determinedly along Samora Machel Avenue. As the road took me through the city's western suburbs, the Acre's central monument appeared for a while at some distance to the left, a towering obelisk on the summit of a darkly wooded hill. But I missed the turning and found myself driving into open country. I continued for some time, in that half listless mood which dalliance often brings, and then turned off on a road which took me to an expanse of water called Lake Chivero, or McIlwaine in pre-independence days. The name Chivero was familiar to me, although I could not decide why. Had I read something in the local newspaper about it? It hardly mattered then, as the road passed through a gate and a sign told me I had arrived.

But the water seemed largely inaccessible, with much fenced private property at the lakeside. Finally, though, I found a way: I followed a faint track through high grass which continued growing even after the water had begun. Quite far out, the grass still showed above the gentle blue ripples of the lake itself.

To one side, four women stood knee-deep while they fished, their slender rods drooping towards the water, the lines hanging straight down. Then a rod was jerked upwards, and a small flash of silver swung towards the fisherwoman. Deftly she disengaged the still-wriggling prize and dropped it into a bag attached to her waist. The patience and silence of the women was regularly punctuated by this sudden movement as another mouthful, hardly more than that, was added to the haul.

But when I called out a greeting, the women did not respond, merely glancing at me in a slightly sullen way before returning to their work. They made a striking picture, with the afternoon sun dazzling on the broader expanse of the lake beyond, as they stood in the shallows, fishing to survive.

'Food, oh yes,' a friendly man told me at a research station of sorts which I came upon a little distance along the shore. A sign had said something about fisheries and ornithology. The man had come to greet me as I wandered between a series of concrete ponds. 'We breed the fish for food here. We experiment with different fish. The small ones that you saw the women catching. Also larger ones like bream. Oh yes,' he went on, smiling politely at me, 'many people depend on the lake for their living. Oh yes, plenty of poor people around Harare.'

I began to see them all along the lake: women carrying wrapped bundles, perhaps the day's catch, on their heads; others in single file with wood; men coming up from the water through tall reeds, two of them carrying rods which they placed upright through the windows of a small car from the 1950s. The rods swayed like aerials as they jolted over low rocks and on to a dusty track.

I came across a village of shacks between the trunks of larger trees at the water's edge. Smoke from fires defined the shafts of sunlight piercing the foliage above; half-naked children watched as I passed; the shacks were made out of corrugated iron and some plastic sheeting; and a small crowd of shouting men and youths pushed a dilapidated station-wagon which ploughed without life through white sandy earth between the trees.

I paused to watch, wondering idly whether they would have success. And it was then that I noticed one of the mirrors had been tied to jagged holes in a fender by a length of wire.

'They smash the wing mirrors of any vehicle that gets too close.'

The words came clearly into my mind, and I saw again the bloated face of Steve's father, his small eyes filled with contempt. 'All their pomp and ceremony,' he said with a lip which curled. 'Their medals and flags. Their cavalcades with all the Mercedes and motor bikes, going hell for leather with sirens and lights. Then get the hell out of it, that's all I can say. Drive on to the pavement. I've seen them smash the wing mirrors of cars just because they think they're too close.'

And now the station-wagon began to buck and roar, and an explosion of exhaust enveloped the small crowd which had been pushing. Figures darted forward to catch up; they clambered through doors which swung open, which slammed; and then, with extreme bathos, the engine died. The noisy men emerged, teeth flashing as they laughed or argued. The bonnet was raised, and they leaned inside to see that reeking object which had frustrated their exertions.

I left them then, these would-be travellers in a reluctant station-wagon, these ragged people from the lakeside shacks, these women fishing in bright sunlight for the tiny silver ones which looked like shards of mirror as they were jerked from the water. Yet I came away with a slight taste of these shards and an idea of swinging truncheons to savour, and drove towards their Heroes' Acre.

But a man at the elaborate gate said I could not go in without a permit. He came marching smartly out of an office to deliver this news. He said, but without any trace of belligerence, that a permit could only be obtained at an office in the middle of Harare. But I was reluctant to be put off: to see what the Acre contained had become an imperative now. I explained that I was leaving town the following morning; and I admitted I had left my visit perilously late. We chatted pleasantly for a few moments. Then he said, and with an expression of real generosity, I thought: 'Look. Come in. I will take you.'

He was a smiling young man, clear-eyed and slim, almost self-consciously neat in his khaki uniform and black beret and boots. He clambered into the car and sat with his hands on his knees. I told him my name and asked him his.

'Pleased to meet you,' he said. 'I am George.'

I asked him if he was a soldier, and his smile deepened.

'No, no, I am only a guide.'

Then we drove round a low shoulder in the wooded landscape, and in this way the various elements of Zimbabwe's most important national monument spread out before us.

George indicated that I should park on a wide area of paving at the bottom of ground which rose with increasing steepness until it culminated in the hill on which the towering obelisk stood. Closer at hand, a large statue the colour of terracotta was flanked by two huge murals. As we walked across the paving towards them, George assumed a more official tone.

'All the material used here is from Zimbabwe. The black granite is from Mukoto. The statue commemorates the unknown soldier; it is in bronze. Now here are the murals. All the artwork was done by ten Zimbabwe artists, and seven from the Democratic People's Republic of Korea.'

We had stopped before the mural to the left of the statue. It was divided into three scenes: the first showed black people being beaten by white soldiers; the second depicted a man with a book surrounded by listening figures ('The conscientising of the people,' George called it); and in the third, people receiving arms and preparing to fight and requesting guidance (again according to George) from their ancestors. The mural on the right completed the story. Here was fighting ('Notice that the boys and girls are acting as informants and ammunition carriers,' said George); and then the jubilation of the cease-fire and families reunited; and finally the victory march, the new flag unfurled, and the head and shoulders of Robert Mugabe rising above this general scene of optimism and the fulfilment of long-held hope.

George raised his arm to point. I followed his direction and saw, on top of the wall on which the mural was attached, a single depiction of those birds of prey, half human in aspect sometimes, which I had seen carved in soapstone in the museum at the ruins of Great Zimbabwe. It sat there in a profound and motionless silence, as if looking down at us. 'The bird of our ancestors,' George explained quite casually, and then he led me away.

We mounted low curving steps to stand before the central statue to the unknown warrior. Three figures towered above us: a soldier carrying a flag, a woman with an automatic rifle who lifted a corner of the flag to her left breast, and a second man holding an armour-piercing rocket-launcher. All three figures gazed steadfastly ahead, chins lifted, expressions indomitable and proud. A few wreaths had been propped against the polished black stone of the base.

'This is for all the freedom fighters, men and women, who were killed or never found,' George said. 'Their spirits can come here and find rest.'

We went further up the hill, on to terraces defined by retaining walls built of stone. The terraces were filled with rows of graves of the national heroes. There were also terraces left open for the national heroes still to come. As we walked slowly past the graves, George began to provide me with short biographies of men like Leopold Takawira, Herbert Chitepo, Josiah Tongogara, Jason Moyo and many others who were buried here. Some had died in prison, others in car and parcel bomb attacks. His official-sounding voice droned on as we moved from headstone to headstone. His face was serious yet relaxed. He knew what he had to say by heart, and the facts came rattling into the gracious ripening atmosphere of the afternoon.

I hardly listened. I saw the bird below me, sitting motionless on the mural wall, the bird of the ancestors, as George had said, but it seemed too small here for any potency. The scale of the Heroes' Acre was monumental, belittling of human individuals; it was on a scale too large for what it said, too large for reality even; and the presence of the carved bird down there could bring no substance to the past. The bird was icon only, severed from the past by the grip of the present, this glorification of independence, this slightly gloating satisfaction over the outcome of a small but brutal war. I remembered my smiling young waiter who had beaten the drums of his own truncated past and who had told me the ruins at Great Zimbabwe had been first built in 1934.

'Committed suicide . . .' George's voice was bland enough as he rattled out the facts.

I looked down at the grave about which he spoke. Maurice Nyagumbo. Born in 1924, died in 1989. Twenty-one years in prison for his part in the struggle for the liberation of Zimbabwe. After independence, serving as a cabinet minister, assisting with the unification of hostile factions within the country — and then giving it all up. Taking his own life rather than live with his shame.

'Yes. He got involved in a motor car scandal of some kind,' George said in a matter-of-fact voice; then he led me at a slightly brisker pace further along the terrace, clearly mindful that the afternoon would soon be drawing to a close.

We trudged up eight flights of stairs cut into the side of the steepening hill. Above us loomed the obelisk, the unavoidable sight of which encouraged George to produce his final drone of facts.

'Forty metres high. The lighted point is symbolic of the eternal flame which depicts the spirit of independence. The tower itself symbolises the spear of our forefathers. And here at the top, from this viewing deck, you can see all the interesting places in Harare.'

While he proceeded to describe these, I looked down the way we had come, to the terraces of graves, the monument to the unknown soldier, the murals, the wide paved area on which my car looked smaller than a toy. The seating beyond, which George told me, seeing where my gaze was directed, could accommodate five thousand 'for funerals and other ceremonial occasions'.

And as I stood there in the early evening breeze and in the last of the golden light, I realised what it was that had made me reluctant to come. It was this sense I experienced now: of a history cut off rather than abbreviated. The place and its scale had forced a question upon me. Had there been life before the anti-colonial struggle? Or had Africa succumbed to the European inaccuracy, as it had succumbed to so much else during that short and tempestuous relationship? A life before the white man came? Hardly one worth remembering perhaps; only a vague caricature of one. Like the small bird on the mural wall, invisible from these heights where I stood beside the symbol of the forefathers' spears. There seemed to me to be a clearer sense of continuity among the fishing people at Lake Chivero, in their preoccupation with survival, than there was here.

I became aware that George was speaking in an African language. I turned and saw two soldiers sprawled on the parapet of the viewing deck, their automatic rifles lying to one side. They had become unspeakably weary of guarding the eternal flame of the spirit of independence.

When I got back to my hotel, I searched among newspapers to find the article which had mentioned

Chivero. I could hear the evening city outside my window, the roar of lorries in the central streets. The headline, when I rediscovered it, seemed to jump out at me, suddenly bizarre.

Man missing after release of crocodiles into lake.

The matter-of-fact prose related how the Department of National Parks and Wildlife Management had put 'twelve crocodiles with a vicious reputation' into Lake Chivero. Now a man was missing, although his jacket had been found at the lakeside. And ordinary people continued to fish 'since they could not afford meat'. I remembered the four women I had seen, standing in the shallows and jerking their rods to bring another mouthful to their bags. I wondered if one of them was Comrade Theresa Sachikonye who was quoted in the article as saying: 'We know that dangerous crocodiles were put into the lake. But we need food, that is why we have to continue fishing. If we are killed, well that's it.' A National Parks employee said they were 'making every effort to inform the public about the crocodiles'.

I stood at my window, looking down into the streets of the modern city, the lights of the cars streaming past and sometimes reflecting in the façades of those buildings built of glass. For a while longer, the western sky glowed red, and then the darkness came.

I stood in darkness, my thoughts dwelling momentarily on the perception of white artists who saw only the harsh emptiness of Zimbabwe's wild country, as if nothing could ever have happened in such a landscape of rocks and trees and the enormous over-arching sky. Like those hot and lonely canvases I had seen in the gallery, all flooded with light; and the implicit revelation in them that stone was stone, and that there was nothing much in Africa before the canvases themselves.

But more clearly I focused on the artefacts of Africa which had cried out the contradiction, and which cried out other things besides: the stories they told; the continuities and discontinuities they laid bare. Above all, certainly in my Zimbabwean experience, the wrenching impact of colonialism had left people without an idea of their own past, leaving them only with imitation and false ruins. And in such hiatus the culture of the powder sniffed seemed not so far removed, as antidote, from those newer artefacts, the bronze guns and rocket-launchers of liberation.

Liberation had become the new past, and also symbol now of psyches out of joint. Yet what of the continuity I had dimly sensed? The rocks and birds of Great Zimbabwe; the blending at Serima of the sacred and unintentionally profane; the re-creation in the new Shona sculpture of the old consciousness when man and beast were one. These things seemed to flow not far beneath the obliterating impact of colonialism. But who had the power to see, or for that matter to dismiss, their connection to the urgencies of now?

4

Davison's World

The sooner one grasps the ordinariness of Africa, the easier it becomes to appreciate that people in Africa, however primitive their culture, are concerned with the same basic tasks — earning a living and raising a family — as people anywhere else in the world.

— Robin Hallett, *Africa to 1875,* 1970.

Even before I had got to Lusaka Airport's passport control — indeed, as I was still settling at the back of a short queue there — I was approached by an attractive young woman with her eyebrows arched. She carried a clipboard tucked against the inside of one elbow. Her almond-shaped eyes settled questioningly on my face as she asked for me by name. When I responded, she said simply and with a graceful smile: 'Welcome to Zambia. I hope you will enjoy your stay in our beautiful country.'

She introduced herself as a representative of the car hire company through which I had arranged a vehicle; and I found her presence immediately reassuring. My aircraft had landed after dark, and in the slight confusions of arrival — the strange clusters of lights seen from the runway, the disorientation of unknown buildings and direction signs, the new sights and sounds which set up vague cross-currents athwart the mainstream of my attention — she provided a focal point. At least I had not been forgotten.

And her experience certainly smoothed my passage through the airport rigmarole. Here were forms to be completed. Here was luggage. Sign here for the car. Telephone here for a nice hotel. Her politely smiling face went before me, and it was not long before we had left the terminal building, and I found myself surrounded by the shining paintwork of taxis and a gaggle of drivers offering bargains into town.

My guide said in her perfect English: 'I'm sure they will have mentioned to you in Johannesburg that your car will be chauffeur-driven. This is to cut down on theft. It is not a good idea to leave vehicles unattended in Lusaka. We lost four self-drive cars in one week recently.'

Faces seemed to loom up out of the shadows on every side, calling out fares. Then one face steadied. It was dark-skinned, narrow, with compact features and hard eyes sliding across my own.

'This is Davison, your driver,' the young woman said, and smiled in her engaging way. 'You can relax. He's the best we've got.'

We shook hands on the crowded pavement. Davison nodded a somewhat terse greeting. He wore a black leather jacket, even though shirt-sleeves would have been more appropriate for the mildness of the night. The young woman had given me a map and a guidebook, and now with another graceful smile, she left me with Davison who was locking my luggage in the boot. Then he opened the door of the car and made a slight gesture which indicated that I should enter. I clambered inside, and in a moment we were driving towards my hotel in the centre of Lusaka.

The vehicles on the road flowed slowly, sometimes swerving unexpectedly, but rarely troubling to dim headlights for oncoming traffic. Davison drove in the same way, and I could see that the swerving was to avoid those places in the roadway where the surface was broken into holes. Lights were left on bright, no doubt so that these impassable areas could be identified more easily and in sufficient time to take the necessary evasive action.

Davison steered the car into Addis Ababa Avenue, a curving thoroughfare with a central island separating the traffic, and along the length of which, above shrubbery with big leaves, many of the street lights were out. Davison chewed gum while he drove, his narrow features defined for the most part by what illumination the remaining street lights offered.

We said little. I had asked him if he had lived long in Lusaka, and he replied: 'I was born here, educated here, and I got married here.' He was surprisingly soft-spoken. His image, vaguely strong-arm in the leather jacket, had promised a gruffer articulation; but in reality his voice possessed a lilting quality of which, even as our time together increased, I was always conscious.

I had established, too, that Davison was almost exactly the same age as Zambian independence, both having been born in the early 1960s. In consequence, Davison had no direct experience of colonialism; he represented the first full generation of independent black Africans. Whether he typified this generation, whether any individual could, it was of course not easy to tell.

Although the hotel — with fountains at the entrance and chandeliers in the foyer — looked too expensive for my purpose, Davison fell immediately into a particular role when we arrived. With curt efficiency, he placed my single suitcase in the care of a hotel porter. Then, his expression showing what I thought to be a certain veiled superiority, he turned to me for instructions.

'What time in the morning?'

'Why not have breakfast with me?'

'Yes, all right. What time?' His expression had not changed.

'About eight.'

'Eight-hundred hours,' he said in his lilting voice. 'Yes, I will wait inside.'

His hard eyes shifted across my face. I said good-night. He turned away to attend to the car which stood with one door and the boot still nonchalantly open outside the imposing entrance to the hotel.

T he long counter where breakfast was laid out had as its centre-piece a huge bowl laden with tropical fruit; and from our table, decorated with fresh flowers and folded napkins, we had a view of the hotel pool at which languid figures already disported. To judge by the switching direction of Davison's eyes, his attention was quite vexingly divided between the pool and breakfast, but the food on the counter had the advantage of being more accessible and he returned to it for frequent replenishments.

Davison cut a slightly shabbier figure in the light streaming in from the terrace and the pool. I saw that his jacket was imitation leather, and comprehensively worn at the cuffs and waist. His features, too, seemed flatter than they had the previous evening, and the whites of his eyes were bloodshot. During the course of the meal, he removed his jacket, and sat in a short-sleeved shirt the collar of which had slightly frayed, and the name of his car hire company printed in red on the pocket. Yet his eyes remained as hard as they had been in the darkness, and continued to slide across rather than engage my own.

He ate, it seemed to me, primarily out of a curiosity to taste the quality and variety of the food on offer. Then he sat back, his arm hooked on the back of the upholstered chair, and ordered coffee in the same slightly imperious way he had placed my single suitcase the previous evening in the care of a hotel porter. He sipped his coffee and listened to me telling him that the hotel was too expensive for my budget and I would have to find a cheaper one. His expression hardly changed, but I thought I detected some disappointment mingled with amusement beginning to register there.

Nevertheless, we chatted amiably enough over the remainder of our coffee. Davison told me he had been driving for a living for nine years. 'Before this firm,' he said, indicating the name on his pocket, 'I was the chauffeur for the Algerian Ambassador here. I drove his Mercedes Benz. But then the Ambassador left. I think he was asked to leave, but I don't know why. My last job for him was to take his car to Windhoek. I drove for two days. I went to Livingstone and then along the Caprivi Strip, and I got to Windhoek in time to meet him at the airport.'

'How did you get back?'

'By some buses.'

As we were leaving the hotel, I said that I knew Zambia was made up of many different tribal groups, more than seventy in fact, with the main ones being the Bemba on the Copperbelt, the Lozi in the west, the Nyanja in the east and the Tonga down south towards the Zambezi River. To which group did he belong?

His eyes slid across my face. 'Nyanja. But I told you: I have been born here in Lusaka.'

We drove slowly in the streets of his home town. I had asked him to give me a tour, and he proceeded to do so. Most of the formal business of Lusaka was conducted in Cairo Road, a wide thoroughfare flanked by the few high-rise buildings which the city possessed. Informal business thrived a few blocks further west as crowded Indian shops, half their wares seeming to be suspended from the ceilings, gave way to the street stalls which surrounded the ceaseless activity of Soweto market: block after block of vacant ground filled with commerce growing up from rich beds of litter and children and frequent patches of mud which marked the deficiencies of haphazard drainage ditches.

Despite the mud — evidence of a lingering rainy season — thick layers of dust covered everything. Each stall was contained within scaffolding cages which held in place roofs of canvas or plastic, and the narrow alleys between the resulting rows showed dark even when the sun was high.

Billboards carried large posters: 'Your family still needs you — use condoms — avoid casual sex.' Beneath such warnings, young men smoked, their shirt-tails flapping in a slight breeze; and one of them stepped suddenly towards the car and said without a smile: 'No cameras here. We don't allow it. First you pay ten thousand kwachas.'

But Davison's mind had lingered with the AIDS poster. 'Too many people are dying,' he said in his lilting voice, but without much expression. 'Now they are digging up the coffins so they can be used again. Yes, I have heard that. They dig up the expensive ones and sell them again.'

'Who are "they"?'

He merely shrugged his shoulders.

The streets were crammed with people. Even away from the markets and the Cairo Road, people pressed together in considerable crowds, especially where food was sold from the pavements. Like at Café Delight: the dust in drifts on the plastic tables, people eating, reggae music from speakers too small for the volume; and some broken pot plants, telephone kiosks out of order, traffic lights which gaped black as vehicles from all directions inched forward, blind people being led by children, and a man in a T-shirt with the ironical slogan: 'Life on the ocean wave'. All this and more in this land-locked country.

'Land-locked, yes. This was our weakness after independence,' an Indian academic said to me. 'When Ian Smith in Rhodesia cut off our supply lines from the south, the country was nearly strangled. Then the Chinese built the railway from Dar es Salaam. You've heard of the Tanzam railway? But until that was opened, life here was very difficult.'

We sat in an office piled high with books and papers. The curtains were stained, the floor unswept, the wastepaper basket overflowing. The academic, a man in his early fifties named Dr Sridutt, wore a white open-necked safari suit. He looked at me through thick-lensed spectacles with eyes which seemed peevish, more petulant than annoyed. We pieced together Zambia's troubled history.

Independence from Britain came relatively painlessly in 1964, but had been followed a year later by Rhodesia's unilateral declaration of independence. Zambia had refused to co-operate with the white settler colony south of the Zambezi. Indeed, it gave support to guerrilla groups in opposition to the Smith regime. Zambia thus became a target for military attack, especially towards the end of Rhodesia's bush war ('There were actually several bombing raids on Lusaka in the late seventies,' Dr Sridutt said), and for sustained economic strangulation.

The economic crisis associated with the actions of a hostile Rhodesia had pushed President Kenneth Kaunda's ruling United National Independence Party (UNIP) steadily towards one-party rule, a process hastened by fears that inflamed ethnic divisions would otherwise tear the country apart. Opposition was crushed, but the economy continued to deteriorate. Widespread discontent plagued the Copperbelt; and in 1990, rioting in the streets of Lusaka (over maize price increases of more than 100 per cent) claimed more than thirty lives.

But the rise of multiparty democracy in Africa could not indefinitely be held at bay; neither could the need for reform in the shape of economic structural adjustment programmes. By the end of 1991, Kaunda and his party had been ousted. Frederick Chiluba became president, while his Movement for Multiparty Democracy took control of the national assembly. In this way Zambia's second republic, which had begun in 1973 with the introduction of Zambia's one-party-state constitution, had come to an end.

'It's the best thing that could have happened,' Dr Sridutt told me. 'But the country is not out of trouble. We're paying now for the experiments made with socialism then, and for the corruption which was rife — and probably still is. But at least we seem to have turned the corner. There's an air of realism now.'

But what seemed to haunt him most, bringing that distraught and peevish expression to his magnified eyes, was the unevenness of development in a country which had been cobbled together for the convenience of a distant empire and a few white settlers, and with little regard for the people who actually occupied the territory.

'Look at this map,' Dr Sridutt said. 'So they build the railway up from the Victoria Falls, from Livingstone, to Lusaka, and from there to the Copperbelt. All development takes place along this line of rail. Nothing happens in the hinterland. Then the Colonial authorities introduce various taxes to force people from the hinterland to present themselves as labour along the line of rail. Nothing since independence has been able to reverse this trend. The trend is called urbanisation. Zambia is the second fastest urbanising country in Africa. South Africa is the fastest. Zambia is for the moment underpopulated, but that is changing. The national population is growing at 3,2 per cent a year. Lusaka is growing at nearly 6 per cent. In 1988 the population here in town was 870 000. Now it is more than 1,3 million.

'The associated problems are many. Housing, unemployment, health. All round the periphery of Lusaka unplanned settlements — we call them shanty compounds — are springing up and being enlarged. Unemployment is very high. Since Chiluba got in, nearly thirty parastatal companies have folded, and retrenchments are commonplace as the civil service is reformed. People talk of the new poor, almost all of them from the old middle class. As it is, more people depend on the informal sector than the formal. There are only about 350 000 formal-sector jobs for a country of around nine million.'

He took off his spectacles and with his eyes closed pinched the bridge of his nose with thumb and forefinger. When he opened them again his eyes looked small and tired as he looked across at me.

'People come to town in search of jobs. They are not always successful. Overcrowding takes place. The demand for food outstrips supply. Water and sanitation systems become overloaded. Health services can't cope adequately. We've had outbreaks of dysentery, cholera, as well as the normal problems with malaria, measles and tuberculosis. And of course AIDS is everywhere; it's a major epidemic. And then there are the social consequences which interlock with all the physical ones: heavy drinking and increasing violence from these most peaceable people. Zambia is a far less violent country than India. But more and more people are now resorting to crime.

'The solution? I sometimes say rural development. Somehow, we have to make people believe that coming to town doesn't represent some sort of salvation. We need to re-emphasise agriculture and small industry away from the line of rail. We need to improve roads and transport. But sometimes I say there are no solutions. I've been here for nearly twenty years. It's too long. I want to work somewhere else. I would like something better, somewhere where the problems are not so depressing.

'Here,' he said, all at once tossing a stapled sheaf of paper across the desk. 'Take my CV. I am talking now purely out of self-interest.'

I saw the names of Indian and British universities on the front sheet of the papers he had tossed across. I looked up at him again, and found him smiling, his peevish eyes expressing at once some mockery and also considerable depths of weariness he had not shown before.

'Go on, take it. Maybe you'll bring me some luck.'

Davison was dozing behind the wheel when I returned to the car. He pulled himself upright, his eyes sliding across my face as he waited for instructions. I told him of a hotel I had heard of not far off the main road south to Kafue.

He nodded. As he started the engine and drove off, he said: 'But first I will show you two things. They are quite near.'

In this way I saw the imposing gateway to the president's residence, two smartly dressed guards with automatic weapons eyeing us as we passed.

I asked where Kenneth Kaunda lived now that he was no longer the president; and Davison replied inscrutably: 'He has a very nice house.'

I then asked if he, Davison, had ever been into the presidency, perhaps to deliver a message or to take the Algerian ambassador there. He glanced at me in surprise, almost in scorn, I thought, as if I had failed to understand a simple truth. 'I have been in the driveway only, never in the house.'

We drove now in a busy thoroughfare which Davison told me was named Independence Avenue. The afternoon sun struck a shaft of blinding gold against the windscreen, obscuring my vision. I was conscious largely of vehicles grinding along in either direction. But soon enough Davison had pulled the car on to an uneven verge and pointed across the road. 'That is our Freedom Monument,' he announced.

We got out and crossed the road towards it. I saw the monument against a background of the concrete shell of an unfinished building, scaffolding still in place, construction cranes motionless above the huge multi-storeyed structure. But already the black marks of rain and humidity had streaked its unfinished sides.

At the base of the monument lay wreaths, some still in cellophane wrapping. The front of the plinth carried the single word, freedom, in raised metal letters against a white background. But vandals had defaced the background, and some of the raised letters themselves had been twisted out of shape.

On top of the plinth stood a statue of a muscular and obviously African man in a pair of shorts, his arms raised above his head, his mouth open in a grimace of effort as he snapped the chain which threatened to entwine his powerful torso. Freedom. Davison's hard eyes looked up at this symbol for a moment, and I wondered what it meant to him, who had been born after the struggle against colonialism had been won, who had witnessed other struggles instead.

Suddenly his eyes swung back to mine, and for once held them, as if he had braced himself for some question he would be unable to answer. Kaunda still lived in a very nice house; and here was the monument, unveiled by Kaunda himself in 1974, the tenth anniversary of Zambia's independence, and a year after the beleaguered country had been declared a one-party state. Did Davison cling to these images as anchors in an uncertain world?

'That building behind?' I asked. 'What is it?'

'It is no longer being built,' Davison replied.

'I can see that.'

'It was offices for UNIP, Kaunda's party. Then they lost the election.'

On the sides of the freedom monument's plinth, bronze reliefs showed people carrying independence placards and people rejoicing. One of the wreaths at its base had begun to disintegrate. Across bare earth behind the monument I saw the concrete beginnings of the grandiose entrance to the unfinished building.

'I have heard that the new government will make a hotel,' Davison said, turning away.

We drove in silence after that. We turned south on the Kafue Road and left the central hubbub of Lusaka behind us, replacing it with the dust and flying chickens of a congested detour. American money was rehabilitating the road, according to a sign, just as Japanese money was doing for the telephone system in the city itself. At each telephone pole, as we progressed along the detour, tangled wire hung down in confused bunches. I thought these bunches represented perfectly the confusion of disconnected voices, all jabbering after the balm of simple communication and a simple surety perpetually denied. Minibuses charged and scraped over the humps in the road designed expressly to prevent them from doing so. The dust had the taste of decomposing refuse.

I asked Davison if he had ever served in the army. He shook his head. Perhaps he had been involved in some way in the death throes of Rhodesia a decade and a half ago now.

But he had not been. He had emerged into adulthood under the protection and constraints of African paternalism and dictatorship, and had driven a Mercedes Benz for an Algerian ambassador who had later left in something of a hurry. Were there disillusionments now, or ambiguities of response, which could hardly continue to be explained or maintained by the old anti-colonial imperatives? Those simple blacks and whites of popular perception had receded into a confusion of voices, the old sureties replaced by a jabber of doubt and alienation now.

The hotel lay sunk in trees and the folds of a countryside all dusty and drooping with the demands made on it by incessant humanity. I stood on the veranda, waiting for my room to be prepared. Cattle grazed in the middle distance. Trees stood untidily in the green pastures. There were banana groves; here some overripe and laden maize, and thatched huts and a flat-roofed structure from which an incessant stream of wailing jive issued, and from somewhere else the scattered shouts of children in the evening time. Power lines looped between timber poles, bringing electricity to the hotel. Some distant hills turned purple. And I saw two women carrying a bed into my room.

It had already turned dark by the time I could enter it. Unfortunately, there was no hot water and the telephone lines were down, they said. But supper would soon be served, and, look, the television was working fine. A programme called Palaver Time.

Is society doing enough, a talking head asked, about the problem of Lusaka's street children? Are the police coping with crime? According to a news report, the head went on, the United Nations is expressing concern at the wave of crime, largely drug trafficking and vehicle theft, which is sweeping Africa, including Zambia.

Later, a deputy minister smiled into the camera. He had been accused of diverting so many millions of kwachas from a health project into his own pocket. The deputy minister refuted this accusation, calling his adversaries toothless wolves, and smiling with exceptionally white teeth while invoking the name of the Lord Jesus who would help to vindicate him, this most maligned deputy minister, and to administer just deserts to his cowardly and ineffectual adversaries.

I turned down the sound, wondering momentarily if Davison had found his way safely back to town, and listened to a million insects crash into the gauze over the windows in their frenzy to get closer to the light inside.

'Life in Lusaka is tough now,' Davison told me the following morning.

The sky showed grey and overcast, and he wore his black imitation-leather jacket zipped halfway up his chest. We were driving towards the city, through the dense dust of the detour, when he offered this information.

'It's tough,' he repeated. 'If you haven't got a job, then you have to work in the Soweto market, or be a vendor in the streets. But then I don't know how you can manage. Life is very expensive these days, especially since the end of the second republic.'

He steered the car over one of the speed reducing humps which straddled the roadway. He had reduced speed to walking pace; even so the underside scraped the crest of the hump; and I saw fine sand sifting down the windscreen and then scattering sideways as he accelerated once more.

'When I went to school everything was free,' he said. 'Also books and stationery. No longer. I earn 22 000 kwachas and pay 7 000 kwachas rent. But I must also pay 1 500 kwachas a term for school, plus more for books. I have one child already at school. And now we are paying for health as well, even when we wait in queues at the hospitals.'

'How many children do you have?'

'Only two.'

'I would like to come and meet your family while I am here. Would that be possible?'

Davison sent a glance sliding across my face. He smiled faintly. 'All right.'

'You can tell me what gift I should bring for your wife.'

He remained silent. Then after a while he said: 'I am having trouble with the bank. I am needing a favour. I am asking for your help.'

His problem, he said, had to do with a gift he had received in the post from a friend in America: a traveller's cheque worth a hundred dollars. But the bank would not cash it because it was unsigned.

'Some of these black people here,' he said with sudden feeling, his narrow features pinched with distaste. 'They are always competing with each other. They are just too clever and important to be helpful. White people don't behave like that,' he added, but perhaps largely to clinch my assistance.

We had, meanwhile, arrived at Lusaka's main hospital. In a city characterised by dishevelled public places, unmown grass on pavements, and a proliferation of litter, the hospital grounds looked conspicuously neat. Lawns were well trimmed; roses bloomed; and to one side a small sign offered this explanation: 'These grounds were adopted for maintenance by the First Lady, Mrs Vera Chiluba, on 27 February 1993.'

Leaving Davison in the car, I went into the hospital's main reception area. A bowl of fresh flowers adorned the circular desk. Rows of seats in the central waiting area were crowded, and everywhere I saw the whites of eyes in dark faces. People seemed suspended in the act of waiting: it was Africa's forte, someone had told me, knowing how to wait. The floor was of raw concrete, and the air smelled strongly of disinfectant. Flies swarmed in the lavatories which carried cholera control instructions: wash your hands; boil drinking water. In the reception area itself, people waited in the dogged way of the sick, hunched over, or looking out at the world as if from their own small citadels of pain. The world was only this concrete floor and the shoes of the passing, and people drinking Coca-Colas on the mezzanine, and nurses hurrying by, and various notices stuck to the glass doors into the wards. Here the Government was announcing a programme on self-employment and job search techniques for all retirees and retrenchees, funded by the World Bank. And there, a scientific seminar jointly organised by the Paediatric Association, the Infectious Diseases Project, and the Sickle Cell Society of Zambia.

A pleasant black doctor said: 'By the end of the second republic, all health structures were in an advanced state of disarray. Deterioration would be a better word. You should have seen this hospital. It was disgusting.

'But now we're living in the new age of pragmatism. We need to identify our priorities and find appropriate solutions. We have to realise we can't do it all at once. If we wanted to achieve all our goals now, we would need amazing amounts of money. Probably about twenty times more than the size of the present budget.'

The way forward, the doctor said, was a new style of management, independent decision-making at decentralised levels, small cost centres; and most important of all, the introduction of what he called 'drastic cost recovery programmes'.

When I suggested that this could place an ultimately intolerable burden on the poorest section of the population, a section which by all accounts was rapidly expanding, he waved his hand in a gesture of broad impatience.

'Everyone must pay,' he said, the impatience spilling over into his voice. 'The ideas of socialism and free services have smashed our health system over the years. We all know what the result is of free medical care: filthy hospitals and empty pharmacy shelves. We've learned our lesson.

'Those who literally cannot raise the cash should be forced to pay in kind. The only people exempt will be those suffering from AIDS. The Government has decided this on humanitarian grounds. We don't want to charge people who are dying.'

The idea of paying in kind was dismissed with a guffaw by a woman I went to see about Zambia's AIDS epidemic. We had begun by talking about the health services in general. 'What on earth are the clinics going to do with fifteen chickens, seventy-eight bunches of bananas, umpteen bags of maize or groundnuts, and a hundred grass mats? It's a completely ridiculous idea. It's bizarre,' she added, mouthing the word with some relish.

She was a large woman, clear-eyed, with a pleasant if boisterous laugh. But her face lost much of its good humour when she turned her attention to AIDS. The walls of her office were plastered with awareness posters and newspaper articles dealing with the disease. She showed me one story headed No Wailing: authorities at the very hospital in which we sat had banned wailing by mourners both inside the wards and in the grounds which were looking much prettier since the First Lady had taken over their maintenance. The vocalising of grief among the colourful roses and neat lawns had been outlawed. It seemed a bizarre combination of imperatives, I thought, remembering the pleasure the use of this word had brought to the clear-eyed woman before me.

'It's going to get a lot worse before it gets better,' she said now. 'My estimate is that around fifty per cent of all deaths in Zambia these days are AIDS related. You want to know how many? Go to the cemetery on Leopards Hill Road. I'd say about a thousand deaths a week. But that's country-wide. A lot of the recently urbanised tend to go back to their villages to die. Nevertheless, Leopards Hill is a busy place.'

I remembered what Davison had told me regarding the theft and resale of coffins. The woman nodded. 'I've also quite frequently heard of people sealing the graves of relatives with concrete to avoid this theft. I suppose on the day of resurrection those poor people will be the last to get out.'

She laughed in that sudden boisterous way so characteristic of people who live habitually with danger or unpleasantness. 'Isn't that bizarre,' she said, her clear eyes dancing on my face, and laughed even louder.

But she seemed more interested in Zambian generalities than in the dark specifics of its AIDS crisis. She was a professional woman with most of her life before her. Her expertise had been harnessed to a depressing reality, but she was more than her expertise. This was the message she seemed to wish to impart. I had provided a sympathetic ear, and she wanted to express to me her other side, her broader understanding, and her hopes for the future.

'Socialist economic policies and the one-party state have ruined this country,' she said. 'It was so easy to live on the over-reliance on copper and mining which we inherited from colonial times. And we failed to exploit our other potential, especially in agriculture. The experimental farming collectives were not a success. And now we're encouraging white farmers to come here. We're encouraging any external investment at all — whether it be in agriculture, commerce, industry, or whatever.'

She told me of the excitement and hope which had come to Zambia at the ousting of Kaunda and UNIP in 1991. 'We knew it was going to be tough. And it has been. And perhaps the spirit of willingness to work for a better future has been dampened by all the corruption. But let me tell you that the freedom is great. The one-party state became very repressive. We feel and enjoy the freedom every day. I certainly wouldn't be talking to you like this if there was still a one-party state.'

As she was saying goodbye, her mind suddenly reverted to the original purpose of our conversation. 'Oh, yes, you were looking for figures. The forecast is that HIV positivity will peak at about 1,6 million people in ten years. Yes, that's out of a total population of around nine million.' Her handshake was firm, and her clear eyes danced in their lively way as I turned to go.

I told Davison to drive me to the expensive hotel at which I had stayed when I first arrived in Lusaka. At my request, he showed me the letter which had accompanied his gift of a hundred dollars. I signed the traveller's cheque, and then re-signed it in the presence of the cashier. She counted out several wads of local currency. As I placed them in his waiting hands, I realised with a slight shock that the amount was in excess of two and a half months of his normal monthly pay.

'Don't spend it all at once,' I said in a slightly jocular way.

He smiled with a sudden flash of openness which revealed his even white teeth. He clutched the money in both his hands. It was the first and also the last time I saw him smile in that way.

In 1970, Zambia had played host to the third summit meeting of the world's non-aligned nations. The late 1960s and early 1970s had been a somewhat heady period of high and stable copper prices and, in spite of the threat posed by the Rhodesian regime to the south, a time also of extravagant public expenditure. And what better occasion on which to lavish a little special attention than this gathering of countries which had learned how to use the hidden agendas of the cold war to further their own ends?

A special monument commemorating the conference had been erected across the street from Zambia's High Court. The latter was an elegant colonial structure in brick and stucco with colonnaded entrance and complacent-looking concrete lions on either side of the wide front steps. By contrast, the monument commemorating the summit was late 20th-century modernity itself. We drove past this edifice frequently as I went about my business in the capital, and I became used to the three spires built out of copper plate which provided a high and angular focus in the otherwise flat civic centre of the city.

Mulungushi Hall, set among trees and with a herd of small buck grazing off surrounding shrubbery and flowers, provided an equally impressive, and certainly more useful, reminder of the summit. Built especially for this occasion, the main hall could seat two thousand delegates, sixty of them around the main conference table, with another three hundred accommodated in a public gallery. We peered into this huge facility one morning, Davison and I, glimpsing the green beige of table tops, forests of microphones, and also glass-fronted booths set into the circular walls presumably offering simultaneous translation facilities. In the main foyer, a model of an open-cast copper mine had been set up; huge sheets of copper adorned the walls; a cafeteria at one end of the foyer was empty, while outside, not far from a collection of empty flag-poles, a solitary man swept sand and buck droppings off the tarmac of the drive.

The museum — what I had come to Mulungushi to see — stood to one side. Yet it was more like a storage shed than a museum at the moment, a young curator with a high-pitched voice admitted to me.

'But,' he went on in a vaguely pedantic way, as if he was addressing a class of schoolchildren, 'have you seen the UNIP building which is unfinished? Yes, that is the one behind the Freedom Monument. There is a suitable place there which we are hoping will become our new national museum at some time in the future.'

He had gentle and drooping eyes, this curator, and when he spoke he invariably did so with his hands deferentially clasped before him.

He now directed my attention to what he called the museum's 'outdoor exhibits'. A battered metal cage which had been mounted on the back of a lorry and used to transport Northern Rhodesia's captured freedom fighters; a grader with which the colonial authorities cleared away road-blocks until it was attacked and destroyed in 1961; and a Land Rover, used by Ian Smith's commandos to attempt an attack on the Lusaka hideout of a prominent black Rhodesian politician, but which had received a direct hit and exploded into this twisted rusting wreckage on display, although the machine-gun mounting on the back still swivelled, as the curator was at pains to point out.

Not far from the entrance to the museum shed lay two concrete lions, the one broken in several places along its back, the other little more than a heap of rubble with only the occasional feature recognisable. I waited for an explanation.

The curator said they had once graced the steps of the High Court building, but had then been destroyed by a grenade lobbed by more of Smith's raiding commandos.

I had a vague vision of these daredevil Rhodesian soldiers, eyes white and bloodthirsty in their blackened faces, tearing around Lusaka in their vehicles wreaking this sort of havoc. But there was a stronger vision. It concerned the lions which graced the steps of the High Court now. Were they new ones? Imported from England? Those complacent feline faces, but without whiskers, coming in an open truck through the numerous tunnels of the Tanzam railway? The curator could not enlighten me; in consequence the vision hardened.

But I thrust it from me as I went into the shed, the curator in deferential attendance, and began to look at some of the many exhibits stored there: typewriters and loudhailers which had been put to political purposes; membership cards of the various political parties which had finally merged into UNIP; posters from the 1991 elections. The Movement for Multiparty Democracy proclaiming 'the hour has come'; and under a photograph of homeless people: 'Zambia has seen enough of this for the past 27 years'. Nevertheless, Kenneth Kaunda occupied a prominent place among the exhibits: old photographs of him, youthful and vigorous, signing papers, smiling in groups, addressing rallies; and a large and ornately framed portrait which, like similar portraits of Cecil Rhodes and British royalty, had left their original places of honour to end up propped haphazardly against the walls and shelves of this shed.

Memorabilia piled these shelves, preserved from the early days when Rhodes's British South Africa Company had administered the old north-eastern and north-western pieces of what became Northern Rhodesia in 1911, and passed under the direct rule of the British Government only eleven years later. Other pictures (painted by a North Korean artist, the curator said) showed bloody fights between blacks and white soldiers in khaki shorts and pith helmets firing their rifles in an organised, regimented sort of way.

I noticed Davison, his shoulders slightly hunched as he thrust his hands in the high pockets of his black jacket, standing before the portraits of Rhodes, Kaunda and Queen Elizabeth II in white dress with blue sash across the bodice.

I wandered among the crowded exhibits, the curator lingering at my side. The past seemed reduced to hundreds of small objects, crowded into the glass cases. Here, for example, was the shell which had stopped the tape recorders.

It looked like a shell picked up on a beach, perhaps on the shores of Lake Tanganyika or Mweru, and if held in the hand at political meetings it jammed the tape recorders of the police informers. These things I learned from hand-written inscriptions on an accompanying card. And this animal's horn, another card said, was placed in the water to cause the security forces in their speedboats to lose direction and not be able to find the freedom fighters hiding in the reeds on the bank.

I glanced once more at Davison standing before a portrait of the reigning British monarch. His narrow features poked out of the upturned collar of his imitation-leather jacket. And it seemed suddenly absurd to me: this juxtaposition of the young Lusaka man with bloodshot eyes and a discarded likeness of a foreign queen as irrelevant now as the old magic perhaps.

'Here is a good example of black magic,' the curator said deferentially, his hands clasped before him as he spoke. This time the magic came in the form of a walking stick and fly switch. I read the inscription on the card. A certain Mr Muchengwa had used these objects to hide himself from police torture, 'and several times when police went to Mr M's house in view of arresting him, but so long as he was holding the switch and walking stick the police were unable to see him while standing very close'. Mr M also at one time ate poisoned food prepared for him by two constables. The constables had died, but Mr M had survived. 'Mr M was doing this from 1959 to 1962,' the card said. 'So you can see this is a highly developed science which some of us cannot do.'

I asked the curator if he believed in this sort of magic. 'Oh, yes,' he replied; 'it is still in the villages, even in the towns.'

In the car, I asked Davison what he had thought of the paintings.

He drove in silence for a while. 'They are not good.'

'Why?'

'All right,' he said, 'because the one of Kaunda doesn't really look like Kaunda. My brother is a much better painter than that. If my brother painted Kaunda it would look exactly like him. But he would need a photograph to take the likeness from.'

By then my earlier vision of the two lions travelling all that way from Dar es Salaam in a railway truck had returned. It was a wayward vision. Perhaps in reality they had been nailed into crates, or they had come from South Africa; but my vision of them was that they had sat unfettered in the open truck, all the way from England, smiling out at Africa as they rolled through the continent's confusions and magic — and also its extravagant pain.

We went, one overcast afternoon, to look at the Leopards Hill Cemetery. The road off which the cemetery lay, although marked as something of an arterial to the south east on the map, seemed insignificant and even countrified, with rank growth having spread inwards across the verges and now swaying over the potholed surface of the road itself. I had become used to the sight of maize growing in Lusaka's suburbs, but this was more than maize; it was a tropical luxuriance of banana trees and flourishing weeds which made the road look narrower than it actually was, and through which pedestrians had made smooth passageways in places.

Before we reached the cemetery entrance, the road became choked with a row of vehicles drawn as far as possible into the foliage at the side. People in their best clothes sat on the backs of lorries and trucks. Panel vans with their rear doors open showed evidence of wreaths. A dilapidated minibus driven by a young man in wrap-around dark glasses had a coffin tied to the roof-rack. I heard singing.

Davison said: 'The trouble is the cemetery is only open from eight hundred to seventeen hundred hours. Sometimes people wait in the queue for two days.'

'Does AIDS worry you?' I asked, glancing at the narrow face beside me in the car.

'People talk about it.'

'But you?'

'Yes, it worries me. People are getting sick. Now here, now over there. I know them,' he replied, but with controlled impassivity, his eyes fastened on the road ahead.

We had edged past the waiting vehicles to turn into the cemetery by way of an unpaved road scarred with craters which always threatened the underside of the car. At the end of this drive, a few trucks and buses stood close to a low building. People seemed to mill aimlessly about, passing in and out of the open doors of the building.

'They are viewing the body,' Davison informed me in an expressionless voice.

But expressions of the people's grief came as a dismal wailing across the distance between us and the building. Old people were supported as they wept. A haze of dust blew in a thin cloud from the graves which lay mounded up with raw earth, and some of them not yet closed, in the lumpy ground on every side. Several funerals were in progress simultaneously.

The lumpy ground and the thousands of graves stretched away, softened only by rank grass which grew unchecked over and between. Plastic wreaths lay on the earth, while the trousers of the suits of the men were plucked at by the wind. Heads were bowed. A man in overalls walked past with a collection of shovels. To one side lay the children's graves, adorned with small plastic chairs or upturned baby baths. All those thousands of mounds, some of them arranged round the rusting remains of cars which had been there longer than the dead. Litter bowled sluggishly along in the breeze. The sky showed a lowering grey. The processions wound through the weeds and dust; and when the ceremonies were over the mourners clambered once more on to their lorries and trucks. Some of the more elderly were lifted bodily into place. And the lorries would grind and crash slowly through the craters on their way home.

We followed in silence. Davison's expression offered no clue to what he thought: unless it be simply that he considered me strange, wanting to visit cemeteries rather than game reserves.

We drove out at last into more ordered suburban streets: an old colonial feeling of repose and substance here. Garden walls concealed what lay within the properties, but sometimes hose pipes trailed over the brickwork, and gardeners watered the flowers and shrubs which grew on the street side of these walls. Or the gardeners would shout jocularly to the women who tended their small stalls of vegetables and fruit set up on the street corners even of such obviously opulent places.

I was conscious of Davison's presence in the car, a sort of brooding expectancy as if he wanted to speak. I wondered if the sights at the cemetery had distracted him. For the moment, though, he said nothing. The upturned collar of his jacket cut a sharp black angle against a slightly hollowed cheek.

As we passed through the centre of town on our way out to the Kafue Road, through the dust of the detour, and to my hotel, I saw hundreds of ravens circling and settling on the roof of a tallish building in the vicinity of Cairo Road. They sat along the ridge of the roof like frequent knots in a taut line. I remembered going up in a lift in one of the buildings in the Cairo Road. The light had fused, and my ascent, a slow and creaking business, had been illumined only by the changing numbers on the panel. And now the ravens circled black against low skies, and sat like knots all along the straight edges of the city's skyline. At ground level, crowds moved forward, a faceless throng perhaps, yet with individual features large beyond the windscreen sometimes. Was their world the world only of entrapment and ill omen?

I asked Davison how long he had driven the Algerian ambassador's Mercedes Benz.

'For three years.'

'Apart from your last trip to Windhoek, did you ever get out of Lusaka?'

'Once to the Victoria Falls,' Davison replied. 'Once to Malawi.'

I made no reply, looking instead at the dusty city, the rubbish piled in gutters, the overloaded minibuses, the flapping shirt tails of young men kicking a tennis ball on an empty lot while others urinated in dark patches against a convenient wall.

'I have waited for a chance to tell you,' Davison said awkwardly. 'I am thanking you on behalf of my family for helping me with the traveller's cheque.'

I asked if he had given his children a treat.

'Yes, I bought food and sweets for the children.'

'And for your wife?'

He shrugged his shoulders. 'But for myself, I bought beer and watched the television.'

As my stay in Lusaka lengthened, the idea of going to Davison's home, and in this way learning more about him, became something of a preoccupation with me. I mentioned it several times, and my suggestions were met always with the same vague nonchalance as at first, or a faint smile and a comment such as, 'Well, unfortunately my wife will not be home at that time'.

What finally turned Davison in the direction I wanted him to take me was a big bag of charcoal bought at the side of the road just outside the city.

We had driven around the outer suburbs of Lusaka for a day. I had wanted to see some of the so-called unplanned settlements or shanty compounds peopled by the newly urbanised, and Davison had proved an excellent guide.

Through his perceptions, I got an inkling of a social hierarchy based on where people lived. Even the most disordered suburb seemed preferable to the shanty compounds. Yet the latter seemed not to be altogether unlike the former.

Kaunda Square, for example, was not a shanty compound, according to Davison, yet the houses were small and decrepit, the roadways bordered with trenches in which dirty water stood. Rubbish rose in strong-smelling heaps adjacent to the inevitable food stalls, and the atmosphere was one of poverty which seemed alleviated to some extent by a cheerfulness possibly engendered, I gathered from Davison's comments, by security of tenure.

Not so different to Kalingalinga, a few kilometres to the south of Kaunda Square; or the sprawling George in the north-western corner of the city. Both these places, said Davison, were shanty compounds. Yet still there was a sense of the places having been laid out, with roads in rough grids, and houses which had a permanent feel, and with some banana and papaw trees growing tall and established in the cramped yards.

'The urbanisation process is too swift,' I remembered the Indian academic, Dr Sridutt, telling me. 'As a consequence there is inadequate sewerage, roads, water supply, waste disposal, inadequate virtually everything, in fact.' Lusaka had suffered a dysentery epidemic in 1992. 'And don't worry, the old bacillus Shigella hasn't gone away,' Dr Sridutt had added wryly.

In George, I saw old women breaking rocks into stones for use in concrete. Their product stood in piles all down the sides of streets. The old women hit at the rocks with hammers, and the dust of such work had whitened their faces. This was a manifestation of a poverty otherwise hidden, although it showed also in the wet squalor at communal taps, in the crumbling away of mud walls, and sometimes in the eyes of under-nourished children.

Other children, especially young boys, flew kites. It seemed an unusual thing, light and carefree, to do in a shanty compound, but Davison told me it happened all the time. The kites sailed in the air like youthful optimism. The rubble and the ditches of dirty water were forgotten beneath. I suggested that the Chinese who had helped to build the Tanzam railway (there had been 25 000 of them) might have introduced the skill. Davison readily agreed with this explanation.

But I had learned not to trust some of the things which Davison said. He had already informed me, for example, that Lusaka's population was now four million. He told me, too, that he had once driven a singer from Lusaka to Zaire's capital city, Kinshasa, in two days. Two and a half thousand kilometres through the central African jungle in two days. I said I doubted whether that was possible. Davison laughed in a slightly cynical way and said: 'Well, it's true. I drove day and night.'

In other ways, though, he was an interesting informant. The divisions between shanty compounds and the more established suburbs or townships, he understood acutely. His own township, he had told me, was Avondale, just off the long road to the airport: it was well established with schools and a clinic, not like the shanty compounds of Kalingalinga or George at all.

'You see,' he said, pointing out the absence of poles or wires as we drove deep into George, so deep indeed that we began to emerge into open country beyond, 'many of these houses have no electricity. Also they must walk to get water.'

'How do they cook?'

'They burn anything in the stoves. Also they use charcoal — if they can afford it.'

I asked what the Davison family used for cooking.

He smiled faintly. 'We have electricity. But often it is not working. So we also cook with charcoal.'

'Is it expensive?'

'It is expensive at Soweto market. But if you buy it out of town — like here — it is not too bad.'

'Like here' was a rough pile of hessian sacks by the roadside. I told Davison to stop. He did so and then reversed to the sacks. They bulged with the shapes of large pieces of charcoal, but were unattended. I said I wanted to buy a sack, and Davison, his face expressionless, tooted on the horn. A woman came running.

'This can be my gift to your wife,' I said.

'All right,' he replied impassively.

But after we had forced the sack into the boot and were driving again, he glanced at me, a quick appraisal with those hard eyes of his, and said: 'But you cannot come today. My wife is busy until the evening.'

'What about tomorrow?'

He was silent a moment. It seemed to me that he shouldered my persistence with a definite heaviness of spirit now, yet a heaviness which he concealed beneath some mild amusement. 'All right,' he said at last, 'tomorrow is a Sunday; tomorrow in the afternoon.'

A brisk storm marked our approach to Avondale the following day. The rain lashed down from dark clouds which only partially obscured the sky. The tarred road to the airport steamed, and we turned off it into mud and pond-like potholes, with the drainage ditches in full spate and sometimes flooding where a pipe under a driveway had been blocked. The car splashed slowly through. But before long the downpour had finished, and the sun shone bright and hot from beyond the broken cloud. The wetness of Avondale dazzled the eyes then, and I saw the dark silhouettes of children waving as we passed.

Davison's house was like a hundred others which stood in a row beside the road. Suddenly we had arrived, with Davison guiding the car into a yard full of mud and then pulling on the handbrake. He clambered out, and I followed, feeling the mud adhere thickly to the bottom of my shoes. I looked around.

The property was shielded from the road by an untidy hedge. An outside lavatory stood close to this hedge, but it was roofless, although a piece of plastic, sagging now with the weight of rain-water, had been draped over the top of the walls. The house itself presented a drab sight of rough unpainted plaster with red earth splashed up along the base. A single deciduous tree stood in the mud to one side, but it carried no fruit.

'Must I take out the charcoal?'

The hard eyes questioned mine momentarily, before sliding away; and the boot swung up while I looked at the house again. Metal window frames had blistered with rust. The door was made of unmatching timber slats sodden from the rain and jammed ajar, with two young faces peering shyly out at me. I scraped as well as I could the mud off the bottom of my shoes. 'These are my two children,' Davison said as he ushered me inside.

Two girls: the elder around ten years perhaps, her eyes lively and her lips quick to smile; the younger hardly three, I thought, a paler skin, and with a wan and listless smile.

Two young men sat on the settee which ran along one side of the small room. A television set dominated the opposite wall. I was invited to sit in an easy chair to one side. The young men were introduced as a friend and a brother. They smiled in a friendly way, but did not rise. Their eyes switched back to the television from time to time. Davison stood before me in a deliberately nonchalant way.

'The big girl is Elíta. She is the one at school. Say hallo.'

The child mouthed a silent greeting, her bright eyes on my face. She had entwined her arms around her father's leg, and she looked out at me quite confidently from this position. And her position seemed strengthened when Davison momentarily rested his hand on her head.

'The young one is Kalunga. Say hallo.'

But the child made no response. Her limbs showed painfully thin, and her eyes seemed rheumy and partially unfocused as she leaned against the plastic-covered settee. Davison sat down beside her, and looked across at me once more in his nonchalant way. Then his eyes too switched to the pale monochromatic images on the television.

Church News: the droning confessions of an alcoholic who no longer drank, thanks to the Lord's help.

I saw a few empty beer bottles standing on a dresser of sorts. A doorway behind the settee had a sheet of metal nailed across it. Kitchen things lay on the floor, including a hot plate with disconnected wires protruding from its base, and various containers with holes punched in and discoloured from the heat of burning charcoal.

I asked Davison why the doorway had been sealed.

'That room in there is for the other people in the house. I rent only these two rooms.'

And from the second room now a young woman emerged, carrying cups dripping wet from the washing. She seemed hardly more than a girl, perhaps fifteen years of age, her small breasts still proud against the grimy T-shirt she wore. I felt Davison's eyes slide across my face. I saw the slight smile in his compact features as he said: 'This is my sister.'

These words became for me the signal of a point of no return, and a sense of bathos even, rather than a signal for any new insight. Yet the possibility of insight crept upon me slowly. The face on the television stammered on about the second bottle each day, but there was no insight there. Tea came in a chipped cup, but there was no insight there.

The floor was of red polished concrete. The walls had once been painted blue but now the plaster was falling off. I could see pieces of faint blue plaster lying on the red floor. And there were holes in the upholstery on the settee, and a large window pane had been broken and blocked with a board, and a naked light bulb dangled from the ceiling. But no insight came from these things either.

It lay elsewhere. It lay, perhaps, in the child Kalunga who looked ill. It suddenly struck me that she might be dying, and I had a vision of those small mounds at the Leopards Hill Cemetery, a few of them adorned with baby baths overturned among the grass and weeds. Those thin limbs and nearly sightless eyes on the settee opposite.

I asked Davison quite bluntly where his wife was.

He said: 'Unfortunately she has had to go out. Perhaps she will return before you go.'

But I knew she would not return. I sipped my tea. I thought pointedly: and she has left a child who is also dying. Davison glanced at me with his hard eyes. I said nothing. I caught a sense of disillusion and collapse in him which was almost overpowering then.

W e drove into the lavish countryside for a few days the following week. Even though we never deviated far from the line of rail, the country became an unfenced wilderness. A few villages lay visible to the right and left, and straggling groups of people frequented the verges of the road, but otherwise the country seemed hardly impinged upon. Late summer grass stood taller than a man and swayed laden with ripening seed. In certain places dense trees, some grown to considerable heights, dominated whole hillsides; in others large tracts of woodland reached away in a shadiness of spreading branches with grass and sometimes thickets underneath.

But on the road, the 20th century laboured up and down. The roof-racks of buses were piled high with flapping luggage. The sight of these vehicles reminded me of Davison's journey back from Windhoek: four days on the buses, he had said, rattling in great heat through the Caprivi Strip. And the lorries belched out their suffocating fumes; the big articulated vehicles, some with South African registration numbers, making the long journey into central Africa. On the ascent out of the Zambezi valley, especially, the big vehicles crawled forward or had stopped at unsuitable angles, rocks behind rear wheels, while sweating men shovelled sand on to patches of oil spilled on the already greasy tarmac of the twisting gradients. Once or twice, in ravines far below the road, I saw twisted wreckage and the remains of smashed loads rusting among boulders and ferns.

In another part of those southern places, we turned off the tarred road and drove into what seemed like another time. Ox carts creaked on a track which offered no comfort to our car. We were seeking missionaries. Davison asked some roadside dawdlers with elaborate bicycles, and they replied readily enough.

But Davison said to me with his slightly ironical smile: 'They are speaking a language I cannot understand. These are Tongas here,' he added after we had passed on. 'The Tongas only want bicycles. That's all right, because I know bicycles are a lot cheaper than cars. But they just like their bicycles. Bicycles and cows.'

Davison, the city man slouched in his black imitation-leather jacket, coaxed the car quite expertly over boulders and on through a golden afternoon towards the missionaries. Or was it Davison, the Nyanja man, shaking his head at the follies and predilections of another tribe? Perhaps a little of both.

The missionaries told me that although viewed as impractical by various health agencies, they (the missionaries) still preached behaviour change as the only effective antidote to AIDS. Yes, the epidemic had not by-passed the rural areas. Did I want to see the young women, some of them hardly thirteen years, both pregnant and infected? Had I not seen the ox carts under the trees, coming to fetch their dead? The traditional practice of ritual cleansing, where a surviving wife or husband would have sexual intercourse with a near relation after the burial of the spouse, had undoubtedly helped to spread the disease among some communities. But there was also the problem of urbanisation and all those young men with shiny shoes and ghetto-blasters who had forgotten about traditions but who were nevertheless extremely promiscuous. And did I know about the fortunes which traditional healers were making out of AIDS patients?

A woman doctor from Ireland spoke to me about the future of Africa in the way that some Europeans feel impelled to do after they have lived on the continent for a while. 'So many of them are really bright,' she said. 'And some of the bright ones are also now becoming influential. I think they'll probably be able to pull something out of the wreckage. Mind you, it's hardly any better anywhere else. In Dublin these days, I can't walk in the hospital carpark after dark. Here, I can do so at any time.'

When evening came in a blaze of pale light awash among scattered clouds, the missionaries gave us rooms, each with a narrow bed and a mosquito net. But they regretted that the source of power had failed: there would therefore be neither light nor hot water until the following day. And even the cold water would soon falter because it was electrically pumped. Davison's eyes seemed especially intense by candle-light. He went to his room early, and I heard him coughing periodically late into the night.

In the morning, and all day, we drove on rough roads through the country of the Tongas. Even when we regained the tar, the going was difficult over the patchwork surface, new patches over old, and the endless potholes which could smash the suspension if taken too fast. The compensation was the country through which the road led. The wooded parkland places: the endless trees with grass between; the long-stemmed trees, branches supporting elegant clusters of foliage; others flat-topped and laden with pods; while still other trees had died, showing ashen and delicate among the living. And over all this sailed the white-grey cumulus, flat-bottomed and piling up, a constant presence in the high and vivid sky.

Nor were we alone on these roads. Frequent companions were the charcoal burners, pushing bicycles loaded down with those lumpy hessian bags, one of which I had bought for Davison's wife. And sometimes we detected the smell of wet wood burning, but we saw no smoke in all those expanses of natural trees through which we travelled. In one of the towns, I found an office marked Forestry. Inside, a pleasant man in a khaki uniform said he was the district officer. He nodded in agreement as I spoke.

'Yes,' he said, 'deforestation is definitely on the way. Our trees will not last. There are sawmills that exploit the trees, but there at least we supervise the cutting. The trouble is there is no replacement programme. When the British ran the department, there was replacement, but it didn't really work. The young trees were eaten by rodents and buck.

'There are three hundred licensed charcoal burners just in this one small area. But there are more illegal ones than legal. We cannot patrol everywhere. We are too few. And anyway the fines are too low: only fifteen kwachas. They cut mopane and ebony. Now they are cutting the teak forests for charcoal as well.'

He stood up and fetched a book from a shelf. He showed me the cover: 'The proceedings of the first international conference on the teak forests of Southern Africa.' Then he showed a place inside where his name was printed as one of the contributors.

'But the recommendations from that conference — it was held in 1984 — haven't worked or haven't been put into practice. The biggest problem is over-population. There are too many loafers in the streets now. Even in this small town, the loafers are terrible. Now they live here, then you see them on the bus to Lusaka. Then in three months they are back. And they all want charcoal. And I think in ten years' time our trees will be gone.'

In another town, little more than an untidiness of fruit stalls and tyre menders, I stopped to look at some art exhibited at the Tonga Museum: wood and linocuts, for the most part, by Patrick Mweemba. I was struck particularly by those depicting the urban experience. A few dating from 1980 in London: a black man walking down Carnaby Street (to judge by the boldly patterned street paving); a figure in African dress talking to a white man with umbrella outside an underground station. The stools and bottles of a bar formed the basis of another design. And here were taxis, and a businessman carrying a briefcase and looking at his watch; and a strange piece entitled Vomiting in the Toilet which showed a torso in obvious discomfort over the porcelain bowl. Some of these woodcuts held images of discord, perhaps even of despair.

I stopped for the night at some chalets built on the bank of the rapidly flowing Zambezi. Davison said he knew of an inexpensive hotel nearby. 'I will stay there,' he said. But he explained that his company had given insufficient expenses for him to pay the bill. I agreed to put up the money until we returned to Lusaka.

'Shall I go then?'

He stood before me in his black jacket, even though the night was humid. He looked tired. I said as much, saying it had been a long day.

'I am not at all tired,' he said shortly.

We arranged a time for him to collect me in the morning, and he turned away, as if relieved to be rid of me for the night at least.

I ate at a small restaurant which served the chalets; but before I did so I saw four men lift stones above their heads and kill a snake. I was walking up from my chalet when suddenly the creature was there before me, slightly moist-looking in the beam of my torch, slithering in the roadway. I drew back, an irrepressible revulsion, and the creature passed, yet seeming distracted, changing direction without warning, pale on its underside as it writhed away.

But beside me, now, had stopped a waiter carrying a tray. He underwent an instant metamorphosis: this polite black man in a white jacket, now shouting as he swooped for stones. I heard running footsteps. A stone cracked against the tarmac just beyond the snake. Cobra! Men were shouting as they ran from the restaurant, and stones began to fly like bullets. The men seemed suddenly alive and agile in a way which spoke of danger. They were no longer waiters. One of the stones hit the snake along its length, sending it sliding sideways along the road. The reptile half turned on its attackers, the flattened head raised. I saw the tongue in the torchlight. Then a stone cracked against its skull at that precise second. The snake coiled itself in a tight and terrible spasm and then lay still.

The men stood over it, prodding with their waiters' shoes. 'It is dead,' one of them said, his teeth white in the darkness.

The snake's head was smashed into a broken caricature of what it had been, blood oozing from the flattened mouth. The action had passed as quickly as it had begun. Trays were retrieved. The men walked about in their neat white jackets, talking in amused voices and smiling.

In the morning, Davison was late. He stood before me with bloodshot eyes. 'I have come when you said I should,' he said in an expressionless voice.

'No,' I replied. 'You are forty minutes late.'

He offered no reply.

'Did you have a party last night?'

He slid his eyes sullenly across my face. 'No, I did not. There was no water in my hotel this morning.'

I let the matter rest.

George Cornhill had a voice of gravel and eyes to which smiling had long become a habit. The eyes were nevertheless firm and rock steady in a now deeply lined face, and he carried about him the expansiveness of a patriarch. But his authority appeared to have mellowed as he had grown older, and although people still did his bidding, the bidding itself seemed no longer absolute. George Cornhill was a self-made man, a rancher of considerable substance who owned several other business ventures in southern Zambia as well. He was assisted in these things by his several sons, one of whom sat with us in Cornhill's large living-room.

Cornhill junior was a relaxed young man, perhaps now in his middle or late twenties, who had a large and intelligent face, and who spoke in the essentially unregionalised accents of the English middle classes.

'Eurafricans,' George said in his voice of gravel. 'Coloureds. That's what we are. In colonial times, the authorities tried to prevent us from joining the African independence movements, saying we weren't African. But what the hell were we? I stood as a UNIP candidate in the

1962 elections. I lost. Then in 1991 I worked for a UNIP defeat. Why? Because the party had become too big, too dictatorial, too corrupt. But the Movement for Multiparty Democracy, Chiluba's MMD, has such a huge majority that it's now virtually a one-party state machine. So now I'm supporting the new opposition. I believe we must have a balance.'

The room in which we sat was large and protected from the glare of the day by an enclosed veranda filled with long twining stems and foliage. Along the picture rails of the living-room itself, the creepers grew. Two large settees covered with embroidered cloths faced each other across the room. A young woman, one of George's daughters, came and went with glasses, and then disappeared to prepare a meal. Cornhill junior took a sip of his drink and stretched his legs out before him as his father spoke once more.

'You want a summary of what has happened to Zambia since independence,' George said to me. 'Here's your summary. At independence we inherited money from Britain which propped up our debts. Our population was relatively small. The weather was good and, thanks largely to white commercial farmers, food production was high. The price of copper was at its best, and we had no unemployment to speak of, not along the line of rail anyway.

'What happened? Essentially four things. Number one: copper prices start to fall; increased production couldn't make up the shortfall, but it did raise worker expectations; there were strikes and riots. Number two: the climate went into an unfavourable cycle, and anyway more and more white farmers started moving south. Number three: politicians maladministered the country to an astonishing degree, and foreign debts went through the roof. Number four: the illegal Rhodesian regime tried and nearly succeeded in strangling us. We had no fuel. Before the Tanzam railway was built, we had what was called the hell run. Tankers coming from Dar es Salaam through huge areas of virgin Africa on dirt roads, half of them − well, that's what it seemed like − overturning, crashing, exploding...'

His greying hair had been cut short, so that it bristled quite fiercely from his head. His views were forthrightly expressed, yet his verve and good humour encouraged engagement. It was easy to tell that he wanted to talk, that perhaps he strained against his sense of isolation sometimes, or even that he welcomed my presence as an opportunity to reminisce.

'Ask your next question,' he said.

So I asked him about himself: how had his life begun?

'I was suckled by an African breast,' he replied. 'My mother was a Tonga. I grew up in the villages until I was ten. Then my mother brought me back to the Englishman who had fathered me. He taught me English. He started to teach me to read and write. Then he died. I only knew him for six months.

'But he left something for my education. I went away to school in South Africa. Those were difficult times. Later I was expelled from a South African university for being a political activist. So I came back here and joined one of the political parties which later merged into UNIP. But between all the politics,' he added with one of his engaging smiles, 'I concentrated on making money.'

The young woman returned to say that the food was about to be placed on the table. George thanked her, and then turned to me once more. His eyes were narrowed.

'When I think back, I realise that my life has been made possible only because of education. Without that money which my father left for schooling, what would I have become? Education is something no one can take from you. Only God: he can make you mad. Money can be easily lost, but not education. And that is what I have worked for. To educate my children, because that is the only valuable thing.'

Cornhill junior smiled affectionately in the direction of his father at this point. 'This explains why I speak a bit like an Englishman,' the younger man said. 'I went to prep school in Wales and then to a public school in Bedfordshire. I did my A levels. Then I did agriculture in Lusaka. I was away from home for eleven years.'

I asked if the experience of an English education had made him into a misfit in Zambia.

'Not at all. I encountered a fair amount of English hooliganism and racism while I was there, and it did nothing to endear that culture to me. In fact, I feel more an African than ever,' he said in his clipped accent.

George Cornhill had risen. As we moved towards the dining-room I remarked on the greenery which filled the enclosed veranda. He nodded.

'It is my wife who has the green fingers. You know, I would have liked you to meet her. She has shared my life right from the beginning, when I came back from South Africa.'

I asked where she was.

'It is such a pity,' George Cornhill responded, 'that she is away at the moment. She is in Lusaka to attend the funeral of a second cousin. You know what it's like these days, all the funerals.'

F or only a short while, as we travelled in the south west of the country, could Davison hold himself together. It appeared to be with considerable effort that he did so. His mood was subdued and his attention elsewhere, his eyes expressing an absentness which I had not seen in him before. I asked if he was keen to return to Lusaka, to be among friends, but he simply shook his head. And then the inevitable happened.

On the morning that we were indeed due to drive back to the city, he again did not appear at the prearranged time. I tried to telephone the hotel at which he was staying, but could not get through.

I sat waiting in the shade of conical thatch perched above a concrete table on the northern bank of the Zambezi just above the Victoria Falls. For the first hour — and it seemed appropriate that I could see the steam rising from the top of the falls — I wrestled with mounting annoyance. After the second hour I resolved to wait only another ten minutes and then proceed with the hire of a second vehicle to get me back to Lusaka, nearly 500 kilometres away, in time for a flight.

I was actually making my way once more to the telephone, when I saw the car turn into the carpark. I stopped and waited. The car drew to a slow halt a little distance from where I stood. Davison emerged. He stood leaning slightly against the bonnet as I approached. It took only a glance to see that he was ill. But my anger superseded that.

'This is not good enough,' I said.

He gazed away at the river, saying nothing.

'This is appalling,' I said. 'Two hours late.'

'I was sick,' he said.

'It seems to me that you are still drunk.'

'I was sick,' he repeated. 'I was even bleeding.'

I looked closely at his face. His features were drawn and strained, and his eyes glared redly at me. His face, dark as it was, seemed drained of blood, as if he was about to faint and fall. But he leaned steadily enough against the bonnet.

'Bleeding where?' I asked.

He pointed briefly at his mouth, and then he said, and it seemed to me out of a pit of misery: 'This is why I am apologising.'

'And now I suppose I must go and pay your hotel bill?'

'Yes,' he replied.

The hotel was a single-storey structure with a deep veranda from which excruciatingly loud music blared. Davison went to collect his bag, presumably from his room, while I waited at a reception desk above which a dead light bulb hung. I had to call a young man from the bar to accept my money, which he did with a faintly mocking air, and then at my insistence issued a receipt. He wrote it out in a slow and childish hand, holding his face close to the pen in the gloomy reception area. Then he spent several minutes looking for change. The music flooded the whole hotel with repetitive and painfully distorted twangs.

But by the time I had finished, there was once more no sign of Davison. I therefore went after him.

The rooms of the hotel all led off a courtyard filled with overgrown grass, damaged palms and shrubs, and rubbish bins which overflowed. I saw Davison standing before one of the rooms in conversation with another man in a black waistcoat. The door of the room was closed. I called none too politely that time was running out. Davison looked at me with an expression of almost total inertia as I approached.

The man in the black waistcoat, obviously attached to the hotel, said: 'He has locked the key inside. We have no extra one.'

Yet I could see that the locks were of the type which excluded that possibility. It would be impossible to lock the door without actually turning the key.

Davison glanced at me with his strained and bloodless face, his red eyes sliding across my own, and I could smell that he had been vomiting.

Then the curtain of the room was drawn aside and I glimpsed a bed in upheaval, and a child of perhaps ten, her big eyes regarding me in slight wonder, her slender hand passing through a key.

The man in the black waistcoat smiled at me with gaps in his teeth. 'She crawled through to fetch the key.'

The situation had become suddenly incomprehensible to me, yet as suddenly sinister. I turned away. The facts drummed in my head, yet I could not get the pieces of this sordid puzzle to fit. The key, the child, the sight of Davison as if he was quite close to death. He seemed to stand in stark relief for me against an idea of liberation which had turned to rags. This young man in his black jacket, the imitation leather frayed at the cuffs and waist, the narrow face strained, his wife already dead from AIDS, I guessed, and his skin oozing with the stench of his own indulgences.

We drove in silence, hour after hour. I drove with the window down and the air from the lavish Zambian landscapes and from the smouldering fires of the charcoal burners swirling through. On Davison's face, beneath the habitual inscrutability, there lay indelible marks of pain and disappointment now.

5

In Paradise

Kinshasa and its environs provide an inexhaustible supply of landscapes, thrills, and memories. Kinshasa is also, and above all, a pilot city, the capital of a great country which purports to be an accurate reflection of the unshakeable will of a people aware of its destiny and eager to assume this destiny to the hilt.

— Publicity brochure. Undated, but probably from late 1970s or early 1980s.

T he man who attended to my air ticket to Zaire said he had lived in that country between 1961 and 1965 'under trying military circumstances', and then again for a year more recently. He had also worked, and all for the same airline, in other African countries.

'Let me tell you,' he said with a certain cheerfulness, 'Zaire is the worst country in Africa. But you can find that out for yourself.'

'Conditions must be appalling,' I suggested, hoping he would say more.

'If you mean appalling in the sense that conditions are terror-striking, yes, then you are correct. The best restaurants in Africa are in Kinshasa, a city where people are starving. Yes, there is a small black bourgeoisie who will speak English to you and slap you on the back because you are a fine fellow, but the vast majority are completely impoverished. They'll be more than willing to hit you over your head for your money.'

Zaire was famous, especially in South Africa, for having had such a bad start to independence. Events in the Belgian Congo in 1960 and the years which followed were frequently promenaded as horrifying confirmation of the savagery of Africa. The collapse of colonialism in this central African country had been swift and brutal; and thousands of Belgians, having lost everything, fled south.

One of these was a woman named Anna, a widow in her early sixties now. She lived in a fine South African suburb in a house filled with her husband's hunting trophies — an elephant tusk, the heads of roan and sable antelope mounted on the living-room walls, on the floor a lion skin with a head which silently roared — and with her memories of an Africa now lost.

'No, I never want to go back to Zaire,' she told me. 'I still love Africa, but I would rather live with my memories now. It was like a paradise there, but not now. Now, it's nearly the end I think.'

Zaire was famous, too, for profound corruption, startling inflation, and an army beginning to grumble about money. Soldiers would make up their wages with bribes and fines at road-blocks. And it was disgruntled soldiers, not too long after my visit, who dragged an already unstable country into mayhem and fire.

Meanwhile, I asked Anna if she could provide me with a contact in Kinshasa, an old friend or acquaintance perhaps. 'Oh yes,' she replied immediately. 'The wife of a colleague of my husband. Her name is Antoinette. She is very nice. She is still quite young. I will give you a letter.'

T he flight from Johannesburg took less than five hours, and I travelled by day deliberately. The sun lifted clear of the horizon as the aircraft taxied out; it was a hazy orange ball, so veiled by smog that it was possible to look at it for several seconds without discomfort. The aircraft turned. Then the surge of power and gathering speed engulfed me as the earth, blurred by speed, fell away beneath the wing. Johannesburg spread endlessly underneath; then came a glimpse of the city centre, glass sparking in young sunlight, far off to the left as the banking aircraft set its nose northwards.

A big landscape soon drifted below: bush country, the bushes like peppercorns littered on a slightly crumpled and interminably dun expanse, but sometimes divided into small rectangles of green and reddish brown. How quickly the urban sprawl had been left behind; in its place this emptiness, with here and there a settlement of sorts — dwellings no more than dots made clear perhaps by the shadows they cast — converged upon by roads. And was that a dam across a brown and sinuous river bed? Then, when the latest settlement had passed, the earth became a patchwork of ploughing, the fields irregular in size and continuing to an escarpment of sorts, a fold, where the country dipped into an unutterable emptiness of bush and small white water courses, devoid of water.

The land down there became an abstraction. I detached myself from the task of identifying things and sank into the sheer spectacle of texture and colour beneath. Smooth and blue-green, this expanse of water down there, this pale surface which extended further than horizons, and at the edges, directly below, a delicate tracing of dark brown and pure white, reminiscent of mud and salt. And now a cream lace spread across yellowish land; the warm colours swimming up and drawing one down into a primeval haze.

But what was this down there beneath the wing? Dense green, and then, miraculously, a rent in the earth, a broad river with islands and channels, a curving feather of spray, the savage scouring of a gorge, neat towns on either side, a criss-crossing of tarred roads, a bridge, airstrips to one side.

'Oh, wow. Vic Falls. Do you mind if I share your window?'

An American girl crowded in, camera at the ready. I was confronted by her profile, her perfume, her nose puckered as she released the shutter, an intimate view of her ear — hair drawn back in straight combed lines above it — and her pendant ear-ring which swung quite gaily as she turned a pleasant face to me and said: 'Isn't it fantastic?'

She took photographs until the spectacle passed out of sight, then straightened up. She stood, a short plump girl, perhaps eighteen, with her knee on the seat beside me.

'Are you South African or European?'

'South African.'

'All I can say is you're lucky,' the girl said. 'Africa's fantastic. Thanks for the loan of your window.'

When she had gone, her ear-rings swaying along the aisle, I looked down again at the fantastic continent, at bush unblemished except by long wriggling wounds, possibly rivers in the wet season showing as pale scars in the dull green bush, and sometimes in the scars a scribbled line, as if by a free-wheeling pencil, indicating a trickle of water perhaps. No roads in the bush, no pathways, only the scars, fed by smaller scars, like the outlines of rib-cages in the bush or the veins of a gargantuan leaf. Later, the earth between the trees turned whitish; then a town somewhere in Angola already; then a substantial-looking river; then mountains, defined by their own shadows, forming a broad ridge, looking hot, hostile, bald, pale brown and olive green. The turning river lay like an endless snake on the land, those Angolan battlefields, and the river was clearly defined yet made with airbrush subtlety, almost a navy blue, and washed with sand banks of the softest green. A whole series of perfect oxbow lakes passed beneath.

Then, suddenly, a straight line, glinting dimly, coming out of infinite distance, turning once with purpose and aplomb, then continuing as undeviatingly as before. Man-made. The Benguela railway. More battlefields remembered.

The aircraft had passed into cloud. Its course had followed that of another river, one which became more substantial all the time, which turned in broad sweeps, flashing on rapids — settlements crowding its banks now, narrow fields on steep land — then swirling through bald yellow country rent by gullies and valleys filled with black trees, then toppling over an escarpment into cloud. Or perhaps it was more like steam through which the aircraft, condensate streaming on windows, now descended.

S team. Certainly like a blast of it as I disembarked. The pilot had said the temperature in Kinshasa would be 27 degrees, a moderate heat, but the humidity clung immediately like a mouldering coat and the light seared the eyes. No sun, only a violent brilliance which beat relentlessly from a white hot sky. No sun, but neither were there shadows.

The disorientation of airports: a few soldiers on the tarmac to ensure that the straggling line of passengers did not stray; then glass doors. Inside the building, a window where black hands slid my passport under the glass; then through customs to be confronted by a throng of black faces, eyes sizing me, lips speaking in French, bodies pressing unconcernedly against me, hands reaching for my luggage. I had arrived in what the airlines man had called the worst country in Africa.

I had seen a little of it from the air. By the time the aircraft had emerged under the clouds, it flew only a few hundred metres above the ground. Nevertheless, I saw market gardens, appearing to be fastidiously kept, and groves of palm and papaw and banana trees, and then streets of square houses built of unadorned concrete blocks. Some of them stood roofless, as if half-completed. Those roofs that were in place, and there were thousands upon thousands of them, showed nearly always in the russet colours of ageing corrugated iron, low roofs in dense crowds and demarcated into blocks by sandy roads. There were signs of informal settlement as well: some backyard shanties and squalor. Directly below for a second a tarred road carried a jam of vehicles, pedestrians, some goats. The aircraft's wheels had already thudded out in readiness for landing, and for a few seconds I looked across an urban expanse which continued westward until its detail faded in a haze, and there, rising above this distant haze, stood a whitish cluster of tall blocks.

I now proceeded towards this cluster, the city centre, sitting in the front of an airlines minibus. The pleasant driver spoke no English and drove with that speed and nonchalance allowed only by long familiarity with the congested roads, the traffic, the crowds of strolling pedestrians.

While the aircraft was still in the clouds, I had got into a brief conversation with a hard-faced man travelling in the seat across the aisle. He was returning from Johannesburg, where he had bought spare parts for his machines. Yes, he had been born in the Congo, on a farm outside Stanleyville. Six years old when the troubles had come: sleeping under the bed and listening to the firing. Now he owned a construction business in Shaba Province. He had recently married and was now the father of a young daughter.

'I think when she is old enough for school I will go to South Africa permanently,' he said, pressing a South African newspaper into his bulging hand luggage. 'The kaffirs have ruined everything here. It is very corrupt. If you had the time, I'd take you to Lubumbashi. Then you'd see. The country has gone down. But Kinshasa's not too bad.'

I remembered this hard-faced man — cold blue eyes, short hair, a faint curl to his upper lip — as the minibus jolted and swerved on the long road into town. He had said that to travel a hundred kilometres in the rainy season in the eastern parts of Zaire could take up to a week.

Not so in Kinshasa. The road into town — the Boulevard Lumumba — was tarred all the way. Kilometres of roadside markets flourished in the mud beyond the ragged verges. People lolled on torn mattresses, blankets, or bundles of sacking in the protection of dilapidated shop-fronts. The grey houses swarmed on the flat land, and the sky seemed sullied with smoke. People walked slowly in the heat, pressing through a chaos of chickens and fruit and meat and smoke and mud and hooters blaring for kilometre after cluttered and clattering kilometre.

Presently a big monument loomed, four concrete cylinders rearing into the glare, and on the top the masts of a radio or television transmitter taking the structure even higher. Black mould from the relentless humidity had defaced the concrete.

What had once been grass and gardens surrounding the monument's grandiose base, now were overcome with weeds, even a few spindled stalks of maize, and some rank bushes with large leaves, fast-growing branches sometimes broken, hanging down in wilted gestures of neglect. This was the Monument to the Martyrs of Independence, and it stood as if at the gate of the city proper.

The roads deteriorated, and the buildings on either side became close-packed and old, discoloured, crumbling away in places. Water lay in stagnant pools and rubbish littered the streets and pavements. I saw naked children sitting on some steps. Yet a few of the buildings had been adorned: each balcony in a yellowish block of flats, three storeys high, offered a vivid display of flowers. Before long, the foyer of my hotel beckoned and the driver's perspiring face smiled politely as I alighted.

My room was on the third floor: it contained an air-conditioner, a small refrigerator, and extravagantly textured wall-paper spattered in one corner with brown blobs almost to the ceiling, like the splash of blood, but which on closer inspection turned out to be brown mould, the result of water or spurting beer perhaps.

The window provided a view of unimposing buildings, not many of which, to judge by the architecture, had been erected since independence, and all of them stained with black mould as the Monument to the Martyrs had been. Between the bases of the buildings I had a first glimpse of the river, an expanse of grey in the white haze, and it was impossible not to think of the early European explorers here, the pompous Stanley and the sauve Brazza. And what of Joseph Conrad's Marlow, inching upstream in his battered paddle steamer in search of Europe's ruination in Africa?

But the immediacy of the city was difficult to resist. Young people laughed in a littered street, the flamboyance and grime, and the colourful clothes of an early Sunday afternoon looked vivid in black Africa's biggest city. There were five million people out there, perhaps more, crowding against constraints imposed only by the sweep and curving of this famous river.

I went for a walk. Not ten metres from the hotel foyer beggars had surrounded me: a forest of upstretched hands, children's voices cajoling, whimpering, and the pleading of big doleful eyes. But within seconds, the beggars were chased away by salesmen with sly and shifting eyes. On offer were watches, jewellery, condoms, crudely crafted artefacts, garish colour photographs (no more than snapshots) of a plump black woman in uncompromising poses.

I waved my arms at them, but they clung to me until I had turned into the city's most prestigious thoroughfare, the Rue du Juin 30, where the tarmac seemed to be drowning in sand, except for the two strips where the wheels of the traffic kept it at bay. Along the pavements stood closed bistros with young men drinking and playing cards at the tables outside. The white hot sky pressed close to the tops of the buildings, some of them not unimpressive, which lined the wide roadway.

Now a young boy with a festering sore just below his right temple attached himself to me. I tried to ignore him, but the boy would not be deterred, speaking in incessant and imploring tones in broken French, and often rubbing his stomach. For nearly ten minutes, the boy softly implored. Then he tried in a forlorn voice to be my guide. If I glanced at the façade of a building, the boy would tell its use — a bank, government or airline offices — even though these uses were usually prominently displayed.

A minibus filled with young men slowed down beside me. The door had been slid fully open, and the youthful faces looked out at me with jeers. They spoke to me in a language I could not understand. I indicated this to be the case, and the youths laughed, imitating my gesture, but with some hostility. An empty beer can bounced on the pavement at my feet. Then the minibus roared off. I thought it might be prudent to return to the hotel. As I did so I noticed that the pleading boy had disappeared.

Again the salesmen and begging children surrounded the entrance. Then the relative safety (these words were in my mind) of the foyer provided a cavernous dimness compared to the hot light of the afternoon. Two women sitting in easy chairs turned their heads in my direction and immediately offered that unmistakable sexual invitation, a series of short hissing noises emitted between tongue and teeth. When I ignored them they laughed, one of them slapping the other's thigh.

I looked at those sections of the river visible from the window of my room. I could see the vague shapes of Brazzaville on the distant bank. I stood there until darkness began to fall — it did so with almost startling rapidity — and the lights of Kinshasa came on. The river flowed like ink and from the darkened waters a hooter sounded in three staccato blasts.

I n the evening, I ventured down to a lounge which oozed without benefit of air-conditioning. I shared the small and lurching lift with a dark-skinned woman with large breasts who smiled brightly and said 'bonjour'; and then, with disarming spontaneity, lifted the sash at the waist of her dress to wipe her nose. She, too, entered the lounge and settled at a table — two tables pushed together — occupied by perhaps a dozen other young women. They suspended their conversations when I entered. Easy enough to engage their eyes; then they would smile or wink or incline their heads in invitation.

A large picture of the President in a leopard-skin beret provided the only adornment in the lounge, the walls of which glistened with moisture. Fold-back doors along one side gave access to a courtyard of sorts, but even this proximity to the open air provided little respite. The heat came in slow waves, forcing perspiration everywhere on to the skin.

'It is hell, no?'

At the next table: a pained expression on the face of a prematurely balding man who said immediately: 'It is foolish to sit at separate tables. I am Michel. I am Belgian, a businessman. What are you doing in Kinshasa?'

'Looking around,' I replied. 'I'm on holiday.'

Michel's expression turned incredulous. 'A holiday? Rome, perhaps; Paris, yes; even Brussels for a good holiday; but Kinshasa!' He laughed.

He brought his drink to my table. His face was fleshy, moon-shaped, and he seemed nervous, looking constantly over his shoulder while he spoke. 'I'm in import-export. I am here for nearly six months now. Plenty of money.'

His gestures seemed exaggeratedly continental. The dismissive hands, the shrug as he expelled breath through relaxed lips to denote dismissal and contempt, but not contempt in any cold sense, rather a sense of exasperated goodwill, as if to say: Oh, my God, look at this — the inattentive waiter, the hotel, the heat, the country itself — it can't be taken seriously.

'Everything here is old and broken — and dangerous,' he said, eyeing me with some concern, and then launching into a catalogue of warnings. 'Don't go out at night, not walking. It is very dangerous. Always in a car. Even then you must keep the doors locked. The whites here are equated with money. However hard we work for it, it doesn't matter. They think of us, they so much as see us, and they think of money. They will easily rob you for ten Zaires.'

I smiled with slight incredulity, but Michel would not be deterred.

'And watch out for the traffic police on Thursdays and Fridays. That's when they start thinking about money for the weekend. Tens of thousands of Zaires for a minor offence, like stopping over a line that isn't there, or driving the wrong way in a one-way street that isn't marked.'

He spoke rapidly, his speech punctuated by this strange mannerism, this constant glancing behind him, in this case at nothing more alarming than the benign-looking portrait of Mobutu Sese Seko.

'When we go into the country, there's never less than three cars, for safety. At night, outside Kinshasa, it's impossible. Road-blocks everywhere. If you come across one, slow down, then speed away. Never stop. As sure as you are sitting there, you'll be robbed.'

Michel's attention had been engaged by the young women who were flaunting themselves for the benefit of a fat-bellied white man who sat with his hands clasped behind his head, observing them. They were speaking to him with their bodies, their eyes. They were flagrantly dressed — low necklines, short hems, lips and nails bright red. Predictably, another warning came from Michel, perhaps this time offered with undertones of regret.

'All these women here have Sida,' he said, using the French acronym for AIDS. 'I have nothing to do with your private life. That is your affair ...' Nevertheless, he told me that the women would find out from the night reception clerks which rooms contained single men and then they would begin to knock on doors.

The fat man, meanwhile, had made his choice, it seemed, and he sauntered with her to the lift. While they waited for the doors to open, he placed his hand on her buttocks. The sight of this seemed only to bring an added restlessness to Michel.

'This is a terrible hotel,' he said. 'We go for a beer at the Intercontinental, no? It's really the only place in Kinshasa. Nice and clean.'

We went out into the street where I was vaguely conscious of watching eyes in the shadows all around. Michel continued to be talkative, offering further insights into his response to his African experience. 'Lock your door,' he said as we drove off into the rowdy night. The city reeked of an acrid smoke. 'No refuse collection here. They burn it in the streets.' We passed through the fog-like smoke along the Rue du Juin 30. 'That's when these buggers got their independence. Since then, all downhill. Two years ago, the girls would stand on the pavements. No longer. They're all dead from Sida.' We began to drive in what looked like a suburb, the streets becoming steeper as they ascended to ground higher than that occupied by the city centre. Michel had begun to point out groups of people huddled on the pavement. 'See them? Starving people. They die in the gutters.'

The Intercontinental turned out to be a large and shining complex, complete with air-conditioned shopping mall. 'You can buy anything here,' Michel said brightly, 'even African curios.'

I laughed, looking at plate glass and chrome, at fashions and artefacts lit by clusters of spotlights. 'But this could be Johannesburg or Brussels or New York.'

'Exactly,' Michel responded. 'That's why I like it.'

He took me on to a terrace with a view of a floodlit pool and the scattered lights of the city beyond. A band played subdued music and predominantly white diners leaned back in their chairs. 'Impressive, no? But very expensive. Now we go for our beer.'

The bar glowed with brass and maroon plush. We sat in extravagant easy chairs, and bought beers at nearly treble the price being asked in my own hotel. Michel spread out his hands in a gesture which clearly intimated: I know, but isn't it worth it?

The aura in the bar was one of wealth, ostentatiously so, and yet one of subtle degradation also perhaps. The young women here were better dressed, more subdued, and they mingled freely with the men at the bar. An elderly white man was being entertained by an exquisite girl — hollowed cheeks and pale brown skin — who laughed at the appropriate times and allowed her escort to light a slender cigarette which she had placed between pursed red lips.

Full African lips, and big dark eyes, and the whites of those eyes, and the sensuality, the promise, as ageing white hands lifted the strands of a necklace from her smooth brown throat and an ageing white mouth left its imprint on her cheek, her own lips parted now, eyes lowered.

'As you can see, there's no apartheid here,' Michel said cheerfully. 'But sometimes I wish there was apartheid. Not here, of course. This is great, no? But out there,' he added, glancing over his shoulder at imaginary dangers.

'The trouble with out there,' I observed, 'is that there is poverty.'

'Yes,' Michel said with a dismissive gesture. 'But ask yourself why. You see, the people don't want to work. This is one of the richest countries in Africa, but they are lazy. It's the Western banks that keep the country going. Why work when you can steal from the whites or the government or whoever?'

He sipped his beer, looking about him with some relish. After a moment, he said: 'But I love Africa. I don't want to go back to Europe. I will go to Johannesburg next, I think. Or maybe Harare.'

For the moment, however, Zaire was paradise. Africa itself was paradise, even now. In the European imagination, it was a place where luxury and ease were still possible, and the climate and views fantastic. Also, there appeared to be plenty of money in export and import.

The provinces were better than the city, Michel was saying — and in direct opposition to the opinions expressed by the hard-faced man on the aircraft that morning. Kinshasa was the worst part, Michel maintained. But in the provinces — he mentioned the names of places which caused him to kiss the ends of gathered fingers in a gesture of relish and approval — there, most of the time, the blacks were primitive, and they still respected the white man. And the fishing in some of the provinces: fantastic, like a dream.

I watched the ageing white man playing with the necklace of the young woman at the bar. But Michel's presence was hard to ignore: his moon-like face, his trivial confidences, and how, in the provinces, the trout literally begged to be caught, trout as big as your arm.

In the morning, armed with the letter given to me in South Africa by Anna who lived alone with her husband's hunting trophies, I sought out the down-town office of Antoinette, and introduced myself.

'Antoinette is too long,' the woman said when she had read Anna's letter. 'You must call me Toni. I am Toni for all my friends. Anna telephoned,' she went on, looking at me with bright and interested eyes. 'I know who you are. I will show you all I can.'

A striking and vivacious person, this Toni. Anna had mentioned that she was a Frenchwoman married to one of Anna's husband's friends and that she had lived the past seventeen years in Zaire. Toni's face had worn somewhat, no doubt under the perpetual fierceness of light, yet teemed with sensuality still, and her body looked youthful in a simple cotton dress, her limbs sleek and brown-skinned.

She said: 'You have come on a terrible day. I am so busy. But we will think of something. Then tonight you will come to Jake and me for dinner.'

A tray of tea had just arrived, so Toni unearthed another cup and we sat together in her office for a few moments while she made a telephone call. Then she turned back to me with a pleasant smile. 'I have made a tour for you. Is that all right?'

A young woman entered with some files. Toni introduced her as 'Christine, my assistant'. Christine's hair was done in intricate plaited strands which converged into an elaborate superstructure, giving balance and poise to her head. She smiled easily, greeting me in careful English. She sat down at a desk in a corner of the office where she began to write in one of the files, her face held to one side of and close to the point of the pen.

After tea, Toni took me down to the street where a minibus, the name of a Zairean tour company printed on the door, already waited. Toni spoke in French to the driver, a good-looking black man with a trimmed beard: it sounded as if they were arranging an itinerary. Then Toni turned to me, her eyes narrowed in the glare, and said: 'Francois will look after you. Have fun.' She stood on the pavement smiling for a moment, then turned and walked back lithely into the office block.

Francois drove in congested streets, hooting often, swerving to avoid carts and people, changing gears constantly; and after a moment turned on the fan which caused humid air to swirl about the cab. The city presented a muddle of potholes and sweating faces and buildings stained with mould. At all the main intersections along Rue du Juin 30 policemen directed traffic. They wore white gloves, surely a relic of colonial times, and were protected from the glare of the sky by small awnings stretched above the pedestals on which they stood. One of them did his directing with a cigarette protruding from thick lips.

We drove up a hill and came to imposing gates with soldiers dressed in camouflage overalls and maroon berets lolling on the inside. Francois told me that the President lived here. A cage of tigers, one of them prowling up and down with an insatiable restlessness, stood to one side. No buildings could be seen from the gate, only the tigers and trees and gardens and a roadway which curved up inclining ground. Did I wish to stop to look at the tigers? I declined. So we drove on, the road hugging the wrought-iron fence of the presidential residence on one side — soldiers armed with automatic rifles at intervals along it — and the grey expanse of the river on the other. Two men stood in a pirogue, poling the craft upstream in the quieter currents close to the bank. Out in the middle, the water buckled like steel sheeting as it swept into the rapids. We turned towards higher ground and came to a monument.

A bronze warrior: three times life size, with shoulder-high shield and spear, and with the obviously African face staring out over the city centre which lay in a haze of humidity on the inside of the river's sweeping curve. The monument was not entirely realistic: the powerful torso sat on a rectangular stomach, the depression of the navel also rectangular. On the plinth were the words: Justice Paix Travail. 1972. A statue of the explorer Stanley had once stood here, looking out over the river as it broadened into the pool which had been named after him. But such things had been torn down in a frenzy of anger and nationalism. I mentioned the tearing down to Francois, who smiled politely. They had pulled them down with ropes, he said. All over the city stood empty plinths; and at the top end of Rue du Juin 30 a row of double-storeyed colonial houses we had passed on the way up now stood empty and derelict, doors and windows ripped out, floors caved in, ceilings hanging in shreds, some of them appearing to have been burnt, but long ago.

The high ground occupied by the warrior afforded a sweeping view. The river shone steel grey, appearing slightly swollen in the fierce light of the day. A paddle steamer, small and toy-like at that distance, thrashed upstream. Brazzaville shimmered on the farther shore. Closer at hand, Kinshasa's cluttered business district, containing Toni's office and my hotel, hugged the southern bank, while to the south of the business district lay the endless sprawl of Kinshasa itself: the low structures, coloured dun and rust, which stretched into an increasing obscurity of smoke and haze. 'We can go,' I said at last. Deferentially, Francois opened the door of the minibus for me.

At the Academie des Beaux-Arts, I was assailed by a throng of objects crowded together on the tables and walls. Here were highly polished wood carvings, mostly stylised, sometimes not dissimilar to the statue of the warrior, and frequently of women; ceramics (masks and vases, plates and table lamps); paintings, some of the oils very fine, an ink drawing of a hunting scene — naked men with spears stalking elephants and antelope; brass work, often abstract or impressionist, again with a preponderance of women as subject. The women's breasts and backsides were invariably voluptuous, almost absurdly so sometimes. The religious symbols seemed as discordant and over-detailed: crucifixes carved into totem poles filled with small primate faces; a copper relief of Christ carrying the cross, the crown of thorns, even the blood trickling down.

Outside the gallery, a rectangular piece of wood had been carved quite intricately on one face and then discarded. A young man, no doubt a student, used it as a bench while he contemplated a geometry problem drawn on a paper which he held firmly in his pink-palmed hands.

In the grounds, more art beneath the palm trees. Sculptures stood in large bronze groups, yet seeming discarded among the weeds and unmown grass. The sculptures presented a profusion of images, exclusively human, often in postures of march or striving or conflict. I waded through the grass to look more closely. Here were two obviously black men in chains, their faces expressing the elemental longing to be free; close by, a figure crouched forward in an attitude of complete exhaustion. Such pieces spoke eloquently of the disaster of slavery and the brutal colonialism which followed in this part of central Africa. But the newer pieces — like a muscular man carrying a flame (same symbol as on the Zairean flag) at which he and his followers looked up as though worshipping — were less satisfying. They seemed reminiscent of the propagandist art of Nazi Germany or Soviet Russia. They were a trite expression of the freedoms which independence had hardly brought to Zaire.

On the way to the harbour — I had requested this stop after visits to a park, some government buildings, the big statue of a tom-tom drummer — we came across a barrier of soldiers across the road. But Francois showed no sign of nervousness; indeed, the soldiers stepped aside to allow the minibus to pass in terms of procedures to which I was not party.

The harbour turned out to be little more than a customs house and a concreted area upon which stood some crates of machinery and a pile of large string bags containing plastic footballs. The harbour area was surrounded by a high wall on the top of which glinted jagged bottles and other broken glass. The concrete sloped down towards the river, ending in a slipway. A few vessels lurched on the water close by. The strength of the current came as something of a surprise, and I watched the ferry from Brazzaville describing a pronounced downstream arc as it approached.

The concrete grew busy with people. A port official with an enormous stomach cracked a whip, but no one took any notice. A policeman in dark-glasses looked about him with an air of supreme authority. But when he turned his back, heads bobbed up and several black bodies slithered over a corner of the glass-topped wall.

The ferry, a dilapidated vessel with circular paddles on either side, turned in choppy water and reversed against the slipway. Ropes were thrown and secured. The stern clattered down, and people streamed up the slipway, chattering and shaking hands while the port official cracked his whip and shouted. Someone had already set up a stall to sell smoked fish. The shirts of the men flapped open and untucked. An assortment of battered trucks and cars ground off the deck of the ferry. Crates of alarmed chickens disembarked on the heads of women, babies on their backs; and then the cripples came off, several on crutches, one in a buckled wheelchair which sped up the slipway under the impetus of a muscular chest and enormous arms.

The smell of fish and of the river was in the air. A million pieces of green flotsam, no doubt torn from the banks at unknown upstream places a week or a month before, rode on the powerful waters. This sight of an enormous natural force, and this sight of an ebullient people beside it, their careless use of so many of the rejects of the developed world — the ferry itself, the vehicles and wheelchair — brought with it a special vision. In spite of the dangers and the pain, Africa possessed the colours, the passions, the age, and the ambiguities of a grand design.

When we got back to Toni's office, Francois stood with one hand discreetly open while the fingers of the other covered the wrist above the asking palm. I felt slightly disgruntled because I had planned to tip him without, in this way, being asked. I gave him 10 000 Zaires, wondering whether this polite and unabashed man had been old enough, in the early 1970s, to tug on the ropes which brought the statues down.

S trange, after the clamour of the day, to sit in a deckchair beside a swimming pool in a garden filled with big-leafed plants and the scent of flowers. Toni and Jake's garden, surrounded by high walls, secluded and peaceful. We drank iced water.

'We are careful how we drink alcohol,' Toni said. 'It is too easy here. I know Europeans here, men and women, who are already through their first bottle of whisky by this time of the day.'

Toni had told me on the way home that her husband, a big blond with pale eyes, was a reserved man who would speak little. But he must have been in expansive mood that evening, because he said to me immediately I arrived: 'That is a terrible hotel you stay at. We have a room here. We will fetch you tomorrow.'

Then later, when Toni went into the house to replenish the water jug, Jake told me he was Belgian, but that he had been born in Zaire. 'I have lived here all my life. When I go to Europe, I stand there with big eyes. It is all too fast. Everybody is running.' He grinned in his slightly self-conscious way. 'I prefer it here.'

Toni returned with the water, and we talked generally of conditions in Kinshasa. I asked if it was safe to walk in the city — the city centre — at night.

Jake shrugged. 'I think so. They will ask you for a cigarette, for money for a beer, even if you are feeling like having a wife —' again the grin '— but fairly safe, I think, although of course I don't guarantee it.'

Big leaves rustled, and a youngish woman in a towelling gown appeared. 'Do I intrude? I have come to swim.'

Toni introduced her as a neighbour, a Swedish woman living alone next door while her husband was away 'in the interior' selling spare parts for lorries. It was decided that we should all swim, and then eat outside. Jake lent me a pair of bathing trunks, and we lolled in the tepid pool, drinking iced water and talking. Night had come quickly, and the faces around me were illumined by the lights of the patio. The

Swedish woman's face seemed very pale and round, with her hair wet and plastered back behind her ears.

She said: 'I am very interested in South Africa. I have read a book called *A Moment in the Breeze*. It is a wonderful love story. The author? I think it is Albert Brink.'

'André,' Toni said, and then she laughed. 'The book is *Instant in the Wind*. I have read him, too.'

'But after that,' the Swedish woman said, 'his books became too — how shall I say? — heavy, ja?'

'Too political,' Jake said in French.

The lights of the patio went out, but the event raised no consternation. 'Another power failure; that's Zaire for you,' Toni said as she went into the house, returning in a few moments with candles.

'Obviously the lights go out often,' I remarked.

'All the time,' Toni replied. 'And the telephones go off, and the water supply. You learn to live with it.'

Talk turned to the disorganisation and muddle — and corruption — in which these Europeans, powerless in political terms, seemed content to live and earn a reasonable living. They told me that bribery was commonplace. Take the telephone system, Jake said. The technicians would deliberately disconnect, only to reconnect for a fee. The solution was simple: pay a set monthly amount to a technician to ensure that your line stayed open. An added advantage here was that the technician would then arrange that no overseas calls were metered — this simply to protect his source of income. 'We can beat them at their own game,' Jake said, winking at me. Things like driving licences, planning permission (if one bothered) and business permits could usually be got for a bottle of whisky, or not much more.

In these ways they spoke of a venality which had been suggested, earlier that day, by the way in which the soldiers barring the approach to the harbour had so easily given way. It had to do, no doubt, with the cupping of palms and the passing of notes. The more formal organisation, and consequent strictures, of Western societies did not work in

Africa. Neither Africans nor Europeans wanted that sort of organisation here. I began to wonder whether the contribution made by Europeans in independent Africa to the continent's corruption was not in direct proportion to their political impotence. I wondered if there might even be a form of spite, whether conscious or unconscious. Through independence (the white mind was saying) you took away our paradise; we will therefore quite happily assist in the fulfilment of your nightmare.

Someone seemed to be reading my thoughts. A voice said: 'But I suppose South Africa is too much like Europe. There are too many rules and regulations, yes?'

'It's changing,' I said.

'I have been to South Africa twice,' Toni said. 'Once I was very sunburned. I am swarthy as it is. I leaned out of the window of the car in a country town and asked a man to direct us to the hotel. He replied: there is only one hotel, and unfortunately it is for whites only.'

Everyone laughed.

I asked the Swedish woman how long she had lived in Africa. Nearly seven years, she replied. Had she enjoyed it? Some parts of the experience she had enjoyed, others not. 'I do not enjoy the insecurity, the unease. You never know what is going to happen. I worry about my husband. I am aware that I do not belong here. They can kick you out.'

'I am aware that I belong,' Jake said. 'I am born here.'

'Yes,' Toni said, 'but you have a Belgian passport.'

'That's true,' Jake replied. 'Which means we can go to South Africa when we're kicked out.'

Again everyone laughed.

The Swedish woman worked as a laboratory technician for an American pharmaceutical company in Kinshasa. But times were hard. They were short-staffed. Several qualified black colleagues had already died of AIDS, others were ill. And her young assistant was studying part-time to become a politician.

'He knows where the money is,' Jake said with a grin.

'Ja, but the trouble is he does his studying in work time. He washes no equipment. He is too busy working to become a politician.'

Over dinner I mentioned the bags of plastic footballs I had seen at the harbour. But did I not know that football was the passion? Was it not so in South Africa, as well? 'What about Kaizer Chiefs?' Jake said. 'That is the big South African club, no?'

They told of a recent match between Kinshasa and a visiting team from Brazzaville. The home crowd had become convinced that the Senegalese referee showed a bias in favour of Brazzaville. Angry crowds had run amok on Rue du Juin 30, attacking anyone they thought might be Senegalese, and also some whites.

'We're always to blame,' Jake said, winking at me.

'But European football is just as bad,' the Swedish woman said. 'These people here are wonderful really. When the bribery and corruption is put to one side, they are very fair. And normally they are very friendly.'

Jake told a story to illustrate their sense of fair play. He had once bought a plant which the seller had assured him would provide a yellow flower, rare for that kind of plant. Jake made the purchase on the understanding that if the flowers were not yellow, he would be refunded. 'The flowers were red. I took it back — perhaps most people would not have bothered — and the seller apologised and returned my money. That is not uncommon.'

When the evening had been concluded and the Swedish woman had gone home, Jake and Toni drove me back to the hotel. At Toni's suggestion, we drove on a road which provided a clear view of the river. A huge moon had risen, its reflected face shattered in the turbulence of the current. The light of the moon described the farther bank as a faint line, and cast a pale sheen upon the façades of mansions lining the road on which we drove. The air smelled warm and of the fragrance of extravagant blossoms. An almost over-gorgeous scene, too gorgeous to be real, more like a dream, one which had been eagerly embraced by earlier Europeans. Now their heirs looked upon it, not from the deep verandas and balconies of mansions, but from the cab of a rattling pick-up.

I remarked on the clarity of the air, with the lights of Brazzaville twinkling far away across the silver river. Toni's reply was enigmatic: 'Always, here, at night the clarity comes, when it is too dark to see.'

I was eating breakfast in the hotel dining-room the following morning when she sat down at my table and ordered coffee. 'Have you booked out yet? Come on, fetch your things. It will save you money.'

In the cab of her pick-up, she kicked off her shoes and hitched up her skirt slightly to drive. She warned in her vivacious way that the vehicle's brakes were faulty; therefore she must drive fast, as she could change down and slow the vehicle with more effect if the revolutions of the engine stayed high.

'I am taking you to see a man who will interest you,' she said. 'He is shunned by the European community in Kinshasa because he has married a Zairean woman. He has — how do you say? — gone native? But he is very knowledgeable. Eighteen years ago the President wanted a museum, and for seven years this man, Adriaan, had money to collect the art, but now the President has forgotten about the museum, although he still pays Adriaan a salary. All the things he has collected are in cupboards and sheds.'

'In the presidential residence?' I asked in some surprise, recognising the direction in which she travelled.

'In the grounds,' Toni replied as she drew up at the imposing gates, tigers pacing to one side, the soldiers looking suspiciously out at the pick-up. One of them approached, his young face stern-looking beneath the maroon beret. Toni spoke to him in French, showing her identity. They looked at my passport. Then the gates opened slowly.

We found Adriaan in a small stifling office. He listened as Toni explained my presence in Kinshasa, and then gestured pleasantly for us to sit in ragged office chairs. Toni would not sit, however; she must attend to business at the office, she said. 'I'll come back for you,' she added. I heard the pick-up drive away.

Adriaan regarded me expectantly, and also with some enthusiasm. 'I have tried to think and understand,' he said. 'In Africa — I am Dutch but I have been here twenty years — it is difficult to ask questions. You ask slowly, slowly. Even then they say: you do not understand; you are white. But slowly I am understanding.'

He was a big man, powerful of build, although now with an air of having gone to seed. His black hair looked oily, matched by a similar beard. He wore thick-lensed spectacles and a checked shirt, the collar lying flat and wide open at the throat. His lips seemed very pink inside the beard, and from time to time he licked them.

'In Zaire there are between four and five hundred different tribal groupings, but not all of them are Bantu. Some are Sudanese. How do you say? Nilotic? Others are stone age, like the Pygmies. You have the stone-age Bushmen in southern Africa. But did you know that all your southern African Bantu people began to move south from the Congo Basin nearly two thousand years ago? Their forefathers had come here from West Africa.'

Adriaan's small office was piled with books and magazines, an untidy collection which grew from shelves, from a small table in one corner, from the desk itself. I suspected him to be self-taught: his African experience had long become obsession.

'There are things we need to understand when we look at the objects they make,' he was saying now. 'We need to understand, for example, their concept of beauty. They do not say: that is a beautiful animal; they say: that is a fat animal or a useful animal. It means the same. Utility is beauty. There is, or at least there was, no independent aesthetic. But they are learning from us, ja?'

It sounded as if he recited things he had read again and again, but he did so with the freshness of new discovery. His enthusiasm was unavoidable: his eyes glowed with intensity, and his gestures were unconsciously those of an embrace.

'Another thing we need to understand is that many Bantu peoples — most of them, in fact — perceive the world as being controlled by their ancestors, not God. They believe in God as the creator of the world. But he is too far away to influence people's lives. What does influence them is that other world between God and themselves, a crowded world of good and evil spirits. And the intermediaries between that other world and the real world are the ancestors.'

He paused here, frowning slightly. 'I think I am becoming too simple — there is more than this — but let us look at the things. I will talk as we go.' He rose from behind the desk, then added: 'But we will not be able to stay long because of the heat. Then we come back for some coffee. There is also tea.'

We crossed a small courtyard to the end wall of a long shed. He unlocked the door, looking at me with a slight smile. 'There are not many South Africans who have been in here.' The door swung open. Two immediate impressions struck me: one of appalling heat, the other of surprise growing to astonishment.

The shed had no windows, probably no ventilation at all, and the underside of the raw asbestos roof glared down. 'Not too bad,' Adriaan said, glancing at a thermometer behind the door. 'It is forty-nine. I have seen it at sixty.'

But the astonishment overrode the physical discomfort. The entire shed was crammed with grey metal shelving in which thousands upon thousands of artefacts had been collected. Thousands of faces, thousands of intricate things. No attempt had been made at display, only storage.

'This is incredible,' I said.

'This is seven years' collecting,' Adriaan said, his eyes shining. 'I can make the best museum in black Africa. But this is like one small handful when you think of what is still out there.'

We walked along one of the aisles between two sets of shelving. Adriaan said: 'They worship their ancestors, pray to them, give them things, talk to them, asking them to intercede. It is all to make their lives safe. They make images of them so that they always remember. Here are some ancestral figures, some for graves, others for households and shrines.'

Figures of the earth, of clay, of wood, with grass and animal hair adornments. Other figures had protective functions: to outstare the mysteries of evil, to entice good, to promote successful hunting, to ensure the survival of the tribe.

Adriaan tapped one of the survival pieces and said, with a certain scorn: 'Too many white people, they become fascinated with the penis, the genitals, in African art. The Africans are sex-obsessed, they say, probably with some envy. But the Africans were thinking only of fertility and the survival of the tribe.'

The hot air reeked of these figures, standing in long regiments in the metal shelving, staring out, sometimes blindly, sometimes with a fierceness which jarred against preconception, sometimes with a grace or whimsy which called for responses only from the blood. Like insights from a reality out of reach, these regiments; but not less real for that, and each figure carefully labelled.

We moved further into the shed. Adriaan told of some deep graves he had once excavated but about which the people now living on the land knew nothing. The graves were not of their ancestors, they said, but of some previous time.

'I thought of two things,' Adriaan said. 'How full that other world, the world of African spirituality, must be. And I also thought of the staggering age of the land, how much life and death and human ritual it had experienced over tens of thousands of years.'

He showed a collection of big wood statues which had adorned the roof and entrance of a chief's abode. The lower parts of the statues had been eaten away by termites. 'It makes you realise how much has been lost for ever. Of the things made from organic materials, nothing can be much older than sixty or seventy years.' He made a gesture which enclosed in its purview all the artefacts by which we were surrounded. 'The whole lot is 20th century.'

Adriaan's shirt stuck sopping to his back, and he used a handkerchief to keep the freely running perspiration out of his eyes. 'How is the heat?' he asked with a sudden grin. I indicated that it was appalling. So we emerged into a day, in the presidential gardens, which seemed by comparison moderate and pleasant.

I asked, while we gulped water and then poured tea in Adriaan's small office, why the President had lost interest in the museum. Adriaan shrugged his shoulders. 'Perhaps the Americans will help one day.'

As our shirts dried, and we waited for Toni's return, we spoke generally about Africa.

'In many places it is in turmoil,' Adriaan said. 'Yet African cultures are old and rich and highly logical when you look closely at them. I think the trouble is that Europe disrupted them in the worst possible way. First there was slavery. It's easy to become indignant about slavery; you know, in the liberal way. But there has been slavery for all time. Africans enslaved to Africans. Chinese to Chinese. But the massive exporting of slaves, the slavery business of the 18th and 19th centuries, that is our heritage here — and theirs. It always will be.'

He looked at me with eyes which burned with involvement, even with sudden anger. He licked his lips. 'Then came colonialism. In the Congo it was brutal. Men were chained together to make the railways and roads. They died in their thousands. People's hands were cut off for failing to collect their quota of rubber. As a result, they took only the worst from European culture, except perhaps in the field of music. And they began to lose their ancient traditions and skills. All the carving is lost now. Zaireans were the most accomplished carvers in Africa. But no one carves any longer, except for the tourist market.

'It was a bad mix, Europe and Africa. For more than a century white people have been telling Africans that what they were doing was wrong, inferior. They became confused. They still are, I think.'

He told me of someone he knew, a Zairean Catholic, a good man who accidentally knocked down an old woman with his car. Then his son died. 'Things were going wrong. He prayed and prayed, but could find no peace. Then he sacrificed a goat and two chickens to his ancestors. Peace came. Do you see the dilemma?

'Or listen to this. I once asked a Catholic priest, a black man, whether he no longer believed in fetishes, and the priest replied: I try never to ask myself that question.' Adriaan grinned at his own story. His teeth were stained from the pipe he now took some time to light. 'But I am sure a merging will come here at last,' he said between puffs of brownish smoke. 'A synthesis. I have heard that the Catholic Church in Zaire has asked the Pope if they can include ancestor worship in the liturgy.'

He began to make a comparison between Japan and Africa. 'You see in Japan, the Japanese chased out the Catholics. They had the confidence. The Africans were not so confident or prepared. They were in most ways so far removed from European thought that they simply assimilated some of it — religion especially — and were crushed by other parts of it. The Japanese were literate before the West became an influence there. They had their own literature and written history to fall back on. That was not the case in most of Africa, certainly not here. It is only since the whites came that things have been consistently written down and preserved.'

He talked insatiably. He struck me as a lonely man, lonely in his ideas. The other expatriates were safe, albeit powerless, behind their high walls. They were not prepared to tolerate Adriaan's ideas because he had 'gone native', not so much by virtue of his marriage, but because he had retained a fundamental respect for life, especially for the logicality of primitive peoples and their traditions and customs. The expatriates would not tolerate him, but it seemed that Toni could.

'Oh, the Zairean Bantu can be dangerous when he is angry,' Adriaan said. 'But he is reasonable. Once during a troubled time — there is much anger against whites still in the heart of the Bantu — I was crossing a street in town and some young men shouted: go home. I turned to them and said: who are you to shout that? Do you know who I am? Do you know how long I've lived here? Do you know what I do? Where is my home? The youngsters apologised.

'But there is racism among them too, and I do not know whether they have learned it from the white man. I think not. I think it was here long before the white man came. I was out in the eastern parts of the country, travelling with my Bantu workers. One evening I went to drink with the Pygmies near by. The Bantu were shocked, because they consider Pygmies to be little better than animals. Yes, I said, I go with them and why do you tell me that white people are racists when you are worse?

'The Pygmies I like. They are pacifists, they countenance no quarrelling among themselves, they are economical and clever — they can make lawyers and doctors — and they are generally happy.'

Toni's sudden presence invaded the office. 'Here, I am so late,' she said. 'I thought by now you would have been walking up and down with the President's tigers. But we go to lunch, yes?'

Adriaan became suddenly shy and apologetic, pulling once at his beard and licking his red lips. He declined the offer of lunch until Toni said matter-of-factly: 'We go African. Come.'

We ate wild pig in a restaurant where formica tables were set out under a pergola, covered with big-leafed creepers, and where the cooking was done in a long shed —

long enough to accommodate the diners in wet weather — from the side of which the pergola extended.

We were the only white people in the crowded place. Rhythmic music blared from speakers tied in among the leaves of the creepers. Adriaan spent some time explaining the menu: here was antelope, wild pig, monkey, chicken and duck, crocodile, snake, porcupine, elephant, fish and goat. 'The crocodile is quite interesting,' Toni said, but in the end we settled for the pig which proved to be like tough pork tasting and smelling of game.

Talk turned, under the leaves and jiving music, to the European partition of Africa, to the profound impact it had caused throughout the continent. Adriaan's face was flushed with excitement as he talked, and as he sparred with Toni. Colonialism, he said, had been an unmitigated disaster because it had been motivated by greed and prestige. The Berlin Conference; 1884; the arrogance, he said, all those stupid goats sitting in the middle of Europe carving up a continent they knew nothing about.

'Yes,' Toni said, 'but it's happened, it's passed, and what have we left? Something quite sinister I think: let us call it the victim syndrome. That is what Africa is saying: we were victims, therefore anything goes.'

'But they *were* victims,' Adriaan countered, leaning forward and licking his lips. 'They had no chance, they lived and died under the white man's derision, under his yoke, under his superiority, under his obsession with power. Africa was like a woman under the boot of a bullying man.'

'But that is too simple,' Toni replied. 'Maybe a bully can also have generous moods. I am not saying colonialism should be painted all white. Neither should it be painted completely black. Most Europeans came to Africa to make a living in what to them was a wilderness. Could life have been so easy for them, these bullies? Did they sit all day watching Africa the beautiful woman doing their work for them, then rape her at night?'

Toni, too, had become animated, and for the first time I saw her as someone who, like Adriaan, lived in a form of isolation which was at once pervasive and almost invisible — until it was broken. Yet perhaps hers was the more awkward position. Adriaan at least had made his choice. Toni had described his wife as a 'lovely laughing black mama'. Toni herself showed more ambivalence. 'In a way I envy him, but I would dread to do what he has done. There is something in me that would not allow it.'

But now, in the restaurant, she turned her animated eyes to me and said: 'See what you have done. You come here and stir us up. Then you sit silent while we quarrel.'

I laughed. Adriaan, on the other hand, became immediately concerned. He did not mean to quarrel, he told Antoinette, it was just nice to talk.

'No, no,' Toni replied, 'don't apologise. I am pulling a leg, that's all.'

I asked her to explain what she had referred to as Africa's victim syndrome.

She spread out her hands. 'Whatever happens there is something to blame. We have bad government in Africa because of colonialism, corruption because of colonialism, broken roads and railways because of colonialism, wars because of colonial borders, famines and stagnation because of neo-colonialism. Some of this is true. But to excuse yourself always because of the way your mother made you sit on the pot is nonsense.'

Later during the meal, I asked Adriaan what it was about Africa which gave him his strongest sense of affinity with it. He contemplated the question for some time, perhaps because he groped for English words with which to express his thoughts.

'The age and the flow,' he said at last. 'Africa is very old. It has stayed in the same form for nearly 200 million years. All the other continents have broken away from it. The last break happened only five million years ago. That was when Arabia split off, and when the rift valleys also appeared. It was in these valleys, and also in southern Africa, that apes began to walk upright and use their hands, at last, for the making of tools. Everywhere I go in Africa I can feel the age of it, and I can feel it to be our birthplace. Africa gives an idea of belonging that I can feel nowhere else in the world.'

'And the flow?' Toni asked.

'It is partly the age, partly the African spirituality. This idea that the past is alive in the ancestors. I imagine sometimes a place in the African consciousness which is crowded with faces and beings, a big crowd, and in the distance, the faces are part man part animal, and I think that this place of the ancestors goes back into the unconscious too, far back into the beginnings of human life and the relationship between this life and the earth itself — I mean the rocks, the roots and bark and berries, the water, the sunlight.'

An expression of near exaltation had come to his heavily bearded face. Nevertheless, I asked another question. 'Do you feel able to connect with this spirituality, this continuity?'

'As a human being,' Adriaan replied, 'I think it is possible. As a Westerner . . .' He shook his head.

It struck me quite forcibly then that this African spirituality was what I had glimpsed in Adriaan's sheds. The sprites and charms and carvings of ancestors, the icons for graves, the clay and grass-work figures, crowding together in the shelves as doubtless they did in the African air. There was magic overlaid by magic and tens of thousands of ancestors, this big crowd as Adriaan had called it, stretching back into the great mists of the valleys of primeval times. But all this in its turn had been overlaid by confusion and doubt now. And the long pain of transition — the poverty, the rage, the pretentiousness — could end only slowly, or perhaps only with disaster.

But for the moment it was enough to be sitting there under the big-leafed vines, 'going African' in the company of the passionate and bearded Adriaan and this lively Frenchwoman who had become my hostess.

S he said to me one morning, not long before I was due to leave Zaire: 'I have taken the day off. I will show you some of the things you haven't yet seen.'

We walked, to begin with, in the market-places of the sprawling city. As usual, there was no direct sunlight, only that merciless glare from a sky made white with low and steaming cloud. Toni wore dark-glasses, and her bag was held firmly under an arm. This was thieves' market, she told me with a smile as we moved among the thronging crowds. Jake had once bought back the spare tyre of his vehicle here, hardly an hour after it had been stolen.

Yet conversation was not easy. The jabber of the market surrounded us, and we walked in silence through the stench and welter of food for sale, the writhing grubs, the chickens, the black meat in crude chunks, the small dead crocodiles, the fish, the smoked monkeys with agonised expressions on their wizened faces.

Then suddenly a commotion: shouts, the scraping of boxes against concrete, the splintering of wood, a few screams. And the crowd swayed away from the epicentre, forcing us backwards in a crush. Across a sea of heads, I saw maroon berets bobbing; a face caught in a sweating grimace; the careless swing of a rifle butt.

'What is it?' Toni asked.

'Soldiers, I think.'

'Come,' she said, gripping my arm and forcing her way with surprising strength in the opposite direction. 'Pardon, pardon,' she said, squeezing through the mass of dark bodies. When we came to less congested ground, she looked up at me and laughed. 'That is the fear. The soldiers. A mutiny. Then who will stop the looting?'

She said she must pay a visit to her tailor, and we drove in her pick-up into the dense houses which formed the great mass of the city once away from the central area. The streets became narrow, congested with dilapidated vehicles and people. The buildings on either side stood low and raw-looking, seeming only half built, and between them many structures made of rusting corrugated iron, of packing cases, of cardboard and hessian, had sprung up. Some of the people still wore what I supposed to be tribal dress from the surrounding countryside — beads, bangles, woven grass, animal skins, feathers — but in no demonstration of conviction or pride. I saw a few people thus adorned scavenging at the perimeter of one of the piles of smouldering refuse which littered the city.

The building in which Toni's tailor worked had the words, Mansu Mode, prominently hand-painted on the front wall. The tailor, presumably named Mansu, smiled deferentially, holding his hands together in front of his stomach as he spoke to Toni in French. She was expansive with him, using her hands and laughing. She introduced me, and Mansu offered a moist and inert hand and a set of dazzling teeth. Several women worked in the small rectangular building — blue walls and no ceiling — and they too smiled up from behind hand-operated sewing machines.

Mansu had produced a skirt. Antoinette took it and held it against herself, flicking out one hip so that the garment swished against her legs. 'What do you think?' she asked.

She appeared to me, all at once, to be a person more vulnerable than I had at first imagined. I watched the pleasant way in which she shooed a crowd of inquisitive children from around the pick-up. But was there, for all the confidence, a loneliness in her head?

I asked her. We were driving again and I spoke to her about intellectual isolation, perhaps even of the type which I suspected Adriaan lived with. The loneliness of ideas and thoughts, did she feel it sometimes, a Frenchwoman living in central Africa?

She replied from behind her dark-glasses: 'I don't really know about things like that. All I do is live. I stay alive. But I am a little bit annoyed that my skirt is not ready.'

She said she would show me colonial Leopoldville which still existed in the sprawl of modern Kinshasa. She drove into an area of narrow roads, avenues of huge mango trees, high walls. Sometimes, through gates, we caught glimpses of mansions both old and new, swimming pools, tennis courts, lavish lawns. The walls surrounding these properties appeared to have been built incrementally, the height added to from time to time.

She laughed: 'Our wall too. Every time something happens, another bit goes on.'

We had lunch in the Kinshasa yacht club, and afterwards strolled on the wet timber jetties, looking at the boats on which the Kinshasa wealthy pleasured themselves over steaming weekends: water-skiing, fishing, picnics on mud-banks in the surging river. Leisure time in paradise: playing in sun-dappled water which in five minutes boiled in rapids.

'But that's just it,' Toni replied. 'People would get tired of paradise if it was permanent. There must be some risk.'

From the far end of one of the jetties, we looked across a channel at an island crammed with shanties. Even on to the narrow sand the shanties tilted, water lapping at poles. Naked children played beneath rickety structures; young women did the washing, malnourished breasts already drooping against ribs; and a man in a torn shirt, short cigarette between thick lips, staggered in mud and reeds. The stench of poverty, suffused with the steam of the height of day, wafted across the narrow water to where we stood.

'Paradise,' Toni said ironically. 'Not for them, I suppose. But they have always lived on the islands, these particular people. They're the river people. Only there are too many of them now, I suppose.'

When we returned to the pick-up, I asked if it would be possible to drive to the university. She put on her dark-glasses once more, and said: 'You must look at your map. I am not certain of the way.'

I worked out a route, yet the road I chose, marked as a main artery on the map, finally petered out into a welter of rubbish dumps, low hills of waste oozing a suffocating stench and coils of acrid brown smoke. People swarmed everywhere. Some of them called to us with a sort of mocking cheerfulness as Antoinette stopped the pick-up and began to turn it in the suddenly narrow road.

'I have never been this way,' she said. 'Your directions are very bad, yes?'

'The university isn't crucial,' I said as she reversed, swinging the wheel. A huge perspiring face had stooped close to her window, peering in. 'If you feel uneasy...'

Her expression became one of scorn. 'I am not frightened. Not at all.' She drove out the way we had come, the roadway ahead and around flooded with sweating Zairean faces. 'You want to see the university. We will find another way. Unless,' she said, glancing shrewdly at me, 'unless you are frightened.'

I smiled.

'Have you ever been frightened,' she asked, 'here in the African paradise?'

I nodded.

'And me,' she said. 'Toni driving into a crowd after a soccer match. The next thing, here was the brick smashing the windscreen. My mother was visiting. She crouched on the floor in the glass. She has not been to visit again.'

We laughed.

I said: 'What did you do?'

'I reversed at high speed. I never knew I could go so fast going backwards.'

Laughter again, and looking at the map, finding a new route, tackling a road where the exhaust fumes of crawling vehicles obscured the distance. The pick-up jolted on a roadway which had once been tarred, but now was filled with craters, the original level of the tarmac marked only by flat-topped protrusions, like hills in an eroded valley; and the big bald tyres of heavy vehicles bucked slowly through this landscape, close enough to touch beyond the window of the pick-up.

We drove for nearly an hour, and for nearly an hour we were surrounded by a chaos of activity and noise. Furniture makers worked among their curled wood shavings in the shade of trees; and the ramshackle premises of tyre menders

171

littered the roadsides; and stalls of all descriptions; and the big buses — more like old army lorries, and of a similar colour — filled with black faces, while youths with flapping shirts clung to the canvas sides.

I remarked that the inaccessibility of the university — it was proving to be an excruciating journey, even though by the map it was hardly fifteen kilometres from the city centre — in some way mirrored the inaccessibility of education to Zaireans generally.

My words seemed to trigger something in Toni. She told me that most teachers in Zaire could neither read nor write French. Then she said: 'My heart is for the children. The children of my servants. I keep thinking: I must do something. I could do something. I could teach them myself. But when the end comes — perhaps it is tomorrow, perhaps next year — it will all be lost.'

At last the urban turmoil fell away behind. We drove up a gently sloping hillside — tall grass, thorny scrub, weeds — and Toni said: 'You perhaps have not noticed. But we are on the university campus now.'

Built in the 1950s, a few years before independence (Toni told me), the buildings occupied the crest of a hill which had long ago reclothed itself in its indigenous dress. An incongruous sight, the slightly pretentious mid-century Western architecture lapped at on every side by unkempt central African vegetation. There had once been lawns and avenues, but these had long ago been overlaid by weeds and lush-leafed creepers. A young couple lay embracing on a long flight of overgrown steps.

'Look at it,' Toni said quite sharply. 'How do you English say: gone to seed?'

A group of languid youths played cards and a board game like checkers outside what appeared to be the entrance to the main building on the campus. They looked up momentarily as the pick-up drove past. I wondered whether the Rector was inside, what he might be doing. I asked: 'Is this term time?' Yes, it was term time; look at it.

'Why do you stay?' I asked her.

'I have property here.'

'Is that your reason?'

'Why must I have a reason? I live here.'

We had turned a corner. Under flat acacia trees, among thorns, a silent jet aircraft stood on flat tyres. The cockpit canopy had been removed, as had the cowlings around the single engine. Wires and pieces of what looked like electronic equipment had been pulled out and hung in a tangled mess against the fuselage. I glanced enquiringly at Toni. 'The Department of Engineering,' she said. We drove on in silence.

A blond-headed young man stepped suddenly into the roadway, signalling for Toni to stop. She spoke to him in French. The young man squeezed into the front of the pick-up. Toni spoke to him in pleasant conversational tones, and he replied as pleasantly. When she had set him down, close to the main gate of the campus, I asked her what had been said. He was a lecturer from Belgium, she told me. He came every year to Zaire to give a five-week electrical course which took five days in Europe. But he liked to come; he had made friends in Zaire, and they had fun when he came. Kinshasa was good fun.

I asked whether the lecturer had offered an opinion on his students, on the state of the university.

'I didn't ask him,' Toni said sharply. 'Perhaps I should have driven him into town so you could interrogate him.'

After a moment she added, still with some irritation in her voice: 'This is what paradise is like. Don't you know that? All it is is exploitation, and then hatred, and then the big fire, yes?'

I t seemed strange, after the exertions of the day, to sit in a chair beside a swimming pool in a garden filled with big-leafed plants and the extravagant scent of flowers. A sense of having been there before, certainly, of remembering the beginning; from that first evening to this last one, all that had happened, all that had been said; a half-hidden sense also of inevitability.

How calmly these friendly people predicted collapse, as if Africa had made them pliant, ready for extremes. 'Except, I am not moving,' said Toni obdurately. 'Not while my property is unsold.'

Jake winked at me. 'I think we will dig the trenches over here and over there.'

I chatted to a widow named Lillianne who had, as she said, dropped in for a sundowner. The Swedish woman from next door dawdled in the pool, her body seeming very white under the patio lights, her wet hair slicked back behind her ears. Jake jumped in and arcs of water sluiced on to the paving. Toni in her bare feet served iced water.

Lillianne said that she did not want to return to Belgium now that her husband had died. But she was due for retirement soon, which meant that she must find another job if she wished to stay.

'The thing is, I like it here. I am used to it. I think it is because there is more responsibility here. You have to think of everything yourself. There is a sense of achievement against all the incompetence. Also, life is easier. I can keep a servant. I have a very good house boy who makes me laugh. I play bridge and golf and I have a pleasant social life...'

'Africa is not so attractive to me,' the Swedish woman said, her forearms resting on the edge of the pool. 'I am beginning to yearn for my home. Even for snow and long winters. That's home for me. Not this. I think Africa is wicked. And,' she added with a coquettish toss of her head, 'sometimes that is not too bad.'

'Africa is too innocent to be wicked,' Jake said, heaving himself from the pool. 'Corrupt, yes. But not wicked, not of deliberate evil intentions.'

Part way through the evening, a dark-haired man, his eyes pale blue but already red-rimmed with liquor, appeared and sat with the company for a few moments. He told them he was sick to death of Africa. He took the beer which Jake offered and drank it from the bottle. He glanced frequently at the Swedish woman, who seemed ill at ease in his presence, as if his subtle arrogance discomforted her.

He dominated the conversation while he was there, talking of his bad experiences as a European pilot trying to work for an African airline.

In Luanda, for example, the air-conditioning in the only luxury hotel was invariably out of order, and more often than not the taps yielded no water. 'I wash in a bucket,' he said, his lips curled. But some of the West African countries were the worst: the chaos, the dangers. 'There they not only rob you, they kill you quite easily. They ambush the cars from the airports.'

He turned his attention to the deliberate overloading of aircraft. Airport officials taking bribes to get another crate, another box, into the hold, regardless of regulations or safety. Airport officials getting wealthy at the risk of passengers and crew on nearly every flight. 'Bastards,' he said. 'They strut about, they tell us we are only workers. But without us, they have no airline. And the government lackeys with their suits and briefcases, forcing their way on to the aircraft, unbooked, saying they are on special missions. Special missions, my arse. They're stupid. They abuse everything. A friend of mine, he left. He couldn't stand it any longer. He went to a European airline. He lives a normal life now. He works under normal conditions. He says he can no longer bear to see a black face. He sees a black face and he feels tension and aggression. I am going that way also. And yet,' he said, 'it can be paradise here, not so?'

That ironical smile, crooked, ruggedly handsome, and the tired and disillusioned eyes. He stood up abruptly, saying he was going to a night-club to get drunk. 'No flying tomorrow.' Then he said, looking directly at the Swedish woman's troubled face: 'And later, if I can still walk, I will find myself a girlfriend.'

I became conscious of Toni's bright eyes looking at me over the brim of her glass of iced water. 'To paradise,' she said. And I had a powerful sense of watching people moving sluggishly through final days.

In the morning, as well, this awareness of pending termination and collapse. It was time for me to go, and my consciousness was of what I was to leave behind: the chaos of Kinshasa streets, the smoking piles of refuse, the aircraft under the trees at the university as if it had crashed there, the friendly expatriates; and also Adriaan, bearded and red-lipped, with his lonely eyes and forgotten artefacts in the white-hot sheds in the president's garden.

When the time came to say goodbye, Toni placed her hands on my shoulders, putting her cheeks against mine, first one side then the other then the first once more, in the French way. 'The time has been too short,' she said. 'But I am thinking we will meet again. Perhaps in your country.'

Jake grinned in his slightly self-conscious way as he extended his hand.

It was indeed in my country that we next met. But at first, I heard nothing. As the soldiers mutinied, and as Kinshasa was sacked, I kept in close contact with Anna who lived alone with only her husband's hunting trophies for company. But Anna received no communication. Pictures of expatriate refugees alighting from aircraft with bundles of belongings and frightened children appeared in the newspapers, but I saw neither Toni nor Jake depicted there. I saw pictures, too, of smashed shops on Rue du Juin 30. Then there were reports of widespread looting in Kinshasa's expatriate suburbs. The local currency had become valueless: while a dollar was worth around 500 Zaires when I was there, by the time the soldiers mutinied more than 32 000 Zaires were needed. Much worse was to follow. Meanwhile, French and Belgian troops had forced the Zairean soldiers off the streets. But by then most of the expatriates had left; most European embassies had closed; and consular protection was specifically withdrawn for people electing to stay on in the pillaged city.

When I heard, finally, that Toni and Jake had stayed on, it did not surprise me. Then Anna telephoned to say that, unexpectedly, they had come to South Africa on a visit. I hurried to see them and to hear their story.

They had been on holiday in Europe when the mutiny took place. Toni had flown back early, to return to her job. (I remembered the young woman Christine with her hair arranged in an elegant superstructure, and how close she had held her face to the files when she wrote.) Toni learned later that her employer was shot at as he tried to reach the airport outside Kinshasa. Toni's flight had been diverted to Brazzaville. She had stayed there for five days, helping the refugees coming across the river in boats and light aircraft.

'We would wait for them on the beach,' she said, looking at me with her bright eyes; 'and they came in the clothes they were wearing, sometimes with no shoes, an old couple with nothing but their toothbrushes and two cats in a basket. I knew them.'

In Kinshasa, about a kilometre away across the turbulent water, the soldiers had been joined by their families and finally thousands of civilians, including young children; and this mob had plundered hundreds of expatriate homes.

'Ours too,' Toni said. 'I couldn't believe it. Smashing locked doors right out of the walls. Everything was taken. We had bought sixty bottles of good South African wine before we went on holiday. It is the best investment when money is losing value so fast. We came back to empty bottles everywhere. Friends told me there were two hundred people coming in and out of my house, like ants.

'But we were lucky. They did not take our bath and lavatory. Others lost all that; and kitchen sinks, tiles, light fittings, even the electrical pipes in the walls.'

The stories became bizarre, tragic, almost surreal. A young woman barricaded alone into her house; the soldiers breaking a hole in the kitchen wall, crawling through in front of the woman's eyes; she gave money; they left; they even repaired the hole they had made; then, within an hour, they returned drunk, battering down the front door, and stole everything. (I thought of the Swedish woman and wondered if she had made it home to one of those long dark winters which she had begun to miss.)

A man had tried to defend his house with a rifle, firing at the looters through a window; the soldiers waited until he had run out of ammunition, then they broke in and, while the man and his family watched, stole all his property — including his rifle. ('They so much as see a white face,' Michel with his exaggerated continental gestures had said, 'and they think of money.')

I heard of the looting of an oil depot, hundreds of drums being rolled away, some of them bursting so that the broken streets of Kinshasa ran slippery with oil. A bicycle factory plundered, people running with cycles on their shoulders because they could not ride; others trying to ride, falling over, crashing, buckling wheels. And booty from an ironmonger's yard, children dragging long reinforcing rods in all directions through the shattered city.

'And now they try to sell everything they have stolen,' Jake said. 'They try to sell computer monitors as TV sets. When you say: that is not a television; they say: yes, all you need is a remote controller and the picture will come. Often they do not know what they are selling. I found a man trying to sell a double adaptor, but he had no idea what it was. And everything they try to sell is either broken or has parts missing. But they say: it comes from a European house, therefore it is valuable.'

Toni looked at me, and there was a hardness in her bright eyes that I had not seen before. (But I remembered how, as we had driven to the university on my last day in Kinshasa, she had shown me some of her concern. 'My heart is with the children,' she had said.)

Now she said: 'For a month I was very depressed and angry. Then I said: but I must go on. I said: I am lucky compared to what is happening in other parts of the world. I have not lost husband or children; none of my friends is hurt.

They stole from us whites, but they did not kill. So far as I know, only one man was wounded when he tried to use his pistol to defend his car.'

She laughed shortly. 'No, I do not have a gun in my handbag. What is the point? We had a gun in the house, but of course it was stolen.'

'It is like starting at the beginning,' Jake said. He grinned in his slightly self-conscious way, even a little sheepishly. 'You try to decide whether you can afford two chairs or only one.'

I asked them why they stayed.

Toni was immediately forthright, as she had been on this question before. 'Because I own property there. If I leave I will lose it. I also have a good job — for the moment. And on top of that, the African climate suits me.'

Jake regarded me with more uncertainty. 'It can happen again at any time. Soldiers are supposed to protect their country and population. Instead, they have ruined it. And they have not been punished. That is the important thing. The President has done nothing to punish them. There is no morality left.'

'That is why,' Toni said, 'even small children now demand money on the streets, or lifts in your car. If you refuse them money they say: fuck you. If you refuse them lifts, they stone the car.'

I asked her if she knew how Adriaan had fared, whether he still worked among his crowded artefacts in the President's garden. But she looked at me blankly now; she shrugged her shoulders; and I could see in her eyes that there was no longer any room in her perceptions for doubt or puzzlement or even curiosity.

6

The Water with the Fish

The friendship of the water with the fish is real while that
of the water with the sand is not. (The first lasts. The
second ends. As soon as the wave withdraws, the sand is
left alone.)

— An inscription in the garden of the Mission of Our
Lady of Help, at Mua in central Malawi.

On the walls of the safari company's office had been
affixed several posters advertising 'the warm heart of
Africa', large colour photographs of wildlife and lavish
sunsets over water of molten gold. A young woman with red
hair and freckles sat behind a computer, holding a telephone
between cheek and shoulder and tapping away with two
fingers at the keyboard. Her name was Rina, and she had told
me quite explicitly that she was having a bad day. While I
waited on the far side of the desk, a smiling African brought
me a cup of tea on a tray and then retired through an inner
doorway.

The young woman slammed down the telephone. 'Oh,
damn,' she said, her voice a small explosion. 'I really can't
wait for these people all day.'

Delays and frustrations accumulated about her like
unwelcome baggage as she tried to find a car for me to hire.
She said, half laughing in an abstracted way, that in view of

the problems she was encountering my first impression of Malawi would inevitably not be favourable.

But my initial impressions had been made some time before her fuming had begun. It had been of seared country, red-brown earth and red-brown vegetation, rolling away as the aircraft landed; and again as this somewhat artless young woman had driven me from Kamuzu Airport into the capital city of Lilongwe, the dust of the long dry season draped over the roadside trees. In response to a half-idle question, she had told me readily enough that she was Rhodesia-born, and had gone to boarding school in South Africa.

'But my parents got out of Zim in 1978. We were living in a particularly unpleasant area. When the war got really bad, we made a duck. I've been in Malawi for about sixteen years,' she added. And I had judged, glancing at her profile as she drove, that such a period would have constituted about two thirds of her lifetime.

Now in the safari office with the over-sumptuous posters on the walls, Rina dealt with a thin young man from a bank, gold-rimmed spectacles lending a fine seriousness to his dark and unsmiling face. The problem was a cheque which had not been stamped with the safari company's official purple stamp. 'Oh, for God's sake,' Rina said, grinding the rubber against the back of the offending document.

I looked into the amber eyes of a leopard which lay sprawled along the branch of a tree, fixing me with a glossy stare from one of the posters.

A voice said: 'The elephants have knocked over a tree in our garden.'

It was an indeterminate English accent the normal precision of which appeared to have been blunted by perpetually warm weather. I glanced up to see slightly rounded shoulders inside a flimsy T-shirt, the skin on an upper arm peeling from the sun, pale eyes above a small mouth coloured pink. Chatting to Rina about this commonplace hazard -- that of the elephants in the garden -- in the way of the blasé expatriate: at once meticulously knowledgeable and slightly scornful of such knowledge. Then talk turned to a young man soon to return from remote Tanzanian parts. 'Oh, he'll be spending the evening with me,' Rina said smugly. 'Bully for you,' her visitor responded. And for a moment, the two young women faced each other with decidedly cool eyes.

Strange that Malawi appeared to mean something so different to these sparring women than it must mean to Malawians themselves. Had Rina and her adversary no inkling of the political unrest which had led to a referendum in 1993 in which most Malawians had voted in favour of a multiparty system? And what of the elections which had taken place not long before my visit? What of the ensuing celebrations, as much for the demolition of what had been by all accounts an authoritarian and intolerant regime as for the establishment of the first new government since independence?

The telephone rang. Rina attended to it. Her face tensed as she listened.

'Who am I?' she said sharply, her upper lip curled in obvious racial disdain. 'Who am I? I'm Mr Elvis Presley phoning from Timbuktu. That's who I am. Where's Simon? I want to talk to Simon about a car. God, these people!' she added, rolling her eyes for the benefit of anyone who watched.

The woman in the T-shirt grimaced faintly.

The smiling African came sideways across the office to collect my empty tea cup. I asked him (I spoke beneath the rattle of Rina's telephone conversation) if he thought it would soon rain. He flashed his teeth at me, but shook his head. 'Not yet,' he replied, and for some reason he had lowered his voice to a whisper.

I stood up. I said to Rina that she could contact me at my hotel when the car had been arranged. As I turned to go, I glanced into the watching eyes of the woman in the T-shirt, and they seemed aloof, preoccupied, secretive. I conjectured about the response she might have developed for the country in which she found herself living. Or Rina, for that matter,

182

African-born. Had it, above all, to do with the passive excitements of game reserves, or elephants uprooting trees in the garden, or draped mosquito nets on perpetually warm weekends at the lakeside?

Perhaps there was something more, which I thought might have to do with the isolation of European sensibilities in Africa, and the loosening of strictures and reserve which such isolation provoked. Was this the lure: the idea of unrestraint, especially in a hot climate? Was this the message I should be reading in the woman's eyes: this promise of the exchange of the damp and peevish urges of suburban England for the extravagant passions of the tropics?

Extravagant was a word which suited perfectly my first evening in Lilongwe. It suited the air itself as the sun set, infused with the reds and golds of dust-laden light, and sent shafts at acute angles across a garden filled with flowering bougainvillaea, roses, crimson bottlebrush; and the large trees with pale trunks standing in a crowd to one side of the pool. It suited, too, the panel-beaten Rolls Royce in the carpark, midnight blue with grey leather upholstery; and the false eyelashes of the young African women on the terrace, the pendant ear-rings and big red lips, the pants with flared bottoms and the sway of hips. And the young bucks strolling in with hands in pockets, wearing loose-fitting lumber-jackets and doleful expressions. Over the loudspeakers drifted the strains of popular music from America. Once, as darkness settled gently between the lights, a black man in a suit hummed along with one of the tunes and suddenly sang in a strong baritone voice: 'You fill up my senses, like a night in a forest...'

I asked John Chikakuda, a man with whom I spent some time while in Lilongwe, whether Malawi was still self-sufficient in food. This had once been the claim, I reminded him, under the government and agricultural policies of Hastings Kamuzu Banda, the country's leader since independence from Britain in 1964 until the recent elections.

'No longer self-sufficient,' John replied. 'And for several reasons. There have been periods of severe drought, especially in 1991 and 1992. You also need to take into account the impact on agriculture and the economy in general of nearly a million Mozambican refugees who crossed our borders during the 1980s. Some are going back, now that peace has at last returned to Mozambique. But many still live in Malawi.'

Easy to see on the map why Mozambicans had fled to Malawi. The long sliver of country had jutted like a peninsula of calm into the storms of one of southern Africa's most enduring battlegrounds. Just after the town of Dedza, for some kilometres on the main route to southern Malawi, the road served as border between the two countries. There were no fences. The road followed a high ridge, and the hills of Mozambique swept away to the western horizon. The people of Mozambique had strained the services on the Malawian side, John told me as we drove this way one afternoon; but they were hardly conscious, most of them, that they had moved to another country. Families and clans straddled the border. They were Ngoni people who in the complex diaspora caused by the Zulu-centred Mfecane had migrated from the south in the 19th century. They lived in villages on either side of the road. On one side only we saw the empty shells of Portuguese trading stores, abandoned and then vandalised in the mid-1970s when independence came to Mozambique.

But there were other factors which needed to be taken into account when attempting to understand the declining position of ordinary Malawians, John said.

'They have always needed cash for what they cannot grow,' he explained. 'That was fair enough. But in recent times this need for cash has dramatically increased. They need it now for education and health services. Yes, economic structural adjustment programmes, cuts in social spending — it's the same in many African countries. But it's hitting the ordinary people hard; it's forcing them out of subsistence agriculture and into the cash economy when the economy isn't really ready to receive them.'

We saw them by the roadside, walking barefoot in the fine red sand of the long dry season. We saw them on bicycles, peddling loads of food or fire-wood from point of supply to area of demand. The flat country around Lilongwe stretched away in all directions, and in all directions the characteristic sight was of untrimmed thatch like rustic hats upon the huts, and of children in the dust, and of donkeys drooping in front of carts. Also on the country roads, more than once, I saw double-decker buses lurching and listing axle-deep in sand-drifts and stones while dense clouds belched out behind the wheels of these incongruous machines.

John Chikakuda said: 'More than eighty per cent of Malawians are subsistence farmers who are being crippled by increasing cash demands. The short-term solution of course is to sell ever larger portions of the home-grown food crop, but with disastrous consequences. Hunger regularly becomes a cruel reality. And not only hunger. Do you realise that one in four Malawian children dies before the age of five?'

We drove on through a landscape which seemed exhausted by dryness, a burnt sienna country crouching beneath a high and unyielding sky.

'The reality is that there is wealth in Malawi,' he went on. 'Considerable wealth. It's a question of redistribution. Before the referendum, people were feeling the squeeze, but what could they do about it? For thirty years the government was boss. Dissent cost jail or simple disappearance. You smile? Two or three years ago, we would not have spoken as openly as this. We would never have trusted each other. Or maybe the driver would be an informer. Then one of us would disappear.'

The man who drove the vehicle in which we travelled — a four-wheel-drive with a long swaying aerial — showed no sign that he had heard the remark.

John continued: 'Now the referendum and the elections have freed the people from that old bondage; and, let me tell you, expectations are high.'

On first meeting this friendly man, I had been struck by the grasp and consciousness he displayed of his country's political life. We had sat together in the small office where he worked for an international development agency. He was a large man, probably in his middle fifties, with slightly bulbous eyes, a thick neck, and small ears in a head which had considerable depth. He spoke in a strong, sometimes sharp-toned voice; but his stance was never aggressive. He talked to me about the new freedoms which multiparty democracy had brought to his country. Newspapers springing up all over the place; the principles of accountability taking root; and the right of the electorate not only to choose but also to make mistakes now being entrenched.

'The thought of having an electorate is itself refreshing,' John remarked. 'It's a big advance on simply having an all-powerful president leading — or chasing — the people like sheep.'

Had Malawians voted on ethnic lines in their election?

'Not so much ethnic lines as regional ones,' John replied. 'The old government had fostered regionalism simply by being so biased towards the central region. People in the northern and southern parts of the narrow country had voted for their regions mainly so as not to be left out in the cold again.'

Banda had even gone to the trouble of shifting the country's capital from Zomba in the south to Lilongwe in the centre. This had happened because Banda hailed from the central region and had wished to consolidate his political base by stimulating economic development there.

The new president, I noted, was from the south.

'Yes,' said John. 'But he is speaking for all Malawians; he is acting for all three regions in the country.'

'Are you from the south?' I asked.

John Chikakuda smiled. 'Originally, yes.'

But it was to the poverty of most Malawians that our attention inevitably returned. 'Famine is never very far away,' John remarked as we drove in the parched and rutted country; 'especially now at the end of the long dry season.' And the spectre of that terrible statistic which my host had so matter-of-factly dropped could not be evaded. It seemed to shimmer in the clarity of sky, and in the reddish haze of dust which hung above whole landscapes of hand-tilled fields. One in four Malawian children is dead before the age of five, John had told me.

We stopped one morning at a village called Mitundu. It lay not much more than twenty kilómetres to the south of Lilongwe, yet it felt remote. People walked or sat in the wide main street. A group of men worked on bicycles which stood upside down on their saddles and handlebars. Red dust lay everywhere, and its haze was thickened by smoke from the food stalls in the market; a clutter of humanity and torn plastic awnings protecting assorted wares, and some vegetables in heaps. The main street was lined with battered shop-fronts: sagging verandas jutting from small façades; corrugated iron closing holes which had once been windows; signs which were hand painted, but long ago. Here, above all, was desolation and dust, a sense of movement having slowed down through sheer tedium and weariness.

Yet, here, in Mitundu, I met a lean young man whose eyes sparked with the energy surging inside him like a perpetual hunger. He introduced himself as Kondwani Kazembe.

He wore a white coat and carried a stethoscope in his slender hands. He was what in Malawi was called a clinical officer, a health worker trained in diagnostics and basic surgery, and then placed in charge of rural health facilities. Kazembe's responsibility was the Mitundu health centre, filled with waiting women and children, and the small attached hospital whose beds were used largely for maternity cases. Yes, he did Caesarean sections. He had also been trained to do basic laboratory work, including blood testing for malaria and worms.

'But we need a microscope here,' he said, glancing to gauge the impact his words were having on me, and at the same time momentarily tugging at his neatly trimmed beard. The glance and the tug brought to him an air almost of conspiracy, and for a second, behind his energy, I saw a man of calculating shrewdness.

But John had pointed him in another direction. 'Show us the nutritional rehabilitation centre,' he said.

So we turned our attention towards a low building set among trees some distance from the health centre. The walls had been whitewashed, but long ago and now the colour of the red sand on which the structure had been built had crept to the window sills and higher. Kondwani Kazembe took us on a tour of empty dormitories, not even blankets on the narrow metal beds. 'There are thirty beds here,' he said. 'At the moment we have twenty children. But by the end of the dry season we'll have sixty. And before the first crops are ready, say by next February, we'll have at least ninety. I'll put three in a bed,' he added, glancing about him.

I asked about blankets.

He leaned slightly towards me, anxious to please. 'They have not been stolen, if that is what you are thinking. The bedding has simply been worn out. The blankets have been used until they were rags.'

The rehabilitation centre had, he explained, been built with the assistance of an overseas aid agency, and then handed over to the Malawian government in the mid-1980s. Since then the facility had deteriorated. 'It's not functioning properly,' was Kondwani Kazembe's way of expressing it. Nevertheless, the idea had been to assist in the alleviation of malnutrition by admitting mothers along with their under-nourished children — ginger-haired and swollen, some that I saw in the sandy yard of the centre. The mothers would then be trained in gardening, nutrition, income generation and the like, while at the same time becoming involved in restoring the health of their children, not by any First World magic, but simply by regular feeding with the correct locally available food. The idea was familiar enough, but Kondwani Kazembe explained it with an enthusiasm and freshness which seemed to fill his narrow bearded face with light and purpose.

Here were the kitchens, he said, leading us into a smoke-blackened space. There had at one time been two homecraft workers, but no longer. In fact, the kitchens were hardly used any longer, except for the heating of water, because the tin chimneys had long ago rotted away and the smoke swirled chokingly under the iron roof, finding no escape. I saw a water tap to one side swathed in a bandage, presumably so that no one would be tempted into using it. Kondwani Kazembe's bearded face smiled a trifle ironically at me in the smoke and gloom.

Most of the women sat and crouched over open fires in the sandy yard outside. Some of the younger children were tied to their mother's backs. I glimpsed flies settling on faces in repose. Other children rubbed their eyes in the smoke of the fires. Pots of porridge bubbled sluggishly. 'Likuni phala. That's what we call it. It's a high protein porridge: one part soya beans, two parts maize, and sometimes another part of groundnuts.'

I asked him how long he had trained to become a clinical officer. He smiled confidently. 'Four years in medical school.' I asked how long he had been in charge at Mitundu. 'Nearly one year.' His eyes flickered with a slight defensiveness. John Chikakuda had got into a conversation with some women under a tree, and Kondwani Kazembe appeared to be suddenly conscious that he was alone with me. He had become guarded and awkward, as if he feared I might catch him out in some way. Smoke billowed between us momentarily, and in the haze I saw his shrewd eyes upon my own, and once more his slender fingers tugging at his beard.

When the smoke had passed, he said: 'Look over there, that is the garden. The fence of reeds is to keep out the goats. But my staff buy the seeds themselves because there is no budget. And over there, that small house with the wire netting around is for the chickens. But we have no chickens and anyway the wire is everywhere broken.'

I looked through the smoke of the fires and the faintly sour smell of the porridge to the slow activities of the village as it stretched on the parched earth beyond. A child was howling in the sand; she wore no garment to clothe the lower half of her body.

'We need support here,' Kondwani Kazembe said. 'We have been forgotten here.'

I expected to see some kindled anger or at least frustration in his expression then. But there was only the politeness, the sense of energy, and beneath it the calculating shrewdness, as if he would do anything to get the support he needed: the microscope, the seeds, the new chimneys, the chicken wire, the rekindled hope.

He said: 'When I came here last year, the hunger was terrible. Children were dying ten a day. I did everything I could. I worked day and night. I kept thinking: these are my fellow Malawians, but they are dying. Here, taste this porridge.'

I put a finger into the steaming ladle which was offered, the eyes of women and children on me as I did so. And then, as I brought my finger to my mouth, the women laughed and turned their eyes away.

'I love my job. I am happy to be able to do what I can. To do something: that is my driving force.'

He stood before me smiling, this Kondwani Kazembe, holding his stethoscope in slender fingers. Two ballpoint pens, one blue, the other red, were clipped into the pocket of his coat. The whites of his eyes were unblemished, his beard neatly trimmed. He struck me, as he stood there in the smoke of the cooking fires, as being like a hard dark portrait of idealism squandered, an indelible etching of waste. I had judged him to be not yet thirty years old; and he was smiling at me in that essentially artless yet calculating way he had.

The car which Rina, the brash redhead of the safari company, had so laboriously arranged for me arrived nearly two hours late. 'It's not my fault,' her voice wailed over the telephone. Simon was usually very reliable, she said. In a few moments, she called me back and laughingly explained that the driver had gone to the wrong hotel. 'It's now on its way,' she said cheerfully. 'Sorry about the mix-up. If you want, you can ask for a discount.'

Once in possession of the vehicle, I was able at my own pace to see something of Lilongwe. Not that there was much to see. The old town, an untidy mess of crowded shops and street stalls, dusty houses and potholed roads, lay to the south east of the meandering Lilongwe River. To the north west had been built the new capital, ostensibly to encourage development in the central region, but at four or five times the cost required to consolidate the capital at Zomba.

The new capital seemed unnecessarily spread out. Modern buildings jutted at random from plentiful bush and trees growing tall in the open spaces between. There were a few banks and commercial complexes, but for the most part the capital comprised the offices of various government ministries. And all this had been so laid out that it lacked an obvious focal point. It was a conglomeration rather than an entity. The streets ran in twisting disorder, conforming to no apparent design. Nevertheless, the frequent traffic circles were adorned with gardens and lavish blooms; and people stood in small crowds waiting for taxis and buses, some of the latter those incongruous double-deckers I had seen out of town, ploughing through the sand. The Lilongwe streets were picturesque rather than imposing, looking like those of a well-to-do and shady suburb, although some of the names attempted a grandness which was otherwise lacking: Kamuzu Procession Road, Presidential Way, Independence Drive, and Africa Unity Avenue. Such places had been made possible by a large and inexpensive loan from South Africa's apartheid regime more than a quarter of a century before.

I discovered another irony. At one end of Africa Unity Avenue stood the United Nations High Commission for Refugees. I was reminded of John Chikakuda's comments about the Mozambican refugees, nearly a million of them straining the resources of this small lakeside country. 'And now that they're going home — some of them at least — others are taking their place,' he had said. 'We've got people from Angola, Ethiopia, Somalia, Zaire and the Sudan. And now we're getting thousands running all the way from the slaughter in Rwanda. I think they come here because everybody knows how well we treated the Mozambicans.'

I drove out of Lilongwe and turned east towards the lake. For a few moments I passed beneath an over-arching avenue of large jacarandas filled with pods, but largely leafless in the long dry winter season. Then an undulating countryside received me, drawing my eyes to distance. The hills of central Malawi enticed the road into slow curves and long successions of switchbacks which looped forward even to the horizon sometimes. Occasionally the way had been forced through dun-coloured cuttings, but for the most part the topography was accepted and the road ran with the country, a blue-grey ribbon unfolding over landscapes of profound aridity. Goats walked against rocks and across stretches of empty earth. Women collected sticks and branches for burning. Children ate what looked like stalks of sugar-cane. And the fronds in the banana groves adjacent to each village seemed wilted, many of them brown and dead.

Over most of the villages through which the road passed hung an aura of disrepair, even of decay. Old rectangular houses and shop-fronts were always in evidence, but invariably as empty shells, sometimes burnt, sometimes simply collapsing. My friend John Chikakuda had illumined this aspect of rural Malawi for me. We had stopped, during one of our drives to the south of Lilongwe, to examine what must once have been an imposing row of roadside shops, but derelict now, roofless, windows smashed out, a veranda roof sagging between supporting pillars. In the centre of the cracked and peeling façade, plaster letters still spelled out a name: Ismael Mohamed.

John had nodded. 'In the early 1970s, Indian traders were ordered to leave the rural areas and move into the towns.

Their old shops are standing empty all over Malawi. The reasoning behind this move was straightforward. It was argued that the Indians had dominated the economy for long enough, and that Africans should now be given the opportunity of becoming shopkeepers. But very few of them did, with the result that villagers not only lost the convenience of a local trading store but were faced with the added cost of travelling considerable distances into town to buy what they couldn't produce on their smallholdings. And this was supposed to be African development,' he added with a certain good-natured contempt.

In one of the villages on the way to the lake, an extensive row of these Indian shops had been slowly smashed, only broken walls remaining, while on the sandy space between them and the ragged tarmac of the road stood an array of grass and pole stalls displaying small dishes of food and lengths of sugar-cane, and some basketwork for passing tourists.

But I could see as I drove that not only the Indian shops were derelict. Quantities of mud had fallen from the rough timber framework of the huts themselves, and the thatching seemed often to be threadbare. Hundreds of people walked by the roadside, the women carrying baskets on their heads and babies strapped to their backs, children carrying water, some men pushing laden bicycles. Buses emitted voluminous black fumes; their roofs were nearly always loaded with assortments of cargo; and small boys grinned and waved as I drove close to overtake. The road went high into the hills, and some of the colour — of the people's dress, of the buses, of the sky itself — was lost in the haze of the heat of noon. I travelled for over an hour in this dun, parched world which lay waiting for the rain.

When the descent began, it did so without offering any view of the lake. Difficult to decide whether this was due to a secretive topography or to the haze as the road swept down towards Salima, a town sprawled on the flat country which hugged the western shoreline.

On the outskirts of the town, I passed a grove of old established trees which had been devastated by the constant demand for fuel, branches ripped off to dry, a man cutting at one of these severed limbs with a saw, smaller wood chopped and piled to one side. Now there were samoosas for sale at the roadside, and hundreds of bicycles weaving before me on the tarmac, and as many pedestrians thronging the wide verges on either side. The buildings of Salima appeared in haphazard groups and then fell behind. I noticed two tourists in straw hats and baggy shorts walking among low tables filled with wood carvings. Roadside markets offered clothing, and vegetables for the first time since Lilongwe (an indication of a supply of water), and many baskets and grass mats, including basketwork helicopters with turning blades, and motor boats of various sizes. These indications of the presence of water served to sharpen my expectation of the lake.

The road ran across flat country studded with trees and dilapidated villages. I drove through bluish smoke from a grass fire, and past a smart new bottle store called The Third World; and everywhere by the roadside there were places of worship and religious activity. The Church of the Nazarene, Seventh-day Adventists, a Baptist mission, the Salima Catholic Parish and the Salima Islamic Centre. The cross of Christianity intermingled easily enough, here, with the moon and star of Islam. The domes of the mosques blazed white in the sun, and their shadowed arches showed pale grey in the light striking off the harsh and sandy earth on which they were built.

These mosques for the most part would have been built by the Yao, I conjectured, an African people who had been pushed west from what is now northern Mozambique during the upheavals of the mid-19th century. The Yao had brought the Muslim faith with them after centuries of contact with the Arab traders of the east coast. The Yao had themselves for centuries been traders, not least in ivory with the Arab merchants in Kilwa, and finally in slaves.

But such thoughts were cut short by the appearance of the lake itself. I had parked my hired car and walked into the garden of the hotel at which I would be staying for a day or two. Only from the garden could I see the lake, its edge ornamented with a few umbrellas and thatched cones, a few yachts and bikinis. But from that first moment I was struck by the stark divide: behind me stretched a dry brown country where starvation stalked; before lay the extreme blue of deep water reaching to the horizon and beyond. There was no intermediate zone where the long dry season and the bountiful water mingled. Only a strip of pale sand against which small waves lapped and then hissed back.

A little distance from the hotel, at a place called Senga Bay, I found a small bar dispensing drinks to groups of people sitting on a low terrace which overlooked the lake. Trees with large leaves turning deep red provided shade, as did some thick-stemmed climbing plants growing over a pergola at the entrance to the bar. The climbers had grown so luxuriant that people were obliged to stoop as they passed underneath. Music thumped gently from loudspeakers, but the predominant sound was of conversation, some laughter, and the small waves washing on the beach. I saw a young man wearing an AIDS-awareness T-shirt; another held hands with a plump white girl in shorts; one table was occupied by boisterous English tourists intent on taking snapshots of each other; another by an Indian family sitting silent but content as they watched their white-bearded patriarch suck up bright green liquid through a straw.

The lake lured and comforted the eyes. A few small islands broke the horizon, a few dugouts rode closer to the shore, and at a distance the small white waves looked like clouds floating in towards the land. The sand of the beach was coloured dull yellow, laced with sparkling black. People strolled along at the water's edge. Some women did their washing, laying out their lengths of colourful fabric to dry on the sand higher up the beach. A couple of young black girls held up their arms so that the flimsy material they held billowed gracefully in the breeze coming off the lake. There seemed to be such languor here, such grace, with the blue water stretching away and no sign of the eastern shore.

Was this what David Livingstone, the first European to explore Africa's second largest inland sea, had found in 1859? Doubtless, not much had changed. The dugouts now being dragged on to the sand, hand-hewn from a single tree trunk, would have been the same then as now. And the languid breeze and the colour of the water. Even the billowing fabric, perhaps locally made but more likely woven in India in Livingstone's time, and traded by Yao slavers at the rate of four yards (of calico) for a man, three for a woman, and two yards for a boy or girl.

There had been a tendency, I had read, for European Christian missionaries to view the Yao in general as always having been slavers, a heartless people; and as always having espoused Islam. Sometimes the linkage between slaving and Islam had perhaps been over-emphasised for the sake of religious competition. But those who made this emphasis had almost certainly forgotten, or perhaps had never understood, the linkages between slavery and Christianity on the other side of the continent.

But nothing I had read concerning the Yao offered adequate preparation for the combination of guile and innocence I was soon to encounter. I had walked down to the edge of the lake to take a closer look at the dugouts, at the few fish flung far up on to the beach. The shouts of the fishermen came like sharp punctuation above the hiss and flow of water on the black-sparkling sand. Then I became conscious of a presence which lingered at my side. I turned to encounter a young man holding out a small carved artefact for sale.

More a boy than a man perhaps, I realised on a second glance, with thin limbs and lively eyes. He guessed I was a tourist. I asked if he had carved the artefact he offered. He shook his head. 'It is made by my brother,' he said. He guessed I was from Germany, and that I wanted to see some hippos. I shrugged my shoulders in a non-committal way. Unabashed, he walked with me along the sand.

I asked where he lived.

He pointed up the beach. 'Yes, I still go to school, but now I am on holiday. So I come to the lake to sell you my brother's nice horse. See. It is the head of a horse. It is ebony. You must touch it.'

He looked up at me with a bright and engaging self-confidence. 'My name is Peterson. I am seventeen. You give address, I write a letter. Then you send me books.'

'What sort of books?'

'History. I like to read Africa history.'

'What about the history of Malawi? Do you learn that in school?'

Peterson nodded. 'Of course,' he said. 'The British. But I want to show you the hippos. It is not far. We can go in your car.'

'How do you know I have a car?'

Peterson laughed. 'You are German tourist.'

I shook my head. 'I am South African.'

'Joburg,' Peterson said promptly. 'I want to go to Joburg and earn the big money. Not like Malawi. My father was a builder. But last year he passed.'

I waited for him to continue, but he said nothing. I asked, expecting vaguely to hear of some test or promotion process, what it was his father had passed.

Peterson seemed momentarily nonplussed. 'Passed nothing,' he replied. 'He has passed. He is dead. This morning I go to the Mosque.'

We stood together in silence, looking out across the deep yet placid waters of the lake. I was conscious of Peterson's eyes resting on my face.

In a moment, in a calculating voice, he said: 'My mother sells tomatoes at the road.'

I said nothing.

Peterson went on in the same tone: 'It will be a good time now in the afternoon to see the hippos.'

I could not help smiling. 'All right,' I said. 'I am a German tourist. We can go in my car.'

Peterson's face was instantly animated. 'Now this is a joke,' he said, laughing quite gaily as he almost pranced along by my side.

We drove up and through that abrupt divide which concealed the lake and brought the immediacy of parched country and stunted trees pressing in on every side. Only reminder of the lake now was the sand sometimes heaped into low dunes through which the road began to meander. When I fastened my seat belt, Peterson watched and then did the same.

He travelled with his elbow crooked through the open window. He looked at once proud and yet tensed in a stance which spoke clearly of trepidation; and I wondered when last he had taken a tourist to see the hippos. It suddenly occurred to me that he might never have done so before. Yet his directions were crisp and clear enough — turn here, drive there — and I had a feeling of going into countryside and into the privacy of villages which rarely experienced a white face, nor even a motor vehicle to judge by the absence of tyre marks on the sandy tracks.

I said: 'So you are a Muslim.'

He looked at me.

'You go to the mosque,' I reminded him.

'Only sometimes. My father went always to pray.'

'And your mother?'

'My mother is a Christian. She goes to Baptist every Sunday in the morning.'

'Are you a Yao?'

Peterson laughed. 'How do you know?'

'I guessed.'

'Yes, I am a Yao. But I want to be a Baptist. I want to go to Joburg in your nice big car. Turn along here to go to the hippos.'

The track had become almost indistinguishable from the country surrounding it. The car swished through a sudden grassy patch towards a cluster of large old trees. Suddenly a mongrel dog rushed out and attacked the wheels. I felt the animal thud against the side of the vehicle. Peterson drew his elbow quickly inside.

Then we were in the trees. Old people sat against the walls of huts. A man stood in the track, his arm raised. All at once the car was surrounded by sullen faces. I smelled beer and perspiration. The branches of the trees had closed above us.

I heard Peterson's voice, slightly tremulous, speaking rapidly in Chichewa. A big face, leaning in, answered in a negative snarl. I placed my hand on Peterson's arm, asking for an explanation.

'They say we cannot go through.'

I indicated to the big face that I wished to reverse. He stood aside. As I turned the car, someone struck the roof with his open hand. I caught sight of the old people against the walls of the huts, watching without expression. I drove slowly out of the trees the way we had entered them, and again the dog charged out, snarling at the tyres.

When we were at a safe distance from these hostilities, I turned to Peterson with a grin. But he was hardly ready to receive it. His face, a moment before so jaunty as he had said he would like to drive to Johannesburg in my car, now seemed to have collapsed. I saw perspiration standing in small shining beads on his forehead.

'It doesn't matter,' I said.

'They have never stopped me like that,' he said in a strangled tone.

'Do you come this way quite often?'

He opened his mouth, his eyes darting across my own, then he slumped lower in his seat. It was as though he had exhausted, at least momentarily, his capacity for hope. He shook his head.

'It doesn't matter,' I said again.

But he sat in a morass of opportunity squandered; and it was out of this morass, his expression plaintive, that he asked me directly for money.

I offered him no response as I drove on the sandy tracks.

He said: 'My mother has no money for my school. I have a sister who is fifteen. We are all alone.'

I reminded him how he had said that the horse's head which he had tried to sell me had been carved in ebony by his brother.

'Yes, but he is from another wife of my father. He is much older. He is my brother; I did not lie. But he is not with us where we live.'

'Where is he?'

'He has gone to be a soldier. He is in Rwanda.'

'With the United Nations?'

'Yes, I think so.'

After a moment, he tried again. 'The school fees are hard, but the uniforms are also hard. I must wear black pants and a white shirt and the shiny shoe. Or I must not come to the school.'

I drove through labyrinths of roads and tracks about which I knew nothing. Had it not been for Peterson's directions I would quickly have become lost. I wondered whether he was aware that he possessed this power. Then all at once we went over a sand dune and the lake, as well as the bar and the low terrace at which my afternoon had begun, lay close at hand.

As I stopped the car, he asked quite urgently whether it would not be possible for me to write him a letter from South Africa and send him some school fees, even for one term. Or at least a pair of shiny shoes.

I said that he should first write to me, then I would decide. I said further that I wished to purchase the horse's head which his brother had carved out of ebony. He conducted the transaction with an expressionless face. I gave him a few extra notes for attempting to take me to see the hippos.

On an impulse, I said: 'Are you sure we went the right way to see the hippos?'

'Yes,' he said. 'Why must I trick you?'

But his face was sombre as I left him standing in the roadside sand. I drove slowly towards my hotel. When I was some distance away, I saw in the rear-view mirror that he looked down at the notes still clutched in his hand and then leapt suddenly into the air, one thin arm raised and stiffened above his head, much like a footballer who has scored a difficult goal.

F rom my hotel room, as the shadows lengthened, I had a good view of a short stretch of shoreline which served as a caravan and camping site. Among the tents and the drifting smoke of fires stood a truck, the body painted an incongruous pink, with large wheels and a greasy young man in bathing shorts working on the front differential. An enormous toolbox stood open to one side, and spanners littered the grass all around. Some girls in bikinis lolled on the sand of the beach, calling out laughingly to the young man from time to time. These overland adventurers; I envied their apparent harmony with Africa, the unhurried pace with which they camped and coped, and the ease of their abandonment to the voluptuous qualities of the lakeside evening. Spanners were soon thrown aside, and there, in a moment, stood the greasy young man, his arms around the waists of the bikini-clad girls, as they gazed together at the dusk coming off the calm waters of the lake.

The air soothed the face like a gentle incense. It was impossible to remain indoors, impossible not to stand facing the lake, feeling the air so easy on the skin, so easy in the big leaves of the hotel garden, hardly sufficient to flutter them. The sunlight caught only the top of a bristling island out there across the water, and then caught not even that, as the world sank towards peace. A fish eagle cried out suddenly as it flew across the darkening lake, and a yacht ran slowly homeward.

When Livingstone first arrived, there had been dhows on the lake, vessels of misery and terror, used for the transporting of slaves from the interior (those areas now comprising Malawi and north-eastern Zambia) by the most direct route to the East African coast and thence to Zanzibar. In one of Livingstone's biographies it is recorded that 'the burnt villages, the numerous skeletons, the floating corpses, and all the other horrors that they saw' so influenced the great explorer that he resolved to build a small steamship for the lake in the belief that 'the trade it would make possible would soon cut the feet from under the revolting traffic that now ruled'.

Livingstone's steamship never reached the lake, but others did. In the lounge of the hotel, old photographs depicted some of them. I saw the flag of the British Merchant Navy, and here was the HMS *Pioneer,* built in 1892 and commanded on the lake by a Rear-Admiral Villiers between 1893 and 1894, dates which coincided with the final crushing of the slave trade in Malawi. I guessed that Peterson would have learned of such British endeavours in his Africa history classes. I wondered if the steel-hulled *Pioneer* had sufficient guns to sink a dhow. I wondered if any had been sunk. I could visualise Peterson behind a desk in his white shirt and shiny shoes, absorbing these events which had profoundly influenced the course of his great grandfather's life.

While I dawdled in the lounge I discovered on a wicker table another reminder of my young Yao friend: a hotel brochure which said that an excursion (maximum three persons) to the hippo pools could be got for a fairly substantial sum, certainly more than I had paid for Peterson's attempt to get me there.

Dinner was served out of doors with candles burning motionless on white and silver decked tables and a full moon rising out of the lake. Palm trees stood black against this spectacle, and the yellow light of the moon danced in a broad path all the way to the small waves breaking on the beach. Perhaps it was inevitable then that I thought of Rina, the brash redhead in the safari office, and the Englishwoman whose garden, so she said, had been romantically disrupted by elephants. This was their Africa, this outdoor dining at the lake, or at least it was an aspect of the continent which they constantly desired.

The aroma of cooking wafted from hot coals stoked in containers under conical thatched roofs. I heard the chink of cutlery and raised glasses; I saw the relaxed faces smiling in candle-light and the attentiveness of waiters passing noiselessly between the crowded tables.

One of the waiters appeared at my elbow. He said: 'There is a guest who is also alone. But the hotel is most full. Perhaps she can join your table?'

'I do not want to intrude,' a young woman said in a foreign accent.

She had blonde hair done in flowing curls which framed her face. Her eyes were direct and unabashed, and they seemed easily accustomed to laughter. Her name was Heidi Lehmann, she said as she sat down; she was from Munich. We proceeded to have dinner together as the moon climbed steadily towards its zenith.

She told me in her pleasant way that she was spending a weekend at the lake, that she had come down from Lilongwe to Salima on a bus with many boxes and bicycles tied to the roof. 'It was so cheap, I could not believe it.' Then in Salima she had found a pick-up which could bring her to the hotel. 'So that is how I arrive, yes? Sitting on my suitcase on the back of the pick-up. We are ten women on the back, but only I am white. You must see the man at the hotel look at me. He cannot believe it.' She laughed musically at her own story.

I asked if she was living in Lilongwe.

'No, no,' she replied. 'You see, my husband has broken his leg. He is in Johannesburg. But my ticket was nearly finished. Yes, as you say, due to expire. So I had to fly alone. He is coming from Johannesburg in the afternoon tomorrow. So I thought, here I am alone. I will make a weekend at the lake.'

She tilted her head and raised her eyebrows in a gesture which indicated that her presence was now adequately explained. Yet she had a great deal more to tell, and during the course of our meal I was able to piece together the details of her and her husband's adventures.

Heidi had trained as a school sports instructor, and she still worked in this capacity not far from her home town. She had, however, married Peter Zimmerman, a German painter and fashion designer. Not long after their marriage, they had gone on a holiday to Senegal, and Peter had been fascinated by the richness of colour and light he experienced there. A relationship with Africa had begun which both had wished to pursue. Their work in fashion design in Munich seemed dull by comparison.

Before long, Peter came to Malawi for a short stay. But Heidi told me with a musical laugh that he had done more snorkelling in the lake, mountain climbing and lying in the sun than he had painting. During this time, however, he had been befriended by a Malawian named Michael Makunganya, and by Michael's family. This led to the planning of a further excursion, for a much longer period, where the idea was for Peter to rent a house in Lilongwe which he would share with his friend, and in which, from time to time, Heidi could join him.

So a few months prior to my having dinner with Heidi, out Peter had flown to a rented house in old Lilongwe town. But in the first week, he had fallen into a drainage ditch and smashed his leg.

'The bones were sticking out,' Heidi told me with slightly widened eyes. 'The first I know is that he is going to Johannesburg because the Malawi hospitals cannot make it right.'

After the necessary operation, Peter had hobbled back to Malawi on a pair of crutches, and had spent most of his time confined to bed in the rented house where Michael Makunganya and his family looked after him. 'He was too stubborn to come home,' she said in her musical way. Under these limiting circumstances, Heidi went on, he had however developed a relationship with several Malawi artists with whom he began to collaborate. A surge of productivity had followed. Already, there had been an exhibition in Berlin. More exhibitions were being planned. Now he had returned to Johannesburg for X-rays, but he had no plans whatsoever to return to Germany. Indeed, he hoped Heidi would give up her teaching job and join him in Africa.

She sat smiling at me over the candle on the table between us. 'It would be nice, but not yet. You see, I am useful in Germany, selling the paintings.' Again that laugh.

I asked her to tell me her feelings about Africa.

'Oh, I like it here. I feel at ease,' she said. 'And the best is that you live by daylight here. After dark, you sleep. That is the natural thing. It is primitive. In Europe, you live after dark. You are going to eat at nine o'clock, and then to a movie after, and then in the morning you wake up feeling stale. The early mornings are the best thing in Africa. Every day it is like the beginning of a new world, yes?'

She possessed an innocence which seemed palpable then as we sat back in the languid darkness of the evening to taste our coffee.

She said: 'I think Peter is a European artist who is touching Africa. It is very strange. The pictures he makes with the other artists — I like them. They are good fun. When you come back to Lilongwe you must come and see. Peter calls himself Vincent of Malawi,' she went on with a laugh. 'You know, like Van Gogh. Dreamland Artists, that is how he calls the group. It is like a factory in the house sometimes.'

I asked her to draw me a map of how to get to Peter's house in old Lilongwe town, and she presented me with one at breakfast the following morning. I accompanied her to the hotel entrance when she left. She haggled vigorously with a driver whose ramshackle vehicle was inscribed K K Boys and Girls Taxi Service. After arriving at a price which satisfied her, her suitcase was pushed into the boot. She clambered into the front seat, seeming at once small yet uncowed behind the large space of the window. She smiled and waved as the driver slammed his door and the taxi lurched forward with a puff of dust behind the rear wheels. She was an innocent at her ease in Africa.

W e talked about poverty alleviation in Malawi, John Chikakuda and I, as we drove through wide gatherings of baobab trees and through parched brown villages not far from the lake. Women turned the wheels at the communal pumps; others walked by the roadside with containers on their heads. The day was hot, and a gusting wind hurled clouds of dust high into the air.

John began by speaking of the now famous letter signed by the country's Roman Catholic Bishops which had signalled the start of open dissent against the previous regime.

'Government agents burnt the press which had printed the letter. Isn't that typical of repression? Mindless brute force — and of course totally ineffectual. The letter was just the start. After it had been published, dissent came spurting out from every quarter, unable to be silenced. This dissent, coupled with growing international pressure, is what led to our referendum on multiparty democracy last year.'

And no wonder the dissent had come with such velocity when the inescapable lot of most people was poverty and struggle, with a debasement of dream and reasonable aspiration alike. They had voted, first, for democracy. And now, via a democratic process, they had voted for a government which, John said, was viewing poverty alleviation as its most important task. The will and the cry of the people had been heard.

But what, in practice, did poverty alleviation mean?

'There's a whole programme,' John said. 'Every sector from agriculture to youth is involved. The best news is that most of the components of the programme don't need a lot of money. They will depend on changes in policy which break the monopolies, stamp out corruption, allow market forces freer play, assist small business and the informal sector, increase community involvement in decision making, increase female school enrolment...'

John talked on enthusiastically, and it was not difficult to see that for the first time in many years he had found something in which he could believe. The new political processes at work in Malawi had given this kindly and thoughtful man new direction and new belief.

We had, meanwhile, driven into a hilly region where hand-tilled fields covered even the steepest slopes. John talked about the increasing pressure on the land, and then he glanced at me with a slight smile. I noticed that he perspired heavily in the hot interior of the vehicle.

'You know what people say, white people especially? Africans have too many children. That's why Africans are all so poor. I agree that birth control and family planning is of crucial importance. But let me tell you that in my experience it's not even worth talking about reducing family size until the problem of high child mortality has been solved. Under the present economic conditions, it can never work the other way around.'

He paused as the vehicle bounced through some large holes in the road. 'That's why poverty alleviation is so important. If we can arrest the tide of starvation and death among our children, if we can assist people to have a stake in the cash economy, then it will be much easier to deal with the demographic problems. We might even discover that Africa is a lot like the West in this way. When universal poverty alleviation finally occurred in Europe, the birth rates started falling.'

I glanced at his profile as he spoke: that small ear in a head of considerable depth, the slightly bulbous eye, and a runnel of perspiration running straight down from his temple into the valleys between the sinews in his neck.

'Africans are quick learners,' he continued. 'When you think of all that has happened since independence it is difficult to disagree with that. Africa has learned from its mistakes, don't you think?'

He shrugged his broad shoulders to signify that a reply to the question was unnecessary. 'But a lot of people in the West talk about this hopeless continent. They talk about the self-destruction of Africa. But perhaps the continent has been written off too soon. That is what I sometimes feel. I find it difficult not to face the future with optimism. I feel that Africa will one day be great. Perhaps sooner than we think. But then, of course, I speak as an African.'

These last words were uttered with a smile and a sidelong glance which denied apology for such a stance as firmly as it did any stiffening to self-defence.

W e arrived at last, as we drove in the hilly region, at a place called Mua and The Mission of Our Lady of Help.

The main mission building comprised two long storeys of brick-built arches supporting a tiled roof, and beyond the arches I saw that white walls had been adorned with warm-coloured and repetitive geometric patterns, as if they had been printed with an outsize woodcut, or perhaps drawn on with a stencil and then painted.

The overall impression jarred faintly: for the building was unambiguously European while the adornment spoke in a muffled sort of way of the continent in which it had been erected. For a moment I could not be sure why this signal should appear muffled, except that the ornamentation seemed more reminiscent of than actually African. An inscription on one of the walls indicated that the mission had been founded by French Catholics in 1902.

We had arrived at an inconvenient time, and the people whom John had arranged to see were not immediately available. I therefore walked in the grounds of the mission, and while doing so saw many things which added to my first impression of faint discord. I was repeatedly struck by the idea that the place was slightly out of focus. The sense was not of Africa so much as of Africa quite consciously depicted, the same sense as that engendered by the patterned walls beyond the brick-built archways, but magnified. Here in the grounds, in short, was a grand and sometimes faintly grandiloquent pastiche.

I came at first to a building comprising three circular modules, like huts, but brick built and repeating as leitmotiv the arches from the European mission. On the outside walls, within each arch, colourful murals depicted what appeared to be a historical progression: pre-colonial village scenes, the manacles of slavery, the hoisting of a Union Jack, and so on. A striking feature of many of the murals was that the source of light had been located in the background, usually in the form of an ochre sun hanging low over the outline of jagged mountains, and that in consequence the subject of each painting, usually clusters of human forms enriched with spears and shields, cast strong black shadows towards the viewer.

The earth surrounding the circles of the building had been cleared and recently beautified with shrubs and flowers, and in one corner a huge python sculpted in grey cement lay along the side of a pond, its head almost bashfully submerged.

The building contained nothing but the dust of new cement and some wood shavings. I watched a man on scaffolding working on a high and intricate ceiling of grasswork and timber. I asked him to what purpose this unusual and beautiful structure would be put when complete. 'This is the museum,' he replied. But I needed more; I needed a glimpse of the rationale. I asked whose idea the museum had been. 'Father Bushie,' the man on the scaffolding said, looking down at me.

In the centre of the museum, where the three circular modules met, a small courtyard was dominated by another piece of cement sculpture, this time a fat-trunked tree surrounded by living plants in pots and some lawn. Even the leaves of the tree had been sculpted in cement. I stood in silence at this manifestation of Father Bushie's vision. (I spell the name as the people at The Mission of Our Lady of Help pronounced it, although I suspected something more French, Booshay perhaps, but Bushie was the Father which these people, and the remarkable surroundings in which I found them, imparted to me.)

Under a large thatched roof a little distance from the museum, a collection of young men worked at the carving of various artefacts. Their voices, and the chip and scrape of their chisels, emanated in contented tones from the space in which they worked. They laughed easily among themselves, and paid little attention to me as I stooped under the thatch and stood among them. There were several large carvings of Christ on the cross lying on the floor. Other religious pieces took shape under dextrous hands and home-made mallets which impelled the blades of U-shaped chisels, blow by expert blow. One youngster in his middle teens worked quietly on a relief — perhaps intended as a panel for a door — which he copied from a drawing on a piece of paper weighted down with stones. I asked the young sculptor who had made the drawing, but he seemed not to understand the question. Then an older man stepped forward and said: 'You buy at that hut over there. Father Bushie make the shop for you to buy. You cannot buy here.'

The walls of the hut which the man had indicated were filled with those familiar geometric designs in the warm colours of Africa; and the thatched roof had been extended to form a generous overhang supported all the way round by timber poles into which numerous human figures had been carved. I saw faces swathed in spider webs. Then someone came running with a bunch of keys. The interior contained hundreds of carvings for sale, some utilitarian objects, and whole armies of faces staring out towards the light which the opened door admitted. But the figures invoked a faint disgruntlement: many of them seemed contrived — those pointed beards of the patriarchs, those stylised madonnas with babies — possessing that sense of caricature so often present in the wares intended for the consumption of tourists. Then a wild animal noised suddenly not far from the door.

The bearer of the keys grinned at the surprise which must have appeared on my face. 'It is the zoo that Father Bushie has made,' he said.

I walked along a pathway as directed. The country fell away steeply towards a ravine on my right-hand side, and I was shielded from the plunge by an ornamented fence of timber and bamboo which in many places had already been eaten by termites. The pathway meandered along the top of this change in gradient, and then presented a set of steeply descending steps. I took them, and in this way I found myself entering the strange and highly labelled world of Father Bushie's Africa.

Timber plaques had been attached to many of the trees. On the plaques was recorded the popular and African name, as well as the scientific. I had a vague image of a man in a habit poring over botanical manuals, his endeavours lit by a hurricane lantern perhaps, the room where he worked filled with the aroma of the leaves and fruit he was trying to identify. It was with this image in my mind that I now descended, my feet on the steep steps. I thought of David Livingstone's adventures, and how the missionary society with whom he first came to Africa had been severely disappointed in Livingstone because he had tended to neglect his preaching in his passion to explore and to discover. Was Father Bushie another of these men with a passion for more besides the lost souls of Africa?

But these thoughts faded as I descended further into the zoo. I found myself surveyed sometimes by the eyes of wild animals and birds, and I could smell the reek of their captivity on the hot air. The zoo had been painstakingly built on various levels down the steep incline, with pathways and steps cut into the hillside. Some fairly large excavations had been undertaken − this was the work of many years − and some of the enclosures were laboriously built of natural materials, although sturdy wire-netting was also much in evidence. I saw in one place a multitude of feathers caught in such wire, and inside an extensive cage a fierce eagle with red legs and cheeks stared down at me from the branch of a dead tree. Attached to the wire a plaque had inscribed upon it a few words in an African language which were presumably then repeated in English underneath: The Bateleur Eagle is so greedy that he does not even waste a feather.

I had a sudden sense of invading a deep privacy. For whom could these words be meant? The imprisoned eagle glared down at me, and the feathers fluttered in the wire. I felt caught in a mesh of contradictions; and incongruities seemed to echo back from the deep trees in the ravine below. Who was this Father Bushie?

The question re-emerged from everything I saw: the crocodiles and porcupines, the pythons lying coiled in a deep pit, the small primates hanging upside-down from the bamboo roof of their cage. And the question seemed magnified by the inscriptions on the plaques. 'Nothing can happen without perseverance' on a cage holding a heron sitting motionless above a dark pool of water. Or 'Because of its caution the bushbuck grew long horns'. Of a red-jowled bird identified on the plaque as a Ground Hornbill the inscription read: 'The load does not burden its owner.' And on the bars of another cage through which the slightly tormented eyes of an animal with large ears looked out: 'The elder's childishness made the villager lose his precious serval cat's skin.'

Sometimes the inscription included an explanation, as in the one I encountered at a fish pond surrounded by water grass and reeds and ferns. The place was labelled The Sacred Pool and the inscription and explanation read as follows:

The friendship of the water with the fish is real while that of the water with the sand is not (The first lasts. The second ends. As soon as the wave withdraws, the sand is left alone.)

The words caught me unawares, as in a sudden revelation. I felt myself groping through a strange light of new insight where nothing was tangible, still less concrete. I stood by The

Sacred Pool, looking at the inscription regarding the fish and the water and the sand, and I knew — this was the revelation — that I had found the image I was looking for, something that would give substance to all I had seen and heard in Malawi. All my experience seemed gathered together now, even from the first moments, even from the brash redhead in the tour office that afternoon who had been having a bad day. She was like the sand. And Father Bushie?

Now a soft footfall sounded behind me on the path. I turned and looked into the calm eyes of a black woman. She carried a crucifix in her hands, and sunlight dappled by leaves fell across the neat white uniform of a nursing sister.

Yes, there was a hospital at the mission, she said, smiling at me. I noticed lumps at the joints of the fingers which held the crucifix. We stood in a momentary silence by The Sacred Pool where the fronds of ferns stooped to touch the surface of the water. I asked my questions.

'Oh, he has been with us for eighteen years,' the sister replied. 'No, not so old. He is a good man. He is gentle. He is our priest.'

'Is he still here, at the mission?'

'Oh, yes,' she said. For an instant her eyes seemed almost amused by me, but in a serene sort of way. 'He will be in his rooms.'

'Could I see him?'

'I will take you.'

I stepped aside to allow her to lead me on the path. She walked at a steady pace, never once turning back. Small animals eyed me as I passed. A large bird cried out. We walked back along the path where the plunge to the ravine was protected by a fence of timber and bamboo, half eaten by termites. I saw a wild animal's skull on the side of a brick-built barbecue. Then we were passing the museum built like African huts but adorned with unmistakably European arches. The sister turned, showing only her profile.

'I will see if he is here.'

We had passed into an area of garden rich with flowers. I watched her descend a few steps, and she seemed to do so painfully. She was no longer a young woman, and it occurred to me that her joints might be stiffening with arthritis. She walked along a veranda, the walls of which were covered with masks carved in wood and highly polished. Even the feathers which decorated some of the masks had been intricately carved in wood. They were permanent representations, even stolid representations I thought, of essentially ethereal things.

The sister had knocked on a door which stood ajar. Then she turned and beckoned me forward. A large man emerged from the doorway to greet me. Behind him, in the room, I glimpsed papers and books, but no hurricane lantern. He thrust out his hand in a friendly yet half-shy gesture. This was Father Bushie.

He wore jeans and an ornate Afro-style shirt which strained slightly over his stomach. His hair was dark, tousled, his trimmed beard showing patches of white. He told me he was a French Canadian who had been living in Malawi since 1967, but at Mua only since 1976.

'But we can sit,' he suggested, indicating a concrete bench among flowers.

The bench faced the carved masks on the wall of the building where he lived and worked. As we settled on the bench, I noticed that he wore open sandals and that his toenails had grown long and hornlike.

I said I had been interested to see the museum and the zoo. He smiled. His dark eyes seemed all at once to be painfully shy.

He said in his gentle voice, 'It is all about conservation; that is what we are trying to teach. Is conservation a new idea in Africa?' He shrugged his shoulders. 'I doubt it. But we are having to reteach it. The zoo is for the conservation of wildlife. And also I am trying to show them the value of their own idioms and proverbs, because they are losing them too. And the museum, that is for their artefacts, their material culture...'

214

These words brought an overlay of reality to my sense of revelation, yet they could not altogether ground it. There persisted that sense I had got from walking in the grounds of the Mission of Our Lady of Help, that sense of Africa having been re-created in Father Bushie's stylised vision of it. Did this explain the shyness in his eyes, the sense of vulnerability which he carried beneath the flimsy overlay of rationality? The zoo is for this, the museum is for that. But underneath there appeared the marks of that fabulous abandonment to mystery, that longing to be like the fish in the waters of The Sacred Pool, whether these waters broke in waves or whether they slid back, always to be one with the water of Africa's great pool, that shimmering intangibility which required constant definition to possess it, and constant conservation.

We spoke about the masks. They had been rendered in wood because they would last longer, but of course they were too heavy to wear. They were replicas of the masks still used in the villages around Mua. The wearers would look out through the mouths of the masks, avoiding recognition. The masks helped to make a distinction between the spirit world and the world of now. There seemed always to be a fierceness and severity in the expressions depicted, while on Father Bushie's face only serenity prevailed.

His vulnerability pained me. The extent of his passion sent a searchlight burning into all such passions, and all the varying relationships which people developed with Africa. I remembered the trite perceptions of the redhead again; and the woman whose garden had been ravaged by elephants; and the German woman, Heidi, whose husband had found such inspiration here. But what did the searchlight reveal of my Yao friend, Peterson, or of John Chikakuda for that matter? Father Bushie said that the mask up there on the wall shaped like a horse's head, with angry nostrils, depicted the chief dispenser of discipline in the spirit world. And what of my own relationship with Africa? These questions rang against me as I looked into the dark and profoundly vulnerable eyes of this French Canadian priest.

No time for answers now. I had seen John Chikakuda on the edge of the garden. For some reason his friendly form, the thick neck and slightly bulbous eyes, cheered me, lessening the mysteries of The Sacred Pool. When he saw me looking his way, he pointed at his watch.

T he afternoon had almost ebbed away by the time we got back to Lilongwe. The sun lay redly behind trees, about to set. So I immediately took a taxi to the old town in search of the rented house of the German artist who called himself Vincent of Malawi.

I sat with Heidi's sketch map on my knees, directing the driver, hoping that we would find the place before darkness came. The traffic in the old town raised dust which sifted in an orange haze over rough streets and the dilapidation of roadside stalls and makeshift dwellings and the smoke of the evening's cooking. We turned several corners according to the map. A dog loped across the road, causing a blast of hooters. Black faces laughed. We went deeper into the town and into the dusk; and then I saw what Heidi had told me to look out for: a tall grass fence providing some privacy to a house which stood on the corner of two untidy streets. The main one had a tarmac surface, but with a ragged verge which rapidly cascaded into a eroded ditch. Was this the ditch, I wondered, where Peter Zimmerman, alias Vincent of Malawi, had smashed his leg and found a novel synthesis with Africa?

It was Heidi herself, her blonde curls cascading in a tangled frame for her lively face, who opened the door of the house for me. She laughed when she recognised me. 'I am happy you have come, ja?' she said, placing her hand on my arm to draw me inside.

The immediate impression was of low ceilings, concrete floors, the eyes of a black child looking up at me, bright canvases everywhere, and Heidi beckoning me through a doorway hung with translucent Indian fabric lit from beyond. She drew the fabric aside.

The room which we entered had a mosquito net knotted above a centrally placed bed. As elsewhere in the house, the walls were filled with canvases in bright colours. The style of these works was two-dimensional and naive, the shapes depicted seeming primitive and vaguely symbolic.

Peter Zimmerman sat on the bed, his right leg in plaster from which steel bolts protruded. His face was unshaven, his hair awry, his eyes grey-blue and smiling easily up at me. He said, with a hint of conscious absurdity: 'Here in Malawi we make our dreams come true.'

Heidi invited me to sit on a chair in one corner of the room. On an adjacent table stood a half-burned candle, an empty wine bottle and heaped ashtray. Peter raised in my direction the beer bottle which Heidi brought him, a good-natured and dissipated toast, and then swallowed a few mouthfuls.

Indicating the crowded walls of the room, I asked him to tell me about his work.

'You like the work?'

I nodded.

'You just say that. You are polite?'

'Not always.'

Peter laughed. 'I work and live here with my friend. Heidi has told you. Michael Makunganya. Last year I came to Malawi, me and another German, but we did not do much. You know, in a strange country, you need a friend, maybe even a private secretary and butler, someone who can show you everything from the inside. I found Mike.'

Heidi appeared through the translucent fabric with a packet of cigarettes and said to Peter: 'You see I told you I had met this nice man at the lake.'

'Ja, ja,' Peter said, smiling at me.

Then he told me that he and Mike had begun by making chairs and shirts together. 'These things I make in Germany. Long before I start painting, I am making crazy furniture, and shirts out of old curtains and sacks and anything I can find. Then later I am asking Mike what is happening in Malawian art. He introduces some artists. They show their work. It is all realism,' he said with a slight grimace. 'All landscapes with water and little trees. I asked them: why do you not paint your dreams? And they said: because the government wants us to paint mountains and lakes and trees. Yes, all this is after I have broken my leg.'

At this point a young African in white shirt and shorts entered. Peter immediately called out to him and embraced him, holding his own hand against the back of the other's dark and curly head. 'I love Mike,' he said, and then introduced us.

'So then we make a dream factory here, me and Mike and the Malawian artists and all our friends,' Peter Zimmerman said.

And Heidi said: 'See, there. Vincent of Malawi and the dreamland artists.' She had pointed out these words which were incorporated into a canvas depicting a pink multi-winged unicorn. The unicorn had pronounced eyelashes, human feet, and appeared to be devouring a snake; and the whole design was adorned with stars and hearts and other light-hearted shapes.

'So this is how we work now,' Peter said, exhaling smoke in a slightly impatient sideways gesture. 'I sit here on my bed, and I draw out the designs. Then the artists come and we discuss the colours. They laugh a lot about what I am drawing. This is good: I like it when we are having fun. Then the artists take away the canvases and put in the colour. Sometimes they surprise me with the colours they use. In this way we make a lot of paintings, as you can see,' he added, his eyes glancing around the walls of the untidy room.

Mike sat on the edge of the bed, his hands pressed flat under his sleek brown thighs. Heidi watched me with her lively eyes, and she accompanied me when I rose to examine a few of the paintings. Indeed, she took me into another room where canvases had also been attached to the ceiling. She laughed in her musical way. In one corner, on an unmade bed,

I suddenly noticed a small black child lying spread-eagled in sleep. 'She will not awaken,' Heidi said.

The paintings swarmed against us. Collections of distorted faces peered out; stick-like figures danced among snakes and fish and smiling sickle moons; detached eyes stared out from a canvas showing figures with pronounced genitals; and here lay pink and green twins in foetal positions, more lavish fishes, even to the point of a vaguely nightmarish exaggeration, inspired no doubt by Peter's days of snorkelling in the lake.

These were unmistakable European images over which black artists laughed before providing them with colours which seemed to resonate on the canvases now, even in the meagre illumination of the unshaded light bulb. The sleeping child stirred. We moved on to confront another wall.

I asked Heidi to tell me about Peter's furniture building and fashion design. She spoke of him scouring the rubbish dumps for objects with which to manufacture his furniture. As a boy he had danced for the Nuremberg Opera, she said as an aside. His fashion designing had won him considerable acclaim. The Munich newspapers had referred to him as the foremost recycling fashion designer in Germany. His boutiques had become famous. He had started painting largely to create backdrops against which to display his fashions. Yes, certainly, he had at one time used some drugs.

Old nightmares recycled into newer dreams, I thought. Pop stars dressed in rags; the anarchistic urges in underground music and punk fulfilled in grimaces now fading to a remoteness of caricature, even to a gradual bouquet of smiles here in the warmer African places; the pallor and restlessness and entrapment of Europe's underside gone to a slight gaiety and dissipation now. Heidi's lively face showed briefly in profile as she led the way back through the translucent curtain.

Peter said: 'To me, painting has always been very boring. I was always thinking of the next one, a new idea, when I still had all this paint to put on. The idea is what I wanted, not putting on the paint. So now it is nearly perfect. It is good that

I break my leg and am forced to the factory of the dreamland artists. Maybe soon I will not even draw. I will make only the ideas, and let the artists do everything else.'

I suggested, but with a smile, that this sounded like the ultimate neo-colonial dream: the white man with the ideas, the black man providing the muscle and the necessary patience for their execution.

Peter regarded me more carefully for a moment. 'Ag, we have thought of that,' he replied. 'Of course, I pay them. Everyone is happy. In Africa this arrangement works. In Germany not. In Germany, if I asked someone to fill in the colours on my paintings, they would say: stuff you.' He jerked up a single finger to emphasise this point. 'But in Africa it works. Ask my friend Mike,' he added, stroking Mike's sinewed forearm.

Mike nodded with an amiable smile.

'Neo-colonialism,' Peter said with a sudden trace of contempt beneath his smile. 'Ask me how I live here. I eat with them, the same food. I shit in the same hole in the garden as my black friends. I do not come here and live apart. I am living like an African here,' he said, cigarette in one hand, and then accepting another bottle of beer from Heidi with the other.

'But you live like this because it is cheap, ja?' Heidi said, laughing in her musical way.

'Of course it is cheap. But it is also like coming close to the only one true thing. There is that sense, here, of a life that is older than all our inventions. That is what makes Africa like a magnet. This life. It's something that is very close to you, that belongs to you here. You feel it everywhere. Now I am feeling that Africa is the only chance we have. I don't know what to do in the civilised countries any more. There's nothing there for your heart or your soul. Maybe only despair hidden far down. Only nightmares. No dreams.'

He sucked on the beer bottle, and I saw the swallowing movements in his throat. He wiped his mouth with the back of his hand. His blue-grey eyes seemed suddenly wistful, as if he longed — and this thought struck hard against my consciousness of where I was — that what he said was true.

'I am trying to go back for the symbols,' he said. 'If you go back far enough, the symbols are all in the same language. It is like masks. Behind all the fancy ornaments and feathers, there are the basic features: the eyes, the mouth. It is the basis I want to find, that moment when all the masks and symbols become one.

'When I make art with Africans,' he went on, his eyes for the first time revealed, 'I feel that they understand what I am trying to do. I feel that the basis I am looking for is somewhere here, that the pathway to go back to the deepest symbols is here.'

Cigarette smoke drifted past the naked light bulb. I thought of the fierceness and severity in the expressions of the masks which Father Bushie had exacted from the African carvers at the mission, and I wondered again, but briefly, about the nature of the water and its differing relationships to the sand and to the fish. Heidi had told me that Peter's boutiques in Munich had been called Anti-Chic and Extra-Stark. The anarchy of punk, the snarling European desperation which had spat so ferociously, but only at its own tail.

Then he had broken his leg in Africa. He had lain in a ditch in Malawi, smashed bones piercing the skin. Michael Makunganya had helped him then. Michael Makunganya smiled at him now, as again the white hand reached out, as if seeking for reassurance. Heidi looked at me with lively eyes gazing from within that frame of tousled blonde hair. The cigarette smoke had dissolved to heavy haze, and from somewhere else in the house a small child began to cough and whimper.

G oing in a taxi in the darkness with the headlights sweeping across eroded ground and crumbling tarmac as we turned towards the newer parts of Lilongwe and the hotel where I was staying, I experienced a powerful sense of being in the middle of Africa. There was something of its complex interplay, like light and shade, which seemed palpable now, in a sudden and unavoidable proximity.

I had said goodbye inside the Dreamland Artists' factory, shaking Peter's hand and accepting Heidi's spontaneous embrace, her cheek against my own. Michael came with me into the dark yard, guiding me to a side gate in the fence of grass beyond which a vehicle waited. I clambered in and the vehicle started forward.

It rattled copiously on the uneven road. There were no street lights, and the interior was lit only by the instruments on the dashboard. I saw the silhouette of the driver before me, and beside him the vague outline of another young man. I sat in the back with two other passengers. Music began to thump deep bass from a speaker behind my head. We had turned by this time into a busier road, and I smelled exhaust fumes, and heard the hooting of traffic in the distance. A large truck, belching smoke, barred our way. With a roar of power, the taxi swung out to overtake. I saw the lights of swerving cars in the darkness before us. The taxi thundered forward. The rhythm of the music seemed unstoppable, impervious to these small events in the reeking Lilongwe night. As the taxi squeezed back on to the left side of the road, the man beside me turned to me and grinned. I saw his teeth flash in the darkness. 'A close shave,' I said. He chuckled. We drove on. It was then that my most powerful sense of being in the middle of Africa enveloped me. I felt that I could reach out and touch the shifting lights in the essence of the darkness all around.

7

Renewal

At this crucial historical juncture, anti-colonial nationalism has already exhausted its potential... Its limited
objectives have led perilously to the bleak realm of graft,
corruption and economic decline. Its former usefulness has
actually turned into a negation of all that Africa has stood
for and indeed fought for. Only through socialism, whose
direction has already been pointed out by the Zanzibar
Revolution, can Africa re-emerge from the shackles of
neo-colonialism and imperialist domination with their
legacy of poverty, starvation and disease.

— A M Babu, 'The 1964 Revolution: Lumpen or
Vanguard?' from *Zanzibar Under Colonial Rule,* 1991.

A frica could not be seen from the beaches of Zanzibar.
Although out of sight, however, its presence was
inescapable. Without Africa, little rationale would have
existed for Zanzibar. Equally, though, without Zanzibar, the
history of east and central Africa might have been profoundly
different. Islam and Swahili had been provided in exchange
for ivory and slaves: this complex reciprocity had begun more
than a millennium ago and could not easily be broken, even
now. There were some who believed, but perhaps with more
idealism than practicality, that Zanzibar could lead a battered
and disillusioned continent towards a bright new world;
others on the island itself dreamed more pragmatically of
trade preferences, and if possible of political independence

from the impoverished mainland country of Tanganyika, a name which many Zanzibaris still used; still others simply went about their lives, often in ways which had survived the onslaught of modern events and ideas.

I had come to the island for a few days, seeking renewal and some sense of orientation before making my own excursions into east and central Africa. Zanzibar would be my entry point; but even in the short time I was there it claimed from me much more than this.

First impressions were blurred: the dark green strip lying beyond the spray to starboard as my ferry had approached; the sight of graceful dhows dipping into the swell; the weathered concrete of the harbour wall; the odour of the sea in the customs house, even in my hotel. All this served to press upon me Zanzibar's most basic reality, that it was above all an island.

Several times, as I walked on the beaches or in the Stone Town, I remembered and paraphrased John Donne's well-worn lines: no island is an island, entire of itself; each is a piece of the continent, a part of the main. Certainly, this was true of Zanzibar, at least from a rational point of view. But there was another view which continually offered to beguile. This was of a pride and isolation which seemed devoid of the interdependency which Donne so eloquently evoked. Zanzibar was a world of its own, those parts of other mains — be they African or of the Persian Gulf — having long ago been melted in the crucible of the island's uniqueness. And it was precisely this sense of uniqueness which made possible the thought of Zanzibar as illustrative: here was a microcosm of human activity and endeavour, the clarity of the archetype dependent on the completeness of its separation.

The entrance to my hotel — intricately carved doors studded with metal spikes — was barred at night, and only a bout of determined knocking could bring a face to the opening crack. Words would need to be exchanged before the clash of unfastening chains allowed one of the half doors to be drawn back. The act of entry seemed always, in Zanzibar, to be like ritual, an escape from the imagined dangers of the narrow streets and a passing into sanctuary. The stairs were steep, becoming even tortuously steep and narrow near the top of the house. In my room, a canopied bed occupied half the floor, and a small shuttered window provided a view of an opposite wall upon which a few lights played vaguely from below.

At a level slightly above my own window, and to one side, I had a view of renovations going on: a glimpse of new corrugated iron, fresh plaster on venerable walls, new timber still pale from the sawing. Indeed, everywhere I went in the Stone Town I saw piles of sand, and heard the scrape of trowel and the rasp of saw.

In the early morning, the mullahs called in a chorus of intoning voices, some distant, some closer at hand. At the southern tip of the island, a mosque still stands from its building in the 12th century. Here in the Stone Town, however, the mosques were not that old. The town itself, in its current form, developed roughly a century and a half ago, and among its crammed houses now are more than fifty mosques, as well as various temples and a few Christian churches. But a typewritten note inside my wardrobe door left no doubt as to which religion predominated.

'Dear guests,' the note said, and it had been repeated in French, German and Italian, 'welcome to Zanzibar. About ninety per cent of the people are Muslims. In respect of their religion, we kindly request you not to wear too low neckline as well as too short dresses.'

The mullahs crowded insistently into the silence of the early dawn. During the day they could still be heard above the noises of the town; and often, as I walked, I caught glimpses into buildings furnished only with carpets, thin men lying on their sides, reading, thinking, or simply finding some renewal during the rigours of the day.

The rigours would have been those of the narrow streets themselves. All day they buzzed with talk and business and music wailing high above the general hubbub sometimes. The streets made a labyrinth between the crumbling walls and intricately carved doorways. Tourists haggled over curios with Indian and Arab shopkeepers. The eyes of women appeared in the narrow apertures of the austere headgear they wore. Bearded men walked purposefully forward in flowing white garb; others sat on stone ledges built into the walls. Bicycles frequented the throng, and occasionally a spluttering scooter swerved past. There were no long vistas: people appeared suddenly only to disappear too soon around a corner of another turning in the maze. Here were secret places, and a secrecy of events which added to the sense of archetype. There was no other place quite like it anywhere, yet it carried in it the pattern of everywhere.

There was also a slight tang of menace. In spite of the relief I had felt in gaining access through the barred door of my hotel that first night, there were no obvious dangers in the narrow alleyways. The people seemed at peace, and the predominant sounds, after dark, were those of children at play. These lively sounds echoed up between close walls to become amplified into big boisterous caricatures of shrieks and laughter as harmless as the caterwauling of arch-backed cats on the parapets and ledges above my window. Yet the menace lingered. The streets had memories, and this idea of history sometimes jarred at unexpected moments, as in the sight of aged eyes surreptitiously upon me, and in remembrances of blood.

A football commentary on the radio danced from set to set in narrow passageways; and further on I saw a black-robed figure, leaning forward as it hurried close beside a high and windowless wall.

Strange that from all the long history in which the island was shrouded, it should be the revolution of 1964 which came the sharpest to me. No doubt this was because the revolution had happened, in part at any rate, in these very streets in which tourists now strolled to photograph their favourite vistas. I could never completely erase the thought of fists and axes smashing against chained doors, and then the amplified echoing of blows and screams in the elegant spaces within.

In Jamituri Gardens, wedged between the labyrinthine streets of the Stone Town and the sea, people gathered in the warm evenings without much more purpose than to feel the slightly fresher breezes on their faces. To one side lay water which dazzled to the horizon; to the other in the brilliance of the sunset stood the so-called House of Wonders, erected by one or other of the Sultans, its wide balconies marking each floor; and a little further down the promenade the previous palace of these Sultans. Since the revolution, however, this relatively modest building with its stained white walls and frequent arches and balconies had served as the People's Palace Museum.

I saw outrigger canoes crossing the brilliant sea; and on the beach in the short twilight men came down to prepare their boats for the night's fishing. Nets were examined and stowed, lamps filled and cleaned. The men shouted and laughed together as they clambered about the vessels listing on the sand, while behind them a dhow with triangular sail went silently by against the crimson clouds which had gathered out there over the western horizon.

In an arched tea house built over the water, rippled reflections lit people's faces from beneath, while in Jamituri Gardens smoke began to rise from cooking fires. Lengths of sugar-cane were crushed between rollers, and the juice tricked down into glasses then sold to the crowds. People sat on the sea wall watching children playing in warm waves. Smoke wafted gently through the gardens, and the smell of food and the sounds of contentment and leisure permeated the senses. As darkness came, the lamps of the food sellers were lit, faces glowing warm brown in their illumination; and a crowd had gathered to watch the exploits of a garrulous fire-eater who as an encore blew out great feathers of smoking flame.

In the narrow streets on the way back to my hotel, a man asked me for my money. I gave only a small percentage and he hurried on his way. The streets and alleys were in a darkness relieved only by the occasional electric light suspended between the secretive buildings. Old men in white sat on their ledges; women in their darker clothes hovered in doorways while the children played. There was no foliage in the Stone Town, except where walls had cracked and crumbled sufficiently for seeds to germinate.

Later that night, the light in my hotel room went out and the shadows on the wall outside my window disappeared. It seemed to me that the whole town had been plunged into a profound darkness. But the noise and shouting outside seemed not to change tempo. I detected no surprise, no consternation. People were inured to such events perhaps, although I saw neither flicker of torch nor candle anywhere outside, but once the flaring headlight of a scooter gave a faint and transient show.

A three-storeyed house in Zanzibar, set outside the cramped confines of the Stone Town and overlooking the mud flats of the dhow harbour at low tide, had at one time been placed at the disposal of David Livingstone. It was indeed from this house, and no doubt crossing the narrow sea in a dhow not dissimilar to the ones which lay on sandbanks now, that Livingstone had set out on his last great exploration of Africa. He had been trying — it had become a Victorian obsession — to find the source of the Nile. He had also been concerned by the brutality of the slave trade which he called 'this open sore of the world'. Of course, sojourning in proximity to Zanzibar's famous slave market had served only to fuel his concern and outrage. The date of his final departure to the mainland had been April 1866; but only seven tortuous years later, in April 1873, had he died at a place called Chitambo situated in modern Zambia.

These details were offered to me by a young man named Suleiman as we stood looking up at the house. I noticed that a few of the shutters protecting the upper-floor windows were in poor repair, and one of them, unhooked and with louvres missing, groaned faintly in the breeze. Suleiman glanced at me after a few moments, enquiring whether the tour could proceed.

We drove north to Maruhubi, where the ruins of a palace with voluptuous conical domes lay mouldering in a garden of palm and mango trees and well-tended grass. It had been destroyed by fire only nineteen years after its construction in 1880 by a Sultan named Barghash. While it stood, the palace, with a tethered cow grazing between blackened columns which once supported aqueducts supplying numerous baths, had been used exclusively for pleasure. Barghash had four wives in town, but here at Maruhubi lived his ninety-nine concubines.

'They say when he came here he used to visit six women in one day,' Suleiman said. 'But I don't know if he could have managed that,' he added with a slight smile.

While we wandered about the ruins, I observed that being a tour guide must have given him, Suleiman, a good grasp of the island's history. The comment encouraged Suleiman to deviate from the official script.

He nodded with a certain eagerness. 'I have also studied history. In school. And also for two years in my teacher training.'

I asked why he worked as a guide if he had trained to be a teacher.

'It is for the money,' Suleiman replied. 'I am saving to go to the university in Dar es Salaam.'

'What will you study?'

He looked at me, as if weighing me up in a new and more personal way. I was all at once no longer a tourist so much as someone to whom he might offer a confidence. He said with a shy smile: 'International affairs.'

In his middle twenties (he told me subsequently that he had been born in 1967, three years after the revolution), Suleiman's features were open and pleasant and set in a rounded face with cheeks which plumped out slightly when he smiled. His ancestry was Shirazi, he said, even though at a glance I would have taken him for African.

'What is Shirazi?' he asked, and answered: 'My people came at first from the Persian Gulf. I don't know when my own people came, but the Shirazi have been here for a thousand years. I think there must have been intermarriage with Africans. Look at my hair. Yes, I am a Muslim.'

Such statements, especially their candour and directness, rapidly increased my liking of my young guide. Fortunately for me, no other tourists had accompanied us, and Suleiman and I were driven alone in the tour company's micro-bus to various parts of the island. The excursion had been advertised as a spice tour; but it became also, thanks to Suleiman's knowledge and interest, an excursion into the history of the place.

From the 10th to the 15th centuries, Suleiman told me, the Shirazis had been increasingly influential on Zanzibar where, incidentally (Suleiman said with one of his faint smiles), the indigenous African population were already converted to Islam. The Shirazis traded with countries as far afield as China, and considerable wealth had come to the island. Finally an independent Sultanate had been established. This period came to an end early in the 16th century with Portuguese conquests all along the East African coast. But Portuguese rule was brutal and subject to constant uprisings — and competition from Arab interests, especially those from Oman — and by the second quarter of the 18th century the last traces of the European power had disappeared from Zanzibar.

Enter the Omani Sultans who, in spite of resistance from some of the indigenous African clans, ruled Zanzibar, first as part of Oman and then as an independent polity until it became a British Protectorate in 1890. Thereafter, the Sultans lost control of the island's revenues, accepted salaries from the British government, and lingered on in a shabby genteel sort of way until the revolution came.

'The most powerful Sultan was Seyyid Said,' Suleiman told me. 'He ruled during the first half of the 19th century. He was the man who developed the cloves industry here, and enlarged the slave trade. No, it was one of his successors who built the palace at Maruhubi for all his concubines. There were many Sultans, I have forgotten how many exactly, but Seyyid Said was the most important.'

We were driving among cloves, the bushy trees stretching away up a slight incline, and Suleiman gave me some of the facts: at one time Zanzibar (including neighbouring Pemba island) had accounted for 60 per cent of the world's clove production, which in turn had accounted for around 90 per cent of Zanzibar's foreign earnings. The harvesting of unopened buds which needed to be hand picked within a limited time would temporarily transform the social life of the island, even when Suleiman had been a child. The schools would close, and everyone came to pick, even teachers and doctors and civil servants. With time, the trees grew large, much larger than those in the plantation through which we drove, and people often fell out of them when harvesting.

'Ten to twenty bad accidents in a big season,' Suleiman said. I asked if he had ever fallen. He smiled his faint smile. 'Not yet. Thanks to God.'

We went through the outward motions of the spice tour, with my young guide showing me whole forests of coconut palms and jack-fruit; a creeper bearing pepper berries; and the delicate ylang-ylang flower used in the making of perfume, and also on special occasions the young women of the island sprinkled crushed ylang-ylang petals in their beds.

He offered such comments with a half-shy openness, as if hoping to deal with these aspects of his subject in a matter-of-fact and manly manner. Yet I could see that his attention was divided now; that he wished to do his duty as my guide, but that he also wished to talk of other things. I did nothing to discourage him.

'But when Seyyid Said died, the trouble began. Everyone was fighting to succeed him. This was in 1856, and in the end the British used their power to get the proper heir, Majid, to the Sultans' palace, and to keep him there. In 1870 Barghash became Sultan. Yes, the one with all the concubines. Under him, Zanzibar became rich and of course he built many palaces. But he too became more and more dependent on the British, who used this situation to force him to abolish slavery and end the slave trade on Zanzibar.'

By then, most of the clove plantations, and indeed most of the land on Zanzibar and Pemba, belonged to Omani Arabs; while the economy of the islands depended on the business skills of another powerful minority, the Indian traders. Beneath these élites, the broad mass of the population, African, Shirazi and a sprinkling of others, and finally manumitted slaves as well, lived on the land as agricultural workers or peasant farmers who had not the slightest control of the price of their cloves on the international market.

His eyes shone as he spoke of these things. I said that his teachers had taught him well. He dismissed this remark with some impatience. 'The history that they teach is not the real history,' he said. 'Not at all. That is why I do not want to become a teacher. I do not like it.' I did not question him further, but I perceived him suddenly as probably more ambitious than teaching would allow. He wanted to become embroiled in politics, I thought; he wanted power and international affairs.

We had stopped at a crossroads for a drink of coconut. I watched a thin man without a shirt swing his knife at the wooden fruit, lopping off one end as if it was a boiled egg. Behind him, in a field, a heap of empty coconuts lay drying in the sun. The liquid had a penetrating sweetness which clung to the roof of the mouth.

Across the narrow road from where we stood, an open structure, built like a rectangular hut with only a rear wall, had been adorned with a green flag. Suleiman explained that it was a country branch of the ruling political party, a place where the youth or the women could meet or gather for meetings.

'It used to be Julius Nyerere's party,' he explained. 'It's the ruling party here and on the mainland. You know that Zanzibar and Tanganyika joined together as Tanzania after the revolution here in 1964? For nearly thirty years we were a one-party state. First it was the Afro-Shirazi Party here, and then, in 1977 I think, it merged into the CCM, the Chama Cha Mapinduzi Party. That's the CCM flag,' he went on, gazing across the road. 'But there are other parties now, since we got a multiparty system a few years ago.'

I told him that I had a growing interest in the Zanzibar revolution because it seemed to me to invade the atmosphere of the island, even now. He looked at me keenly. I said, too, that what he had said about the history of the place made sense as a preamble to revolution: increasing poverty in the face of powerful élites who controlled access to land and economic power.

He nodded. He tossed his coconut into the field and said: 'There were peasants who owned land, but as cloves prices dropped many of them got into debt, and they were often forced to give up their land to repay their debts. More and more people were poor, and now landless, and becoming angry. Especially after independence from Britain.'

A busload of tourists had descended on the crossroads for their obligatory drink of coconut, and the thin man without a shirt showed a fine deftness in face of this sudden upsurge in trade. A few cameras whirred, but for the most part the tourists looked about them with slightly vacant expressions, revealing the boredom and discomfort which often attend the regimentation of group sightseeing. One young woman with auburn hair and wearing the shortest of shorts made no secret of her dislike of the cloying liquid.

Suleiman and I stood to one side at the crossroads. I saw how the four roads cut away in straight lines through a denseness of vegetation, and the green flag opposite hardly fluttered in the humid air.

'You see, the Africans and Shirazis were disorganised. So it was the Arabs and Indians who won the elections just before independence, and it was to them that Britain handed over the power. But only for a few weeks.'

We drove on. I had, among the palm trees and low huts of the Zanzibar countryside, a sudden sense of reliving the past. The revolution had destroyed the élites and yielded a one-party state. Now the one-party state also had slipped into history as multipartyism gained momentum. But what would multipartyism yield? The seeds of another revolution? It was a sudden inkling of renewal, almost a premonition, which I caught, a sudden glimpse of the cyclical nature of human affairs as manifested on this small and archetypal island.

Suleiman pointed out cinnamon and avocado pears, and once he asked the driver to pause at the roadside to allow me to smell some lemon grass, a few blades of which he crushed between his fingers.

Then he said: 'The killing started in the countryside, and afterwards it went into town.'

'Do you think, looking back, the revolution was a good thing?' I asked.

'In some ways. It returned the land to the people. There was also free health and education. But the killing was not a good thing.'

We travelled in silence for a moment. Above the trees by the roadside, presently, I saw a different flag, blue and white this time. Suleiman told me it was the flag of the CUF, the Civic United Front, one of the parties to emerge since multipartyism had been introduced in 1992.

'It is looking for more independence for Zanzibar,' he said. 'The union with the mainland has not always been good for Zanzibar. That is the feeling.'

'I think this Civic United Front is your party,' I said.

His response surprised me somewhat. He bowed his head with a shy yet strangely spontaneous smile, as if my comment meant something to him, and offered a swift nod.

I spoke with Suleiman again the following day. I went to the office of the company for whom he worked and booked a tour of the Stone Town which, I was told, Suleiman would soon be conducting. Meanwhile, I had thirty minutes to wait; so I dawdled in the small air-conditioned office, chatting to the charming Indian man who had accepted my money.

On an impulse, I asked him if he would recommend to me someone I could talk to who had lived through the revolution in 1964.

He looked at me in mock alarm.

I pressed the matter, saying I would be interested to hear what conditions had been like, what the mood had been in the narrow streets of the Stone Town, then, when the status quo of centuries had been overturned.

'The mood?' he said. 'No one will talk to you about that. It's still a very sensitive issue. Don't think about those times, Sir,' he added, and smiled once more in his charming way. 'Just enjoy our beautiful island. Now here is Suleiman for the city tour.'

This time we were not alone. We were joined by a Canadian tourist named Dave and his short-sighted wife, both immensely overweight. Dave was probably in his late forties, and I noticed that his breath came in short gasps for a moment after the effort of getting into the small bus. His wife peered at everything through thick-lensed spectacles. She wore a trouser suit in a grey fabric which shimmered over her bulk when she moved. She peered at me without the slightest curiosity and said in a distracted way: 'I'm afraid I'm dreadfully blind.'

Suleiman was courtesy itself, even apologising about the humidity of the morning when they both began to display dark patches at their armpits.

The bus was able to take us to various points on the outskirts of the Stone Town, and after that we walked among crowds in the maze of dark alleys and sunlit little squares. The Canadians shambled along, mopping at their faces. In the fish market, a vendor opened the mouth of an eel to show its sharp teeth. The fat woman in grey squinted at it in some distaste. Outside, at stalls selling fruit and vegetables, she said: 'There's certainly lots of colour.' Dave, who had announced (in reply to a question from Suleiman) that he was a prison warder, took a few photographs. When Suleiman offered to show how chickens were slaughtered, the fat woman said: 'Somewhere or another in Africa, probably north of the equator, we had to watch a goat being sacrificed in our honour.' Dave had short-cropped hair and pale eyes, and perspiration glistened in the folds and creases of his substantially proportioned neck.

When I told Suleiman of my conversation in the office of the tour company, he laughed. 'I have never heard of a revolution being called a sensitive issue,' he said. But he seemed slightly ill at ease with me, as if anxious not to be seen to be favouring only one of the tour party in his charge. He wore a crisp blue shirt, and his cheeks often plumped out as he talked and smiled with the Canadians.

At the Anglican Cathedral, built with some arrogance on the site of the former slave market, a group of workmen seemed to be permanently employed to keep the coral-built structure from crumbling away. But their work was rendered more difficult by tourists who swarmed everywhere inside and outside the graceful church. The Canadians were hurried away by a special church guide: I could hear the intoning of her monologue as she marched my fat companions off down the aisle.

While I waited, I found a polished timber cross made, so an inscription said, from the tree at Chitambo under which Livingstone's heart had been buried.

'But even after slavery had been abolished here in Zanzibar, in 1873, the same year that Livingstone died, the trade went on.'

Suleiman stood slightly behind me as he spoke, but his eyes were keen with interest and also with expectation of my response.

'They hid the slaves in caves, and then shipped them out, up to 18 000 a year, to Madagascar and Mauritius and even further away. Only occasionally did the British ships catch the slavers. And on the island itself, in the houses and on the plantations, slavery continued right up to 1917. There were still many people who, when the revolution came, remembered being slaves earlier in their lives.'

When the Canadians returned, Suleiman took us to a nearby cellar which had once been used as a slave chamber. A few slits at ground level admitted some light and air, but it remained low ceilinged and dingy. The place seemed afflicted with memories of misery, with a choking claustrophobia, and also with a muffled rationalisation for revolutions. All at once, and for no apparent reason, the oppression of the place was rent by the fat woman who uttered a short and raucous laugh.

On the way to the national museum, Suleiman asked Dave whether he enjoyed being a warder.

'In Canada, it's OK. The pay's OK. I wouldn't care to do it in Africa though,' he added, clearly to indicate that he was quite capable of making such judgements, even in the enervating heat of Zanzibar.

Suleiman smiled politely, then changed the subject. 'Have you ever been diving, to see the coral?'

'Nope,' Dave said.

'I can't swim,' the fat woman in grey said.

Suleiman offered a lighthearted reprimand in reply. 'I suppose you haven't even brought your costume.'

The woman shrieked with laughter. 'Can you swim, Dave?'

'Yep,' he answered.

'The coral is really beautiful,' Suleiman offered.

'I believe so,' the woman said, 'but I can't even swim.'

The museum resembled a mosque, its white domes stained black from rain and humidity, and contained a wide assortment of exhibits. The Canadians lingered at the section devoted to the building of those most gracious of craft, the dhows. I passed deeper in and found pictures of prominent historical figures. Here hung a large portrait of Abeid Karume, founder of the Afro-Shirazi Party who had led the revolution on 12 January 1964, and who had subsequently presided as the first president of Zanzibar until he was murdered in 1972. The strong African face, thin lipped and with a trimmed moustache, stared down at me from above a tunic buttoned at the throat.

In another place I came across the long line of the Sultans, with Barghash — the one with the concubines — looking suitably dissolute. And here were those who came after him, kept on by the British for 'ceremonial purposes' as one historian put it. They were pompous-looking men with vaguely frightened eyes for the most part, including the one who had been ousted during the revolution and who, Suleiman told me, still lived in an obscure exile somewhere in England.

'The Sultan and many Arabs and Indians escaped in dhows,' he said, standing with me in the museum for a few moments. 'The Sultan ran to the British who took him to England. Many of the others went to Oman and India. But, since 1992 and multiparty democracy, they have begun to return.

'This is good for the economy, I think. Here is an example. Now they are importing rice from Pakistan and India which is cheaper than the rice grown on the mainland.' He half laughed in his shy way. 'I don't know why this should be though, when you think of the costs of transport.'

I remarked that I could find no exhibits or photographs depicting the revolution itself.

Suleiman smiled. 'I have never seen a picture of what happened there. I have read about it, and I have heard stories. Once an old man told me that some Arabs had been caught and cooked alive in the copra ovens.'

In the airless silence of the museum I heard quite clearly the fat woman's sigh. 'I'm so hot, Dave, I think I'm going to die.'

'People say the revolution weakened the economy,' Suleiman went on, 'but I think not as much as the corruption which came afterwards. I have heard that the son of one of the first revolutionary leaders ended up much richer than the richest Sultan. I have heard, but maybe it's an exaggeration, that he could have fed the whole of mainland Tanzania for ten years with all his money.'

The heat of the morning as it pressed towards midday began to take its toll on the tour. The fat woman in grey looked faint, and Dave himself held a handkerchief more or less permanently against his throat. We drove along a busy thoroughfare called Creek Road, with the Stone Town on our left, and on the right a few ugly tenement blocks of about eight storeys which, said Suleiman, had been designed by East German architects after the revolution.

'They try to make Zanzibar look like East Berlin,' he said with a smile. 'And everyone helped with the building. Doctors, teachers, even President Karume, came in the early morning to do a couple of hours' work.'

I said that his words reminded me of what he had said the previous day concerning the clove picking, and how everyone had become involved.

'Yes, it was like that,' he said, his keen eyes glancing across my face. Then with some irony, he added: 'This was a different harvest though.'

We passed a crowd of Zanzibar buses, an assortment of lorries and smaller trucks with the backs rebuilt of timber, sometimes with small individual doors serving each row of seats, and with canopies standing up on shaped timber supports. Our own more modern bus trundled by a circuitous route to the sea front and past Jamituri Gardens where I had spent my first evening on Zanzibar. On the town side stood the House of Wonders with its wide balconies, and further on the stained white walls and arches of the Palace of the Sultans, now called the People's Palace.

'Don't force me to go inside,' wailed the fat woman in grey.

Dave said it would be better if they walked a little under the trees in Jamituri Gardens, trying to find a breeze from the sea. 'Will they have ice-cold Cokes anywhere hereabouts?' he asked Suleiman, as they staggered from the confines of the bus.

Suleiman nodded encouragingly, and followed after them with a patient and solicitous expression. But in a second he had turned swiftly back to me.

'If you are really interested in speaking to people about the revolution, I think I can help.'

I thanked him.

'I will come to your hotel at five o'clock,' he said, then turned his attention once more to the perspiring Canadians, their garments manifesting large dark stains about the armpits.

The Palace of the Sultans, now called the People's Palace, had been converted into a museum which I entered to escape the hottest part of the day. It proved to be an efficient haven. Although the building faced north west, and the afternoon sun was magnified by its own flaring reflection on the slightly heaving surface of the sea, the interior was protected by deep verandas and thick old walls.

I found a pamphlet in the reception area which provided a few facts. The palace, but in much simplified form compared to the later amendments and additions, had been built in 1828 by the first great Sultan of Zanzibar, the Omani ruler Seyyid Said; and it had been used uninterrupted as royal residence until that fateful day in January 1964.

As museum, 'it contains a unique collection of antique furniture, paintings of the Sultans, and artefacts from many parts of the world, mirroring the international role of Zanzibar during the nineteenth century', I read in the pamphlet.

The ground floor had been given over to illustrating 'the formative period (1828 – 1870)' while the first floor still showed signs of 'the period of affluence (1870 – 1896)'. Barghash of the numerous concubines had been a central figure here, especially in his embellishment of the palace and his building of many others about the island. The first floor contained a State Room and Banquet Hall, still quite lavishly furnished.

But the end was already in sight. As Zanzibar came to full flower, the European partition of Africa robbed her of much of her commercial hinterland. In a single act of defiance, one of Barghash's sons tried to assert his independence. In the brief revolt which followed, British naval vessels badly damaged the palace, 'and it was rebuilt on a more modest scale' (according to the pamphlet). It remained the residence of Sultans, however, who now had little power and even less wealth. Certainly, there were social dynamics brewing on the island which, even then, were laying the foundations for revolution, but the Sultans had not much part to play, except as faded figureheads of past wealth and injustice.

They had lived during the decline on the second floor, and it was here that the museum carried a certain gloomy pathos. Some of the windows were protected by shutters, but the louvres were broken now, or missing, admitting strangely shaped shafts of afternoon light. The floors were quite often of red polished cement; some carpets appeared new and gaudy, obviously mass-produced; others were threadbare. I found a bathroom done out in pale green tiles, with pink bath and basin. The main bedroom seemed singularly tasteless, furnished with Western furniture from the 1950s, an ugly enough period, with small tapering legs splayed out at an angle beneath veneered pieces which seemed hopelessly overweight for such slender supports. In the dining-room, a highly polished expandable table would have seated ten, and the china tableware bore the monogram of one of the later Sultans. They lived here in this somewhat vulgar middle-class way: these anachronisms on a seething island, these once proud autocrats reduced now to living off modest hand-outs from the British taxpayer.

I stood in the silent rooms, with sunlight slanting in through broken shutters, and heard, no doubt from the first floor, from the period of affluence, the tinkling chimes of a European-made clock. I wandered slowly back towards this sound and, not far from the stairs, I found a man in an office whom I asked about evidence of the revolution.

He seemed to be of Indian extraction, with straight-combed silver hair and weary-looking eyes. He had looked up from a crowded desk to greet me. His demeanour had been without defensiveness; and now, with a friendly smile, he replied to my question.

'The major evidence, here in the palace, may well be negative,' he said. 'If you look carefully, you will be struck by the many things that are not here. Small objects like cutlery, jewellery, and so on. They could hardly have been packed up and taken away by the Sultan and his family. It all happened much too suddenly. There were crowds at the gates. In fact the gates were broken down. What I'm saying is the palace may well have been looted; there would quite probably have been some theft. But we need also to remember that the Sultans lived modestly, and no doubt the revolutionary forces soon put a stop to any looting.'

He leaned back in his chair, regarding me quizzically. 'Why are you so interested in the revolution? In over a thousand years of history, the revolution is not perhaps such a major event.'

I told him what I had felt about the island being an archetype, small enough for human affairs to appear to stand out in a logical sequence, even for revolutions to be understandable, and for the post-revolutionary fervour and disillusion to appear as part of a single coherent roadway to the new freedoms, and new dangers, of the present.

He looked at me with eyes which seemed wise as well as weary. 'You capture the idea of humanity fairly well,' he said. 'There is never a standing still. There is always a new renewal laid over the foundations of the renewals that have gone before.'

T he sun, no doubt still blazing over an unseen Africa, had penetrated the small open space in front of my hotel only with a thin and dazzling sliver, when Suleiman came to fetch me at five o'clock. He wore a clean shirt, I noticed, and his face expressed that half-shy keenness he had often shown me, and enhanced now with a slight glow of expectation.

'I have arranged for you to meet some people,' he said as soon as he arrived. 'I think they are expecting you.'

We walked into the twilight maze of the Stone Town until we came to a congested square with several alleys leading into it, and small motor scooters from time to time emitting fumes as they wobbled through. We sat down on one of the ledges built into a wall, and Suleiman spoke Swahili to a slightly built man with a peppercorn beard tufting from a sallow skin. In a while the man disappeared into one of the shops.

'I think it is arranged. Fareed is making sure...'

While we waited I examined the square in which a constant flow of people merged and then diverged into the separate alleys. Posters for the Civic United Front enlivened the grimy walls, printed in the same blue and white colours of the flag I had seen while driving with Suleiman in the countryside the previous day. Political newspaper cuttings had been stuck to the wall around the posters, and some paint had been daubed on a wall further on. Then Fareed came back, nodding his head: 'They are ready...'

Suleiman led me a short way down one of the alleys. In a moment it had opened into another square, but this one was almost deserted, except for a few men who stood watching our approach. They smiled in friendly fashion. We went into a room open to the square on one side, like a garage. Some sort of machinery had been stored in one corner, and typed pages were stuck to the walls. I guessed this to be a party office. I was shown a chair. I sat down to be confronted by a roomful of watching faces.

In a voice which quavered slightly, Suleiman introduced me in Swahili. There was a brief exchange. Suleiman said to me: 'They want you to tell them about yourself.'

I did so in English. The faces before me seemed to represent the whole population of Zanzibar: sallow-skinned Arabs like Fareed; Shirazis like Suleiman; Indians like the one I had met in the palace museum; one old Indian man with broken teeth who as I spoke beamed approval in the sociable manner of the deaf; and the features of Africa, flattened noses sometimes, full lips, the whites of eyes vivid in dark faces and in the twilight of the office in which we sat.

When I fell silent, a thickset man behind a desk nodded but did not smile. 'How can we help you?'

I said I had become very interested in the revolution. The faces regarded me doubtfully. There was a silence. The man behind the desk — he wore a close-fitting embroidered cap — shrugged his shoulders.

'A revolution is a revolution,' he said. 'I was away studying in England at the time, so I didn't witness it. But you can rest assured that it was bloody. For three days it was chaotic in the countryside, and here in the Stone Town. People died in the streets. Sometimes they died in their own houses.'

The watching faces seemed close to my own. I saw that one of the typed pages on the wall had to do with the procedure of meetings. Glancing up, I saw Suleiman's intent eyes shining with interest. The old Indian with broken teeth beamed at me, his eyes rheumy with age, and I wondered if he had lived through the revolution. And here before me, on the other side of the desk, the man in the embroidered cap looked at me with his hard clear eyes, and then he raised his eyebrows.

'Is there anything else you want to know? I mean, anything specific?'

I said there was not.

This response had the effect of encouraging him to speak. He told how the Sultan and ruling classes of landowners and merchants, but largely the landowners, had been overthrown. It was like any other revolution, the man said, in Russia or China, when people were fighting against one another, when people of the same race found themselves on different sides of the class divide.

I wondered suddenly whether this man's father had been a slave, but I did not enquire. I said instead: 'But surely both sides of that divide are represented in this room now.'

'Oh, yes.'

'And with the new liberalisation,' I went on, 'the ruling class is steadily returning. In a way, they are a part of the liberalisation process, a part of the move away from rigid socialism and the one-party state — and presumably a part of this party, the CUF.'

The man's eyes glinted with amusement. 'The revolution is over,' he said. 'The quest now is for independence from the mainland. Complete independence. Only when we've got it will we decide what sort of union, if any, we want with Tanganyika.'

'The revolution made matters worse,' someone among the watching faces said.

The man at the table glanced across them. His hard eyes steadied on one particular face. With a half shock of recognition, I thought I saw the silver-haired man from the museum, but the light had deteriorated and I could not be sure.

'Speak,' the thickset man at the table said.

'Let us set the stage for our visitor then,' the silver-haired man said.

I heard a faint stirring among the gathered men as they settled down to listen. Suleiman's eyes engaged mine for a second, then he looked towards the speaker.

'Let us begin,' the silver-haired speaker said, 'in 1956, when clove prices collapsed, and times were hard for everyone. The peasants could hardly make enough to keep themselves alive. The squatters — often manumitted slaves — craved land. And the working class was embittered and angry over declining wages. All this contributed to the revolution.

'But let us look at what happened after the revolution had taken place. The land was taken over and redistributed, three acres to a family. In other spheres, though, the state assumed more and more control, especially in agricultural trading monopolies and in import and export. The state set the prices paid to the new peasant class for cloves very low, even when world prices improved in the years after the revolution. This was done to keep production costs down and profits high. In this way the state swelled its coffers for socialism. But the result was that by 1978 the peasants were getting only about seven per cent of the actual price being paid for cloves on the world market.'

There were some exclamations of disbelief from the listeners. It seemed suddenly astonishing to me that I should witness such an event, the men settled into positions of listening, and Suleiman's plump face tense with excitement. The silver-haired man looked directly at me as he continued.

'The result of all this was inevitable. The peasants on their three-acre plots stopped trying. They picked only what they could reach while standing. There was very little climbing into the trees, and when they did they simply broke off the branches and threw them to the ground. This caused disease to spread through the plantations. I was doing research in the countryside then, and I saw whole lines of clove trees dying across the hillsides. Zanzibar's share of the world market dropped to a paltry ten to fifteen per cent. The mainstay of the economy for over a century had been destroyed in less than twenty years.'

'What happened to the revolutionary leadership?' asked a younger man with African features. 'Why did it fail in this way?'

'Do you remember the first President, Abeid Karume?'

'He was murdered in 1972,' the younger man replied.

'But by whom? By leftists unhappy with post-revolutionary progress. These leftists tried to carry out a coup, but failed, although they managed to carry out a few assassinations. Perhaps the real problem was simply that Karume wasn't a leftist. He was a populist. He didn't understand Marxism. In fact, he despised intellectuals of any kind. He used to say of them: all they do is think.'

This caused a sudden ripple of mirth in the darkening room. Teeth flashed. The old Indian with broken teeth leaned towards me with a simple friendliness enlivening his rheumy eyes. The laughter must have broken about his deafness like a vague rumble on every side. He placed his hand on my arm.

'You are very welcome here,' he said in a gentle voice, determined to add his endorsement to the general air of jollity and acceptance.

'The rest of the story is well known,' the silver-haired man went on. 'By the late seventies and early eighties, Zanzibaris were sick of socialism. The liberalisation of trade, and of the economy generally, started here long before it happened on the mainland . . .'

But the meeting had broken into good-natured chatter. The man at the table looked at me with his hard eyes smiling slightly, his eyebrows raised.

'Is this what you expected? This has always been the Zanzibari way: there is a tradition of talking, and because we are so small there is, I believe, a tradition of wanting to control our own destiny. We feel the frustration of being absorbed into a large country with problems utterly unlike our own.'

I asked what British university he had attended.

'Leicester, and then Birmingham.'

We shook hands in that way which causes the hands to come together in a definite clap. His own felt cool and slightly clammy.

Outside in the square, darkness had begun to descend. Some old men played draughts, sitting together at wooden tables. I heard the shouts of playing children in the alleys on every side. People nodded towards me as they dispersed. Then Suleiman's youthful face appeared, smiling shyly. I thanked him for a remarkable experience, and said I wished to give him some American dollars.

'To help with your saving for university,' I said. 'You must go, and you must do international affairs, and after that you must become a politician.'

He laughed in his shy way, his cheeks plumping out.

'That's what you'd like, isn't it?'

Suddenly he moved closer to me, and I could tell that my gift had meant something to him. He said nothing, however. Instead he nudged me with his elbow, a strange yet spontaneous gesture of acceptance and comradeship. He nodded quickly, his keen eyes glancing once more across my face, and then he turned to hurry away along a dark and litter-filled lane.

I n the morning I returned to the museum. The silver-haired man smiled and said: 'No, it was not me, but I know who you mean, I think. The interesting thing about Zanzibar is that for its size there are many educated people.'

We spoke about the situation concerning land. It had been returned to the people through the revolution, but already it was passing into the hands of a new land-owning class.

'The buying and selling of land has been going on illegally for at least fifteen years now. That's how I bought mine.'

The smiling eyes, weary and wise, regarding me across the crowded desk. 'But this has happened several times in the island's history, this changing ownership of the land. There have been definite ups and downs,' he added, indicating this process with an undulating motion of his hand. 'Yes, certainly, with greater liberalisation a new land-owning class will emerge. Perhaps even now the seeds of another revolution are being sown.'

He laughed at his own words. 'But you yourself know these things. It is one renewal on top of another. Go anywhere in the Stone Town and you will see buildings being renovated, new beginnings being made.'

But I went at first to the old dhow harbour to while away some time. The timber vessels were crammed together, lying four deep against the crowded wharfs. They were motorised now, yet the masts still stood erect, and some of the larger boats still plied the ancient routes to India and back. I watched one dhow, amid a cacophony of shouting, prepare to leave for Mombasa on the mainland to the north. Black sailors clambered everywhere, hanging to the stern and prow, standing on the roof of the cabin the windows of which were flung wide open. Perhaps it was here that the Sultan had rushed when the revolution began. I tried to imagine the scenes of women with their faces covered but for the frightened eyes, and children crying, and all the urgencies of flight, while behind them the Stone Town filled with the dust of charging feet and the bashing against doors.

The Stone Town lured me, and I walked in it for the last time. The revolution had been the sharpest in my thoughts for the few days that I had lingered on the island. But it had at last been overlaid by new ideas. The sense of Zanzibar as archetype remained; it was the thought of the inevitability of renewal, however, which now predominated.

Here, behind the protection of coral reef and regiments of palm trees guarding the long beaches, a clear sight of the cyclical nature of human affairs came into focus. In the Stone Town's labyrinth of alleyways and small squares, especially, I caught this potent sense of endless repetitions, although each with its own variations. The carved doors of the Indian houses had arched tops; those of the Arabs from Oman were square. And this new focus seemed enhanced by the renewal of the Stone Town itself, the constant sound of hammering, the new brick work, the new expanses of plaster set amid the ruins and crumbling away of the old. Children played in mounds of sand and piles of builders' rubble, eternally at play and laughing with life and hope among the materials of new building and the rubble of decay.

8

Into Silence

The part of Serengeti into which the Olduvai gorge is carved was once occupied by a steadily sinking inland lake. It was gradually filled with material descending from the surrounding volcanoes... Thus a splendid calendar of past history came into existence, the gorge today providing us with particulars of deposits hundreds of thousands of years old. It is a unique site for uncovering our earliest history.

— Professor Gerhard Heberer, quoted in Herbert Wendt's *From Ape to Adam,* 1971.

Gathering speed, the ferry to Dar es Salaam stood up on its metal stilts and stalked its way over the swell. Once out of the lee of the island, the vessel pitched and rolled quite violently in seas which had been gathering momentum for thousands of kilometres. But by now, to starboard, the thin dark shore of Africa could already be seen on a horizon which rose and fell in the vista afforded by spray-splashed perspex portholes.

There were no empty seats on the ferry, and mounds of baggage littered the aisles; nevertheless some of the passengers adjusted their aircraft-style seats and tried to recline in spaces too cramped for such endeavours. In the first class section forward of the central bulkhead I could see a television set offering glimpses of a football game in which swarthy players flung out their arms, and snarled, and occasionally embraced. A young African with a polystyrene box offered cool drinks and packets of sweets for sale, sometimes staggering in the aisle as the ferry lurched into a particularly deep trough.

The air in the enclosed space smelled of stale bodies and diesel fuel. Outside, the sea surged past, an inhospitable environment in which I suddenly saw three men sailing an outrigger canoe, the sail above them stretched taut and bulging in a wind which snatched flecks of foam off blue-green crests of water mounding up on every side. As the ferry rose upon the crests, the coast showed in more detail, a darker strip above, bright yellow closer to the sea.

These beaches grew steadily closer, and the trees beyond showed deep green. On one beach, a few moments later, I saw hundreds of people, like dark ants on the sand. The people seemed to bristle on the beach, and the smoke of fires rose in pale smudges. Boats had been drawn up. As we drew closer, I saw the cork floats of seine nets. A catch had just been dragged ashore and now the people ate. I wondered if there was a noise of shouting or of contentment on the beach. I saw some dhows making sail against the sun, and hundreds of birds turned and fluttered above the beach. Then the tone of the ferry's motors changed, and the hull of the vessel subsided into the water.

The swell diminished as we moved up the harbour channel. I saw buildings appear between the trees of the shore, terracotta roofs among the green, and then soon the buildings were that of a city, tall, stained with mould, and the cranes of the harbour stood in rusting rows, and large vessels lay moored against the docks and others listed on sandbanks. The ferry turned and edged towards a wharf crowded with black faces. Ropes coiled out. Men leapt across the closing gap. The ferry bumped gently, and then lay still.

Doors clashed open. I smelled fresher air and new odours. But it was only as I stepped up and out of the ferry that the noise of the harbour and of the city beyond came unimpeded to me. It drummed and clattered on every side. Black hands grabbed at my luggage. A sudden turmoil and urgency swept in upon senses attuned to slower going. I saw my suitcase lifted on to a dark head which immediately turned along a crowded pier leading to dry land. I followed, jostled and impeded, and now assailed by the dirtiness of the city. Such an extravagance of dirt and smells and hooting vehicles all jammed together up there beyond the harbour wall. My suitcase bobbed on a torrent of heads and shoulders surging on the pier.

Where the pier merged with the edge of the city, a face smiled in recognition, and a hand reached for my arm.

'Welcome to Dar es Salaam,' the doctor said. 'Is this your suitcase? Come this way. My son is waiting with the pick-up.'

The Tanzanian doctor, whom I had met elsewhere in Africa, turned out to be as good as his word. 'Tell me when you're arriving, and if I'm in town I'll take you to my home for a meal.'

We drove in a smart double-cab truck, with lightning stripes painted in bright colours down the sides, through the packed and reeking city centre, and then headed north on congested roads towards a place called Mbezi Beach. 'It's bearable out there; at least there's room to breathe,' the doctor said amiably from the front seat.

His son, a taciturn young man who when he uttered his few words did so with a vaguely North American accent, steered the vehicle through a clamour of traffic, newspaper vendors with armfuls of different mastheads, and roadside salesmen who shouted their wares at close range, their competitive faces vying for space at the open windows.

The doctor crooked his arm on the back of the front seat and turned his head to talk to me. He was almost completely bald, with the rim of grey hair which remained cut extremely short. Seen in profile, his nose showed straight and strong, and his chin protruded slightly, almost turning up at the end, a characteristic which gave to his face a slightly conspiratorial, slightly mischievous air.

'I am sure you will enjoy Tanzania,' he said. 'It is a beautiful country.'

Its roads were less so, though, the doctor continued with a chuckle. Indeed, the roads soon became atrocious, and once we got to Mbezi Beach, the roads became tracks which plunged into treacherous quagmires or ascended over jutting rock outcrops which characterised that stretch of country.

'This is why we've got to buy these vehicles. High clearance four by fours.'

'What we need,' his son said tartly in his North American accent, 'are six by sixes.'

After an hour, we had covered the 15 kilometres which separated the doctor's home from the centre of Dar es Salaam. He ushered me with some pride through a huge house, still unfinished and only partly furnished, and up a flight of stairs to a first floor balcony. Here, a soft breeze struck perceptibly cool against our faces.

'It's always pleasant here, compared to town,' the doctor remarked. 'There's always a breeze from the sea. You can just see it, over there.'

A patch of deep blue showed between green foliage. Closer at hand stood several houses in various stages of completion, with rough tracks laid out in a grid between them. A few goats grazed placidly on tufts of bright green grass.

'The policy on land changed in the mid-1980s,' the doctor said. 'That's when these plots became available for private ownership.'

The policy, apparently, had been part of the liberalisation of the economy, an acceptance of the inevitability of private land ownership, but an insistence that it should be available to all. For this reason, prices had been kept extremely low.

'If they hadn't been, the complaint in parliament would have been that land ownership at Mbezi Beach is only for the rich. So we paid ten US dollars for the plots here.'

He glanced my way to see if this surprised me. I said that it seemed remarkably low. In reply, he offered one of his slightly mischievous smiles.

'In reality, though, the land was still only for the relatively well off and influential. I had to pay an extra one thousand dollars to various land officials in bribes.'

His wife appeared on the balcony at this juncture, a graceful woman who had brought out a few beers and cool drinks on a silver tray. The doctor poured her a beer and she sat with us for a while. The heat of the afternoon had begun to subside; the sun slanted across from behind the house, casting long shadows, and then the sun disappeared in its steady evening descent.

The doctor and his wife spoke among themselves, she telling him of the high prices she had been obliged to pay to an Indian shopkeeper for curtaining purchased for one of the newly completed rooms downstairs which they were now in the process of furnishing. They changed from English to Swahili for a moment, and then, as if by way of explanation, the doctor turned to me and said:

'I think the first strictures on Indian business people — those imposed after independence — were necessary, otherwise our so-called independence would simply have meant a new Asian dominance in place of colonial European.'

'They have nice material though,' his wife said.

'When I was at school,' the doctor went on, 'there were only three secondary schools for Africans in my whole region. But there were more than ten for Indians, even though they comprised only a fraction of the population. That was the difference. But by 1985, when liberalisation of the economy began, the Africans had caught up educationally. I still don't know whether we can really compete. The Indians are cleverer than us. But they also take money out of the country. Perhaps they have not much confidence in the future. But we must never forget that there are now some black business people who are very successful.'

He sat silent, brooding momentarily, then he snatched suddenly at the mosquitoes which had begun to whine about us. 'I hope you're taking something for malaria,' he said to me in a doctorly way.

'Education is paramount,' he went on. 'That is what Africa has learnt. That is why I have spent money on the education of my children. My one daughter is an accountant; the other an economist. I have a son who is a civil engineer. They have all been educated overseas. Now my younger son — the one who drove us from town — he is studying business management at a Canadian university.'

'And you?' I asked. 'Tell me about your education.'

'You're looking at the product of mission schools and Commonwealth scholarships,' he said. 'Otherwise I might still be herding cattle.'

He was of the Chagga tribe centred around Moshi on the southern slopes of Kilimanjaro, and he had grown up in a peasant community, one which forty years before his birth had fought the Germans and lost. His boyhood during the 1940s and 1950s, however, had coincided with a transition much more complex than that engendered by defeat at the hands of colonial troops.

But for the moment, his mind lingered in the hills of his home near Moshi. 'Kilimanjaro,' he said. 'It really is unspeakably beautiful. Are you going to see it? You are going to Arusha, further west. Then you must go to the Serengeti, to Ngorongoro Crater, to Olduvai. There you will see Tanzania at its very best.'

I steered him back to his own story.

He said: 'I have lived with changes all my life. As a boy, I remember our African soldiers coming home from the war with guitars and cigarettes. We'd never seen these things before. I think that's when the old African culture got its biggest crack. The soldiers also came back with new ideas about freedom and independence. Some of them came back as sergeants. They were as good as whites, wanting what whites had, and wanting the vote. And many of the soldiers had learned skills in the army which immediately elevated them.'

His wife offered another beer, which he accepted, sucking in the rising froth between pursed lips. Only when the liquid had settled did he continue.

'We used to look up to and admire the drivers of trucks. That is what we aspired to. And many of the soldiers became clerks because they had been taught to read and write. These were the new middle class, getting good jobs and earning money. And it was easy enough to see that education was the key.

'But my father had a more personal reason for pushing me into school. His own father had prevented him from going because he saw school as a form of slavery: giving children away to the whites. As a result my father remained illiterate all his life, and he sometimes used to express real anger against my grandfather's superstitious beliefs which had so limited his own horizons.

'The missionaries came to our area only in the late 1930s, and I started going to their school when I was nine years old. I walked about ten miles each way, barefoot. I only got my first shoes when I was nineteen. I finished school at twenty. Then I went to Makerere University in Kampala, and after that to Edinburgh for my postgraduate studies.'

He drank from his beer.

His wife said with mild sarcasm: 'Now that he has told you his life story, perhaps we can talk of other things.'

The doctor laughed pleasantly, looking affectionately at the woman with whom, he told me presently, he had shared more than thirty years of his life. Darkness had seeped imperceptibly into the warm evening.

'It has not been too bad,' the doctor's wife said, 'all those years of marriage. But I suppose you know,' she went on, looking directly at me, 'that most black men have no sense of responsibility. They are leaving women and children all over Africa now.'

The doctor smiled in a knowing way. 'We have this feminist argument all the time,' he said. 'And I always say to her: polygamy is in our culture.'

She made a dismissive sound with her tongue. 'Our elder daughter is twenty-eight years, but not yet married. Why should she marry? Only to be made pregnant, or given a disease, and then left at home with no money?'

'There are many things that need to be understood,' the doctor countered, 'and the most important is that Africa is at a crossroads between the old and the new. Do we go forward to the Western way, if that is forwards, or back to tradition? People talk of a synthesis between the two, but that will take a lot of time.'

'Is all this,' his wife asked, 'to explain why men have no responsibility?'

'Now if we accept that we are at this crossroads, then we have to admit that polygamy was part of the old culture. And it worked reasonably well. There was independence for each wife, and a house of their own.'

'What sort of independence, always being subservient to the man? Never mind all the crossroads talk. Men have no responsibility because they are losing their power.'

'And women are wanting power,' the doctor said.

'Of course,' his wife said. 'Why not?'

'Ultimately women will regret that they have taken too much empowerment.'

'Why?'

'I have seen them regretting it already. All these career women now, most of them divorced. I know they regret it. I am a doctor. A woman has her place.'

His wife laughed in a low musical way. 'But these women threaten the men,' she said. 'And men fear losing power to women. A man wants to be the head of something. But a man is a man. He protects. He chases the thief; he kills the cow. But why should a woman know her place? If she wants to work, let her work. If not, why did you go to all the trouble of educating your daughters?'

The doctor replied: 'But then again there is nothing in their education that stops them from being women.'

His wife laughed again. She slapped the top of her thighs with open hands and stood up. 'Come, my husband, let us see whether your daughters have prepared the food.'

The doctor turned to me. 'Now we will eat, and afterwards my son will drive you to your hotel.'

D ar es Salaam seemed above all to be crammed with a restless and insatiable dynamism. The cause of this dynamism, or at least one of its causes, was not difficult to identify. Urbanisation had descended upon the city in the past few years like an uncontrollable storm. Figures were difficult to confirm, but it seemed that the population had exploded by at least a million since the collapse of the ujamaa (familyhood) villages for which Tanzania's African socialism had become famous, or notorious, in the 1970s. But the villages had broken down in many parts of Tanzania, and the people had come streaming into town.

For kilometres along the main access roads to the city centre, trade was almost exclusively in building materials: cement blocks in heaps, forests of rough-hewn poles, windows and doors in wood or iron, bags of cement protected inside packing-case shops, pyramids of yellow sand outside.

'All this was just bush,' an old man said to me. 'No houses. Look now. The old president, he wanted to make Tanzania like China, with all the people in the villages. But it didn't work. Now there is a new president, and the people are in town. Thousands and thousands.'

Here was a city of survivors from the rigours of experimental socialism in the countryside, all in their varying ways intent upon the new intricacies of staying alive in an urban situation: carrying cardboard, selling a handful of onions or an armful of watches, shouting out the destinations of the ramshackle assortment of what looked to me to be home-made buses which snarled and jostled in the reeking streets.

'Ujamaa made sense when it came to rationalising the supply of social services and collectivising agricultural production. Tanzania was — and still is — a predominantly rural country, and one of the main aims was to get people scattered all over the place to live more compactly in villages.

The advantages when it came to the provision of schools and clinics must be obvious. But the difficulties arose because of the way it was done. Moving people is always a recipe for disaster, especially if they are forced to move. But the ultimate failure was an economic one. The hope was that by pooling resources in the villages, people would be better off, and more efficient. But the problems of supply seemed insurmountable, with seeds and fertilisers often arriving too late for planting. And having built the schools and clinics the problem became how to keep them supplied with books and medicines, as well as trained personnel. There can be no doubt that Nyerere was a man of great vision. Look how he used Swahili to unify the country. But the management of the economy wasn't equal to the ujamaa vision, and the vision failed. Nyerere admitted this when he gave up the presidency in 1985. And people began to drift back to where they had lived before. Yes, and into the towns.'

Such versions, with variations, came from the theorists and intellectuals, while in the streets outside their offices the great clamour of Dar es Salaam, the 'hell-hole of East Africa' according to one expatriate I met there, went on unabated.

At the city's Kariakoo Market, a large modern structure with cantilevered roof set down in a dough of unpaved streets and mud and rotting refuse, the busiest stalls were outside, set up under ragged tarpaulins and sheets of plastic. Within the market building, over-loud music with an eastern flavour screeched from loudspeakers, while on the various floors predominantly Indian vendors displayed their wares: conglomerations of baskets, pots and pans, and large mounds of different-shaded rice, and beans, and small dried fish swarming with flies. Outside, under a tarpaulin, I watched a young man with deft fingers working on the interior pieces of a large portable radio. Others had built elaborate structures out of the running shoes they sold; still others toted ties and shirts and cloves of garlic. A bus jolted through a crater of mud, sending out a stream of brown liquid towards pedestrians who dodged and shouted. On one busy corner stood three Maasai women with large ear-rings, dressed in purple fabric with one shoulder bare, selling their traditional medicines to anyone who would buy. The industriousness of Kariakoo was palpable; no one lolled or loitered; everyone pulled or pushed or lifted or shouted out their wares; others hurried through on missions to purchase; everywhere there was this ceaseless activity, an almost frenzied scurrying to survive.

The downtown skyline bristled with television aerials. My doctor friend told me that Tanzania's first service had been introduced only in 1993, and then by a private company rather than the state.

'They show nothing interesting,' he admitted, 'but if you can afford it, you have to have a set. It's the new diversion. We've probably been shown more cowboy and catch-a-crook movies in the last month than you've seen in your entire life. But it's part of liberalisation. Plenty of private radio stations too, and twenty-four different Swahili newspapers alone. You've seen how they display them on their arms. But televisions carry status as well of course. They're damnably expensive.'

The aerials thrust out from among the washing and grimy parapets of every building, and screens flickered in numerous eating and drinking places all over town.

The streets beneath the aerials seemed to burst with traffic, the pavements with stalls, and pedestrians surged in the narrow spaces between: Africans in tribal dress; men in turbans; others in white smocks reaching down to their thin black calves; Africans in smart Western clothes, the men sauntering in dark-glasses, the women sometimes heavily made up and mincing on high heels. Open book stalls seemed popular, with trestle tables crammed with titles, spines up, and salesmen always willing to coax. Books on Leninism, economics, engineering and business practice, I noticed, and a 35-year-old guidebook to Tanganyika. Some covers had been lost, replaced with hand-written substitutes. A dusty window display in a side street offered blackboard dusters and boxes of chalk, school stationery, including slates, and textbooks in splayed piles. The street sweltered, and sand from the sea lay in a thin layer over broken tar.

Suddenly a shining four-wheel-drive vehicle belonging to a European aid agency skidded on the roadway. A man dressed only in a pair of shorts spun sprawling into the gutter. People shouted out, but generally in amusement, and the truck moved on.

Closer to the sea, the New African Hotel, a multi-storeyed concrete shell, was being rebuilt with the help of a spindly construction crane which seemed to list slightly against the glare of a humid sky. And across the road, the city's big Lutheran church appeared to be crumbling away. The clock in the tower had stopped. The terracotta roof was bare of tiles in some places, black timber ribs exposed, and walls showed grey-green in places with damp and mould. Close around its perimeter, however, cramped stalls sold dark-glasses, baked beans, watches and plastic radios from Hong Kong and Taiwan, no doubt imported via Zanzibar.

'This is my home town. I'll always come back here,' the doctor's son had remarked as he drove me, that first evening, to my hotel. He had told me, in his taciturn way, a little about his life in Canada, the shock of the cold, the snow and ice and short grey days; and the deeper shock of First World aloofness and self-sufficiency. 'I'll stick it out, for my father. But I know that this is where I belong: in Tanzania, and better still in Dar.'

To a pale extent, I could see what he meant. The richness in the aura of the city was undeniable. There was a sense of antiquity here, but not so much in the city itself. Its origins had been in the 1860s as a summer residence for the Sultan of Zanzibar. Afterwards the Germans had developed it as the capital of their East African colony. Not so much in the city itself, therefore, but in its people: the mixing of the Middle East and India with the endless flow of Africa from its own heart, whether in chains or not; the rattle of Swahili; the shape of the mosques and minarets; and the antiquity of ruins up and down the coast which lay as foundations to the character of the modern city. The ruins at Kunduchi were probably the closest.

Palm trees grew on the sand as it descended to meet the water of the harbour channel. Grass grew in patches between the trees; and on the grass in the evenings hundreds of people sat and talked like swarming bees as the short twilight came and went. Ravens scavenged in the filth which the tides had arranged in layers on the beach, contour lines of rotting and regurgitated rubble. The people looked out at the ships moored in the wide harbour, one or two of them appearing to have sunk at their moorings. The people were city dwellers taking the evening air, that ancient air filled with the reek and immediacy of black Africa lurching into an uncertain future, yet touched also with their (the people's) own antiquity.

The colour of the harbour descended to a luminous blue; the palm trees grew out of the sand at angles and thrust black fans of fronds against a white but fading sky; and people talked and laughed together in a hesperian contentment. There was this calming beauty in the evenings here.

'Maktaba,' the taxi driver told me, 'is Swahili for library. The maktaba is on UWT Street, and I shall now take you there.'

As we proceeded, we became wedged in a convoy of big trucks. The machine before us belched out black smoke against which we were obliged to shut our windows, and flecks of oil appeared on the windscreen. Through the fumes I was able to make out two stickers on the rear of the vehicle: the first said 'in God we trust', and the second, 'no hurry in Africa'. But my taxi driver showed none of the patience implicit in either statement. His hand hovered over the hooter, and once he rolled down his window and thrust head and shoulders into the fumes to see if he could find a way past. He could not; his fingers drummed against the wheel.

'These trucks, they are full of food. They are going to Rwanda,' he said. 'But this one in front,' he added with considerable irritation, and also to explain the slowness of our progress, 'it will break down soon. Yangu imeharibika. Can it go one thousand miles to Rwanda?' He gave a derisive snort.

Soon enough, though, we had reached what a board at the gate identified as the national central library. I paid the driver, and for the tip I gave he offered a final Swahili lesson: 'Asante sana. Kwa heri. Now I am saying thank you very much and goodbye.'

My endeavours in the library were, at least to begin with, not as informative. The first obstacle came in the form of a solemn young man whom I encountered immediately upon entering the building. He shook his head when I asked if I could proceed to the reference section. He also shook his head when I asked to speak to a librarian.

'You must speak to me,' he responded quite severely.

I said I was interested in finding out as much as I could about the ruins at Kunduchi.

He looked at me blankly.

I took a map from my bag and opened it on the counter behind which the young man was stationed. I showed him Dar es Salaam; and there was Kunduchi not far to the north on the coast road to Bagamoyo.

'Do you want maps?' he asked.

I shook my head. 'Here at Kunduchi are ruins. I would like to find a book which tells me something about them.'

The young man glanced about him, at something of a loss.

'Please let me see a librarian,' I coaxed. 'Or perhaps you have a guidebook or some encyclopaedias.'

'Encyclopaedias? Are you a member?'

I explained that I was a visitor.

He looked at me with solemn suspicion. He beckoned for my bag which he asked me to open. He peered inside, but gingerly, without touching it. Then with a show of some reluctance, he said: 'You can follow me.'

In this way, I was taken to a large open-plan area, filled with shelving crammed with books, and the chairs and tables between as crowded with at least a hundred schoolchildren, boys and girls in their middle and early teens, all in white shirts. My young man told me to wait at a table, while he disappeared among the shelves.

The schoolchildren turned the pages of encyclopaedias, one volume for a table of five or six. The library was quite silent, except for this slight rustle of pages, and the chirping of birds outside. The library was also gloomy, with none of the fluorescent tubes in the ceiling lit. Perhaps they were under repair: I saw several squares in the ceiling missing, while others had been broken, with a few jagged pieces still in place. The gloom in the library sharply contrasted with the brilliantly sunlit garden outside. Then I saw a bird swoop in through an open window and disappear through one of the holes in the ceiling.

The schoolchildren turned their pages, and my young man returned with a few volumes of an ancient set of encyclopaedias. Dust flew out when I opened one of them. The entry for Dar es Salaam read: 'Originally a small village, it was made a German station by Dr Carl Peters in 1887. It was captured by the British on 4 September 1916. Population about 10 000 Europeans and 50 000 natives.' The entry for East Africa contained no reference to Kunduchi, and the young man had not brought the volume containing entries beginning with KUN.

I closed the book. 'I'm afraid I must insist that I see a librarian,' I said. 'These encyclopaedias are very old.'

The young man viewed me with open hostility now. He turned and walked away, striking the end of one of the shelves with his open hand as he went. I moved briefly among the schoolchildren, who did not raise their eyes to engage mine even for a second. The books on their tables were falling apart, loose pages thrust back, covers adrift and at awkward angles under the opened volumes. On the shelves behind them — and I leaned in among the children to get a closer view — the lettering on the spines of ancient sets had long ago been worn away.

I sat down once more at my table, surveying the sea of bowed heads, the thousands of dusty books in the long shelving, and saw another bird fly into one of the dark holes in the ceiling. I watched for the birds then, and all at once I saw birds everywhere, at least twenty of them sitting on the tops of book shelves and cupboards, flying from point to point, seeming to be far more at home in the library than the schoolchildren were. The silence and the mechanical turning of hundreds of pages had begun to unnerve me. I saw a small bird defecate neatly as it flew.

'My name is Alfred Fuime. I am a librarian. I am afraid we have no maps.'

An older face this time, with laughter inherent in the eyes. Yet he was being firm with me, and in the background I glimpsed a satisfied expression on the face of the young man who had met me at the door.

I said I had been surprised to see these schoolchildren who had come to the library to learn about the value of books being obliged to use encyclopaedias which were broken and at least sixty years old.

Alfred Fuime hesitated. Then he said: 'We depend on donations from the UK. The books that come are second hand. You see, we are poor. The government cannot afford too many books. And we have no maps.'

I explained my quest: not maps but information on the ruins at Kunduchi, or sometimes they were called the Masanani Ruins, not far from Dar es Salaam on the coast road north to Bagamoyo.

'Ruins,' Alfred Fuime said. 'They must be old. I think you must try the museum. I can show you how to get there. It is down at the end of Samora Avenue.'

I agreed to go. But as a favour, before I set off for the museum, I asked Alfred if we could look, more out of curiosity than anything else, in the library catalogue. 'Over there,' I said, pointing to a row of timber cabinets standing against one wall.

He looked at me as at a nuisance he had not quite the heart simply to dismiss. He laughed. 'All right. But I know of no books about ruins.'

We stood in front of the cabinets, confronted by hundreds of separate little drawers, each containing hundreds of separate cards. I suggested we try the subject index. We tried ruins. We tried Masanani and Kunduchi. I stood beside him as his fingers separated the cards, and I could sense him hoping that we would fail so that I would be satisfied and go away. Several times he said that the museum would be a more fruitful place for me to look.

'Now let's try archaeology,' I said.

He did so more with patience than expectation. He felt, I could see, that he had already proved his point. But his searching fingers had exposed a card which said: Archaeology Tanzania, and a number. I wrote down the number on the back of my hand. Then we moved along the cabinets until we had located the drawer in which our number would be found. We pulled it open to its full extent.

Alfred Fuime's face was without expression, yet I thought I detected a new attentiveness in his eyes now. He leaned over the drawer of cards, his fingers poised, and then almost immediately straightened again. 'Look at this,' he said incredulously.

The card he had exposed, one card out of tens of thousands in the catalogue, provided this information: 'Guide to the Ruins at Kunduchi; Hamo Sassoon; Tanzania National Culture and Antiquities Division; 1966.' And another number which I wrote down on my hand.

'See that mark there,' Alfred Fuime said in a low excited voice. 'That means the book is in the basement.'

'What luck,' I said.

But he brushed my remark aside. He moved now as a person in total command, and as a person, I thought, who was beginning to savour the power which he saw was possible over inanimate things like books and cards.

In the basement he made me wait at a table. He spoke with some authority to a fellow librarian. He took hold of my hand and turned it so that the number could be copied on to a piece of paper. But the basement librarian, a small man in rimless spectacles, began to copy down the wrong number. Alfred Fuime snatched away the pen and crossed out the first number I had written on my skin, leaving only the second. Then they disappeared into a narrow alley between impossibly crowded shelves. I heard them talking together in the bowels of the basement.

While I waited, I saw at low windows high up in the wall, some tufts of grass and sunlight, and some ravens boldly pecking at their reflections in the glass. And I looked too at the numbers I had written on my hand, the one crossed through several times in an emphatic and impatient way. The birds and the numbers: these were the intricacies I had discovered in Tanzania's national central library. No wonder its solemn door-keeper had proved so jealous and obdurate a guard.

But the reward was generous beyond my expectations. The reward was Alfred Fuime himself, emerging from the depths of the basement, some cobwebs adhering to his tight-curled hair, a slender book in his hands.

His face had been transfigured. He looked at me with some pride, certainly, and also some satisfaction. But the central expression, even in the stance of his body, seemed to be one suggestive of a crucial discovery of something valuable in himself. He handed me the book as if it was some treasure he had unexpectedly unearthed; and impelled by his triumph I rose to shake his hand.

People told me it was dangerous to go alone to the ruins at Kunduchi, and the warning was repeated by the driver whom I hired to drive me north along the Bagamoyo road.

We set out in the early morning, driving for kilometres past evidence of the building explosion which had come to Dar es Salaam in recent years, and then into a green and well-watered landscape filled with vegetable gardens and palm and banana trees. In the ramshackle village of Kunduchi, my driver stopped first at the local office of the ruling Chama Cha Mapinduzi party, tattered green flag drooping from a pole outside, and then at the police station.

'I am making sure that we are allowed to go to the ruins,' he explained after he had disappeared into the police station for a few minutes. 'The police say it is very dangerous. We will have to take some askaris because of the robbers. The trouble is no job in Tanzania. People see strangers, especially white tourists, and then they make the robberies.'

But when the soldiers came out to join us, they seemed perilously young to face such hazards. And they were unarmed, except that the older one carried a whistle and a truncheon. They wore khaki uniforms and black boots and caps. They smiled with shining white teeth; and they stood to one side, chatting with the driver, as I looked at the ruins.

We had left the car at a hotel which provided a dazzling view of the sea with the sun freshly risen beyond it. Then we had walked past a straggling line of fishermen's shacks, and into ragged-looking coastal bush. Here, the grass had been cut back to reveal the grey-black walls of the ruins, often with weeds sprouting from their tops.

'The coast of Tanzania and some of the offshore islands,' I had read in the book which Alfred Fuime had found for me in the library, 'were inhabited from the 13th century onwards by followers of Islam who built their mosques and tombs in stone. These people are often referred to as the Shirazi ... and (they) established themselves on the Somalia and Kenya coasts and then moved southwards.' Certainly they moved to the major east coast trading centres like Kilwa and Lindi, but also to Kunduchi which the book described as a 'medieval village' which had thrived during the late 15th and early 16th centuries. But this date coincided with the arrival of the Portuguese, and no building took place until the Portuguese were ousted once more in the 18th century. Then the erection, especially of so-called pillar-tombs, had begun again.

The historical and architectural details of the ruins seemed to fade, however, in the light of the simple immediacy of these grey-black walls. The building blocks had been quarried from coral reefs. As the surface of the material had weathered so the swirling patterns in the make-up of the coral were revealed. These patterns showed the imprint of a mass of shells and passageways for small marine creatures which lay just underneath the man-made shaping of the various blocks.

The ruins stood among venerable trees, including a single large baobab which clawed untidily at the sky. The crumbling walls were dappled with sunlight passing through foliage which shuddered in a breeze. Some of the structures still held inscriptions; and glazed porcelain bowls (from China, the book in the library had indicated) had been set into at least one pillar standing guard over a stepped and disintegrating tomb.

Oddly, the place brought to me no thoughts of robbers bursting from the undergrowth, but rather an aura of quiet continuity. I could hear the pleasant voices of the soldiers and the driver droning to one side. I sat on the wall of one of the graves, looking at the ruins as they spread away under the baobab tree, even to a few arches of the mosque still standing and the *kiblah* facing north to Mecca and choked with rambling weeds. Here was an inkling of the continuity of Africa: the interlocking of peoples, the inevitability of change and ruin and moving on. I had noticed a few newer graves in the grass as well, hand-written inscriptions in Swahili and Arabic, also a few dates, the most recent reaching into the 1960s and early seventies. The inevitability of change, the overlaying of life by more life, as in a coral reef, the irrepressible logic of the continuum. Where could it all have begun?

Tanzania offered many things, and it held a clue to such an imponderable as well. So it was in this direction, towards the vast interior and a gorge called Olduvai, that I now turned.

B y the time the bus was ready to leave, there was no longer any space left inside even for standing. The luggage compartments underneath the floor had been stuffed to capacity, while mounds of excess were covered with a tarpaulin and tied to the roof with ropes. I had arrived early, thus securing a window seat not far from the front. I was soon joined by a large woman who, to prevent too much of herself from overflowing into the aisle, sat very close. Then the aisle filled up. Then the woman got into a disagreement with a blue-eyed hitch-hiker over whether the sliding window at which I sat should be opened or closed.

My view through this contested aperture was of more buses preparing for departure, men lashing bicycles and 44-gallon drums and plastic baths on to the roof-racks. A youth had stationed himself on the roof of one bus, named New Generation, perhaps to ensure that things were not stolen before the journey could begin; in another bus the multi-toned hooter was being vigorously tested; and close by someone hit at something behind the rear wheels with a large hammer. In a while I saw New Generation, but now without the youth on the roof, jolt over rough ground towards the street which streamed along one side of the bus-station. Other buses immediately took its place: Living Stone had a badly dented roof, as if it had overturned; One Way looked in slightly better repair, but the name could have inspired little confidence in those passengers wishing to return. Salesmen made hissing noises through their teeth to attract the attention of passengers at the windows above them, then offered their assortment of wares: armfuls of towels, sweets and biscuits, handkerchiefs, nuts, colourful shirts, golfing caps, ties, and wall clocks. And as background to all this stood the grimy buildings and thickets of television aerials of downtown Dar es Salaam.

The morning grew warmer, and the interior of the bus sweltered. I saw generous beads of perspiration develop on the upper lip of the large woman next to me. The blue-eyed hitch-hiker — he was an Englishman having his African adventure, I guessed — half lay against a huge rucksack, his eyes closed. His face looked petulant, and I could see the pale blue veins on his eyelids, as on the lids of fair-haired children. Other backpackers staggered down the crowded aisle, banging people's heads with their bulging packs. Now, newspaper vendors sauntered underneath my window, displaying whole armfuls of newspapers, each masthead carefully displayed. They reminded me of bunches of flowers, like bouquets to the new freedoms which liberalisation and multipartyism had brought to Tanzania. I bought a copy of the *Daily News* to help to pass the time. The picture on the front page was grotesque: it showed a young man being stoned by a grinning mob.

All at once a squat Indian man swung up into the driver's seat and started the engine. The passengers hummed slightly with expectation. But then the man swung down again and disappeared. A mother with hair plaited into long strands sticking out all over her head unhurriedly dandled a screaming child, and someone played a few soothing notes on a mouth organ. Only after fifteen minutes did the driver return and our long journey begin.

But for some time the reek and humidity of the city adhered to the vehicle as it ground up Morogoro Road and through the informal shanty towns beyond. Hard to believe that Tanzania was still essentially a rural country as one looked out over the endless jumble of low roofs coloured in a myriad shades from shiny galvanised to deep coastal rust. But at last the countryside began. And especially after we had turned off at Chalinze on to the main road north did the country spread before us, with the occasional dilapidated village huddled not far from the road, some of them looking deserted now, monuments to the experiment and ultimate failure of ujamaa.

'Brutal force was used,' a professor at the university in Dar es Salaam had told me. I remembered his words as the bus wound north on lonely roads. Brutal force; broken homesteads; humanity being bent to an ideology as more than eleven million Tanzanians shuffled with their belongings into villages which could not be sustained.

'Tanganyika made a relatively easy transition to independence,' the professor had told me. 'There were no major tribal divisions to bedevil post-colonial politics here. And the new class that came to power was educated, not too arrogant, not too numerous, and almost entirely dependent on the West.

'But things soon began to go wrong. The first economic plan drawn up by the World Bank wasn't working. Then the Zanzibar revolution exploded in their faces. By the middle-1960s, the policies of the West were declared a failure and Nyerere embarked on a path of socialism. But it was imposed from the top. That was the trouble: it was imposed, rather than dependent on some dynamic from the population itself. And the imposition didn't work.'

The bus droned on the road. The large woman next to me had placed a scarf over her face to sleep, but in a while it slipped off on to her ample bosom, and her face in repose was open-lipped and peaceful as a child's, and I could see that she was considerably younger than I had at first imagined: no more than twenty-five years. But I remembered the professor's words, brutal force, and looking away at hills I saw fires marked by drifting smoke in the big and empty landscape. The army went into the countryside, forcing people into the villages. The professor had stayed in one of these villages, and the people had spoken to him and he had written down their words.

'A group of party leaders and soldiers forced us to leave our homes. Two weeks before the rains we had to move. During the rains we were building new houses in the ujamaa village instead of planting. So we went hungry that year, because the lorries with the food often did not come. There was a school but no teacher. No medicine in the clinic, not even a bandage. We longed for our old homes.'

Meanwhile, the state steadily took control of every aspect of national life (the professor had said), including state trading corporations which held monopolies, and between 1964 and 1979 the bureaucracy grew from 30 000 to 280 000, and corruption also grew until it gripped the country's throat with vice-like claws. Salaries which were once adequate soon became no longer so. Inflation fuelled corruption. The end came in 1983/84. There was a drought in combination with the collapse of the ujamaa system. Everyone was starving, even the bureaucrats.

'It took me once two weeks to buy a loaf of bread,' the professor told me. 'There was no bread in the shops. There was nothing. I had to borrow half a loaf here, half a loaf there, to keep going, and I was a professor. Then Nyerere said: I have failed; let the World Bank come back in. So here we are with liberalisation of the economy, some fairly crude ideas about multiparty democracy, and enough newspapers to cover all the walls of the buildings of this university.'

I shifted my position in the cramped space available and picked up the *Daily News*. In the foreground of the picture was an open hand. A rock had just been released from it, clearly aimed at the head of a youth sitting dazed among rocks already thrown. In the background a sea of watching faces showed white teeth. More pictures, the caption said, could be found on page three.

But the bus had slowed down. Passengers crammed towards the windows on my side of the bus to see an articulated vehicle which had tumbled down a steep bank, the cab crushed and crumpled like a paper bag. Soon afterwards, the bus stopped in a small village to be immediately surrounded by vendors, their wares displayed on trays carried on their heads. The large woman next to me had awoken and she leaned across my legs to bargain brusquely for a pair of wooden combs and a bunch of grapes. Then the bus rolled forward once more, climbing into hills whose summits had become shrouded in drifting mist.

The young man sitting dazed among the stones 'became the latest victim of mob justice when he allegedly attempted to steal a door mirror from a car'. When detected, he had tried to escape but was caught 100 metres down the road where a mob had 'started enforcing the now standard sentence for suspects in the city: wanton beating with any object in sight'. The pictures on page three showed the victim trying to protect his face while young men kicked at him, and another assailant, both feet high off the ground, jumped at his head. He was, according to the report, about to be doused in fuel and set alight when 'patrol policemen arrived and rescued the battered suspect'.

Other stories concerned several children who had been killed when playing with a hand grenade in north-western Tanzania, close to the Rwandan border; two people killed by lions in the southern part of the country; and another two people who had committed suicide, one by drinking pesticide, after discovering their partners' infidelity. I breathed in the cooler air of the high country through which we travelled and remembered my doctor friend and what he had said concerning Africans being at a crossroads; like all those grinning people, schoolboys and girls among them, who had stood watching as a photographer took pictures of a youth being kicked and stoned.

The woman who shared my seat touched me on the forearm. 'I want to read your newspaper,' she said. I passed it to her; and when she smiled I saw that she had a front tooth missing.

The bus droned on. Mountains rose quite close to the road now. Intermittently, I noticed that the driver turned on his windscreen wipers to clear away a fine mist of rain. People hung and perched in postures of exceptional patience all down the aisle. Outside, once or twice, I saw rice fields glinting water, and people stooped over as they worked; and beyond the fields stood an amphitheatre of mountains with forbidding rock faces and densely wooded ravines between. As such distractions came and went, the bus droned on.

I took out my map to check what progress we had made. We were travelling north towards Moshi and Mount Kilimanjaro. I recalled that this was my doctor friend's home territory; and I fell to thinking about the speed of change which had overtaken so much of inner Africa especially. In a single lifetime from a pre-industrial peasant community, a herder of the family's cattle, to the rigours of a Western-style medical career in a city caught in the confusions and stresses of massive urbanisation. It struck me all at once as astonishing that the mountain country outside the windows of the bus, its upper reaches obscured by a grey-white mist, had been so greedily devoured by a European power in competition with other European powers. What had impelled them in this unseemly scramble? Certainly, the old arguments had been well used: they were searching for raw materials and for expanding markets for their capitalist economies. But beyond this there had been a madness of acquisition for the sake of acquisition, and also a deadly competitiveness. All too often territory which one power vacillated over, another took, regardless of its usefulness or otherwise. It sometimes seemed no more complicated than the hoisting of a flag — but with what profound consequences for the people of an entire continent.

I saw brown fingers with red-painted nails touch my forearm once more. The large young woman smiled. 'Where are we on the map?'

I showed her, pointing out Moshi where we would turn west towards the town of Arusha. 'But I think it will be too cloudy to see Kilimanjaro.'

She ignored my comment, saying instead: 'Show me Rwanda.'

Opening the map more fully, I pointed out Kigali and also the borders of the cramped central African country.

'It is so small,' the woman said, 'for all that trouble. It is not a good place.'

'We are quite far from it,' I remarked.

'Yes. Quite far. How far?'

With my pen as a measure, I estimated 900 kilometres, 'if we could get in an aeroplane and fly straight there'.

She laughed, and I could not be sure what had amused her: whether it was my method of estimating, or the thought of us getting into an aeroplane to fly into the middle of the fragile yet sullen calm which seemed to have followed Rwanda's terrible storm.

I asked my companion where she was going on the bus.

'Home,' she said. 'My home is Moshi.'

I told her I had a friend, a doctor, who came from the Moshi district. 'He tells me the mountains there are very beautiful.'

She nodded, her eyes resting momentarily on my own. 'We will soon be in Moshi.'

'What have you been doing in Dar es Salaam?' I asked.

The question seemed to take her by surprise. She hesitated. 'Business,' she replied at last. Then later, looking demurely at me, she said: 'I went to beg for food.'

Her clothing, and the polish on her nails, belied this statement, but I offered no rejoinder.

Presently, she touched my arm again. 'My name is Flora.'

I introduced myself.

She smiled in her demure way, showing the gap in her teeth. 'You will get off in Moshi?'

I shook my head. 'Arusha.'

'It will be dark when the bus comes to Arusha. You must get off in Moshi. Come to my house,' she added in a soft and persuasive voice.

I thanked her for the invitation. 'But it will not be possible. I must get to Arusha as soon as I can.'

My rejection hardly deterred her — perhaps she was used to such rejections — and she smiled back at me from the steps of the bus as she disembarked at Moshi. I watched her struggle with her suitcase down on to the uneven ground. Then she clambered into a taxi, one of dozens of white vehicles with blue lines painted down the side.

Flora had been right about the approach of darkness. For a few moments, as we travelled on towards Arusha, the clouds parted and the sun hung low, easy to look at in the smoke and dust of the horizon as it set. After that the night came quickly, and our route became dominated by deviations and heavy traffic. Fine dust lay between the teeth and drifted in the beam of headlights, and sometimes the oncoming beams were splintered, splaying out like stars from behind the intricate branches of trees and roadside undergrowth. Flora's demure smile lingered with me in the darkness: she was a young woman making her own way at the crossroads, and certainly making her own meaning out of the idea of begging for food.

The taxi driver in Arusha apologised for the general darkness of the town, saying that not many street lights were in operation at the moment, nor indeed had been for several years.

B ut by day, the town assumed a more detailed character. At night, the streets had offered only glimpses into lit doorways, some passing traffic, and the occasional pool of light in which people loitered; but now the vistas of the central streets showed generally dilapidated buildings, and beyond the central streets the town spread out among plentiful trees, and beyond the trees and the ending of the streets on the northern side the first slopes and then the pale volcanic shape of Mount Meru towered above everything. The proximity of the mountain, which often had snow and ice in the high places, ensured a generous supply of water which sluiced through the town in small rivers. From one of the bridges I used regularly, I often saw women doing their laundry on the rocks, and once a man stripped naked to wash his clothes and then to bathe himself in a nearby pool, while at the same time calling out quite blithely to the people passing on the bridge.

The higher reaches of Meru were often obscured by cloud, but several times while I was there the skies cleared at dusk, and the steep conical summit, forbidding rock scarred vertically from the times, long ago, when the volcano had overflowed, held the sunlight long after the town had clattered towards darkness.

Arusha's pride stood at the top end of town: the International Conference Centre comprising three substantial office blocks named Kilimanjaro, Serengeti and Ngorongoro. The blocks had been set in a triangle, and the space thus enclosed given over to neatly kept gardens. The windows in the raw concrete buildings looked slightly reticent behind externally mounted louvres; skywalks linked the three blocks; lighting was mounted on clusters of red poles; and 'we bring the world to Tanzania' had been painted over the main entrance. Closer to the carpark, a gathering of poles could certainly have accommodated the world's flags, but the poles were empty now, looking like the masts of unused yachts in a small harbour. Originally built as the headquarters of the short-lived East African Community, the centre had survived on 'a myriad of international conferences', as one piece of publicity material put it. Men with briefcases strolled about; and in my hotel in Arusha town I noticed people with name tags and paper-stuffed folders talking earnestly of sustainable development, international co-operation, economic structural adjustment programmes, and other weighty matters. They also talked of such things in the conference centre's restaurant with its piped music and garish back-lit batiks showing African village scenes and African women as beasts of burden.

The offices housed a variety of tour operators and airlines, as well as many aid agencies working in Tanzania and in east and central Africa generally. In one of these offices I experienced a phenomenon I had vaguely sensed in Dar es Salaam on a few occasions, but which would dominate my stay in Arusha.

A pleasant African man started talking to me about the designs of Islam in Africa. He was a Christian — or at least he worked for a Christian organisation — and he said that it was essential to understand the mind of the Islamic fundamentalist.

'There is a fatalism in their thinking which makes them unafraid of suffering or death. Armed with this basic equipment, they hate the West and everything the West stands for. Yes, I believe they do have quite definite designs on Tanzania.'

He told of a recent campaign in which certain Tanzanian Muslims had called for the Bible to be banned and for Christians to be prohibited from eating pork. He also told of a Pentecostal church which had been burned down. But the bladder of the perpetrator became inflamed and swollen so that he could not urinate. Only after he had repented among the congregation of the church building he had destroyed could he urinate again. But the lesson had been learned, and no other churches were burned down.

I asked why Muslims, fundamentalist or otherwise, would have designs on Africa or Tanzania? 'You have to understand that the aim of Islamic fundamentalism is world domination,' my informant replied.

Ironically, in the newspaper the following morning I read an editorial which identified the preaching of religious hatred as one of the greatest threats to Tanzania's enviable record of internal peace and unity. The other major threat was posed by an irresponsible media. 'These elements must find no accommodation among us,' the editorial declared in forthright style. 'They are carriers of a deadly disease that has destroyed nations near and far.'

Not long after I had arrived in Arusha, I met a missionary named Keith, who wore what seemed to be powerful spectacles and sported a prominent moustache. He turned out to be a pleasant and helpful man, an American of Dutch extraction in his late thirties who had spent twelve years in Africa, and he provided some insights of his own.

He told me that his job was in the training of missionaries, especially teams of new missionaries to work in unreached places, 'unreached, that is, by the Christian message'.

Keith pointed out that some areas had been far more popular among missionaries than others. 'In Kenya, for example, with its accommodating climate, there really had been overkill, except of course in the north east, near Somalia, where it is still too dangerous for missionaries to settle.' It was easy enough to be cynical about such things now, he went on, but the idea had definitely been to do missionary work where the missionaries 'wouldn't get sick, or killed, or eaten'. His own mission, for example, had in the early days restricted missionary settlement to above the malaria line at an altitude of around 5 000 feet. But even with these restrictions, three-quarters of Africa had been 'reached'. 'The remaining twenty-five per cent is going to be very difficult, even with all the modern technological aids available, like aircraft, radios, and sophisticated drugs; but that's where we're pointing now,' he explained.

He then reminisced about his own experience for a while. He had worked in the southern Sudan until it became too dangerous, in Kenya at mission headquarters there, and in Tanzania. Even when times had become hard around the middle 1980s, he had liked Tanzania best. 'But in many places now, Africa is returning to itself,' he added.

I asked what this meant.

He gave this explanation: 'During the cold war, many African governments were propped up either by the communists or by the West. But now that the cold war has collapsed, the battlefield has become of little consequence. As a result, Somalia is now run by feudal lords; in parts of the Sudan there is no government administration at all and a great many people have reverted to tribalism; while in remote places in Zaire the old barter system is replacing the use of money. This is Africa returning to itself. As a consequence, Africa has become a power vacuum, and I believe there is in the hearts of Africans a spiritual equivalent. On both counts, Islam is moving in. Yes, as a Christian I am taking this very seriously indeed. Yes, I see this as the new struggle on the African battlefield vacated by the forces of the spent cold war.'

Such thoughts seemed not to have been far from the mind of the Tanzanian cleric who preached the sermon on Sunday. I accompanied Keith and his family to a service held in an

Arusha hall and attended for the most part by expatriates. The preacher spoke of a declaration of war, and the need for Christians to prepare for the fight to come. 'We are entering a time of apocalyptic turmoil,' he said with such conviction that I thought I might be getting a glimpse into what it must have been like in Europe during the Crusades. Without mentioning Islam by name, he quoted Joshua as telling the Israelites that they should now choose who they would serve, whether those gods on the other side of the river, or the one true Lord. As for me and my house, Joshua had said, we will serve the Lord.

Before the sermon began, Keith had leaned towards me while surveying the congregation in the little hall. 'Mostly mission people,' he said in a low voice, 'and a few from the aid agencies. But you need to remember that Arusha is administrative capital for several outfits. So a lot of the people you see here are in administration, pen pushers and so on.'

The comment seemed typical of Keith who reminded me more of a cowboy than a missionary. He certainly wore check shirts and boots, and there was something about his demeanour, and his enthusiasms, which smacked of the frontier. He had a keen appreciation for and knowledge of Africa, especially the lingering wildness of it; he owned what he called 'a rig', a strong-looking four-wheel-drive truck — he showed it to me standing in his garden — in which he crashed about the hinterland, no doubt looking for unreached tribes, but at the same time loving the rugged terrain, the terrible roads, the unconscious grandeur which could suddenly engulf him on the continent's least trod byways.

Yet he was serious about his work, unflinching in his belief that to train teams of missionaries to work in the unreached places of Africa remained his deepest purpose. And these places were not always where one expected to find them. He introduced me one morning to an attractive young American woman who had trained with an international missionary team about to be installed in a predominantly Hindu suburb of Nairobi, Kenya's capital city four hundred kilometres to the north.

I said to him once that I would like to learn more about his experiences and his beliefs. 'Sure,' he had replied. 'We must sit down and talk.'

With Kilimanjaro to the east and some of Africa's best game reserves to the west, Arusha had no shortage of tourists. Some appeared in large parties, many of the men wearing the latest safari fashion, those multi-pocketed and multi-zippered khaki jackets without sleeves, and a few of the women in imitation leopard-skin tights. They drove off in the early morning on their safaris, returning only at dusk. But they also found time to do some shopping in the curio shops and teeming pavement stalls. Most popular wares came in the form of wood or ivory carvings, richly coloured batiks, and Maasai beadwork.

The proliferation of tour operators, and the competition between them, was another manifestation of the extent to which Arusha depended on tourism. Frequently, in the streets, dog-eared cards would be pressed into my hand which advertised safaris and day trips at 'best prices in town'. And men would stand in the doorways of shops adorned with posters of wildlife and snow-covered mountain peaks, attempting to entice passersby inside.

I had been enticed into one of them to organise a safari of my own. Two women sat behind desks in a tiny office behind the plate-glass shop-front. I wanted to go to Olduvai, I said. They told me I would need a driver and a four-by-four. 'The roads are very rough. And you must go to Ngorongoro Crater on the way,' the younger woman said pleasantly. She had a small cheerful face and dark hair. 'My family is from Goa, and I do not know if I am Portuguese or Indian,' she added with a laugh. 'But I know that Arusha is my home town.' The older woman was African, her hair plaited and then wound into coils which rose in arcs all over her head. Even after my business had been concluded, and a date for my safari set, I dawdled in the shop.

While we chatted, a loose grouping of soldiers jogged past in the street outside. I presumed them to be soldiers because of the rifles they carried and the formation they kept, but they wore no uniforms. Suddenly they began singing and lifting their rifles above their heads.

'The militia,' the young woman said. 'But you must be careful. A tourist just the other day was locked up for two days for taking photographs. They also pulled the film out of his camera.'

I asked if the presence of all those soldiers made Arusha a safe place to live. Was there a lot of crime?

'There is some crime,' the older woman with plaited arcs of hair responded.

The younger one said, 'There are drugs. Cocaine. They call it brown sugar. There is a special street here where they sell it. Also bungi. I'm not sure what else is for sale. The cocaine is brought in by men from Somalia.'

'How do you know they're from Somalia?'

'You can see,' she said. 'They're thin, and they've got very curly hair and light skin, a bit like Arabs and Africans mixed.'

The older woman, whose name I had learned was Hawa, now looked directly at me. 'I have adopted a child whose parents are cocaine addicts,' she said.

Adoption was not a common procedure among Africans, she told me, because normally orphans were looked after by the extended family. But not when people found themselves in the disruptive throes of urbanisation. The mother had found her way from the villages to Bujumbura, capital of Burundi, where she started using cocaine. The man, meanwhile, was doing temporary work in Mwanza, the Tanzanian town on the southernmost shore of Lake Victoria.

'So they make the baby,' Hawa said in a matter-of-fact voice. 'Then the man finds more work in Arusha. But by now he too is becoming an addict. The child is so neglected and she nearly dies. So I take pity, I who have already four children and am divorced. But I cannot leave the child to die. The parents tell me they have no interest in her, and they sign the papers. Now I have heard that the father has lost his job. These people will be dying just now,' Hawa added with a dismissive shrug.

I walked in the congested streets of the town. Young men would rush out of ramshackle stalls, calling 'change your money, change your money', or offering some artefact — Maasai spears were popular — for sale. The streets had been scoured of litter; and I remembered that Keith, the American missionary, had explained the reason: 'Everything gets recycled several times. What people can't eat, wear or sell, they burn as fuel. There's very little waste in the towns and villages in Tanzania.' I passed the entrance to the YMCA, where a poster advertised a programme for Arusha's street children, proclaiming that hundreds of children were living in the streets, even in Arusha, where they were subject to all the dangers of lawlessness, alcoholism, drug abuse and AIDS.

Now a strange figure on tall stilts marched past, taking long and purposeful strides. The figure was dressed in a white tunic and long red trousers; and a mask in the form of a lion's face stared straight ahead. People paid little attention, except a beggar sitting against one wall, his artificial leg propped up beside him, who rattled his tin after the figure as it strode diagonally, and with little regard for the traffic, across a busy street.

I went into a bookshop, finding works by Dale Carnegie and Norman Vincent Peale among such titles as *Third World Options, Towards Ujamaa, The African Cause,* and *China's Rural Economic Reform.* Two books in particular detained me. The first, entitled *The Rise of Babylon,* depicted Saddam Hussein as a man seeking to control the world, with the symbol of this power being the secret rebuilding of 'the mightiest and wickedest city of the ancient world'. Startling photographs, the back cover promised. The second, *Shrine of Tears,* was a novel by 'a leading East African playwright' which told the story of 'a young African generation searching for assurance for the future in the cultural rubble of their past and present'.

Outside the shop, I discovered a thin youth, hardly more than a boy, dressed in a piece of red fabric knotted at one shoulder in the style of the Maasai, and wearing plastic sandals on his feet. He held a stick in his hands and gazed with a sort of steadfastness of attention at the books displayed in the window.

Then I saw the figure on stilts again. It seemed to lean forward slightly to cope with the inordinate length of its strides. It seemed other-worldly and slightly unnerving in a street crammed with curios and exhaust fumes.

Later, on my way back to my hotel in the late afternoon, I heard the beating of drums behind a hedge. I found a way through, paid a small fee, and discovered a performance of sorts. The audience sat on a sloping grassy bank interspersed with trees which cast long shadows in the slanting rays of the sun. An open space at the bottom of the bank served as stage, and the performers changed costume behind a long piece of fabric stretched between two children's swings. In front of the fabric a group of musicians played an assortment of animal-skin drums and a marimba with calabash resonators. Another player hit sharp tinny notes from a dustbin lid, while from time to time young women emerged from behind the fabric to dance, their bare feet raising puffs of dust sometimes.

The faces of the performers grinned and grimaced with a definite sense of exhibition. There were attempts at a certain sauciness which sat awkwardly on the girls with their big breasts and strong thighs and bare feet stamping and sliding in the fine sand at the bottom of the bank. The attempts at humour appeared to be more successful, especially when one of the jesters, a man dressed in grass skirts, kept falling over. The audience laughed appreciatively. I wondered if this was part of the cultural rubble I had read about in the bookshop.

The dancing grew wilder as the tempo of the powerful beating of the largest drum increased, the bass sounds reverberating out to mingle with the human voices of the performers, male and female, and with birds calling in the last of the sunlight. The frenzy seemed to mount, and at its height, sustained by vibrating hands on the vellum of the drums, the dancing changed as the young women took up imaginary hoes, and stooped forward in exaggerated gestures as they tilled the earth. I remembered, then, flying over some or other part of Africa and looking down at the marks of such tilling which went on for hundreds of kilometres, all the corners and hillsides between rock and stream covered in this ribbed patchwork.

Suddenly the red and white figure on stilts stalked between the dancers on the stage and up the bank where the audience sat. A few of the people looked up at the lion's face as it passed. But he was on business of his own, picking his way between the watchers and disappearing into the trees and shadows beyond.

Now on to the stage had been carried a large box marked danger. One of the men in a grass skirt and beads about his neck removed the lid. He pretended to walk away, and then approached the box again, this time with exaggerated caution. He slid a hand into the box, withdrawing it like lightning. The audience buzzed with anticipation as they saw the pale and writhing underbelly of something in the box. After protracted displays of timidity, the man simply thrust an entire arm into the box and withdrew a writhing python. He held it just behind the head, and the snake's fat body coiled about his stomach and legs.

The man pretended to wrestle with the snake. He wrestled it to the ground. He sat in the sand, his legs stretched out before him, and thrust the snake's head several times into his mouth. He lay down with the snake, almost in a coital position with the snake between his legs, and the crowd cheered and whistled.

Then he let go. The snake writhed rapidly away, striking repeatedly at the source of its torment. It lay still in an untidy coil. The man in the grass skirt followed; he began to taunt. In response, the snake reared up and struck powerfully, its small head darting forward again and again, but the man kept himself just out of reach.

He called for a volunteer from the audience. A youth with a pale skin and curly hair came forward. The man held him by the elbow and presented his forearm as a target for the snake. The naked forearm of the Somali youth was thrust in gradual increments closer to the head of the enraged snake. The tension became palpable. Then the snake struck. The crowd screamed.

The crowd rushed forward to see, and the volunteer was paraded, blood dripping from his forearm. His face passed quite close to where I stood: dark-eyed, smiling, the expression about his mouth suggesting some pride. He raised his arm for all to see and the blood dripped once or twice on to his shirt.

The man in the grass skirt had picked some blades of broad grass not far from the stage. He sucked at the wound, spitting out a stream of blood, and placed the leaves as a dressing across it.

Then he picked up the snake by its head and swung it around his neck. He bowed and the audience clapped. Their feet had raised fine dust which mingled with the approaching dark, even though the gaunt summit of Mount Meru still stood in a pale yellow warmth of departing sunlight.

The man in the grass skirt had dropped the snake quite carelessly back into the box, pushing one of its coils in with his bare foot, and repositioning the lid. The blades of grass had stemmed the flow of blood, and the show was over for that day.

'I grew up thirty minutes from Manhattan,' Keith the missionary told me. 'Greater New York. New Jersey, in fact. Out in the suburbs. And part of being Dutch in New Jersey was the church. Christian Reformed. Around ninety per cent of the people in the CRC were of Dutch stock, and we were pretty much missions orientated. We had a big mission in Nigeria, for example, and others in the Far East and South America. So I did grow up hearing about missions.

'But when I went to college I got away from the Lord. I got myself in quite a lot of trouble with drinking and drugging, and with women. But when I went home again, I found nothing had changed, and I slipped back into a routine of going to church.

'I had graduated with a business administration degree, and until I was twenty-five I was very business orientated. I managed some sports stores for a while, then I became a headhunter, looking for top quality personnel. But I got tired of dressing up in business suits every morning. So I moved into asphalting, maintaining the private roads and carparks of big companies, painting the lines and signs on the tarmac, putting in speed bumps, general cleaning and maintenance, and even changing the directors' personalised name-boards in their private bays. There was money in this, and I was going along very nicely...

'Then one day in church, a man who had been a missionary in Southern Sudan told some missionary stories. Then he said: the hardest thing about becoming a missionary is making that first phone call. Whatever I did, I couldn't get this out of my mind. So on the Tuesday I made the phone call, and twelve months later I was in Africa.

'When I went to the mission for my first appointment, I can remember, I was bearded and quite long-haired, and I wore a pin-striped suit from my headhunting days. But I must have done OK, because a man said: where do you want to go? I replied I would go where there was the greatest need. They said that would be in Southern Sudan. But before I got there, they changed their mind. The greatest need was in Nairobi where they needed a decent finance manager. But in the end I got to Southern Sudan.

'I worked in Sudan for a short while only. We kept moving away from the advancing rebels, ending up in Juba. There I got an urgent radio message to phone home. I thought something had happened to my family. But the mission wanted me in New York. They said it was the area of greatest need. So I settled down in New York to restructure the mission's accounting system.

'In 1986 I got married. My wife — we had first met in the Sudan — had done a masters in community health. We wanted to start community health evangelism. So when my stint in New York was over, we chose the Tanzanian islands in Lake Victoria where not much missionary work had been attempted before. All our work was done with boats to the islands we could see from our house.

'But then the mission's central finances were self-destructing again, and I was called back to Nairobi. I went on condition that this would be the last time I was taken out of the field to repair administrative structures. They accepted this, but then asked me to take over their outreach missionary training programme.

'My wife and I decided to do it. It was exactly where we were at: simple living, simple Christianity, living among people rather than preaching to them in the old missionary sense. But I gave head office an ultimatum: they must base the training programme in Tanzania.

'So here we are, doing missionary training on a practical level. The new missionary is a part of a team, but he or she lives with a family in the community where the team will work. The motto is: observe don't judge. Try to understand the culture; bond with the local people. The witness is not so much what you do and say but what you are: you are being a Christian, being like Christ. The accent is on building relationships rather than learning a language to preach in. The emphasis on the former makes the latter more possible. Never before has there been so much good literature that is relevant to this bonding approach. Then once a week, the individual missionaries get together with the team, to pray, to worship, to sing, and of course also to study God's word, seeking His direction.

'In a way this new approach is a return to basics. This is what it must have been like a hundred years ago when missionaries were placed in the field and simply had to rough it. There was really no way out. As time went on, the approach became a lot softer. More amenities were provided in the field to encourage people to go to primitive places.

'At first we thought our new approach would frighten people off, but the contrary has proved true, and we have more applicants than we can handle. People are wanting the rougher, more basic experience. They don't want Coca-Cola machines in the middle of Africa.

'There are very real dangers, though, for all missionaries, and especially those who attempt to bond with the communities they hope to serve. I am thinking about spiritual warfare situations. But the team approach is giving individual missionaries much more confidence. We try to include in the team someone with medical experience, someone familiar with mechanical matters; Bible school graduates add doctrinal depth, and we have found it very important to include a musician.

'You are asking about spiritual warfare. I thought you would. Let me start my reply like this. Most missionaries get together once a year or so for conventions. I've been to plenty of these. But it's after the public sessions have ended, it's over coffee in the evenings, that the real stories begin to come out. Stories about demons, the casting out of evil spirits, confronting the forces of darkness at work in the people. In Africa, I'm sure you know, the spirit world is very real.

'It is the combating of these forces of darkness that constitute the warfare. How? You visit the brothels, the bars, the witchdoctors, not so much as missionaries but as friends. You can then pray for them by name. Also, by making these potentially threatening people your friends you reduce their threat, but at the same time it is essential that you keep yourself holy. But it's not kids' stuff; you have to realise what you're getting into. Then it's all a matter of prayer and more prayer.

'Let me give you an example. When we were working on the islands, we came to one island which had two villages. In the first village we started a church and the people were very receptive. But nothing we did in the second village inspired any interest. We thought that the time was not yet right, and we left it. Then one day we received an urgent message.

'The primary schoolchildren in the second village had become demon-possessed. They were cutting themselves with strips of roofing iron and trying to drown themselves in the lake. We took some fellow missionaries and went to investigate.

'We found that the headmaster of the village school had been caught in some act of immorality. When the villagers tried to oust him, some Muslims came from the mainland and put a curse on the village, causing the children to self-destruct. There were eight-year-old girls who were demon-possessed. One child had a man's voice speaking in Arabic and English, languages rarely heard on the islands. The voice coming out of the child kept mocking us, saying you can cast a few of us out, but we'll simply return. We heard that two thousand four hundred demons had been brought from Medina.

'I wish I could tell you that the story had a happy ending. The child with the man's voice attacked one of the missionaries, breaking his spectacles. Even today, there's an evil cloud hanging over that village.

'If I told this story to some people in the mission, they wouldn't believe it. Some of the older missionaries tended to ignore such things. But our new missionaries confront it all the time. We're trying to be more open and, in the training, to offer coping advice. The answer is prayer. You need to bathe the whole affected place in prayer.

'We see very clearly in Africa that there are forces of light and opposing forces of darkness. There are actual geographical principalities of darkness where, because God is not dominant, evil is. Africans appear to live their lives in fear of the spirit world, of fickle gods and vengeful demons.

'You want to know what makes the struggle to spread Christianity different from the struggle to spread Islam. The answer is based on this premise: that the Bible is infallible. In the Bible it says there is only one way to the truth, through the death and resurrection of Jesus Christ. There is a way through every culture that Christianity can gain access, and that way is via the idea of sacrifice. Sacrifice is common to all cultures and religions. It is a basic human principle, and of course it lies at the heart of the Christian message.'

The headlights of the four-wheel-drive flooded the road for a short distance ahead, and sometimes picked out the red-shining eyes of wild animals not far from the verges. My driver was a young man named Salum Athuman whose pleasant face with trimmed beard and moustache I could make out in the glow from the dashboard. We drove in silence. As light came, at first in a vague outline of hills, and then with that colourless illumination of early dawn, I felt that I was being released from the clamour of the life of a restless continent and that we were, for a time at any rate, driving into silence.

Yet the life continued all around us. We were driving in the Great Rift Valley and the country had become littered with baobabs and with cattle already on the move. Schoolchildren straggled along the road, heading (said Salum) towards a town named Mto wa Mbu where in a while we stopped for breakfast. The market was still empty, with hessian awnings over many of the stalls hanging in shreds, and the dust of the previous day settled in a cool dry sheen. We went into a half-dark shop to buy bottled water. Then we drove in narrow streets to a guest-house of sorts. A woman was sweeping the veranda, and chickens scratched in the sand and bottle tops beyond. We sat sipping cups of sweet tea and eating an unleavened bread called chipati. The steep western wall of the Rift Valley showed dark beyond the low mud houses of Mto wa Mbu.

Across the street, two Maasai men in costumes knotted at one shoulder, their thin sinewed calves protruding from the bottom, stood in conversation with a shopkeeper. Salum offered this possibility. 'Maybe the Maasai have come to buy a cow. They have stayed in the village overnight. Now they are buying something from that shop for their journey. No, they cannot live in this village. They live with their cattle,' he added, waving his hand vaguely in the direction of the country, littered with baobab trees, through which we had just driven.

The scene seemed so elemental, almost biblical: this primitive village, two nomads passing through with their covered heads and sticks, the unhurried transaction while chickens scratched and roosters crowed in the early morning, and goats raised dust at an intersection further down the street. But I could also hear a radio in the guest-house, and a replication of what sounded like a newsreader's voice coming from radios near and far across the village. I asked Salum if anything interesting was being said. He shrugged his shoulders. 'They are talking about more refugees from Rwanda.'

We drove on through an overcast morning, climbing out of the valley through a forest of baobabs and getting to the rolling high country beyond. Fields of yellow maize stalks stretched away. Women carried firewood tied to their backs like rucksacks. Occasional vehicles churned through thick sand and over slabs and broken ledges of rock in the road. Red dust lay on the trees and houses and grass tufts by the roadside. But the country went still higher.

We climbed into the misty bottom edges of the clouds on a tortuously turning road. Lichen hung in generous beards from the branches of huge trees which stood ghostlike in the mist. A large bird flapped across our path: Salum said it was an Augur Buzzard, and showed me a picture later in a much-thumbed bird book which he pulled from beneath the seat of the four-wheel-drive. Meanwhile, we had come to the summit of something, and we began to catch glimpses down into a sunlit valley beyond.

'This is Ngorongoro crater,' Salum said, 'which is twenty-five kilometres across.'

On a stony track we drove down into it. The track clung to the steep sides, descending towards hot and dusty plains dotted with what I saw, as we got closer, to be thousands of animals in herds. The sun blazed into the crater, and I could see the animals raising dust as they turned or ran. We drove down among the antelope and zebra, and herds of buffalo staring at us from beneath their heavy horns, and hundreds of wildebeest up to their bellies in grass, and a pink cloud of flamingos settled on the shallows of the soda lake. But I saw too that some of the animals were cattle, herded by thin Maasai boys with their knotted cloaks and spears. They mingled with the game, forming part of the predators' prey, as they had always done.

The morning grew hot as we drove on towards Olduvai, Salum looking quite forbidding in his dark-glasses and the white teeth of his ready smile. Once out of the crater on the western side, the country quickly became arid, and at various points across the huge view I saw raised dust marking the passage of slowly driven cattle.

'This is Maasai's country,' Salum explained.

At Olduvai I listened to a hot wind blowing through thorn trees which screeched, and to a rattling sheet in the iron roof of the site museum. The gorge had been scoured out across the plain, revealing in its sides the clear gradations of nearly two million years of fossil-laden sediment built on to a lava base. From the museum and viewing site, the gorge plunged away with strange configurations of uneroded earth jutting from the general depression. A guide in a red beret had immediately come to my assistance, and he now began to recite the ages and contents of the various beds of sediments which had been laid down.

A few old Maasai hovered about, requesting with their gestures that I take their photographs. At a small shop, where I noticed Salum had bought a cool drink, T-shirts shouted the message: Olduvai, cradle of mankind. The guide in the red beret raised his voice when he thought my attention had begun to flag. Salum stood looking out over the gorge through his dark-glasses.

I tried to imagine the old silence of the place, the ancient plains, the naked creatures gradually becoming clothed, the silence broken only then by their slow manufacture of another stone tool. Very possibly, this lonely place was one of the cradles of mankind. I thought of the clamour of the harbour at Dar es Salaam, and the birds in the library, and the two protecting soldiers talking at the ruins, and the long bus journey to the mountains, and the man in a grass skirt wrestling the python, knowing that all this may have begun at Olduvai. Here in the museum was a replica of the skull of Zinjanthropus, discovered by Mary Leakey, and dated at one and three-quarter million years.

We drove down to the place in the gorge where she had found it. Beds of brown and yellow sediment glared hotly about us. The guide in the red beret recited his facts. In relatively recent times, certainly long after all these relic-rich sediments had been laid down, the surface of the earth had buckled once more and the water from the rainy season had been forced to flow to a new drainage point: it had done so by carving out this rent in the plain. The wind blew over the top of it now, and I suddenly realised that the clamour of the present had at last receded.

We had got back, for a few moments, to the silent places before the chaos of now, before Islam and Christianity had occurred, and long before the cold-war battlefield had turned to vacuum underneath our feet. We were, in the heat and silence of Olduvai, at one of the portals to those primeval times when the struggle for the continuing thread of our collective life was contest and triumph enough.

9

A Street Called Harambee

Why is it that the unitary system of government that our Founding Fathers bequeathed to us has suddenly become unpalatable? Would the partitioning of Kenya into tribal states... be the solution to endemic corruption... and (the) relentless impoverishment of Kenyans?

— *Finance,* a fortnightly journal published in Nairobi, October 1994.

B road was the way which they called Harambee, with its tree-shaded pavements and gatherings of important buildings along either side. It ran from west to east through Nairobi's city centre, beginning at the Uhuru Highway and ending at Moi Avenue in a welter of commercial enterprises like John & Joe's Fast Foods, Eros Dispensing Chemist, Walk-In Bookshop and Sunbeam Supermarket. But starting at the Uhuru Highway end, Harambee Avenue offered an impressive glimpse of Kenyan power: the Parliament buildings themselves; the office of the president; Kenyatta International Conference Centre; the ministries of foreign affairs and finance and education, police headquarters, and a number of lesser government agencies mingling with the head offices of prominent finance houses.

Traffic jammed the street, and the wide pavements bore streams of pedestrians about their business: plentiful men in suits carrying briefcases; fashionable women; slower-moving youths with alert eyes and multicoloured footwear; some tall Somali beggars in their robes; a middle-aged cripple with tiny twisted legs jutting from beneath his body; and newspaper vendors at strategic points, surrounded by heaps of newspapers and magazines spread out in rows on the pavements.

One cover in particular claimed the attention: black with red trim and a single word emblazoned in white italics: *Majimbo*. 'From harambee to majimbo, that's the story of the politics of independent Kenya,' someone told me as my stay in East Africa's most successful country lengthened.

The city had a modern feel. Buildings soared above the streets to provide head offices to hundreds of organisations active on the continent; while two airports provided scores of flights a day to almost any destination, both local and abroad. Many of the shops were of contemporary design and seemed well stocked; and the telephones, as well as water and electricity supplies, were reliable. 'Black Africa's only city that really works,' old settlers said with a mixture of relief, and also with a grudging respect which they invariably tempered by acknowledging their own part in this success.

The town bore some reminders of its colonial past, not least Karen Blixen's house which had been carefully preserved. During the time of this famous writer's sojourn in Kenya, the house had been in the countryside to the west of Nairobi; now it nestled on the outskirts of one of the city's most opulent suburbs. Another writer who came strongly to mind as I roamed the busy streets was Shiva Naipaul, author of a book on East Africa entitled *North of South*. He had stayed in the New Stanley Hotel, a solid enough pre-independence structure, at the beginning and end of his travels. He had also experienced, unpleasantly, the shoeshine facilities on Kenyatta Avenue, and the open-air pavement terrace outside the front of the hotel.

These facilities still survived, although at least sixteen years had elapsed since Naipaul's visit. Of course, the shoeshine men offered no service to footwear made of canvas and rubber and plastic, as much more footwear now was made, including my own. Nevertheless, one of the men learned to recognise me, admiring my rapidly deteriorating casuals each time I passed, and offering to buy them from me at a price he always invited me to name. 'Should I go barefoot?' became my stock response, which raised some mirth among the company loitering on the pavement.

The New Stanley's open-air eating and meeting place had probably changed even less. Where Naipaul noted that 'a thorn tree, rising centrally from the terrace, threw a dappled green shade across the metal tables' now a giant grew, its pale branches reaching at least six storeys up the façade of the famous hotel. The tables and umbrellas were still of metal, and the patrons seemed quite similar. The European and American safari seekers had been joined by tables full of excited Japanese seeming over-endowed with video cameras and thick-lensed spectacles. The street beyond presented a churning stream of black faces, not many of them finding their way on to the terrace. I did notice a grey-bearded African listening sagely to the utterances of a group of philanthropic-looking white women. No American pot-smokers shared my table, as they had shared Naipaul's; but I caught a glimpse of a more brutal American reality in Africa. A gangling young blonde at a nearby table wore a T-shirt which bore the slogan: I got stoned at the University of Mogadishu, Class of '93; and the drawing of a soldier with rocks flying towards his helmet.

But beneath these Western preoccupations, and some signs of opulence, a certain disgruntlement pervaded Nairobi. Individuals might laugh uproariously, as they frequently did, yet en masse the city's face was morose. Had it to do with the remains of the settler regime, even its architecture, as if this stood as a constant reminder of the depth (and, some would argue, the cause) of the plight of ordinary Kenyans? Yet what was the extent of their plight? It hardly mattered that they were better off than their counterparts in any sub-equatorial African country except South Africa. What mattered much more was that they were less well off than they had been. Nairobi still possessed some of the worst slums in sub-equatorial Africa. And while I was there, a television news item showed a tall city building being evacuated after an organisation calling itself The Oppressed had told police they had planted a bomb there.

Perhaps Kenyans were looking for a scapegoat for their misfortunes now. Many certainly blamed their colonial past; others attacked the economic structural adjustment programmes being imposed by the World Bank in exchange for loans; others looked closer to home and blamed the current political leaders, blamed corruption, blamed more than thirty years of single-party rule.

Nairobi resonated still with Jomo Kenyatta, Kenya's freedom fighter turned president who had died not long after Shiva Naipaul had sat under the thorn tree outside the New Stanley Hotel. Kenyatta Avenue and the Kenyatta International Conference Centre I had already encountered. I also discovered the Kenyatta National Hospital, the Kenyatta University, and the Jomo Kenyatta International Airport. Next door to parliament, the gardens of which were graced with a statue of Kenyatta, stood Kenyatta's burial place, a mausoleum of sorts with what looked like a glass roof. The entrance had been marked by twenty national flags on twenty poles, and guarded night and day by bronze lions and armed soldiers in red uniforms. Not far away, on a broad square behind the Kenyatta International Conference Centre, another statue depicted Kenyatta seated on a tall plinth, his hands on a mace, while he gazed towards his own tomb. The statue was surrounded by a ceramic-lined pond with fountains; but the fountains were defunct, and some of the coloured lights which had illumined them lay dislodged from their mountings and broken in shallow water.

Yet this self-aggrandisement and leader-aggrandisement of the earlier years of independence seemed strangely anachronistic already. In the first flushes of Uhuru, nations had become synonymous with their leaders, and life presidents and one-party states synonymous with freedom from the fetters of colonialism. Now, though, the pendulum had swung quite wildly in the opposite direction.

'For one thousand American dollars,' my friend Wilfred told me once in his mocking way, 'I would go to South Africa and buy a rifle with the telescope on top and come back here and make a few assassinations.' He looked at me with his bloodshot eyes. 'Just give me the American dollars.'

Yet beneath the bravado of anarchy, of bomb threats which turned out to be hoaxes, there seemed to be a yearning for a leadership which would not listen to the Western banks, would not prevaricate, would not repeatedly fail the people in their growing economic need. Under the magnification of such yearning the unity of Kenya seemed precarious. Like many other independent African states, Kenya had been as haphazardly pasted together as the old colonial dependency which preceded it. No wonder the cracks were showing now, yet they appeared to have been revealed as much by internal waste and corruption as by the callous concerns of the demon called neo-colonialism.

Build Kenya — don't bribe, said stickers at the airports, and sometimes attached to walls in Nairobi itself. On one of these walls, indeed on the modest façade of a colonial-style building erected in 1913 and serving as city offices until superseded by the tower block built directly behind it now, had also been affixed a coat of arms. Rampant lions held upright an African shield and crossed spears; and the motto beneath was expressed in a single word: Harambee.

A friend of mine who had spent some time in Nairobi suggested that I make contact with Wilfred, a man of indeterminate profession, 'a bit of a reprobate, in fact, but a really nice guy', who knew the city backwards and would prove to be an excellent guide. I therefore wrote to Wilfred, and he replied that I should make contact with him when I arrived. 'Unfortunately, I am not well off and have not a phone. But here is a map for you to come and see me in my humble abode which you will see when you get here is made from the offcuts of wooden planks.'

The map took me to the northern outskirts of Nairobi, and then walking down among banana groves to a house built of creosoted timber. The gutter along the front had been tied on with rags and pieces of electrical flex, but the roof seemed in reasonable repair, and the windows and front door freshly painted a light turquoise.

Wilfred greeted me with two young sons hanging shyly on to his legs. 'Karibu ni Kenya,' he said with a slow smile.

He had high cheekbones and a sloping forehead from which his greying hair had begun to recede, and his small eyes were bloodshot, although he did not strike me as being a man who drank habitually. We sat in his lounge while the television set droned in one corner. He asked after our mutual friend while we drank tea brought in on a tray by a pleasant-looking woman in her bare feet. 'My wife,' he explained, while he dandled his sons who still clung to his legs. From the start, his demeanour was a strange combination of reserve and ease. He was perfectly willing to assist me in any way possible, he said. Yet another part of him seemed detached, always slightly guarded and watchful, even after I had spent a considerable amount of time with him over several days.

Our conversations would often take strange turnings when it came to his personal life, and such exchanges were always conducted with his expression close to good-humoured mockery, as if he enjoyed saying things more for effect than for accuracy. He told me, for example, that he had been an avid reader of the novels of Wilbur Smith, but that he no longer had time to read.

'I am filled with the worries of making ends meet. Look at my hair. It is already grey. I am only thirty-six. Not old. But my worries are very great.'

On another occasion, I asked about his parents. Did he have any brothers and sisters?

'My brother is a lecturer in Norway.'

'What does he lecture?'

Wilfred shrugged his shoulders. 'That's his business,' he said. 'And anyway we are no longer friends.'

'Why not?'

'I asked him to help me to get to Norway but he did nothing about it.'

'What would you have done in Norway?'

He looked at me with his bloodshot eyes. 'Anything would be better than Nairobi.'

I asked him what he did for a living.

He parried the question. 'Because I am poor you should know that I do not work for the government.'

Wilfred had a 1960s limousine with big tail fins. The vehicle puffed out white smoke; and the front passenger door could be opened only from the outside. Nevertheless this low-slung chariot served admirably in my exploration of the city. Wilfred's engagements during the days were erratic; between them, and with some remote amusement of his own, he volunteered to become my driver and guide.

It drizzled on the first day we had agreed to meet. Nevertheless he insisted on taking me to a high point along Cathedral Road for a panoramic view of Nairobi's skyline. We stood in the damp air while he pointed out the landmarks. In the foreground lay Uhuru Park, built by the youth service and the army in fourteen days. The sloping ground at our feet had been cut into tiers, on many of which the grass covering had turned brown and thin during the dry season.

'This is where the people sit when they are addressed by the president,' Wilfred said, and then added in a vaguely amused way: 'And for no extra charge you can come here at night — it is best to come alone — and they will hit you and take your money.'

I asked if he came to listen to the president.

'Yes, of course,' he replied. 'I want them to see that I am a loyal Kenyan.'

Beyond the trees and ponds of the park, the tall buildings of Nairobi's heart jutted into the soft grey sky. It was obvious that many had been recently built, and the presence of several construction cranes testified to the city's continuing development.

'You see the tall round one? That is the Kenyatta International Conference Centre. I will take you there. Right to the top.'

So we drove down into wet and congested streets, grinding along Harambee Avenue in Wilfred's limousine with its big tail fins and emissions of white smoke, and then turning into a special parking area. Wilfred spoke to the attendant in swift Swahili. The attendant stooped to peer in at me for a second, then allowed us to pass. 'I have told him you are an important man who will from next week be driving in big black motor cars with small flags in front,' Wilfred explained, and then laughed at his own effrontery.

The main foyer of the Kenyatta Centre had been fashioned out of raw concrete, with ceramic water features near the stairwells, and louvred timber ceilings. People hurried through, on their way to either a Dubai Sale or Chinese Commodity Fair being held in the various conference facilities. We tried the Dubai Sale, and found ourselves in a market-place filled with cheap plastic toys, television sets, huge portable radios, ornate headboards, an offering of glassware and pots from Pakistan Good Luck Enterprises, and, among extensive displays of clothing, a heap of Martin Luther King T-shirts with 'I have a dream' printed under his silk-screened image. High up on one wall, the obligatory portrait of President Daniel arap Moi was largely obscured by an array of twenty-four loudspeakers all aimed at the crowds milling between the stalls on the expanse of floor beneath.

Wilfred had picked up a T-shirt and held it against his shoulders. 'I also have a dream,' he said in his slightly mocking way. 'But it is not about civil rights. It is about lots of money.'

We went up in a lift to the 28th floor and then climbed flights of narrow stairs to the 30th. From here we could look out to the edges of the city where the open country began, still dull yellow at the end of the dry season and rolling away.

Closer at hand the buildings of central Nairobi thrust up like a gathering of stalks about us. A brisk breeze blew into our faces as we strolled on the roof of the tallest stalk of all.

'It is now thirty years since independence. I was a small boy then,' Wilfred observed, looking down, 'and I was told that with the hated white man no longer in charge we would all have freedom and money. But what has been achieved?'

'A lot of this,' I suggested, indicating the view.

'Yes, but this is only for the rich. For the poor? I am among the poor. Things get worse. The rich are all in government, or holding hands with the government. The civil servants and the middle class,' he said with a slight curl of his upper lip. 'All the bribes and special deals. I can tell you stories. But I have heard the new talk now: they are a self-destructive class, corrupt and finished. Maybe Kenya will have a revolution.'

He glanced at me with a slightly impudent expression, to see how I took this possibility. Then he added: 'But more than likely we will have majimbo, and we will all go back to our tribes and paint our faces.'

He turned and looked at me then, his bloodshot eyes holding mine for a moment. 'I was too young, but people have told me about the hope. Mau Mau was like a revolution against the British. Kenyatta was the leader. He went to Lancaster House to talk independence. But look at it now. The economy has gone down. And most people are not straight any more, including myself.'

And then, in his mocking way, he had said that for US$1000 he would be willing to buy a rifle in South Africa and carry out a few assassinations.

'But come,' he said with a short laugh. 'I must take you to the museum. I want to show the pictures of Mau Mau and also the guns they made.'

On the way down in the lift, he said: 'I could go to jail for twenty years for talking to you like this. Or they would take me on to the roof and push me off,' he went on, allowing his imagination some rein, 'and then the poor — you know, people like me — would have to clean up. They would have to scrape my brains off the pavement with a spade.'

I smiled at him in the dim lighting of the lift, and he considered me for a few seconds, as the lift clanked down, then once more he laughed out loud.

In the museum, scurrying out of the rain, we encountered queues of schoolchildren, elephant tusks, skeletons of animals now extinct, and a dusty musty smell of age and taxidermy. But Wilfred led me immediately beyond these distractions and into a room given over to the struggle for independence which had taken place in Kenya during the fateful 1950s. In glass cases were displayed the home-made hand guns, rifles, knives, and ammunition belts used by the Mau Mau freedom fighters. Photographs showed white troops on patrol; a young soldier sitting behind a machine gun in 1956; a sign at a place affording a splendid view which said bluntly 'it is most dangerous to picnic in this area because of terrorist gangs'; some white people marching in a Nairobi street in 1955 described as 'a demonstration against the Mau Mau'. In the end, I had read elsewhere, 11 000 Mau Mau had been killed, while 100 whites and 2 000 pro-British Africans had lost their lives.

On one of the walls, a large oil painting depicted the Harry Thuku Incident of 1922. Thuku, according to a printed inscription, was a mission-educated young man who had led the East African Association which had become more and more militant, protesting against the hut tax and labour laws which sought to harness Africans to the labour market by forcing them into the cash economy, a familiar enough story in colonial Africa. When Thuku was arrested as a trouble-maker, his followers staged a demonstration which resulted in between twenty and fifty people being shot and killed. The painting was of bloodied bodies, a crying child, and groups of soldiers or police and white settlers in the background. The expressions on the faces of the Europeans were furtive, grave, patently guilty.

'The tragic and painful event,' said the inscription, 'marked the beginning of a struggle which culminated in Kenya attaining political independence and sovereignty on 12 December 1963.' Other inscriptions took up the story. 'Immediately, with the unique spirit of harambee, Kenyans embarked on building and developing the Kenyan nation.' Over the years, the spirit of harambee had enabled Kenyans to achieve great prosperity in various social and economic sectors.

One of Wilfred's fingers had encroached upon the inscription I was reading. He pointed at the word harambee, underlining it several times. I noticed that his nail had been chewed to the quick. 'I suppose,' he said, his mocking voice not far from my ear, 'that harambee means working together.'

'And majimbo?'

'That means all the main tribes should be governed by their own gangsters.' For a second he showed his small white teeth in a sarcastic smile.

I sat one morning on the pavement terrace outside the New Stanley Hotel, waiting for Wilfred who was to drive me to an interview I had arranged. The generous branches of the thorn tree stretched horizontally above me. A plaque informed that it was an *Acacia xanthophloea* which had been planted here in 1961. A notice-board had been built around the trunk of the tree; and I saw several airmail letters from Europe and America addressed simply to John Smith or whoever, The Thorn Tree, Nairobi, Africa, affixed to the board and waiting to be claimed.

Although not long after breakfast, the tables were crowded, as were the pavements and streets beyond. Difficult not to think of Shiva Naipaul as I waited, drinking Kenyan tea and watching the other customers. I had also bought a magazine to while away the time. The dramatic black cover with red trim I had first seen in Harambee Avenue now lay at my elbow. *Majimbo* (in white italics): the real issues.

I noticed a middle-aged man with a trimmed white beard reading a German newspaper at a nearby table. He did so in a slightly irritated, distracted fashion, his mouth curled downward at one side. Opposite him a young black woman in a gold necklace and low-cut dress sat inert, half asleep yet waiting, rather like a cat.

Naipaul, I recalled, had written that Germans in particular were keen on their sex-safaris in Africa; but my interest in this author while I waited for Wilfred had become more general, more directed to overarching impressions. Africa, he had asserted, was swathed in words, words, words, and swaddled in lies, 'nothing but lies'. Indeed, Africa was described (he had been writing in the late 1970s) as a hopeless case, a doomed continent, unrelieved by the faintest glimmer from any quarter at all, filled only with corruption, pretension, fake thoughts, fake ideologies, and above all with words, words, words.

'What did I think?' he writes with considerable cynicism and anger. 'That words must be taken at their face value? That they have meanings which should be taken seriously? Had I not learned, after all this time, that nothing in Africa had meaning? That nothing could be taken seriously?'

Words like harambee and majimbo, for example. I opened the magazine at my elbow.

Majimboism was a form of ethnic regionalism which had first appeared on Kenya's political horizon in the early 1960s, inserted there by white settlers and other minority groupings nervous of the power being wielded by Kenyatta's majority-backed Kenya African National Union. However, Kenyatta's considerable personal charisma had smoothed the way to Kenya becoming a unitary state, with ideas of minority protection shelved. But in recent years the whole majimbo idea had again been revived. It was also being blamed for the tribal violence which had recently swept through parts of Kenya's Rift Valley province, ancestral home to the predominantly pastoral Kalenjin, Maasai, Turkana and Samburu tribes. The victims of the violence appeared to be Kikuyu who had settled in what was being claimed as the pastoralists' country. As I read, I came across words such as 'secession', 'Balkanisation', and even a term like 'ethnic cleansing' was being used.

Several pages of the magazine had been devoted to a calendar of events, beginning late in 1991 with evictions and displaced people wanting to reclaim land by violent means, to accusation and counter-accusation relating to tribal clashes in the Rift Valley which had continued throughout 1992 and the early months of 1993. Meanwhile, on numerous other pages, the debate continued.

'Majimbo is good for most parts of Kenya because it will disperse economic, political and infrastructural resources from the centre,' said the protagonists.

'Majimbo was coming at a time when Kenyans were yet to heal the scars left by ethnic violence,' came the reply. 'Politics in Kenya today are based on ethnic allegiance. Tribalism threatens to tear apart the economic fabric of the country. The creation of majimboism would involve the displacement of more than four million people.'

But, someone else argued, 'majimboism does not mean that people will be chased from their current areas of settlement, but that they will have to fully participate in the activities of the jimbo where they are living, and cooperate with the locals to minimise conflict.'

Why is it, asked a short editorial, that after only three decades of independence, some Kenyans are so determined to change the constitution? Why is it that the unitary system of government that the Founding Fathers bequeathed has suddenly become unpalatable? Would majimboism be the solution to the endemic corruption, mindless tribalism, senseless state terror, maniac dismemberment of institutions, and relentless impoverishment of Kenyans?

In an acidity of language, the questions multiplied. For Naipaul, Africa, and East Africa in particular, had appeared to be a place of words and of words falsely used. For me, sixteen years later, Kenya's battery of words, and the questions in which they were couched, threw up an outline not so much of doom and hopelessness but of a complex metamorphosis. Even the fervour of the journalism in the magazine spoke of the painful chemistry of crucibles. I caught a glimpse of a country, a nation of sorts, stuck together under the optimistic banner of harambee but now beginning to buckle and melt. The heat of anticolonialism had lost its potency. What new or rekindled energies lay under the crucible now?

'Majimboism,' I read, 'is an ideology revolving around mystical outbursts about ancestral lands and perpetuation of kinship ties.'

An old phrase — Africa returning to itself — found its way into my mind. But the phrase seemed too close to the idea of easy European vantage points in a continent which all too often denied access to high ground, I thought, looking up suddenly into the familiar face of Wilfred with its slightly mocking smile.

'So now we can go to Karen's house,' he said, tossing the keys of his 1960s chariot on to the metal table, a gesture which seemed to describe some sort of challenge, as he sat down opposite me.

'You haven't forgotten that first I have an interview?'

He shook his head. 'I have not forgotten. At Gigiri. Let's go.'

'Yes, definitely, Africa is at an awkward stage in its development,' the thin black man said, leaning back in his chair and regarding me across the polished conference table which stood at one end of his large office. 'It's essential that we clearly understand this.'

His face wore the habitually alert expression of a man in authority. He had asked a couple of his aides to join us, and presently a young woman entered the office with a tray of tea things which one of the aides took charge of.

I said I appreciated the time which had been allowed me. I intimated that it was a privilege to be at Gigiri, at the regional headquarters of so many United Nations agencies, and especially to be in this office now, listening to an authority on

African affairs. I asked my host if he could elaborate on Africa's 'awkward stage'.

The thin man nodded. He asked one of his aides to fetch copies of a few documents which he said I might find useful. Then he turned his alert eyes once more in my direction.

'In part,' he said, and his accent had the flavour of America, and of the Caribbean, embedded in it, 'the continent finds itself embroiled in the aftermath of the cold war. Yes, the vacuum theory. Before, if there was a problem, it was stabilised relatively quickly. Neither the East nor the West could afford to have large-scale instability all over the continent. Think of it in terms of the analogy of a pendulum: it was rarely allowed to swing, always manipulated back to its central position. In this way a false equilibrium was established here.

'Now,' he went on, donning a pair of half-spectacles to glance at a few booklets his aide had brought in. 'Now, of course, the pendulum is being left to swing, simply because there are no hidden agendas in place to stop it.

'But our analysis also needs to take into account another very important process: the demise of socialism in Africa. Multiparty democracy, and all sorts of variants of this idea, might look like the obvious replacement. But the truth is that multipartyism doesn't automatically mean democracy. Multipartyism in Africa so far has meant taking the lid off, freeing societies of the restraints and downright repressions of one-party-state dictatorships. But how will the concept develop further?

'In the Western sense, democracy focuses on individual choice and individual responsibility and, perhaps most importantly, on the rights of individuals. Even so, let us never forget that the Western democracies do not embrace everybody; there are marginalised minorities throughout America and Europe. So democracy with a stress on the individual must never be forced down Africa's throat as if it is some ideal panacea. New models will almost certainly be developed here. Let me give you an example. Perhaps the traditional importance of leaders and leadership in Africa will have a profound modifying effect on the shape of the new political structures which ultimately emerge.

'But whatever happens, the process will not be completed in two years. It will take much longer. It's a lengthy process of argument, a process of developing a new mindset, and coping with new expectations. Now think of the pendulum analogy again. My own belief is that Africa will achieve a new and this time unforced equilibrium by the first or perhaps the second decade of the next century. It will, for the first time in nearly two centuries, be an African-inspired equilibrium.

'Yes, of course, we must ask what is going to happen in the interim, what is already happening. To attempt some answers, though, I think it is very important that we separate the wider processes involved in the pendulum's swing from the effects these processes unleash. The things that are happening in Rwanda, in the Horn and elsewhere, these should be seen as effects. The wider processes are the collapse of the cold war, the demise of socialism, the bite of economic structural adjustment programmes, the increasing pressure on natural resources, the multifarious impact of urbanisation...'

I said I could understand the difference between cause, this complex process of transmutation upon which Africa had been launched in the late 1980s, and the effects which were sometimes emerging in terrible outpourings of travail. 'But it sometimes seems,' I went on, 'as if Africa will have ripped itself to pieces before equilibrium has been achieved.'

The man's response to these words was immediate. His eyes showed hard, unflinching, alert. 'Anyone who tries to rob Africa of this broad process of finding a new equilibrium is misguided,' he said.

I looked out of the window at the trees and lawns of the huge United Nations complex at Gigiri. I saw rows of vehicles in a carpark, rows of office windows diminishing at an angle to our own.

'It's a process that has to be got through, worked out by Africans themselves.'

The narrow face, when I looked at it again, remained unchanged, the eyes locked steadily against my presence as he looked at me over the straight upper edges of those half-spectacles settled low on a narrow nose.

'Africans are going through a major learning process now, facing new freedoms and new uncertainties. What they least need is the manipulation — based on cold war and economic considerations — which characterised the post-Uhuru period. What they most need, though, is the sort of assistance we're trying to develop here. If I didn't believe that, I wouldn't be occupying this office.

'Although it's hard to credit after all the mistakes that have been made, there is still a tendency for aid agencies to give Africans what the aid agencies think will be good for them, without listening to hear what the Africans themselves need. Our role is much less on provision and much more on unlocking the potential which invariably exists on the ground, even among the poorest communities. Let me give you some examples . . .'

We talked for a long time, until one of the aides, glancing apologetically at his watch, interrupted to say that other appointments were beginning to be delayed.

My host rose with a resigned gesture. 'I am being reminded that I must also do some work,' he said as we shook hands.

I took with me along the busy corridors of the building in which we had talked a vision of this man's unflinching eyes, and an echo of his words. The pendulum must be left to swing. It was a process which had to be got through, worked out by Africans themselves. The process was theirs. This new ownership, if they could grasp it, constituted the roots of the travail, and the hope, of their renascence.

T he Ngong hills lay in a low and voluptuous line, clearly visible beyond the well-tended shrubs in the garden of Karen Blixen's house. The Danish writer had felt that here, during the day, she had 'got high up, near to the sun'; and there was still that sense, that mixture of sharp heat with a clarity of air which characterised Kenya's high altitudes. The clarity of air seemed remarkable, considering the growth of Nairobi since the early decades of the century when Blixen had lived here. Now her name adorned the suburb by which her house, once the relatively isolated centre of a coffee plantation, was now surrounded.

'Karen is where only the wealthy live,' Wilfred had told me as we drove through the shaded roadways past large gates, often with guards and dogs in the driveways beyond. 'Not even you could afford to live here,' he added, glancing at me with impudent and curious eyes.

I laughed.

He pointed out a few electric fences, a few security lights on poles, more guards with truncheons patrolling. 'You know what they say,' he told me. 'One third of the people in Nairobi earn a living by protecting another third from the third third.' But I was thinking of an article I had read in the magazine with the dramatic black cover and red trim: burglars had killed a thirty-year-old white woman in front of her fourteen-month-old child in a Nairobi suburb. Her husband, a pilot engaged in flying relief flights into Rwanda, had survived by feigning death. 'Every time such a tragedy happens to a white in Kenya,' observed the writer, himself a white, 'nostalgic articles appear in the British press juxtaposing the latest brutal killing with Happy Valley, the Kenyan paradise that gave us Born Free, White Mischief and Out of Africa (Blixen's book). This dream world belonged to a time when Kenya was pronounced Keenya, where whites tamed the wild and lived − or over-lived − a life of sensual luxury, and where All of the Natives were Happy All of the Time.'

Wilfred, of course, had other thoughts entirely. 'We natives do not live here,' he said, enjoying his parody of self-pity. 'We natives are the poor. We live behind the universe.'

He drove in silence for a moment or two, then added, and now with a trace of darkness in the slightly mocking voice: 'That is why, even today, when the natives come into the houses to scrub the floors they must walk on their bare feet so as not to wake up the memsahib.'

He laughed at his own words, as if to make a joke of it. But his laughter was almost without sound, and it revealed his small white teeth in something like a snarl. 'The mzungus are too proud, and they are too fussy for their women.'

Blixen's house seemed to have sunk somewhat as the garden in which it was set had matured. The pitch of the tiled roof was modestly low, the house itself built of grey stone-textured blocks, and made to look at once larger than it really was and more secretive by the wide verandas which surrounded it on three sides. The windows were all but invisible in the deep shade; and shrubbery had grown to chest height beyond the low veranda walls, sometimes obscuring altogether what must have once been a clear view of the Ngong hills. Some of the pathways around the house were made of gravel in which the footsteps of the occasional tourist scraped and crunched.

The interior was quite silent. Close to the entrance point, large photographs of the American actress and actor who had performed in a film on Blixen's life adorned the walls. But beyond these the house had been given over to more authentic artefacts: pictures of Blixen as an old woman, cigarette between gnarled fingers; dark wood panelling on the walls; a large fireplace with moulded stone surround; a window seat seeming to be stained with ink; and in the study a hand-cranked telephone and old Corona typewriter on the desk. The desk was repeated in a photograph, but this time, sitting behind it, was a young woman seeming lithe, with dark hair and large eyes, and a slender hand against the side of her face as she smiled at the camera. I wondered who had taken the photograph; perhaps her lover, Denys Finch-Hatton?

But these likenesses of Blixen as a young and old woman brought strongly to me the power inherent in literature of lifting life out of time. The slender hand against the face had turned to the gnarled old fingers holding the smouldering cigarette. Yet it was the slender hand which endured; it was the slender hand which marked so many of the most limpid pages of *Out of Africa*. She had lived in Africa from her late twenties to her mid-forties; and it was her perceptions then which mattered most to me now.

I knew that her images of Africa were idealised by eyes jaded by the mustiness of Europe, especially a fading European aristocracy about to be blown to pieces by the cataclysms of the 20th century. Yet I knew too that her eyes had been extraordinarily intelligent, and also that she had been moved by the surface of Africa: the mountains and the plains, the animals, the Maasai with their robes knotted on the shoulder and walking in their vast landscapes. In a sense, the sharpness of the air here, and the clarity of light, had unleashed her. Was there some sense of abandonment even, I wondered, standing at the doorway to her bedroom? Those days when Kenya was pronounced Keenya and people sank into self-indulgence and flagrantly sensual luxury.

Were those her riding boots over there? Was that her pith helmet on the chair, with the ribbons to tie under her chin? Was this the bed, white and unruffled now, in which the young woman, married to a feckless and syphilitic man, had lain with her lover?

But she had lost him. He had killed himself in his Moth aeroplane. It seemed a brutal irony, especially since, earlier, she had written: 'To Denys Finch-Hatton I owe what was, I think, the greatest, the most transporting pleasure of my life on the farm: I flew with him over Africa.' She had buried him in the Ngong hills, not long before she left Africa for ever, but later she heard that a pride of lions had often been seen sitting on his grave up there in the hills, surveying the plains below. 'It was fit and decorous that the lions should come to Denys's grave and make him an African monument,' Blixen writes. 'Lord Nelson himself, I have reflected, in Trafalgar Square, has his lions made only out of stone.'

But Shiva Naipaul rails against this whimsical manifestation of the young woman's grieving. 'Primal Africa pays homage to the English nobleman,' he scoffs. 'Displaced aristocratic yearning has achieved its apotheosis.' Blixen, Naipaul asserts, is European nobility finding a belated throne in Africa by asserting 'a mystical kinship with the land and its creatures'. In all her observations of Africa, there is 'an assertion of implicit overlordship', an implied claim that only someone of her class could have appreciated the beauty of such a place, and have known so gripping a sense of loss when the time came to leave it. But such appreciation, says Naipaul, and such a sense of loss, merge to form at last an illness which has its roots in the white sense of overlordship in primitive places.

I stood at the cordoned door to her bedroom, looking in. I knew that the Africa which she saw had disappeared as surely as had her vision. I was standing at the doorway to another time, and the time seemed redolent with precisely the kind of romanticism which Naipaul so incisively criticised. Had they shot down Harry Thuku's supporters (I remembered the large canvas in the museum) at about the time when Karen Blixen was flying over Africa in Denys's timber and canvas Moth?

Yet what of Naipaul's perceptions of Africa? In the end, he too had left it. Indeed, he had fled, as much from what he repeatedly describes as a doomed and hopeless continent as from some irritating pot-smokers who threatened his privacy on the thorn-tree terrace in front of the New Stanley Hotel.

What lay between these extremes of romanticism and special relationships on the one side, and perceptions of doom on the other? The answer seemed, for an instant, to stand clear and unwavering before me, but before I could clearly articulate it, Wilfred's irreverent voice had invaded the silence. I turned to face him. I saw his pride, his secrecy, his humour, his bloodshot eyes. I remembered how his sons had clung to his legs when we had first met. I saw his habitual mockery and a glimpse of his small white teeth as he smiled.

'You must not stand here so long,' he said, 'staring into the memsahib's bedroom. You are only supposed to tiptoe past on your bare feet.'

B road was the way that led to destruction, the woman in spectacles said, preaching in Kikuyu; but the true way, the way to life, was very narrow. On the broad way, there was dope and alcohol and too many contesting ideas and opportunities which tended to confuse people. And very often the church was failing, and people were rejecting the church. But here the problem was that God had been left inside the Church, instead of being brought into everyday life to help with all the problems. Yes, everyone knew that the world was full of problems now.

The preacher's voice had become strident, as did the woman's next to her who translated into Swahili. My private translator, a short cheerful man with thick-lensed spectacles who sat beside me in the pew, speaking incessantly into my ear, said: 'I think you can safely say that this theme — of many problems besieging ordinary people — is another manifestation of the disappointments and confusions afflicting post-Uhuru Africa. The disillusionment in Kenya is like an epidemic these days.'

My translator's name was Larry, and he had been living in Kenya for the past ten years, and before that elsewhere in Africa. He had driven me up into the highlands, but still within sight of Nairobi, going above the coffee plantations and into the tea, the fields a vivid green and seeming trimmed and tended on the gentle sloping of the hills. He had asked if I would be interested in attending a special church service in Limuru conducted by women. 'It should be quite interesting,' Larry had remarked, 'and it'll end with a misumari. Actually this is Swahili for nail. But it's a term they also use for special collections, a sort of fund raising effort for a specific purpose. These misumaris can develop into fascinating — and sometimes lengthy — occasions.'

We must ask God to help us with all the problems. We must not allow anything into our lives that would cut us off from God. Ask God to help you, the preacher said, looking at the congregation through spectacles which glinted suddenly.

Then she raised her arms, fists spontaneously clenched. God bless you all. On that note the sermon ended.

But another woman, announcing herself as the president of the women's league, had already risen to take the preacher's place. She said a few words in Kikuyu, a few more in Swahili. I caught the words 'women's liberation'. The women in the congregation laughed, while the men smiled in that slightly awkward way of people caught out.

'But the truth is,' Larry translated, 'that without women the men would starve.' Applause rippled around the church, coming from the hands of both women and men. A warmth of expectancy had begun to light the expressions of the people around me.

'This is the spirit of harambee,' Larry remarked close to my ear.

The president of the women's league, in her best clothes and her floral headgear thrust low over her eyes, as if to accentuate her determination, continued with her introduction. 'If this is true,' she said in her determined voice, 'that men would starve without the cooking abilities of women, then what better note could I find to launch this appeal. It is for funds to build a kitchen so that for church functions our women won't have to cook out in the open in all sorts of weather.'

After applause had crackled through the church once more, a momentary pause settled on the congregation, as if they were gathering themselves for what was to come. Then the singing began. A few musicians sat to one side, one with a guitar, several more with instruments of percussion. But the singing swelled above their guidance. The singing seemed to be circular in shape, a central theme coming round again and again, like a rondo. At the front of the hall, some women had arranged themselves at a trestle table, while on one end of the table stood a basket for donations.

Members of the congregation began to move forward to place their contributions into the basket. At intervals, one of the women emptied the contents on to the trestle table. Deft hands unfolded and straightened the notes, others counted, still others recorded a running total in notebooks. The singing subsided.

The president of the women's league acted as controller of proceedings. She called for specific groups within the congregation by name; she motioned to the musicians. And then the singing would start again as the group rose and slowly came forward. Imperceptibly, the dancing began and the percussion grew louder.

I asked Larry about the specific groups.

'They invite people whom they think will be willing to help,' he replied, speaking quite loudly above the repetitive music. 'They invite people whom they have helped in the past. Sister churches from nearby areas; even churches in direct competition with their own. This is very much a community ritual. Look at those men, for example.'

Obviously wealthy, reaching for rolls of notes in the pockets of their suits, these business leaders (as Larry called them) danced slowly forward towards the basket on the trestle table, raising their arms, clicking their fingers, and shuffling in their expensive shoes through the dust raised from the timber floor.

'Bank managers, pretty big names in insurance, the Coca-Cola distributor for Limuru and surrounds.'

The congregation could estimate the size of the donations by the colour of the notes tossed into the baskets; and the business leaders received a spontaneous round of applause and a few ululations for their generosity, as the congregation rose in unison to sway to the heavy beating of the drums.

'The dancing is interesting,' Larry said into my ear. 'It was done in the early days, before independence, I believe. Then it died away. It was frowned upon as vaguely pagan, certainly as something un-Christian. Now it's coming back.'

I asked why.

Larry shrugged his shoulders. 'What you're seeing is Kikuyu dancing. The singing is unmistakably Kikuyu. There are some people here, of course, who are not Kikuyu. You can see that they enjoy it, but at one level — let's be frank and call it a tribal level — they are excluded.'

'But why the resurgence?'

'Perhaps,' Larry said in a voice raised above the level of the singing, 'it has to do with all the disappointments and confusions which have come to so many ordinary people over the years. Perhaps they are turning back to the older sureties, the tribal ones.'

The president of the women's league was looking directly at us as she called for another specific group. We went forward with our contributions.

At the trestle table, with the pink-palmed hands straightening, counting, recording, I turned and faced the audience. People were dancing and clapping, raising dust from the old boards, fluttering their hands above their heads. On their faces lay the pleasure of the dance, and under that the pull and deeper joy of ritual.

'Tell me about harambee,' I said as we sat down.

'This it it,' Larry shouted above a renewed outburst of singing. 'Har-am-bee. Pronounced bay, incidentally. If your car was stuck, people would come and help. Har-am-bay, they would chant, the accent on the last syllable to coincide with the effort of pushing. Pushing in unison, working together. It was used habitually in many parts of Africa by men digging holes or making roads. You've seen them, I'm sure, perhaps when you were a boy, standing in a row with their picks poised above their heads. Coming down in unison, working together.'

I remarked that it had become a political concept.

'Yes, of course,' Larry shouted. 'The people were supposed to push in unison and work together while the bureaucrats and politicians ran away with the rewards. It's a matter of finding out how long you can abuse someone else's spontaneity and willingness. I think that point's been reached now. The old willingness has been replaced by distrust and disgruntlement.

'And where do ordinary people turn to then? To multiparty democracy?' Larry grinned and shook his head. 'To the sureties of the past. They are the sureties of the blood, of kinship, of the tribe.'

A dancing woman had reached down to take hold of my hands. She drew me up. She said: 'You are too much talking and no giving.' She laughed as she danced. I raised my hands above my head, as if in surrender to the manifold powers of a collective persuasion.

After church, Larry and I were ushered into a vestry where some smiling women brought us generous plates of food. From the window I could glimpse green hills of tea rolling away and half shrouded in mist at midday. We were in a part of the highlands which lay more than 7 600 feet above sea level.

Our host in the vestry was an old man, an elder in the church, who had been a supporter of the Mau Mau freedom fighters. 'Of course I am a Kikuyu,' he said through Larry who once again acted as interpreter. The old man's father and brothers had been in the forest, fighting with the Mau Mau. But the old man himself had continued to work for the settlers so that he could supply the fighters with what they needed, including piping and other hardware which they had used for the making of those guns which Wilfred had been so keen to show me in the museum.

The old man's hands shook slightly, and he spilled rice on the vestry table around his plate, but his eyes were still steady, and he proved to be an informative host.

He spread out his hands when I asked him about majimbo, and the rumours that the pastoralists in the Rift Valley — the Maasai, the Turkana, the Samburu, the Kalenjin — wanted more autonomy to rule themselves.

'When the horse and the donkeys are in a race, you have to rein in the horse to give the donkeys a chance,' he said. 'We the Kikuyu fought for the independence; the Maasai and the Kalenjin didn't fight. The British protected the Maasai. They put them in the reserves, like animals in the zoo. They are the royal Africans, the British said, they are like us, the aristocrats. But the Kikuyu were the clever ones, hard-working and fighting for independence.'

All this, Larry translated with patience and good humour, sometimes adding explanatory asides, as when he pointed out: 'I'm sure you know this, but the Kikuyu are Bantu-speaking agriculturalists while the pastoralists are Nilotic. There have always been antagonisms, and these have been exacerbated by independence.'

It was as if the old man understood what was being said, for he added with a gracious smile: 'Kenyatta told us: you are all Kenyans. You are all free of the British. And you can own land anywhere. So many Kikuyu went to farm in the Rift Valley.'

Larry spread out his hands. 'That's the cause of a lot of the trouble in the Valley now. The traditional land of the pastoralists is being farmed by the agriculturalists.'

Another piece of the picture jarred into place. As time had passed and economic well-being declined, the hopeful nationalism of Uhuru had begun to collapse. There was on one level a loss of faith in Uhuru nationalism. But on another — and this was the piece of the picture which forced itself upon me now — there was almost a sense of relief. I had seen the old man's gracious smile. I detected in him no real bitterness. The old antagonisms — those which had preceded independence and the colonialism which came before — were a crucial part of the old sureties. To re-identify the adversary was to re-define the undeniable comforts of tribal allegiance.

Not long before I left Nairobi, Wilfred arranged for me to see something of the city's slums. We had driven past one of the largest conglomerations — at Kibera to the north of Nairobi Dam on the Ngong River — on several occasions, the slums showing as a density of rusting iron roofs and walls all pressed together in a sprawling mess from which dust and smoke perpetually oozed.

'That is where the poor live,' Wilfred had remarked, 'even poorer than me. That is the other side of the universe. Never mind about harambee and majimbo, you must go and see how the people are trying to live. Yes, there is slum clearance. There you can see the new housing in blocks. But you must pay a lot of money even to get on the waiting list. Unless you are a friend of the bureaucrats who keep the list, then perhaps the amount will not be so high.'

While we spoke of these things — and while he promised to organise my visit through a woman he knew who worked in the slums — I looked down at Nairobi Dam, the water reflecting the blue of the sky, and saw a few small craft, their sails puffed out against the backdrop of dust and shanties descending almost to the water's edge.

Wilfred followed my gaze and laughed in his silent way, showing those small white teeth and glancing at me with eyes full of mockery once more. 'Never mind the mzungus in their boats. You have to let them play, otherwise they get restless.'

Agnetta, the woman to whom Wilfred introduced me, explained some of the problems encountered by the hundreds of thousands of people living in Nairobi's slums. 'The first problem is the numbers,' she said. 'Half a million live in Kibera alone, and there are new people coming in all the time. Another problem is abandoned children. The number of street children — they are without parents or guardians and live in the streets — increases as the economy declines. Actual figures are impossible to get, but I'd say between thirty and fifty thousand at the moment.'

Agnetta worked for an all-Kenyan agency which was attempting to alleviate some of the hardship and squalor in Kibera, and she agreed to take me to the agency offices there to talk with some of her co-workers.

We drove in at the top end of the slum and headed slowly down towards the dam on Ngong River at the bottom of the hill. We went down in an agency vehicle, a minibus driven by a taciturn man who grumbled softly under his breath about the state of the roads. Several times the underside of the vehicle jolted against rocks and ruts in the broken surface; and sometimes waste water presented the driver with a quagmire which dragged at the tyres or robbed them of their traction. Such situations served largely to increase his irritation while he slammed through the gears and wrenched at the steering wheel, his thin shoulders contorting slightly with the effort.

Agnetta sat in the front seat, turning back towards me as she spoke. She was young, well dressed, professional. I asked her where she had met Wilfred. She looked vaguely surprised. 'Didn't he tell you? He helps us sometimes with the street children.'

Faces stared in at us as we laboured past. The streets were crowded: children laughed or sat silent in the rubble; women stood in queues at communal taps, or operated ramshackle stalls selling food and occasionally toiletries such as soap, combs, body lotion, aerosol cans and bottles of pale pink scent; men hammered pieces of iron on to rough timber poles, or sat drinking on the low verandas of shacks with hand-painted signs marking them as hotels or bars. In the side streets, often not much more than a metre wide, sagging lines of washing flapped, and groups of sullen-eyed youths whiled away the time.

Agnetta locked her door. 'Now with the tribal violence in the Rift Valley, lots of people are coming to town. Lots of youth. We are wondering when the tribal violence will happen here. Meanwhile, there is just violence, robberies — the Americans say muggings — even murders sometimes here in these streets.'

Dense smoke had filled up the roadway ahead, and Agnetta explained that the people were encouraged to burn their rubbish. 'It's impossible to get cleansing vehicles into Kibera,' she explained. 'And if the rubbish isn't burned it rots, attracting flies and blocking up the drainage furrows. Yes, there are children dying of diarrhoea all the time.'

The stench of the smoke and of the seething mess of Kibera seeped into the vehicle. The roadway descended, with the driver muttering under his breath, through rust and collapsing shanties and the faces of poverty at the windows against which red dust was sifting down. I saw the whites of eyes in a thousand dark faces. They were the eyes of a country facing hard and uncertain times, declining economic fortunes and high inflation, new tensions and strictures, new demands, and with old slogans like harambee as talisman turned impotent now.

At the bottom of the hill, through dust and smoke, I glimpsed for a moment the placid blue water of the dam. Then we turned off and bounced over an uneven field with crooked goal posts at either end, and stopped outside the offices of the agency for which Agnetta, and I had now discovered Wilfred, worked: low buildings, walls stained with the colour of red earth up to the window-sills, a few broken windows; and more faces inside, more whites of eyes in the sudden gloom of the unpainted interior.

They had heard I was coming, and had gathered to tell me what they did: a social worker, an agricultural extension officer, and a round-faced young man with sullen eyes who told me he had a bachelor of social sciences degree from Kenyatta University.

Agnetta began, sitting poised in her good clothes, her stockinged legs crossed, her hands clasped around one knee as she leaned forward slightly in her earnestness. She spoke about empowerment, about small loans to groups of women for the establishment of income generation schemes, and about the agency (for which Agnetta and the others worked) gaining permanent representation on a sanitation upgrading committee.

The social worker said: 'We are also involved in education. One of the problems is that basic school fees are now more than 10 000 shillings a year, but people don't often earn more than 3 000 shillings a month. The result is that thousands of children no longer go to school. So we have started some informal schools with very small fees. We also run a street children's rehabilitation programme that leads either to one of our informal schools or into the state system if the money can be found.'

I asked if the rehabilitation programme was what Wilfred had become involved in.

Agnetta smiled. 'He's so good with the kids. Like a father. He comes nearly every evening. It's that regularity and stability that of course they desperately need.'

Some tea was brought in. A woman poured in condensed milk while I stirred. The round-faced social scientist told me he had also done economics and political science and that he was now working part time towards his masters. His sullen eyes seemed to be sizing me up.

The agriculturist explained the principles of organic farming and composting. He said he was also doing an experiment with pot gardening for use in the cramped slum conditions of Kibera. Also, not far from the dam, a group of women ran a community vegetable garden, learning simple dietetics at the same time.

'I always find it astonishing,' the round-faced social scientist interposed, 'that there is not more anger here.'

'Is there some? In Kibera, I mean.'

He laughed, a trifle bitterly I thought. 'Kenyans don't want trouble. They've heard too much about the wars all around them.'

Agnetta began to suggest that I might wish to visit the community garden, only a short walk away, but the social scientist spoke over her.

'The levels of civic education are too low, that's the trouble. Even when they vote, they vote only for a man who appeals as a leader, never mind his policies. In fact they would vote for whoever offered them some food. It's the politics of poverty.'

I asked him why poverty seemed to be overtaking Kenya at such a rapid rate.

'The World Bank,' he said belligerently. 'Economic structural adjustment.'

He waited for me to reply. I said nothing. So the tirade tumbled out, his round face tense with anger.

'These programmes have a totally inhuman face,' he said, his voice ringing in the gloom of the office. 'What does the World Bank care about ordinary Africans? Nothing. Health and education are the two services which are hardest hit. Now the World Bank talks about cost recovery! Stealing from the poor to repay their precious loans. Shifting an intolerable burden on to the backs of the common people. The city slickers in New York simply haven't taken cognisance of the fact that most Africans live in poverty anyway.'

'But there have also been excesses here, in Africa,' the agriculturist said. 'There has been a lot of waste and corruption. There still is.'

'You ape the neo-colonialists,' the social scientist retorted, his fists clenched in his lap. 'Economic structural adjustment is a conspiracy to maintain the client-patron relationship between Africa and the industrialised West. Why don't we set the price of coffee, for a change?'

No one offered a reply.

'Will you have more tea?' Agnetta asked me in the silence which followed.

The social scientist stood up in disgust. He walked towards the door. 'It's time the West — including South Africa, if that's where you come from — started talking about reparation. Reparation for slavery, reparation for colonialism, reparation for apartheid. Africa is sick and tired of being treated like a problem child when all the time it has been robbed. Robbed,' he repeated, glancing angrily around the room and then closing the door firmly as he went out.

Later during the day, as Agnetta and I drove slowly out of the slum, the dust lying thick on our skin and on the seats of the minibus, I thought momentarily of Wilfred on the day I had first met him in his offcut house, his sons clinging to his legs. I remembered his mockery and irreverence with a sudden affection. But I would remember above all how nearly every night he would come here, to this place behind the universe, offering some stability to young children lost along the way.

Then our vehicle became trapped behind a smallish tanker with the words Kibuku Beer emblazoned on the back. The tanker jolted in the roadway ahead, increasing the dust billowing through the squalor of the slum.

Suddenly our driver spoke. 'Strong beer,' he said, turning to grin at me. 'One glass and you out.'

But there in my mind stood Wilfred with his mockery and his sons, while in the foreground it was all dust and dreams of oblivion as the pendulum was left to swing.

10

One Hundred Teddy Bears

The scale and ferocity of the massacres in Rwanda have shocked and dumbfounded the world. In the West, there is total incomprehension that one of the smallest and poorest countries in Africa could erupt into such a volcano of violence.

— Anver Versi, in *New African*, June 1994.

As the sun rose, long shadows stretched across the open space of the apron and out on to the runway itself. Rows of small aircraft stood to one side, bathed in the early light. Apart from these brightly painted machines, however, the expanse of concrete and tarmac lay empty. In a while, a woman in a bright red *doek* appeared on the apron and bent forward, but languidly, into the task of sweeping the expanse with a standard-sized broom. The sky which arched above the airport — Nairobi's Wilson — showed flawless and deep blue in the west where a sense of night still lingered. But the shadows had shortened considerably by the time the pilot, Andy, arrived.

We shook hands; and he told me he must attend to some paper work while we waited for another passenger, a surgeon from America.

I went into the low terminal building and found a cup of coffee. The small waiting area had begun to fill up, largely with tourists, many of them in khaki waistcoats with multiple pockets and zippers, who spoke an awkward English to the Kenyan airport officials but other languages among themselves. Binoculars and cameras dangled from not a few shoulders; and as the sun climbed, slanting in dazzling shafts through a row of east-facing windows, dark-glasses were lowered from the tops of heads to protect eyes unused to such searing light. Outside, the small aeroplanes had begun to take off, surging forward on the runway and disappearing behind buildings and into a slight depression in the shape of the land, then emerging once more much further on, already airborne and insect-like, wings glinting as they turned towards their various destinations.

The surgeon stood by our small aircraft, seeming slightly nonplussed as Andy tried to fit in all his luggage. 'I'm real sorry,' he said, 'but I did tell them I'd be bringing medical supplies.'

Andy reassured him in a pleasant way. 'This shouldn't be a problem,' he said, putting his weight against a holdall still bulging from the fuselage.

The surgeon turned to me. 'There are another six trunks,' he said. 'Luckily the UN is flying those in. I think they left late yesterday.' But I saw a sense of amusement in his eyes, a readiness to laugh at absurdity when he encountered it. He stepped forward to help with the holdall.

When it was safely inside, Andy said we could soon be on our way, and hurried towards the terminal building to obtain his final clearance. The surgeon and I stood together by the aircraft which bore the markings of a missionary organisation.

'These fellows do great work,' the surgeon said. 'By the way, my name is Rollin. I'm from Durham, North Carolina.' His thinning brown hair lay in a light thatch about his forehead, and he gazed at the activity on the apron with eyes sharpened by interest and new experience. 'You won't believe this,' he said, combing at the hair on his forehead with his fingers, 'but this is my first morning in Africa. I flew in yesterday. I've never been anywhere near this continent before.'

He seemed to be in his middle forties. His eyes were keen and intelligent, and I saw that years of confidence and good humour had left small wrinkles which fanned readily and often across his temples, creating the impression that his eyes were smiling somewhat earlier than the rest of his face.

'OK. All set,' Andy said. 'But before we go, I always like to commit the flight to the Lord.' So we stood next to the small aeroplane, our heads bowed, while Andy prayed in simple language about the safety of our journey west across the Rift Valley and the Serengeti plains and the southern reaches of Lake Victoria, and then on to the Rwandan capital of Kigali.

Rollin sat in the back with some of his luggage. I looked out through the faint blur of the propeller as we taxied out and then roared into the air. Not long after take-off, we made a steady banking turn. Immediately beyond the perimeter of the airport I saw that open country began; and on this country, in single file, I had a glimpse of slow elephants walking with their early morning shadows flung out beside them. I turned to make sure that Rollin had noticed. He already had a camera in his hands. The shadows of the elephants looked more recognisable than the small grey mounds of the animals themselves, as we saw them from above. 'Gee, fantastic,' Rollin shouted appreciatively. 'Look over there. Are those giraffes?' Then the animals had slipped behind, and we were climbing into an endless blue.

The Ngong hills appeared as a crumpled weal across our path. They seemed to swing up to meet us, and the aircraft juddered in currents of air already rising from warming rocks. But before long the landscape had settled and smoothed into the Great Rift Valley. The noise of the engine precluded general conversation, but Andy indicated a pair of earphones which when I had put them on allowed me to hear his friendly voice, and I was able to reply via a built-in microphone.

He told me he had been flying for the mission in east and central Africa for the past three years. His wife and child lived with him in Nairobi. Yes, he had flown to Kigali several times since the Rwandan Patriotic Front had beaten back the government troops defending the city.

'The airport's been shot up a bit. And I hear the town itself is a mess. But people are flying in and out without any major problems now. I think United Nations personnel are doing the air traffic control.'

The country beneath us stretched away in an endless brown and yellow sprawl. I saw a few homesteads converged upon by a network of paths, a few patches of agriculture, but for the most part the country lay empty and exposed to the sun. There were no trees to speak of, only this rolling quality of the immense land, as if some huge brown lake had gone solid, the swells petrified into smooth low undulations having no end.

Andy told me over our private intercom system that he had only half-filled the tanks with fuel, in anticipation of the surgeon's bulky luggage, and that therefore we were heading for Mwanza, a Tanzanian town on the southern shores of the lake, where we could refuel. He smiled across at me. Then I heard some static as he spoke to the tower at Mwanza; and presently the ragged edge of the lake loomed out of the haze of the distance, like a huge blue piece of jigsaw puzzle the outer edge of which passed beneath us as we descended.

A brisk wind blew at Mwanza airport. Rollin, the surgeon, took photographs of the men who refuelled the aircraft with a hand-operated pump. While we waited, a commercial jet landed. 'From Dar es Salaam,' Andy said.

'Where's that?' Rollin asked in his cheerful way.

Outside the airport building — white walls, yellow doors and windows, a dull red roof — I noticed two small blonde children playing with plastic guns which kept rattling out puny-sounding gunfire. Rollin and I stood under the wing, sheltering from the fierceness of the sun.

'A terrible business in Rwanda,' he said, his eyes wincing against the light. 'Of course, we've seen it all on TV. Tribalism, huh?'

When the jet departed, with a blast of heat and noise, the windows and doors of the airport building seemed to bulge with black faces eager to witness the speed and power of this event. Immediately afterwards we also took off, tearing into the wind, and set a direct course for Kigali. The islands of the lake grew small below us, and those areas of the water's surface darkened by wind seemed not to move or change at all.

Tribalism, at first glance undoubtedly. Suddenly the whole world knew about the Tutsis and the Hutus, about a ferocious ethnic antipathy which had burst out in April 1994 when the Bantu-speaking Hutus had begun to massacre the Tutsis in great numbers. But other arguments claimed that tribalism alone could not account for what had happened. To begin with, the origins of the Tutsi people had never been clearly established. Were they immigrants from the north, perhaps Ethiopia, which might explain their physical differences: the tall slender frames (as opposed to the shorter, more robust Hutus), the slightly paler pigmentation, the straight noses? Or were they of the same original stock as the Hutu (they certainly shared a common language, Kinyarwanda) with the physical differences being the result of different economic activity, diet and habitat (pastoralism as opposed to agriculture) and several centuries of physical and political separation?

Imponderable questions. Far clearer was the relationship between the two groups: the Tutsi, comprising less than fifteen per cent of the population in Rwanda, were warriors and leaders, a ruling élite which had established a monarchy; the majority Hutu were subservient, filling the role of servant, serf or client.

Andy said into my earphones that we would soon be crossing the border between Tanzania and Rwanda. Lake Victoria we had left far behind, and the country over which we flew had begun to break and lift into hills with steep and wooded valleys between, the uneven landscape all pale and shimmering with heat which sent up currents of air to wrench quite violently at our small aircraft sometimes.

But from the bloodied perspective of 1994, these tribal or, perhaps more accurately, caste considerations could not be isolated from the impact which colonialism had made on them. The Germans, and particularly the Belgians who came after, supported the Tutsi supremacy and, it is often claimed, through the typical colonial device of divide and rule had sharpened the antagonisms and overlaid the old Hutu stoicism with a new concept, discontent.

Equally damaging was the colonial view of the races in Africa: that the Bantu peoples (the real Africans, according to this colonial view) were hard-working but somewhat dull-witted, while the taller, more elegant peoples, the so-called Hamitic strains from the north, from the Nile civilisations, and possibly even from outside Africa, were superior fighters and quicker-witted and were inevitably responsible for what achievements the dark sub-Saharan continent could boast. Now, in 1994, people were asking: how much of this essentially racialistic thinking of the white man — sometimes known as the Hamitic myth — had rubbed off on the Hutus and Tutsis themselves?

Yet, as the time for independence approached, the Belgians had found themselves embarrassed by their own mythologies. Having actively supported the Tutsi minority for nearly half a century, even to the extent of excluding most Hutus from reasonable educational opportunities, the Belgians were now obliged by the simple demands of looming universal suffrage to change sides, throwing a new Hutu hope of power into a cauldron already bubbling with old divisions, and newer perceptions of discontent which finally erupted in a Hutu uprising in 1959.

Andy had tilted the nose of the aircraft for our descent, and the harsh hills of Rwanda seemed to rise to meet us, hills filled with terraced fields and the glinting iron roofs of thousands of homesteads scattered about in one of Africa's most densely populated countries. Difficult to imagine what terrors these crowding households had witnessed in recent months. But the very air seemed angry, and our aeroplane jolted and bucked quite violently. Rollin, the surgeon, was asleep in his seat, seeming sublimely innocent; Andy's hands gripped the joystick firmly; and I hung on to a metal bar which ran diagonally across my field of vision.

Andy smiled across at me. 'It won't be long now,' he said sympathetically into his tiny microphone.

While we came down through the heat and turbulence of a central African noon, my thoughts stayed on the background to the bloodshed. It had devastated Rwanda only four months before my visit. The country's head of state, and his Burundi counterpart, had died when their aircraft was shot down as it approached, on the same path that we now did, Kigali airport. This incident had been a signal for the horrors to begin.

Tribalism? Ethnic differences? Caste? Whatever the interpretation, the antagonisms between Hutu and Tutsi had been compounded by the machinations of colonialism which in turn had been compounded by the corruption and sectarian interests of post-independence leadership. The Hutu uprising of 1959 was followed by a Hutu victory in the pre-independence elections. The Tutsi monarchy was overthrown; and Tutsis were massacred; and more than 100 000 of them forced into exile. But within ten years, the Hutu majority government had been replaced, amid continuing fighting between the two groups, by a Hutu military dictatorship under Major-General Juvenal Habyarimana. Conditions hardly improved, and Tutsis continued to stream into exile, many of them to join the Rwandan Patriotic Front which had several times attacked Rwanda with a view to 'liberating' the country from Hutu domination.

And perhaps with considerable justification, since Habyarimana's regime was, according to several reports, one of the most corrupt and ruthless in Africa. Yet it was Habyarimana who, at least in recent years, had worked to reduce the tensions within the country and the threat posed by the Rwandan Patriotic Front (RPF) from without. Progress was being made: agreement, after a serious invasion by the RPF in 1993, had been reached regarding the establishment of a coalition government, the appointment of RPF ministers, the merging of the two armies, and a sizeable reduction of President Habyarimana's powers.

Had the president been outmanoeuvred by the RPF negotiators? Had he, in the process, been isolated from his own Hutu base, especially from the Hutu extremists? The answers seemed hardly to matter as I clung to my metal bar and saw, as Andy indicated, the outline of Kigali ahead, a small city extending over several wooded hills. The president had been flying home when his aircraft had been blown out of the sky by a fiery rocket. He had been in sight of the runway, as we were, the painted markings on the dark of the tarmac clearly visible. So it was here, on this approach through tumultuous air, that Rwanda's latest nightmare of genocide and then of storming war began.

From the glass entrance to Kigali Airport's terminal building, Rollin and I watched Andy take off, his small machine soon lost in the immensity of sky. We then turned towards glass doors. One of the most attractive airport buildings in Africa, someone had told me. It was certainly modern, with cantilevered concrete fins adorning the upper storeys, and with open staircases and quantities of glass demarcating the various areas within. We passed across a wide and empty floor, laden with Rollin's luggage. We noticed clusters of bullet holes in walls, plenty of smashed glass, long rows of gashes in the plastic tiling on the floor, soldiers aiming low as Rollin described this phenomenon, his keen eyes soaking up the detail. We came to a barrier beside a small glass kiosk. In a moment a young woman appeared; she asked for dollars for the airport tax, and then directed us to a collection of low platforms where our luggage would be searched. Rollin glanced at me expectantly.

A few soldiers stood in the main part of the terminal building. A slender man with a straight nose told us to wait. Then he disappeared. We arranged Rollin's luggage on one of the platforms. The slender man sauntered back and indicated that each piece should be opened.

'Medical supplies,' Rollin said.

The slender man ignored him. He took out boxes of equipment, and opened them, revealing a few stethoscopes and hypodermic syringes. He took out cartons of drugs and undid the flaps. He held rubber gloves up to the light pouring in from the expanses of broken glass.

Rollin said with a slight edge of irritation, almost a reprimand, colouring his voice: 'I'm a surgeon. I've come here to help you people, you know.'

The slender man ignored him. He had started on another piece of luggage. Here was Rollin's dressing-gown, a pair of slippers. The slender man was leaning forward. He had uncovered a plastic bag filled with soft and unfamiliar objects. He pointed. I saw a collection of bright, bead-like eyes inside the plastic.

'For the children,' Rollin said. 'In the hospital. They are just toys. Jouet?' he added in tentative French. 'Teddy bears.'

The slender man with the straight nose smiled slightly and let us pass.

'I suppose I'm lucky he didn't have them all slit open,' Rollin said as we emerged on to the city side of the most attractive airport building in Africa.

After the genocide came war. The genocide left hundreds of thousands of Tutsis dead; and then RPF forces, the majority of them Tutsis, swept down from the northern border with Uganda, fighting back the Hutu-dominated Rwandan army, as they had done in an assault the previous year, and again before that in 1990. Then, they had battled to within 30 kilometres of the capital, but this time they swept right through it, chasing the government forces clean out of the country in the south. The soldiers in the streets, as Rollin and I passed through them, were therefore those of the RPF.

These cataclysms in Rwanda had produced wave after wave of refugees. Tutsis fleeing the extermination towards their own advancing RPF; Hutus running from that advance, fearing reprisals more than the disease and hunger of the wretched camps which had sprung up in Tanzania, Zaire and Uganda. And the international aid agencies had scrambled in everywhere. Plenty of white faces in Kigali, plenty of sturdy four-wheel-drive vehicles emblazoned with a plethora of logos. I learned later that more than ninety aid agencies had their headquarters in the capital. One of them, in particular, was of interest to both Rollin and me.

We had lingered rather indecisively outside the airport building, hoping for a bus or a taxi which could take us into town, but finding nothing. 'Non taxis' was the only assistance we got from a group of young soldiers in camouflage fatigues with their guns tucked under their arms.

Then a voice said: 'G'day, gents. Need a ride?' The face beneath dark-glasses was chewing gum; the beret was a pale United Nations blue, and on the shoulder had been stitched a tag which said: Australia.

'Samaritan's Purse,' Rollin said. 'Americans, yeah. They're running part of the hospital. Their HQ is a house in town. I have a map here.'

As the RPF had pushed south, this organisation, the Samaritan's Purse, had found work to do behind the advance. Their doctors and nurses had been working in Somalia and the southern Sudan, but it had become too dangerous to continue there; so an advance party had gone into southern Uganda and made contact with the RPF. The task which the RPF asked them to perform had been to provide, within three days, medical services to 75 000 people huddled in a camp at Rutari, hardly 30 kilometres north of Kigali. The Samaritan's Purse had moved in. Then, within hours of the taking of Kigali, a Samaritans advance party found itself in the capital's shattered hospital to begin work on reopening some parts of it. The refugees, largely from the Kigali area, who had fled from the butchery, soon returned home, and the main Samaritan's Purse operation had moved to the capital. Some workers stayed in Rutari, however, to minister to the needs of hundreds of orphans discovered in the camps as the people left.

The organisation's representative in Nairobi had agreed to my visit, had indeed offered accommodation in a city where hotels were not yet operational. And of course Rollin, in private practice in Durham, North Carolina, was travelling under their auspices, having been asked to give three weeks of his time to work in the aftermath of one of Africa's great catastrophes.

We arrived at the Samaritans' house towards the end of lunch. The house itself was large, a suburban family home in happier times, I imagined, and the garden must once have been a delight. Now, several tents had been pitched on the lawns, and a collection of trucks and minibuses stood on gravel to one side. A concrete service yard at the back of the house held drums of fuel, a large generator, and containers of water from which stainless steel purification pumps protruded. Rollin and I were allocated a room which led off a narrow veranda not far away, and we were immediately urged to drink no water other than that purified through the shining pumps.

In one of the spacious living areas of the house, formica tables had been set out, and at these tables, finishing lunch, sat about twenty people. Introductions brought a succession of faces into brief focus. Don, a handsome man in early middle age, spoke with a slow accent and a crooked smile. He was the team leader, I gathered. A young woman with short dark hair and an olive skin, a Filipino perhaps, who had adorned her stethoscope with a brooch of plastic flowers. Ed, a logistics officer of some sort, who left me with a vision of clear and darkened eyes, as if they were permanently dilated, and a tense mouth. A grey-haired nurse, a lively-looking women who thrust out her hand and said: 'I'm Emilie from

Chicago. I do the paediatrics.' A man with a weathered face and pale eyes was introduced to me as Willard, a missionary in Rwanda for many years, whose house had been blown up in the war. His musical drawl was marred by a slight stutter, hardly more than hesitation as he began a new sentence sometimes. A gathering of young people smiled my way. A few of them were Canadian, they pointedly told me, as if conscious of being outnumbered by their North American cousins; and one of them, a newly graduated dentist, said he had come to Africa for a post-graduation break — 'well, it is like a holiday really' — before returning to the more serious business of going into practice with his father. One youngster sat slightly to one side, his hair tousled and curly, his eyes a little doleful when he lifted them towards the general conversation. Some smiling young nurses sat joking with an electrician who carried a small Bible — I could see the gold wording through the fabric — in his shirt pocket. These were the Samaritans, finishing their lunch, taking a second cup of coffee, preparing for the work of the afternoon.

'The hospital bus is leaving in three minutes,' Emilie from Chicago called.

Rollin had appeared in a pale green tunic with short sleeves, his stethoscope in one pocket. He had been taken under the protection of a much older man, a rasp-voiced orthopaedics man from New York, who now began to warn him of the intrigues by which the hospital was bedevilled. 'Now that we've got the hospital going, everyone's there. Italians, French, and of course the Australians doing the medical side for the UN,' I heard him say.

After the hospital bus had left, not many people remained in the house. Ed, the logistics officer, collected up some documents and disappeared. The curly-headed youngster with doleful eyes hovered awkwardly about. Don put his hand on my shoulder.

'You can ride with me. I've got a few chores to do round town. Also, we need to fetch Rollin's extra trunks from the airport. I've just heard they've arrived.'

As we walked out of the back of the house, on to the concrete where the fuel and water filters were, Don hesitated. 'Do you smell it?' he asked. 'The death smell. Every afternoon, as the day warms up, it oozes out of the walls. You're in this back room here, aren't you? We've put on four coats of special sealant, but it won't go away. That's the worst room in the house, I'm afraid.'

We clambered into a station-wagon and reversed into the roadway beyond a hedge. Don told me that the house had been used by a Belgian agency of some kind, but this agency had evacuated at the start of the troubles. When the Samaritans advance party arrived in Kigali, they had found it to be full of corpses. 'Some were just worms and bones,' he remarked in his slow way. No doubt, he conjectured, a few Tutsi families had found the place empty and used it as a refuge, until they had been discovered. 'There were fourteen bodies in your room alone; they'd been dead a month, but the blood was spread so thick, at least three inches across the whole floor, it was still wet.'

We drove down a hill towards the centre of town. A few lamp standards had been knocked over, and I saw a blackened vehicle tilting into a roadside ditch. Don showed me some of the sights. A government building up to the right with holes blasted through the walls, the metal roof torn away and crumpled like paper. Then a bridge with a roadway beneath. Here, Don said, thousands of Tutsi women and children had been forced to jump on to the tarmac below. 'If the fall didn't kill them,' he remarked, 'they were hacked to death with machetes where they lay.'

Don's hair had begun to grey slightly at the temples, and his handsome face looked nonchalantly ahead as he steered the station-wagon around a traffic circle and along a street with shops and commercial buildings on either side.

Here, the signs of recent fighting were everywhere apparent. Walls had been blackened by fire; plate-glass smashed but still hanging in shards in its frames; more burned-out cars, already with rubbish gathered in drifts about them; bunkers dug into the pavements with low sandbagged parapets above; bullet holes looking like craters erupting on the sides of dirty city walls. Soldiers sat at street corners, their weapons across their knees. The streets were crowded: people walked, sat on pavements, shouted to each other, and sold vegetables among the mess and aftermath of war.

'It's only in the last few weeks that the city's started to fill up,' Don said. 'When our people first got here, the place was empty. Corpses only.'

A t the airport, Don smiled his crooked smile at me, and I noticed that his eyebrows were quite bushy, jutting out somewhat above his handsome face. 'I don't know how we're going to do this,' he said cheerfully. 'Just recently the RPF has put guards everywhere. We used to drive freely in and out to the freight depot. No longer. But I think I know a way. Let's give it a try.'

We left the vehicle in the empty public carpark, and entered the airport building, walking rapidly towards a side entrance. The trick, Don said with his crooked smile, was to show no hesitation. A soldier even stepped aside to allow us to pass through the side door. Then we scrambled up a bank and found ourselves inside the security fence. Large transport aircraft of Russian and American design were parked on the apron. The freight depot had been taken over by a specialist aid agency. Crates and cartons were stacked into neat rows. Forklift trucks trundled to and fro. A few clerks tapped away at portable computers. Order reigned. Don passed the time of day with one of the forklift drivers. To one side, I noticed a man in dirty white overalls assembling what looked like small radar dishes. We rode on the forklift and found the six trunks belonging to Rollin.

'Excellent,' Don said. 'Now the problem is, how do we get our vehicle in.'

'Tell 'em you're collectin' free booze for the victorious troops,' the forklift driver said in an English working-class accent.

Don offered his crooked smile, his eyebrows protruding above the good-looking face.

We returned to the station-wagon by the way we had come in. Don drove slowly towards the guarded gate of the freight depot. A UN truck pulled up behind us. Don stopped and got out. He talked to the soldier in the passenger seat. In a moment the soldier, a Canadian, had joined us in the station-wagon. 'I don't know what works and what doesn't,' he said. 'I've only been in the country for thirty-six hours. But let's give it a try.' He sat on one of the side seats, his firearm across his knees. As Don drove slowly through the gate, the Canadian soldier waved to his Rwandan counterparts who let us through.

The eyes of the soldiers at the gate seemed sullen and distrusting, but above all confused. Who were they to apprehend, who to let pass? Who was friend, who the adversary? They did not know; and their eyes seemed slightly reddened by such confusions.

On the way out, Rollin's trunks stacked up on the floor of the station-wagon, Don simply waved and drove once more through the gate. For a moment he kept his eyes on the rear-view mirror, then he drove on the highway into town in silence. Groups of soldiers stood everywhere along the way. In a moment he turned his head to glance at me, his eyes alight with mirth beneath those jutting brows.

'The things we do, eh?' he said in his slow way.

But my sense was of something else entirely: a disturbing juxtaposition. That efficiency in the freight depot beyond the fence: the order, the expertise, the smiling superiority. And on this side of the fence: the groups of poorly trained soldiers, some of them no more than boys, milling about, fingering their weapons, uncertain and uncomprehending; and the city itself, perching on its hills in the lingering sunlight, spread out before us as we drove, and smelling even from that distance of chaos and death. Chaos and confusion had slightly reddened the eyes of the soldiers at the gate. But was there also some shame mingled there, even some anger at being seen in such confusion, with that other world over there, beyond the fence, as oiled and ordered as the clerks at their portable computers?

In the short twilight of that equatorial place, I sat on a flight of stone garden steps at the front of the Samaritans' house, looking out over the hills of Kigali and those lying in a faint blue haze beyond. A few points of light had come on in the city, but Ed the logistics man told me that these were the result of generators, most of them operated by the relief agencies, rather than the normal power supply which had been disrupted during the fighting. 'But I've heard that some parts of town will be reconnected in the next few days,' he said.

He had lingered with me for a few moments in the twilight, quite businesslike in manner and taciturn. But I wondered if there was not something in him which had been damaged. He gave me that sense. Had he undergone some pain, some transmutation, to leave his eyes so open and so hard, his mouth so tense? I thought him to be in his middle twenties, and I guessed he might be genuinely awkward rather than simply taciturn, and that his gruff exterior concealed a sense of private loss with which he sometimes strained to come to terms.

He said: 'I've got some stuff to move tomorrow. Don thought you might be willing to help. I'm leaving at seven thirty.'

'I'll be ready,' I said.

After he had gone, I sat on the steps, looking out over the city and listening to one of the Samaritans strumming a guitar. They had come out on to the deep veranda of the house to experience the slight cooling of the air as the sun went down. I noticed that the young doctor who had adorned her stethoscope with a brooch of plastic flowers sat stooped over a letter, the back of her pen between her lips. Emilie from Chicago walked in the garden, listening to the Voice of America on a tiny radio which crackled sharply as she held it to her ear. Then two young men, fresh from showering, began a game of table tennis on the veranda.

Someone sat down next to me on the step. I looked into the face of the youngster I had noticed at lunch, tousled hair curling on to his forehead, eyes more soulful than doleful I now decided, who had seemed set a little apart from the general gathering of Samaritans.

'You don't mind if I sit here?' he asked in a determined voice, as if to pre-empt any hostility on my part.

I said he was most welcome and, to open a conversation, I asked what work he did with Samaritan's Purse. Was he a medical person of some kind?

'Oh, no,' he said with a doleful smile. 'No, I'm not with them at all. I'm really just a guest.'

'So what are you doing in Kigali?'

He looked at me and smiled. 'I'm here because Jesus told me — you know, just out of the blue — to go to Rwanda.'

'Had you heard about the country on television?'

'I can't remember. All I know is that Jesus was telling me to come. Can I tell you the story?'

I indicated, perhaps with too resigned a gesture of my hands, that I would be willing to hear it.

'You must never resist the power of Jesus,' he said in earnest reprimand.

'Let's hear the story,' I replied.

He began, I thought, in a confused way. He began by saying that he had dropped out of college to study the Bible, and how he had gone from church to church. I wanted to ask him about his childhood, his parents, more about his background, but these elements of what might be impelling him were securely hidden behind a newer reality: he was impelled by Jesus.

'I dropped out of college and was studying the Bible, just me and the Lord, when I was led to join this particular church. And right from the start the pastor was telling me I should go to Bible college. So I went, but I stayed only one semester, because it was at this point that Jesus told me clearly to go to Rwanda. But I said to Jesus: how can I go? I've got no money. And Jesus said: sell your truck, sell everything.'

As background to these words, I heard the bright hollow plopping of the ping-pong ball, the strumming of the guitar, the easy drone of conversation. The city's hills were blackening before me. Had it been Don during the afternoon, or the Samaritans' representative in Nairobi, who had told me that most of these people paid their own way, or paid substantial portions of it, to serve wherever the need was greatest?

'So I sold everything,' the young man beside me said earnestly, 'and came to Rwanda.'

Now again there was a period of confusion, as if we were passing through a blind spot in his memory, because all at once he was in Burundi. 'And then I got jumped almost on my first night in Bujumbura and I lost all my money.'

But he had managed to get back across the border where he had lived with a family with four deaf and dumb children on a terraced hillside for three days. Then the military discovered him and told him to move on.

'They began to threaten the family because I was staying there,' he said. 'But the people told me this had never been heard of before. When I heard that, I knew what was happening. It was the work of the devil. The devil was trying to oust me from Rwanda. But Jesus strengthened me.'

Another blind spot, filled with garbled detail I could not understand, found him near the terrible refugee camps at Goma in eastern Zaire. The soldiers wouldn't let him cross back into Rwanda where Jesus wanted him to be.

'So I just walked,' he said, his soulful eyes enlivened by the drama of it. 'I heard them cocking their guns. I said: if they are going to shoot me now, so be it. But they let me go without harm. They even laughed as Jesus guided their actions. Then I hitch-hiked to Kigali where Jesus led me to a cocktail party. A man at the door said: who asked you to come? I replied that Jesus had. The man said: yes, I can see that.'

Here, the young man beside me smiled in his melancholy way. Even in the darkness I could see the sadness in his eyes. 'You see, I was dirty,' he explained. 'I was wearing only my jeans and a shirt. But at the cocktail party I met the American Ambassador, who gave me a bed for the night and then a note to these people here, the Samaritans.'

I watched the moving lights of vehicles on a nearby hillside. Then someone called us to supper. The guitar had stopped, and the garden lay heavy with the scent of foliage and flowers.

'But I don't think I can stay. I feel I will only stay here for one or two more days. Jesus has told me that I will get a job on Monday. I need to have a job. This can be the test. If I don't get a job I'll have to try to get back to the States. But Jesus has told me there is a huge Christian revival coming in Rwanda,' he went on, his voice tinged with a barely discernible plaintiveness now. 'Not in a few days, maybe only in a few years, but I know that I'll be a part of it.'

After supper, I discovered this young man asleep on a bunk in one of the bedrooms turned dormitory, while the rest of the house still talked, wrote letters, or played cards. He lay on his side, his mouth open; and a small Bible, the pages obviously much-thumbed, had slipped from his slackening fingers.

I sat on the deep veranda, talking to the missionary named Willard. The night was black beyond the pillars, the air calm, yet seeming restless with the heat still weighing upon it. Willard looked exhausted, his pale eyes drained; and with his slight stutter came small spasms to the muscles in his face. Yet his voice remained gentle, a musical drawl reminiscent of the American South, but with other influences admitted also, no doubt derived from his long African sojourn.

I said I hoped he would talk to me of his interpretation of the events which had overtaken Rwanda, and especially of what he considered to be the continuing causes of the long conflict between the Hutus and the Tutsis.

347

Willard looked steadily at me for a moment, then he leaned forward slightly, and in his eyes I saw a desire to glance over his shoulder, although he did not. 'We don't use those terms here,' he said in his gentle drawl, 'even when we think it's safe to do so. We usually talk about the shorts and the talls.'

I remained silent. He licked his lips, while muscles twitched at the sides of his mouth. 'It's about power,' he said. 'But it's also about tradition. The talls just have to govern. Nothing else will satisfy.'

He spoke to me in a low voice, quite calm except for the occasional stutter. He said it was futile to attempt to understand what had happened in Rwanda without admitting events in the neighbouring country of Burundi, especially the lengthy persecution and the massacres of the shorts there.

He shrugged his shoulders. 'But then again I sometimes think of the word symbiosis. I don't know if they can do without each other. Someone just the other day, here in this house, suggested that a solution might be to place all the talls in Burundi and all the shorts in Rwanda. The response from a woman working in the kitchen here — she's a short — was interesting. She said: yes, but who then will rule the shorts?'

He was smiling. He licked his lips, an unconscious mannerism, and went on in his musical voice. 'Psychologically they need each other. The struggle is ingrained. Perhaps this is the truth. In a way, life would be meaningless for the one side without the existence of the other.'

I asked where he had been when the troubles began.

'In my house,' he replied. 'We were trapped there, for the first four days. Then we were evacuated by other missionaries.'

He looked out into the blackened garden, his tired eyes lit with sudden memories. 'I knew we were in a dangerous position,' he went on. 'We were harbouring shorts from Burundi and then talls from our own churches in Rwanda. They would have killed us all if they had known. We could hear the massacres going on all around. I spent a lot of time preparing the people in the house to face death.' He looked at

348

me again, the muscles about his mouth jerking in a sudden spasm. 'But God brought us peace,' he said in his soft and musical way.

But when the RPF had swept through the city, their house had been destroyed. 'We had rented it for years from a previous government official who of course was a short. The RPF apparently had a list of properties belonging to the old government. They blew them all up. We lost everything. There are not two bricks left standing on top of each other. I can show you if you'd like to see.'

I said that I would.

Willard looked again into the garden beyond the pillars of the veranda. Distant dogs had begun to bark. 'In these days it comes forcibly to one: how easy it is for things to be gone. Except,' he added after a moment, 'the knowledge and presence of God.'

Rollin's face wore an expression of slight distaste for a moment. The curtains of our room hardly moved in the night air, and the unmistakable stench of death lingered in our nostrils. 'Have you heard what they found in here?' he said. 'And they buried them in the garden just outside the window,' he added with a wry grin.

I asked, as he unpacked his dressing-gown and slippers and then began a search for a pair of pyjamas, what had persuaded him to come to Rwanda.

'The Samaritan's Purse people asked me. My wife and I prayed about it. And it seemed right to come.'

His luggage began to disgorge its varied contents as he searched.

'Mind you,' he added, 'I don't know if I'll be much use. My career has been with pretty sophisticated equipment. Don't ask me when last I prodded an abdomen rather than examined the scans. But I did some prodding today, I tell you. Boy, the hospital is pretty depressing. Low tech all the way. No modern equipment. And do you know they're still using first generation antibiotics — stuff that was being used in the

States over fifty years ago — that's if they've got any antibiotics at all. There are no pain-killers and very few sterile dressings.'

He lifted out the entire bag of teddy bears which I had first seen as we passed through customs at the airport earlier that day. It seemed suddenly far distant, days or even weeks away from the present here, in this reeking room with the generator about to be switched off and us plunged into perfect darkness.

'But I admire what the Samaritan's Purse folk are trying to do,' Rollin went on. 'They're not trying to run the hospital in a First World way at all. They're trying to get it going so the Rwandans can run it themselves, with the sort of rudimentary resources they're obviously used to.'

I lay propped up on one elbow, staring down at the bright faces of the teddy bears inside the plastic bag. A few of the shiny eyes glinted from the naked light bulb suspended from the ceiling of our room.

'I must tell you the story of these bears,' Rollin said. 'A friend back home, when he heard I was coming to Rwanda, passed me one hundred dollars. He said: it's the kids who are suffering most; get something for the kids. So my wife and I went to a dollar store — do you have them in your country, where everything costs a dollar? — and got these one hundred bears. They're all the way from Durham, North Carolina,' he said, tossing them on to the top of an open suitcase. 'The nurses in paediatrics are quite excited about giving them out to the children in the ward.'

When the generator stopped, a profound silence seeped into the room, now blackened and without form. I felt too weary to sleep. I thought of the bright eyes of the teddy bears, and of sick children in a hospital with scant medicines, not even pain-killers. I strained my ears to take something from the silence. But there was nothing, although I did hear Rollin's breathing change as he fell asleep. The smell of the room came to me with every breath, and I lay in the darkness and tried to imagine the terror, the shrieks, and then the ultimate silence wrought by the staccato barking of gunfire or the thud and slice of machetes. I heard water like blood dripping somewhere one soft drop at a time.

Ed had borrowed a brand-new truck from the United Nations, and it required some effort to climb the footholds leading to the cab. Of German manufacture, the vehicle boasted power steering and various other refinements which Ed made no apology about appreciating; and during my stay in Rwanda I became used to the sight of him high up in the roomy cab, driving from point to point and generally going about the business of being logistics officer for the Samaritans working in Kigali.

I found him not particularly communicative when I joined him in the morning to help with the things which needed to be moved. We drove down into the city and to a large warehouse where Ed hooted at the gate until a Rwandan, loping from the rear of the buildings, let us in. His exchanges with me in the high cab were gruff, often monosyllabic, but I thought that this might be because we were not alone.

The young man with curly hair and doleful eyes, the one who had sat with me on the steps the previous evening, accompanied us. I had overheard him talking to Don, asking with the awkwardness of slight embarrassment whether there was anything he could do to recompense for the nights of accommodation which the Samaritans had provided. Don, with a crooked smile and a friendly pat on the shoulder in reply, had not been slow to direct him Ed's way.

Our task at the warehouse was to unload the back of Ed's truck and stack the contents on to wooden pallets which we dragged in from outside. Ed worked in the rough way of someone who wanted the job done quickly, slamming down the pallets and dragging off the boxes with an energy which suggested anger as much as it did impatience. Then someone called him on his two-way radio and he stood to one side.

While we continued with the work, I asked the curly-headed young man how Jesus spoke to him. What were the signs which he took as the divine voice? The young man paused with a box from the truck still balanced on his shoulder. He looked at me with his lips sucked between his teeth, then he told me that first the thoughts came to him, followed by confirmation from the scriptures.

'Jesus gives me the thoughts,' he said. 'Then He puts the chapter and verse numbers into my head. I have never learned scripture so I could quote long pieces out of my head, like some people do. Now the Lord is using my ignorance to lead me to His will. That's how He led me to Rwanda.'

I asked, leaning on a pile of cartons, whether he could remember the verses which had been involved in this momentous decision.

He nodded. 'These I have learned by heart. The first book of Kings. Chapter nineteen. I saw all the killing and suffering on television. Then the Lord gave me the scripture, and I knew.'

'Will you say the verse? I'd be most interested.'

He looked at me with his soulful eyes brightened in the dim interior of the warehouse. He stood among the cartons, his face illumined by the light from the large doors which stood open to one side of where we worked.

He cleared his throat. 'And he said, go forth, and stand upon the mount before the Lord. And, behold, the Lord passed by, and a great and strong wind rent the mountains, and brake in pieces the rocks before the Lord; but the Lord was not in the wind: and after the wind an earthquake; but the Lord was not in the earthquake: and after the earthquake a fire; but the Lord was not in the fire: and after the fire a still small voice.'

On these last words, the young man's own voice had wavered slightly, and I wondered if it was not perhaps with doubt now that it did so. Then he turned away to continue the unloading of the cartons. Later during the morning, we dropped him off at the gate of an aid agency where he said he would probably be able to get a job.

After he had climbed down from the high cab and given a wave, Ed remarked in his blunt way: 'He should be put on the first plane back to the States. I don't think he's really in control of himself.'

I asked, as we drove on, whether Ed had seen others like the young man, people who were so convinced of their calling to one or other of the world's unhappy places that they neglected too many of the basics in their haste to fulfil their destinies.

'A few,' Ed replied.

'And what makes you do this sort of work?'

He shrugged his shoulders. 'I grew up here. Did you know that?'

In short sentences Ed's story emerged. He was the son of missionaries in south-western Rwanda. He had gone to school in Kenya, at the Rift Valley Academy. Certainly, he had done some studying in America, but then he had returned. He had joined the Samaritans because he felt he could be useful to them, especially in Rwanda where his local knowledge had proved invaluable.

'I was in the advance party which first entered the country during the war. We set up the clinics in the refugee camps at Rutari. That's where we got involved with the orphans. We knew there were children without parents in the camp, but only when the refugees had all gone home, did we realise how many. They're still there, and still under our care. The next big effort will be to move them down here, where conditions can be properly controlled. Most of them are probably from around Kigali anyway. Yes, they're Tutsis. Many of their parents are undoubtedly dead.'

I looked across at him, his strong fists gripping the wheel which was fixed horizontally before him in the high and roomy cab. Suddenly he spoke again.

'It's generally accepted,' he said, as if anxious to get it out into the open, 'that a million people have died. Some reports say the figure is even higher. Of these, about four hundred and fifty thousand were slashed to death by machete. I say it's unforgivable that the world stood by.'

I asked if friends of his had died.

'Yes, of course,' he replied, 'but that's not the point. The point is the world did nothing. I'm sure there were delicate political issues and considerations, but still I say it. Unforgivable.'

His pupils seemed dilated, his eyes very clear, and his mouth was tensed, thin-lipped, and twisted out of shape somewhat with repressed but hardly silenced anger.

I went that afternoon with Rollin and the harsh-voiced doctor from New York to see the place that was being prepared for the orphans from Rutari. The doctor from New York drove our minibus over rutted roads, while Rollin took photographs of everything through the side window. I sat in the back and watched grey-tinged clouds gathering along the horizon.

The orphanage, a row of low houses set among old trees, stood on the outskirts of the city, overlooking a steep valley whose sides were patched with banana groves. The Samaritans had done some extensive cleaning up at the orphanage, and the yards and interiors looked habitable, although evidence remained of more violent times, buckled metal doors, smashed locks, hundreds of broken windows which had been repaired with plastic sheeting.

'There were a lot of bodies here when we first started,' said the electrician, whom we found working on a generator installed under some iron sheeting at the back of the orphanage kitchens. 'I think it must have been used as some sort of execution place. Dozens of bodies had been buried by bulldozer.'

He had a friendly and sincere face, the electrician, one cheek marked with grease, and I noticed that he still carried a small Bible in his shirt pocket.

'We're having trouble with our big generator,' he said pleasantly. 'You won't believe this, but it was stolen by one of the hotels in town now that they're gearing up to reopen. They've returned it, but not in the same condition it was in when they took it.'

Rollin plied him with questions about the bodies. How many? In what state were they? Had they been buried deep in the ground?

The electrician said: 'When we first got to Kigali there were thousands of corpses all over the streets. The smell was terrible. There were no living people anywhere. There was no movement, and no sound.'

The New York doctor grunted in disgust. 'It makes you wonder about humanity, doesn't it?' he said in his harsh voice.

'I wrote in my diary: the city of death,' the electrician said in his sincere way. 'You know, I've been reading the Old Testament recently. Things haven't changed much, have they? Cities were built up and conquered and then smashed down. Nothing much has changed.'

'Are there any body parts still lying around?' Rollin asked, fingering his camera.

The electrician regarded him in silence for a moment, then he said: 'I saw a few bones yesterday.'

He took us to one of the mass graves, the marks of the bulldozer still evident on raw brown earth from which young banana trees vigorously sprouted. Almost immediately, Rollin had found what he was looking for: a few bones thrusting out, some still with ragged clothing hanging to them. He crouched to take close-ups, identifying each protrusion as he did so: part of a child's pelvic girdle, a shattered femur, and so on.

The New York doctor grunted in a mixture of disgust and amusement. 'What are you going to do with that sort of picture, for goodness sake?'

'For lectures,' Rollin said, while his shutter clicked once more.

The electrician stood in a vaguely embarrassed silence, his pleasant face turned as he gazed away into the steep-sided valley beyond the grave. The New York doctor's face was drawn into a grimace, I thought as a reaction to the stench, but it was difficult to decipher grin from grimace in a face which seemed habituated to harshness of experience as much as to absolutes of interpretation. A few birds noised suddenly in young banana trees.

'It sure makes you wonder,' said the harsh-voiced doctor, his expression now turned to definite disgust, 'whether human beings are anything better than animals.'

'Animals don't do this,' Rollin said as he straightened up, rewinding a completed film.

'That's right,' the New York doctor responded with an unexpected laugh. 'This sure isn't human behaviour, this.'

As we went on our way, bumping on unkempt roads in our minibus, I saw that clouds had piled high above the hilly landscape of the city. As the afternoon wore on, the atmosphere turned humid, expectant, and the air heavy. The soldiers at the frequent road-blocks had hardly the energy to wave us through. Once or twice, Rollin tried his French on them, grinning cheerfully through his window, but the soldiers replied only with stares of incomprehension.

I sat in the rear of the bus in silence as the two doctors drove through the city, choosing the byways sometimes, admiring the banana and papaw trees, conjecturing on the lavish flowers blooming everywhere, stopping for more photographs of war damage, blown-up houses, bent electricity poles with tangled wires torn adrift. Once off the tarred roads where pedestrians walked in their thousands, the people who lived in the city seemed to evaporate. Perhaps they stayed indoors. Only children enlivened the open spaces and played among the extravagant foliage hemming in the suburban byways.

One small child jumped up and tried to touch Rollin's arm which he had crooked through the open window of the minibus. In response, he lowered his hand and allowed the child to touch it. Suddenly a dozen children had surged forward. Small boys slapped at Rollin's hand with their own. The children began to cry out with excitement, chasing after the friendly hand as the minibus gathered speed.

'Aren't the little ones cute?' the New York doctor said in his harsh voice. 'But the trouble is they soon grow out of it.'

It suddenly struck me that the little ones knew more surely than their elders perhaps that they stood only on a thin covering of soil, that they could be sucked underneath at any moment. The deepest urge was surely for a tactile experience of life, the hand of a white man dangling from a minibus, the sound of skin slapping against other skin, before they were sucked down. It was this urge which caused the momentary rush and noise beyond the windows of the minibus, the faces of the children strangely unsmiling as they chased, the eyes and mouths wide open in the fiercenesses of this imperative: to find some footholds in the treacheries of their thin covering of soil.

Thunder rolled fiercely. The children screamed and danced in sudden fright. Had it reminded them of guns? More surely, I thought, they understood a deeper truth. A million corpses lay underneath the covering of soil on which they danced, a covering which was stretched too thin and taut to last, so that all the misery and horror would burst out at the first good rains or slightest provocation.

T he orphans ran out to greet us and to wave as Ed's big truck rumbled in among dirty buildings set in a compound at one end of the village of Rutari. Ed returned these exuberant greetings in his slightly grim way; but Emilie, the paediatric nurse from Chicago, brimmed over with an enthusiastic response, calling out brightly to the children who flocked, laughing, to her side of the high cab.

For she had immediately claimed the window seat when we had set out from the Samaritans' house in Kigali earlier in the day. 'I can't bear sitting in the middle,' she explained. 'I feel that I miss too much.'

At breakfast, Ed had announced he had something to do in Rutari, and Emilie had asked to come along for the ride. 'Anything to get out of town for a few hours,' she told me, her face jovial, yet her grey eyes promising considerable reserves of stubbornness. 'Sunday, after all, is our day of rest.'

Ed ground through a city which seemed more thronged with people and dilapidated vehicles with each passing day, then turned north and sent the truck charging and hooting along the narrow roads. Pedestrians and cyclists scattered before us. Ed drove with his lips compressed, his window rolled down to admit the blowing air. He slowed down, but reluctantly, only for the road-blocks, and even then he did not stop, relying on the prominent UN markings on the vehicle to get us through.

The country seemed at once lush yet strangely derelict, the vegetation showing signs simultaneously of the new growth of spring and autumnal decay. The round hills swept up on both sides of the road. The hillsides had long ago been denuded of indigenous trees, filled instead with frequent clumps of bananas and close terraced fields sometimes scarred with erosion. There was also dereliction of a more immediate kind: hillsides which seemed ravaged, the grass worn down and the rotting remains of wattle-and-daub abodes still littering the steep slopes. The remains of refugee camps from 1990, Ed said in his taciturn way. They were refugee camps from a time already several wars ago. Then we turned off the tarmac and climbed up into the hills towards Rutari. We seemed to climb perceptibly closer to the clouds already sailing in the sky, with the air becoming cooler all the time. The road was rough, and it seemed that the bouncing of the truck and the freshening air lifted a load off both my companions.

Emilie said she had one more week to go, and then she was returning to the United States where she was doing a course on ethics. 'I'm looking forward to that, and have I got some questions for my lecturers after working in Rwanda for two months.'

Ed told some stories about the problem of maintaining a water supply to tens of thousands of refugees high in the hills at Rutari. At last he had gatecrashed a meeting of a high-ranking American general when he spent a few hours at Kigali Airport. The result was that the Americans had helped with water tankers.

'Water was also a problem when we started work at the hospital,' he said, his eyes animated but his mouth still tight-lipped. 'The hospital had been shot up a bit and looted, and there were quite a few squatters living in the wards. The water supply pipes had been smashed, and every lavatory in the whole place was blocked.'

'The filth was definitely the worst part,' Emilie said in her lively way. 'Especially for me, used to the shining wards in Illinois.'

I learned that she had been one of the first medical Samaritans to arrive in Kigali after the advance party had cleaned up the house now used as headquarters and billet. She had opened the children's ward. She had spent days on her knees, scrubbing floors; and some more days. standing on chairs, scrubbing walls.

'But it's amazing how quickly our role has changed. First we were cleaners. Then we were hands-on nurses. Now, as more Rwandans are recruited, we play a supervisory and advisory role only. Mortality rates are right down. When we first started they were depressingly high. I got to a point where I couldn't stand so much death. But I must say I'm quite proud of the wards now.'

The truck growled up the steep inclines towards Rutari. Views began to extend into the soft vaguenesses of distance, and I could see the hilly landscapes stretching away and dappled with the shade cast by dozens of individual clouds. Closer at hand, Ed pointed out the places where the tents of the Rutari refugees had been pitched, but not for long enough to seriously damage the green hillsides of these high places.

Emilie was saying: 'But there's always something else, isn't there? I suppose you've heard about the teddy bears.'

I looked at her in mild surprise.

'He seems a nice man, the new surgeon,' she went on. 'But teddy bears! He wants to give them out in our wards. Surely he should know better. Some of our children have been blown apart by grenades, some are dying of malaria and AIDS and pneumonia, others have bullets lodged in their brains; and now we'll also have to contend with children going blue and choking on teddy bears' eyeballs.'

Ed laughed. 'Do black babies go blue?' he asked.

'Or whatever,' Emilie said. 'I just think it's misguided and inappropriate.'

'I often think the same thing,' Ed responded, 'when we get the Christmas presents made by American children. You know the sort of thing: shoe boxes decorated with wrapping paper, and containing pencils and candy and things like that, stuff we could certainly get cheaper in Nairobi. And never mind the organisation and time involved in distributing thousands of these shoe boxes. But if it helps American kids to become more aware of conditions elsewhere, then maybe it's worth the effort.'

It was with these words that Ed had steered the big truck into the compound at one end of the village of Rutari and the orphans had run out to greet us.

They were of varying ages, from children still toddling to young teenagers in school uniforms. Their faces were well-fed, bright, although a few individuals lagged behind, uncertain, fingers in mouths, a few hands fearfully clutching at genitals. Emilie had jumped down, and the children flocked around her as if to feel her liveliness and warmth more closely. It seemed a suddenly moving sight, the grey-haired nurse from Chicago, surrounded by these laughing victims of Rwanda's latest bloody tumult. I remembered all the fevered explanations then: the theory of old social stratifications exacerbated by the European-inspired Hamitic myth of inferior and superior tribes; the theory of a traditional ruling élite crashing headlong into universal suffrage; the theory of the merciless struggle for power among corrupt post-colonial groupings. But they seemed each one to pale at the concreteness of the sight before me: the lively Emilie, her practised hands lifting a face here, a thin forearm there, or drawing down a score of lower eyelids to check the colour; and the children prancing around her, anxious for the warmth of laughter and some blessing, however transient and scant. And above them the clouds already gathering for rain, that sense of darkness washing through, that heaviness of air, and a presentiment in me of half-eaten faces, no more than skin stretched across the skulls of nightmare.

Ed's gruff voice broke across such visions. 'You're South African,' he said. 'I've been meaning to ask you. Do you follow rugby much?'

'A bit,' I replied, looking at his tense face in the cab, his hands still on the wheel, and feeling myself pulled back to him, as if from a considerable distance. The laughter of the children still swirled through Emilie's open door; but Ed's face claimed precedence now.

'I consider myself an American. No doubt about it. But I think American football is the pits. I have two religions: Christianity first, but rugby comes a close second.'

His large clear eyes regarded me intently. He said he had first played rugby at the Rift Valley Academy, introduced to the game by a South African who was teaching there. He told me he was keen to organise a game in Kigali. There were Australians among the United Nations contingent, as well as dozens of aid agencies from Britain and France and other rugby-playing nations.

I asked this small-built and wiry young man what position he liked to play; perhaps scrumhalf?

He shrugged his shoulders. 'I much preferred fullback. I liked that sense of being the last line of defence. Or flank,' he went on, 'where the whole point is to tackle the opposing scrumhalf. I liked the tackling.'

I ventured to remark that he seemed somewhat like that in real life as well.

A slight smile eased his tense mouth. 'You might say that there are similarities,' he said. Then he opened his door and jumped down.

'When the elephants fight, it is the grass which gets torn up.' This was the missionary Willard's voice, stuttering slightly on the first phrase; but the words had come at first from Japhet, a Rwandan clergyman from the north of Kigali.

We stood, the three of us, beside Willard's battered pick-up in the middle of town. We were waiting for some visiting missionaries to emerge from the offices of an aid agency. Japhet was a youngish man, neatly bearded, and he had offered the comment about the elephants to illustrate the plight of ordinary Rwandans, his own congregation not excluded.

I asked Willard whether Japhet was a short or a tall. We spoke in English, a language of which Japhet had no knowledge. Willard replied: 'He's a short. But does it matter? I could show you talls in similar circumstances. Our church leadership reflects the population percentages of the country as a whole. Now, of course, this leadership is either dead or in the refugee camps. Japhet is one of the few ministers remaining with their congregations. He is also working in the refugee camps in Goma in eastern Zaire.

'Let me tell you that Japhet is a courageous man,' Willard went on. 'Every time he comes to town he probably risks his life.'

'Why is he here?'

'This time it is to buy seeds for his congregation. The planting season has arrived, and if the people don't go into the fields, we will soon have famine on top of everything else.'

I looked at Japhet, and he, possibly conscious that we discussed him, offered a sudden smile which showed glistening white teeth. Willard spoke to him in Kinyarwanda, and Japhet replied in the same language.

Willard said to me in his quiet voice: 'This man has fled his home three times since 1990, and in Burundi last year he and a colleague were the only survivors of a massacre at a Bible college in Gitega.'

Japhet nodded his head politely, his stance deferential.

When the visiting missionaries appeared, we set off to see Willard's house which had been bombed. The missionaries, a middle-aged man and his wife, sat in front with Willard, and he apologised in a vague and stammering way that I would therefore need to travel behind. I set his mind at rest, and he offered a grateful smile.

The back of the pick-up was full of furniture, but Japhet and I found corners to perch in as Willard drove through the thronged streets of downtown Kigali. The furniture — to furnish a room Willard had claimed for himself and his wife at the back of his church — he had bought at a ramshackle street market. 'Yes, I know it's all stuff from the looting,' he had said with a shrug, 'but where else can I buy?'

As we drove, a light drizzle began. Willard looked back through the rear window of the pick-up with some concern, but we waved him on. The drizzle had come as anticlimax to another ominous gathering of clouds which produced little more than a heaviness of air and a sultry expectation. Thunder had rattled for a while, but no storm materialised, only an oozing drizzle. The fine drops of water lodged in Japhet's beard like small stars. We grinned at each other.

The streets seemed narrower from the back of the pick-up than I had experienced them before; and also, sitting against the direction of travel, the contents of the streets came unexpectedly upon me. We drove into the middle of things before I knew we were there. In this way, I had close views of the smashed glass of shop windows and bullet holes sprayed across masonry, and also the sudden sight of a crumbling block of flats, first floor windows showing black from recent fires within. Charred strands of curtaining hung behind broken panes. Japhet sat with his hands folded around his knees.

I had a close view, certainly the closest I had been afforded so far, of the people thronging the streets of Kigali. I tried to imagine what lay behind the eyes, what their thoughts must be, what they had experienced and whether these experiences had jolted the foundations or the superstructures of their lives.

Then I found myself looking directly into the painted faces of three young women. The pick-up had stopped at an intersection, and the women stood within touching distance of my side of the vehicle. They smiled at me in slightly mocking enticement. They were boldly dressed, their clothes tight-fitting, the curve and cleavage of their breasts exposed, their lips and cheekbones highlighted with red. I greeted them simply because they looked so directly at me. They laughed in reply.

As the truck moved forward, one of the women reached out and trailed her fingers, the nails a vivid red, down my forearm. I remembered the children chasing after the minibus when Rollin had placed his hand within their reach, and how they had slapped against it, again and again as they ran, as in some urgency for touch before they were sucked down. And these Kigali women also, standing in the anticlimax of the drizzle, one of them with big red bows on her shoes, as they regarded my departure with partly amused and also slightly sneering smiles.

We drove past a succession of caved-in shops, men standing on verandas which no longer had any covering on skeletal roofs. Other men walked on narrow sidewalks of wet and recently dug soil. Had they buried people even here, their bones waiting for the torrents? The faces of the living seemed too close for comfort; and all at once, like a confirmation, I saw a face deranged, the eyes loose, the mouth plagued with wincing tics. Was this the result of terror, of some unbearable moment filled with an inner collapsing of control? Beneath the face stood the thin body of a man, but seeming twisted out of shape and covered with a ragged shirt and soiled trousers open at the front. This twisted man stood so determinedly in the roadway that Willard was obliged to drive around. When the loose eyes, half rolling, saw me, a tongue was thrust out and thin hands began to clap. Applause and intimations of madness for us as we drove slowly by.

We went up a steep street which Willard later told us had seen some of the fiercest fighting in the battle for Kigali. Shattered military vehicles still crouched where they had exploded and burned. The houses on either side were pock-marked with bullets, and sometimes whole walls had collapsed. A few faces looked out from behind cardboard and scraps of rusting tin as we laboured up the steep and unpaved incline. The drizzle had stopped, but this arena of war still glistened and shone in its wet aftermath. Japhet looked out at these things with an impassive face. He drove with us on that overcast day simply because he had not yet been killed.

Yet the words he had uttered and which Willard had translated, those words about the elephants and the grass, returned forcefully to me then. The madness of war, the sense of being sucked down, the torrents of rain that threatened but would not come, the face of God somewhere in the mayhem of massacre. But also the closeness of things from the back of the pick-up, everything within touching distance; and then the pick-up was stopping in the yard of Willard's house that was no more. For a moment I saw the hills of Kigali stretching away in the grey afternoon, then the pain and immediacy of the present claimed me when I saw what remained of Willard's old home.

Only rubble. Roofing crumpled and torn aside, screw holes become rents. Splintered wood. An electrical conduit pipe looping into the air above a chaos of bricks and plaster, some pieces still showing the colour of the walls or the remnants of tiles from the bathroom.

Willard stood in silence. The visiting missionaries uttered sympathetic sounds. But Willard stood for a moment unhearing, his gentle face caught as if in the light of flames. He licked his lips, the tip of his tongue held for a moment exposed, and his features gripped in a flurry of small spasms which dragged repeatedly at the corners of his mouth.

I turned away. Japhet's sombre face was before me. 'When the elephants fight...' I said. Japhet did not understand the English words. He nevertheless smiled in a solemn way and nodded politely.

E milie, the paediatric nurse from Chicago, showed me through the children's wards at Kigali's central hospital.

Those children who could walk accompanied us. Others followed only with their eyes. Narrow beds filled up the wards, and the space between was crowded by the presence of mothers and other family members. The children were housed in two long buildings, with a concrete courtyard between. Crude wooden coffins had been stacked in one corner of the courtyard; and at the taps in the centre I paused to watch a woman washing the naked body of her son while flies still swarmed at his buttocks.

Emilie moved confidently through the wards. She wore jeans and running shoes, and a pale blue T-shirt. A stethoscope dangled from her neck, and a two-way radio had been hooked on to her belt. Her short grey hair bobbed as she strode about. She spoke cheerfully to everyone she met, using a tall young man with a pleasant, slightly introspective face as her interpreter, and evincing smiles and laughter as we passed between the beds.

'This one had a bullet in his head; in fact, it was lodged there for a month before he was brought to the hospital. And this one here, a hand grenade went off in his face. Didn't it, my little friend? He's a naughty one, this.'

I glimpsed a big bright eye peering out from between bandages stiff with dried blood. An older child in a Woody Woodpecker T-shirt looked up at Emilie with a face disfigured by scars in a variety of colours from pale pink to dark brown.

'Burns,' Emilie explained, running her fingers over the child's features. 'We've dealt with plenty of burns here, haven't we, you rascal?'

At one end of the wards, smaller rooms housed children still in the contagious stage of tuberculosis. 'But why are they running around all over the place?' Emilie asked a nurse. 'I just hope God protects us all.' Emilie's young interpreter spoke to the nurse in Kinyarwanda, adding a few phrases in French. To Emilie he spoke a careful English. He had told me, as we waited for Emilie to attend to a child who had screamed itself breathless, that his name was George. He had a wry smile which spread itself slowly across his narrow features.

In the ward on the far side of the concrete courtyard, small children lay motionless, one of the mothers fanning her child with a ragged towel.

'Malaria, dysentery, pneumonia, AIDS, malnutrition. Take your pick. Some of these poor babies have the whole lot. George, remind me: we need more oxygen. There's not enough to give everyone though.'

Two small children had died in the night. Emilie looked briefly at the shape beneath a sheet. She placed her hand on the mother's shoulder. The body of the other child had already been packed into a cardboard box. 'We have nowhere here to dispose of bodies,' Emilie said, 'and anyway the mothers usually want to take them home for burial there.'

With her hand still on the young woman's shoulder, Emilie spoke gently with her through George. Even though he spoke to her in a language I could not understand, he seemed to catch Emilie's intent exactly, her sympathy and gentle reassurances. But the woman could not be consoled. She sat by the side of her dead baby, her eyes wide open, her hands knotted in her lap. She kept looking down at her hands, as if astonished that she no longer had anything for them to do.

'Although they don't show it, the mothers are always emotionally devastated,' Emilie said. 'This mother is hardly more than a girl herself. It's her first child. What a short and brutal life these people live.'

I went with Emilie to the outpatients' department, walking in the sunlit morning but seeing that, as on previous days, clouds had already begun to invade the blue. The hospital buildings showed the marks of stray mortars going through brittle asbestos roofs on which, at one point, a large red cross painted on a piece of fabric had been anchored with sandbags at each corner.

At outpatients, I heard the harsh voice of the New York doctor admonishing a woman. 'She leaves her son here and goes shopping. That's how much she cares.' The son was a boy in his middle teens, his left ankle swollen to twice its normal size. The New York doctor prodded at it, so that the boy winced. Rollin appeared from behind a drawn curtain and began to take photographs of the ankle, then he made a few notes. The X-rays showed no break, the doctors said among themselves. The New York doctor spurted a few drops from the front of a syringe and then thrust the needle in. The boy cried out as much in fear as in pain. One of the young American nurses, her calm face suffused with love like an angel's, slipped him two small biscuits which he clutched in his trembling hands.

Rollin said: 'I'm bringing the teddy bears after lunch.'

Emilie replied in a resigned voice. 'If you must.'

Rollin laughed, winking at me. 'I'll see you then.'

Back in the children's ward, we drank tea on our feet. Emilie had a short meeting with the staff, using George as interpreter. The contagious TB patients should be kept separated. The wards were looking tidy and clean. More oxygen was urgently needed. The nurses stood around her as she spoke, their faces dark beneath white caps, their eyes large and attentive. When she told them this was her last week, before returning to America, they said with regret: 'Who will come to help us then?' Emilie said briskly that the time was soon coming when they would be required to run the hospital themselves, as they had in the past. 'But the Belgians were here in the past,' the nurses said. 'Well,' Emilie replied, 'maybe the Belgians will come back. Now we must prepare for the doctors' rounds.'

George stood beside me, finishing his tea. He said in his careful English: 'I work here because I can speak three languages. I have just finished school. Yes, I was nearly dead,' he went on with his wry smile. 'Sixty pupils were shot. But I cannot tell you what it was like. There are no words. You had to be there.' He put his cup on a table. 'But now I want to go to university when it is again open. I wish to study biochemistry because that is what I have already started at my school.' We went out into the nearest ward.

The young Filipino doctor who had adorned her stethoscope with a brooch of plastic flowers stood by a bed, her face resigned. Beside her, a nurse was writing on a clipboard. 'Here is the problem,' the doctor said. 'The child can be discharged, but the mother is saying there is no food at home. There is an agency called Food for the Hungry. See if they can help.'

A moment later, she was cutting away the dressing on a child's foot with a pair of office scissors. Toes had been amputated. 'This is good progress,' she said in her mild American accent. 'Actually, the child can be discharged. But the question is: can the mother be relied upon to clean and dress the wound twice a day. Does she know how? Of course, the child should go to the local clinic for this attention. But where in Rwanda is there a local clinic in operation?'

Another mother at another bed: showing clear disappointment at news of her daughter's discharge. 'Who will carry the child?' she asked in a woeful voice. 'How did they get here in the first place?' asked the young doctor. 'There's an agency called Care International; see if they can help.' The nurse wrote painstakingly on her clipboard.

A metal bottle of oxygen was wheeled in. Emilie said matter-of-factly: 'That's all we're getting for today. Where do you want it?'

'Here,' the doctor said. 'These two can share. They look as if they're saveable. I'm afraid that one over there isn't.' She opened her hands, palms upwards, to indicate the hopelessness of the situation.

That one over there was being fanned with a ragged towel, the forearms of the mother working mechanically, her face a mask of patience and inscrutability. The child seemed indescribably small, indescribably fragile. Its colour was a yellowish grey. It lay on its side, its eyes and mouth open. I wondered if it had even been born by the time the massacres in Kigali had begun. From time to time the mother rose to place the back of her hand against the baby's cheek. Then she sat down once more, and the slow fanning was resumed.

The doctor had moved on. 'Why is this woman still here?' The young mother still sat with her dead child in the noisy ward. But now the body, at first lying under a sheet, had been made into a small parcel with a piece of blanket and string. The woman turned slow eyes upon the doctor, and the doctor looked away.

'Can something be done?' she said, and her voice sounded vexed. 'Where does she live? We must get her home. Oh, this poor girl.'

The nurse with the clipboard spoke to the woman and then, briefly, to George who translated in a low voice to Emilie. Emilie went out into the passage and unclipped the radio from her belt. 'Emilie to Ed. Ed. Ed, do you read?'

Ed soon came. He drove his big truck to the entrance of the ward. Emilie brought the young mother out with her parcel of blanket and string. She also carried a small plastic bag, no doubt of personal things. 'Ed will drive you home,' Emilie said gently.

The bereaved mother looked up at Ed sitting in his high cab and provided the name of a destination. Ed nodded. Then Emilie took the parcel and passed it up to Ed who took it carefully. I looked at this tableau, with only a sullen sky beyond: Ed with his mouth tense, holding the parcel with one hand while offering the other to the young woman as she climbed up towards the cab. There were no words. But I could see that Ed's eyes were in pain, dilated with anger and pain, and even a thirst for pain, I thought, as if he could not bear to be bypassed. So he rushed again and again, but with his terrible self-control, into the torment of the place he owned as home. Now the young woman was sitting in the cab, high off the ground, her head at an angle of pride and bewilderment. I watched as Ed handed her the parcel. He did so with a tensed dignity, even with an unconscious grace, as a man would give a gift to a woman; and the young woman turned her head slightly to thank him. And I saw Ed clearly then in another setting: those steadfast eyes, the last line of defence, the outstretched hands refusing to be bypassed, the resolute tackle, flesh on flesh, bone on bone, as many times as the game dictated.

Emilie said: 'I think we'd better go in and practise getting glass eyes out of children's throats.'

But for a moment I lingered. Ed changed gears and the truck ground away. The sky beyond the high vehicle as it turned was filled with low and darkening clouds.

T he teddy bears were spotted early by those children who could walk, and they surged forward in excitement. Rollin took photographs as the toys were handed out. Emilie walked down the middle of the wards with the plastic bag, dispensing bears. 'I'm doing this against my better judgement,' she told me, albeit with a smile. 'And if you like — ' this time she addressed Rollin — 'you can buy them all back at the market on Saturday and repeat the process again next week.' Rollin laughed. I saw beads of perspiration on his forehead, gathered there in response to the airless heat which preceded equatorial storms. The wards had become gloomy as the afternoon darkened, but for a few moments they were lit and vivid with enthusiasm over the one hundred bright-eyed teddy bears which had travelled all the way from Durham, North Carolina.

Rollin took photographs of the tentative outstretching of small hands to grasp the bears. Other children were too ill to reach out, but followed the movement of the bears with their eyes. A few could not even manage that, and Emilie propped up the bears against a thin arm or a small body. She laid a cheerful bear beside the yellow-grey child being fanned with a ragged towel. The eyes did not even flicker, but the fanning mother smiled her thanks. Would oxygen have helped?

The boy with burns held his bear up before him, staring quizzically into the bright glass eyes. Emilie walked up the length of one ward, and down the other, giving out the gifts. By the time we had got back to the starting point, some of the bears had already been forgotten. They lay ignored beside sick children, and some had already fallen to the floor.

'No eyes been swallowed yet?' asked Emilie.

Then she took a step forward. The yellow-grey child had flung on to its back, its tiny arms spread in an attitude of surrender, its eyes staring upward. Emilie placed her fingers against the side of the child's throat. Gently, then, she took hold of the mother's hands so that the waving of the ragged towel would stop. The woman looked up at the ceiling, casting aside the restraining hands and fanning still, as if to ignite a miracle, but with her face set rigid now in a sadness beyond despair.

I looked out into the courtyard and at the crude wooden coffins in a heap; and I saw, with a shock of fear, fierce rain bouncing off concrete, sluicing in gutters, thickening the air just above the ground. I heard Emilie's gentle voice behind me. There seemed to be no respite anywhere. Death upon death, the sucking under, and now the tearing away of Rwanda's thin and tenuous soil. Thunder crashed against the low buildings of the hospital, and the rain came with fearsome force against the brittle roof.

11

Face of Innocence

I am a Ugandan child aged 16 in Ntare School. While most of us African children regret why we were born on this poor and war-torn continent, I have a feeling that regretting will do us no good. It is a pity that due to wars, poverty and low life expectancy of Africans, we children no longer have our forefathers to make consultations with; but thanks to the documented and theoretical history provided to us by the educated class... we have the mistakes and achievements made by our forefathers on which we can supplement ours and compare the two for a long-lasting solution to our problems.

— Anonymous letter in Kampala's *The Sunday Vision,* October 1994.

W e stood by the roadside in a deep pre-dawn darkness made even more profound by an overcast sky. The damp air of the mountains struck cold through clothing, and our breath, caught in the distant light of the approaching vehicle, emerged as transient wisps of steam. The figures of my companions were also discernible, roughly dressed for walking, and standing against the rocks and wet vegetation piled up beyond the verge. One was a young Scottish fellow carrying a rucksack. The other two were American, a man and a woman who had taken a day off from their duties as medics in a nearby camp for Rwandan refugees. The young Scot smoked a cigarette, standing with his shoulders hunched;

373

and I saw that the American man, who had introduced himself as Geoff, wore an ear-ring and a chiffon scarf at his throat. The woman stood with her back to me, her short hair sticking down like brown straw from beneath the cloth hat she wore.

When the vehicle stopped we clambered in to be greeted by smiling Ugandan rangers. 'We see gorillas good today,' one of them said, showing large white teeth.

The vehicle bounced forward. We passed through the sleeping village of Kisoro, and almost immediately began to climb. The road had become no more than a track, and we were obliged to hold on to whatever we could find to stay in our seats. From behind us as we drove the light of dawn began to appear. Looking back, I saw the beginnings of an outline of a huge vista stretching away and filled with mist. But our attention was primarily directed forward and up, to see if we could catch sight of the old volcanoes towards which we climbed.

I had seen them the evening before, from the garden of the hotel at which I spent the night. They had showed clear and dark against a fading sky: in the east, Mahavura; then the slightly smaller Gahinga; and finally Sabinyo, gaunt and conical and free-standing, like a beacon. Mist had rolled and settled about the bases of the volcanoes, while the steel-grey sunset had flung light upwards in chill shafts. The cold and damp had come up out of the wet ground of the garden where I stood. Flocks of crows circled and rasped in the big trees standing tall and dense-leafed about the hotel; and I heard the cries of children diminish as group by group they were called into the small houses of Kisoro, and the bleating of a goat which continued unabated until long after the darkness was complete and even the shapes of the volcanoes had merged with the night.

Once, in the deepest twilight, I heard a sharp metal sound, repeated several times; and not far away I discerned a man testing the mechanism of an automatic rifle.

It came to me as a half brooding and melancholy thought that I was standing on the continent's central spine, that long arc of mountains and lakes which began in the north at Lake Albert (more recently named Mobuto Sese Seko) and then curved through the lakes called Edward (Rutangise), Kivu, Tanganyika and Malawi. To the west of this arc lay the immense basin of the Zaire River stretching for 1 500 low-lying kilometres before Kinshasa was reached, and after that city the great rapids which took the river crashing down in steps to the sea. To the east of where I stood, the Indian Ocean lay 1 000 kilometres away. Perhaps it was the combination of great beauty with great isolation, a sense of profound embeddedness, which brought the melancholy.

The American woman with the short hair sticking out from beneath her cloth hat said as we had ascended: 'These roads sure remind me of the ones in central Zaire.'

'More like the roads in Zambia or Angola,' Geoff with the ear-ring countered.

The young Scot asked the question which perhaps the Americans had been hoping for. Yes, they said, they had worked all over Africa. Geoff had also worked in South America. But Africa was his first love. 'It just has a grandeur you can never get away from.'

Outside the jolting vehicle, grey light had revealed a mountainous landscape, and by the track side, a view of low walls built of lava which divided the steeply sloping ground into fields. The soil in the fields showed moist and black, and already rows of women, and a few men, worked among the lush green of the rows of crops.

'Look at it,' Geoff said. 'Isn't this primeval? You see it like it's been for hundreds of years, maybe for ever. Hand-tilled fields; women with babies on their backs; a huge landscape of absolute grandeur.'

When the vehicle could go no further, we got out and stood on a grassy bank, gazing down into a thousand valleys, each one filled with early mist. Behind us, the gaunt slopes of Sabinyo caught the first rays of the sun. At the base of the highest slopes, the forest began. The tops of the densely growing trees provided a yellowish sheen to the folds and slopes and ravines up there on the sides of the old volcano, especially in the young sunlight as it spread rapidly downwards.

Geoff adjusted the knot of his chiffon scarf and then pointed. 'You see the summit? That's the junction of the three countries. The ridge running down there, pointing north, that's the border between Uganda and Zaire. And beyond this ridge here in front of us, running east, is the devastated country of Rwanda. Now, see the forest on the northern slope. Right there. That's where the gorillas are, and that's where we're going.'

'It's wonderful to be here, out in the open again,' the American woman said. 'We're having a welcome day off from dysentery.'

'Is this your first time to see the gorillas?' Geoff's question was generally directed. We all nodded. 'Just you wait till you see them,' he said, crinkling his nose in an expression of affection and delight. 'Oh, man, they're real neat.'

When the rangers were ready, we began to walk. We followed each other in single file along a path which ran through deep grass above the line of the last of the lava walls and fields all blackened with ancient ash. The air pierced the lungs in refreshing gulps. Wet grass swayed against our legs. The sun grew warm. And it seemed, as the mist below evaporated, that we could see halfway across Uganda from our pathway trailing up towards the forest.

One of the rangers carried a machete, the other an automatic weapon, and I could hear Geoff expressing his disapproval about the latter. 'The trouble is I've seen too often just what guns can do to animals and people.' The young Scot, long hair held in place with an elasticised head band, asked whether Geoff had been in the Angolan war. 'I saw some of it,' Geoff replied. I heard him say that he used to fly out to Windhoek, 'a funny little colonial town', for his periods of rest and relaxation. And then he told the Scot: 'I've come to know Africans pretty well, and do you know they're very emotional. In Angola, for example, I developed a friendship with one of my helpers, a really nice young guy. We got on very well. I was teaching him the basics of some medical stuff. But when it came time for me to move on, this fellow became withdrawn and silent, quite sullen really. Strange, huh? The sad thing is I heard he was killed not long after I had left. Land-mine.'

We had entered the bottom edges of the forest. The air went cool, the light pale green. Lichen grew thick on the trunks of the trees, and our pathway cut through a profusion of undergrowth and ferns. We climbed steeply now, using moss-covered rocks as steps sometimes; and our voices had been reduced in the new environment to low murmurings as we moved expectantly forward.

After an hour, we stopped. Geoff gulped down some water, while one of the trackers went forward alone. When he returned, we moved off the pathway which in any case had grown faint. I heard the swish and slice of the machete cutting through the undergrowth. We walked neck-deep in ferns. The tracker had begun to call to the gorillas, a sort of humming sound made with the lips closed. A breathlessness had come upon us.

'I can definitely smell them,' Geoff whispered. 'They're very close.'

We had come upon a new pathway which tunnelled through the undergrowth. We began to crawl on hands and knees. A sudden bark broke the silence. We waited. We crawled forward. I caught a glimpse of something moving beyond thick foliage, then it was gone. We changed direction, crawling forward. The wet machete was sent forward once more, the wide blade passing close to my face en route. I heard a new pathway being cut. Our hands and knees were black with volcanic ash, and even the dust on the fronds of the ferns showed black. Again the bark, but from a different direction, and sounding further away.

'I knew I should have worn my good cologne,' Geoff said in a low voice, looking back with a grin at those who followed.

Then with that swift thrill of the unexpected, something charged through the undergrowth at us, then stopped. We lowered ourselves in submission, as the rangers had instructed, and kept our eyes fixed to the ground. The front ranger began again to hum his greeting. We were half lying on the wet earth, close to the roots of the undergrowth. Slowly we looked up.

I saw the big dark shape, seeming silvered between front and rear limbs. I saw the young: small black bundles frolicking among roots, disappearing up a bank. And then, for a second, the adult turned its shaggy head. I saw its face. I was lying on wet earth and decayed vegetation high up on the central spine of Africa, and I saw the out-turned nostrils exhaling breath, the black eyes, the furrows of curiosity and puzzlement between them, the eyes themselves bright, unabashed, fierce yet composed, and engaging mine so that I felt compelled to bow my head once more.

When I looked again, the gorilla had gone. But in my mind I carried the imprint of that brief glimpse I had been afforded into a face of unutterable innocence.

I undertook the long drive north to Kampala, Uganda's capital city, with a man named Joseph. As I had arranged, I found him waiting for me in Kisoro village when we returned at midday from our walk on the volcano. Joseph offered his hand with a friendly smile, asking if I had enjoyed the gorillas; and then we set out immediately.

The scattered houses of Kisoro soon fell behind. High on our right, we had a good view of the three volcanoes, some cloud now strung out across the face of the mountain I had not long before descended. Closer at hand, we passed the refugee camp where Geoff and his American companion worked as medics. Blue plastic sheeting had been fastened over innumerable low structures made of grass; and on the verges of the road scores of women, some wrapped in colourful cloth, walked in single file with bags and baskets of food balanced elegantly on their heads.

Then we drove into the hills and valleys of a high and voluptuous country, intensively cultivated even where the land was steepest, and with some moist mist blowing every now and then across the road. Joseph turned on the car's wipers for a few seconds to clear the windscreen of the gatherings of fine drops.

The road, brown and often muddy, twisted through valleys and then climbed in zigzags to the hilltops. The vistas stretched away in a beguiling softness to the eye, and they were all filled with the intricate quality of patchwork. Thousands of fields followed the contours of the hills. No land was wasted. The fields changed in colour from the rich black-brown of earth freshly tilled, to the silver sheen of young crops growing, to a lushness of maturity and then the slight yellow hues which heralded the harvest time. Beans, millet, Irish and sweet potatoes, but largely beans, Joseph explained.

The houses of the people were scattered between the fields; and the people themselves could be seen on the pathways, or at work in the fields. Much of the country had once been littered with lava, and heaps of grey rock had been collected into the corners of fields, or served as walls between the changing gradient of the contours, or stood in neat rows along the length of other fields, leaving broad uncluttered passageways for the crops. The moving of these stones had been the work of centuries; and everywhere, through vista after vista, the sense in the gentle light was of a venerable husbandry still preserved.

I asked Joseph to stop the car once, and I stood for a few moments on the edge of the tumbling away of a steep valley. The gentle landscape filled my eyes. White smoke spiralled up from the burning of excess vegetation (wastages, Joseph called these smouldering piles) at many points across my view. An outline of hills stood pale and indistinct beyond the hills that I could see. A fine drizzle sifted down. And the calling of the women as they worked the soil came from near and far, like a powerful yet consonant singing with distant descants, sounds which punctuated a silence which had reigned in a vast fecundity since last the volcanoes had sparked and roared.

For over an hour we drove through such country. Then we went into places of indigenous forest and tall bamboo, and Joseph advised me not to take photographs as the army had a base somewhere in there among the trees.

We got to Kabale in the pouring rain. On the approach to the town, the road ran through meadows where fat cattle stood up to their bellies in tufted grass, and rows of trees bowed laden with rain, and the fences were made of stout timber poles; and in another place, I saw a pit for the hand-sawing of timber, with mounds of sodden sawdust to one side.

The tarred road began in Kabale, and the rain had filled to overflowing all the indentations down the main street. We splashed quite briskly through these, and then Joseph stopped the car outside a row of small shops. 'We should buy food here,' he said in his pleasant way. 'We will only get to Mbarara in the evening.'

I met a friendly man, a pharmacist from Pakistan, as I wandered through the shops. He had a salt-and-pepper beard, and he wore half spectacles without frames and a black and white turban. A child sat on the counter, and from time to time the shadow of a woman passed in the background. It seemed that he had married a Ugandan, and I asked if he had spent an extended period in Kabale.

'Yes, yes, long time,' he replied. 'Uganda is my country now. But with Amin, we ran away to Nairobi. I was young man then.'

I remarked on the beauty of the country: the mountains, the extensive agriculture on the steep hillsides, visible in the distance even from the door of his diminutive shop. He nodded quite vigorously. 'Oh, yes. Fine country. Sometimes it remind us of north Pakistan.'

He used the plural now because we had been joined by another man, his round face unshaven, who wore a loose-fitting smock and strong sandals. 'A missionary,' the shopkeeper told me. The man in the smock smiled in a slightly oblivious way, and I realised he could speak no English.

'He is staying with me,' the pharmacist explained, looking at me over the top of his half spectacles. 'Often men come from Pakistan, paying own expenses, to be missionary for three months in Africa.'

'Nairobi,' the unshaven missionary said, and then pointed at his sandals.

'Pilgrimages,' the pharmacist interpreted. 'The missionaries walk to Nairobi, preaching on the way. The mission is to bring peace to the world. Yes, Islamic religion. Islam is everywhere.'

He went to fetch something behind the counter of his shop. The missionary smiled at me with his round face. I saw a few drops of rain make perfect circles in the frequent puddles littering the surface of the road. The pharmacist returned, paging through a substantial-looking book. 'Addresses of Islam,' he said, showing me some of the pages with English addresses, clearly assuming I was from that country.

Next door to the Pakistani pharmacist's shop, I found one devoted to the hiring of videos. A Ugandan woman with almond-shaped eyes and near-black skin asked me my business, and then allowed me to browse among the modest collection of films. I came across Cat on a Hot Tin Roof, Rocky V, The Sound of Music, Exorcist III, and also The Raid on Entebbe. The cardboard slipcase protecting this last cassette was well worn, suggesting extensive use.

'I have seen that film a few times,' Joseph said as we drove on a good tarred road towards Mbarara. 'Also many times I have watched The Rise and Fall of Idi Amin. This is our history.'

I saw the splashes of colour of school uniforms worn by walking children strung out along the roadside. The uniforms were orange and white in a landscape of deep green under low grey skies. Sometimes rusting corrugated-iron houses showed between the banana trees, with black-skinned women on the paths which wound towards them. On the road itself, numbers of United Nations and Red Cross vehicles lumbered towards Rwanda or the Rwandan refugee camps in eastern Zaire. Tarpaulins flapped against the loads they covered as the rain came down once more.

Our minds lingered on 1976, however, when hostages from a hijacked French aircraft flown to Uganda's Entebbe Airport had been rescued by raiding Israeli commandos. I asked Joseph if he had been old enough to be aware of these events.

He nodded. 'We saw the tanks going to the airport, but I think that was after the Israelis had already left. We knew nothing for sure. You didn't talk too loudly about things like that. They could kill you just for talking. That is why everyone wanted to see the film, to find out what had happened.'

Joseph told me then about his life. He had been born and attended school in a village which actually straddled the equator; but at eighteen years old he had moved to Kampala to attend a driving school, having decided by then that driving would become his career. This was not long after the expulsion of Asians from Uganda in 1972, and not long before the Entebbe Raid.

'For a long time I didn't know what was happening. I just went on living. But you heard things. Sometimes there was shooting. And by then most people knew that Amin was killing everybody he thought was against him. He also killed the educated, the intellectuals.'

I wondered if some of his memories were not now mixed up with scenes from the films he had seen. He spoke about a chief justice who had angered Amin by releasing a foreign journalist whose writings had not flattered the Amin regime. The chief justice had been drugged and taken to the soldiers' barracks and killed. 'Killed, just like that,' Joseph said, clicking his fingers. 'Yes, there is this scene in the film, The

Rise and Fall of Idi Amin. I will show you when we get to Kampala. Do you want to see?'

I nodded. I could see that his eyes had become slightly inflamed, as if haunted by a memory of the tortured times through which he had lived. Yet his assessment of events in Uganda's post-colonial history seemed thoughtful.

'The expelling of the Asians did no good,' he said as we drove through steadily driving rain. 'The worst thing Amin did was to give the Asian businesses to people who could not run them. Peasants became the owners of warehouses full of hardware, for example. But there was no responsibility, no experience in replacing stock or keeping books. So very quickly — in three years — there was nothing in the shops. Another problem was that when it came to spares for machinery, even motor cars, most of the sources of supply in East Africa were owned or run by Indians. There was not much co-operation with the new African owners in Uganda. This is understandable, I think,' he said with a slight smile. 'But it meant that times were hard.'

Uganda's president since 1986, Yoweri Museveni, had now invited the Asians to return and reclaim their property. Many had done so. Some of the Africans who had gained by their expulsion were embittered by this turn of events, Joseph said; but most people were pleased to see the Asians back. It meant well-stocked shops and renewed competition. 'They're good for the economy,' Joseph commented, nodding his head.

'Life is improving in Uganda now,' he went on. 'People are getting confident again. The government is encouraging foreign investment. Also we have solved the problem of the soldiers. The trouble has always been with them. Obote's soldiers, Amin's soldiers, then Obote's soldiers again, after the war with Tanzania. The soldiers had power only through their weapons. But that problem has now been solved.'

I asked him how, but for a moment he remained silent. A line of heavy vehicles threw up dense white spray which smothered our windscreen as Joseph pulled out to pass. Some of the trucks were piled high with green bananas, and on top of the bananas men sheltered under their ragged coats held up like tents against the weather.

'Two things have happened,' Joseph said. 'First, they have learned about political science. Second, they have learned about the firearms. Do you know that after the overthrow of Obote in 1986, the country began for the first time to govern itself?'

He explained that in each village now democratically elected resistance committees had been established. And it was first the members of these committees who had learned about political science and weapons. But now thousands of other people had also learned.

'In political science the people learn why there was colonialism, why dictatorships came so easily to Uganda, what is democracy, all those things. Then Museveni also said: the people have always been harassed by those with guns. Therefore the people must learn to use the guns as well. That will take away some of the soldiers' power.'

The landscape in which we travelled rolled forward into the mists of the rain. I remembered how, from the hotel garden in Kisoro on the evening before my climb to the gorillas, I had seen a man outside his hut testing the mechanism of an automatic rifle. Perhaps he was the secretary for defence of the Kisoro resistance committee, balancing the power of the military with a weapon-based power inside the community itself.

Joseph was telling me of these things as we drove down from the mountains towards Mbarara in the evening time. His voice was essentially one of optimism, one belonging to a man who had seen dark days but who looked at the future with more confidence now.

'We are governing ourselves; we are solving our problems. Before, we had cheap politics that was all about personal power and ambition. No longer.'

Variations of these words he repeated several times as he steered the car into lower lying and drier country. Although not yet forty, Joseph's hair was receding; his eyes showed habitually friendly and patient; and he had slightly protruding front teeth which brought a prominence to his mouth, especially when he smiled.

The chairman of the resistance committee was often the poorest man in the village, he told me. This was because he could understand all the problems being faced by other villagers. The villagers would invariably choose a man like that when it came to the voting.

This form of Ugandan democracy seemed to fascinate Joseph. At any level democracy fascinated him, and I wondered if he looked upon it as some sort of knack, like the ability to balance which suddenly comes when one is learning to ride a bicycle. He described the workings of the constituent assembly at national level which was currently engaged in debating the pros and cons of multiparty democracy.

But for the community processes he reserved something almost like reverence which was coloured with a glowing pleasure, as if it amazed him that mere human minds could have thought through such inventions to keep at bay the terrors of dictatorship and anarchy. He offered a vivid description of how things worked in the villages.

'They hold a big meeting of the villagers where members of the resistance council are nominated. Those nominated must leave the meeting. They must excuse themselves. Then the people who have nominated them must speak about their choices. Why have they made the nomination? Then there is a public debate on any possible weaknesses in the candidates. Then the candidates come back to the meeting and each talks to the people for five minutes about what they plan to do.

'For the voting, the candidates stand in a line with their backs to the public, and all the people line up behind the candidate of their choice to be counted. Now here's an important thing,' Joseph said, his face caught in the pleasure he derived from such procedures. 'No voting is allowed to take place after six p.m., so that nobody can say they couldn't see properly who they were voting for.'

When we got to Mbarara, the rain had stopped, although the sky was still overcast. Only in one small westward place, the clouds had broken to allow through a few slanting rays of sunlight. Marabou storks with large wattles hanging at their throats sat preening themselves on top of the hotel's façade. The darkening air felt warm as I got out of the car, certainly warmer than the chill of the damp mountains on Africa's spine the evening before.

I got into conversation with a man from Northern Ireland in the hotel bar and we ended up having dinner together. He introduced himself as Gordon, and told me he had something to do with the administration of mission hospitals in Uganda, and how they linked with and in many areas formed the backbone of the state health system.

We began our conversation by commenting on all the rain which had fallen in the south and through which, we discovered, we had both driven. But the conversation quickly broadened into a range of other topics. Gordon had an open face and sharp blue eyes beneath a shiny pate. He had originally come to Uganda from Hillsborough in County Down in 1967. For the worst of the Amin years, he had moved away, but now he had been back for nearly eight years.

'Things are definitely on the up here now,' he said. 'Just look at how the buildings are being repainted in Kampala. You're driving there tomorrow? It's like a small renaissance.'

When I asked why he thought this was so, he replied in an accent which still had a lilt to it: 'If you ask me, I think it's the returning Asians who are responsible. Some Africans are already expressing concern at how many are coming back, and no wonder. They're already dominating the economy once more.'

We talked, inevitably enough, of those years when Amin had been in power: 1971 to 1979. But the whole post-colonial experience had been a nightmare for this most beautiful of places. At independence, Uganda had been the richest country in east and central Africa. By the early 1980s when

Obote returned himself to power via an unfair election, professors from one of Africa's finest universities, Makerere in Kampala, had been reduced to begging on the streets. But Obote proved to be as ruthless as Amin, perhaps even worse, and it was not until Museveni had taken control in 1986 that the situation in the collapsed country began to stabilise and then gradually improve.

'He's an impressive man, this Museveni,' Gordon told me. 'I've heard him speak twice, once at the cathedral and once at Makerere where he said that Uganda faced three serious tasks: maintaining security, building the economy, and fighting moral degradation. He said the first two tasks were being attended to. But he said that moral degradation might well undo everything that was being done. He was clearly talking about corruption and graft. I thought it remarkable that he spoke in such a candid way, implicitly criticising most of his own civil service. He's a new breed of leader, an intellectual, not particularly interested in self-aggrandisement. Have you noticed his likeness doesn't appear on the bank notes? That's unusual for black Africa, so far as I can recall.'

But over dinner talk turned once more to Amin. 'He was like a chief of the last century,' Gordon said, his bald head reflecting the few lights hung above the nearby buffet. 'He wanted and he enjoyed absolute power. He was an uneducated jester, and also a ruthless butcher. He killed hundreds of thousands of his own people. Yes, he was tribal in outlook, being a Kakwa from the north west of the country. He was also a Muslim. But I don't think it was tribalism, and certainly not his religion, which motivated his darker side so much as a colossal self-indulgence. He found himself in a situation where there were no constraints. He could do anything he liked.'

But Gordon seemed at pains to objectify this view. He remarked that it brought understanding no clearer to dismiss Amin as a product of savage and undisciplined Africa. 'I'm tired of that view which seems to me to be almost completely racist. Hasn't Europe had its share of men like Amin this century? I'll tell you an interesting thing. When I got back to Kampala in the early 1980s for the second time, a Ugandan lawyer suggested ironically to me that I was coming to Africa to escape the tribal warfare raging in Northern Ireland!

'You will remember that my country was burning at the time. But the comment took me by surprise. I wanted to say: hang on, tribal warfare is for primitive people, for Africans. But when I thought more clearly about it, I realised there was considerable truth to the gibe.'

In the morning, Joseph and I continued on our way to Kampala. The chaotic streets of Mbarara looked fresh from the rain, and hundreds of people rode on their bicycles in bright sunlight, clogging the main road or weaving on the muddy verges between the stalls of food and tethered chickens flapping on the ground. Large bunches of green bananas had been piled on straining trestles, and Joseph stopped once to haggle in a friendly way and then to buy. He placed the bananas in the boot.

I asked him, as we drove on, about his family. He told me he had five children ranging from thirteen years to seven months. 'We are working all the time just for survival,' he said. 'But we are given the family by God, so it is not a burden. It is the normal way of having a life.'

We drove through scintillating morning air and a luxuriant landscape. The broad leaves of banana trees flashed green, and in the fertile earth stood harvests of millet and sorghum and sweet potatoes. Lush creepers grew up electricity poles, and sometimes clung to the tapering pinnacles of the frequent anthills. New silver pylons without wires marched across the verdant country, following the same path as the line of timber poles covered with creepers.

Joseph was enjoying the drive. He had lowered his window so that crisp air rushed into his face. He looked across at me with a friendly smile. 'Do you notice? No road-blocks. All the way from Kisoro, not one. That is a sign of peace. I remember in the old days: there would be twenty road-blocks between

Kisoro and Kampala. Asking for ID. Asking for money. I used to get fed-up. No, they never tried to shoot me.

'But sometimes the soldiers became uncontrollable,' he went on. 'Especially when Obote came back after the war with Tanzania. They would walk in the streets, shooting anything they wanted. I have seen them shoot the dogs for fun while taking money from the people. Most court cases against the soldiers were dismissed. The soldiers were looking for money. Looting had become the only way. There was little money, and what there was had lost value. The Uganda shilling — it was worth nothing. But now. Now it is better. See how the people are building?'

We had glimpses of rough timber scaffolding as we drove through straggling villages; men on planks and balancing on drums before half-completed walls, trowels and bricks in their hands. We had a brief sight too of the flat blue of Lake Victoria in the distance before us, and then our way descended into acacia country and the roadsides became littered with driven herds of long-horned cattle. I had a sense that we drove through antiquity now: the ancient landscape flattened with age and filled with the yellow of blossom on the thorn trees, and the cattle themselves, their sharp horns curving skyward. Their ancestors had come to Africa five thousand years before the birth of Christ, an astonishing thought as the sunlight glanced across their well-fed flanks. Since then there had been considerable interbreeding, especially with imports brought to the east coast by Arab and Indian traders from the seventh century AD. Now the coats of the cattle were black or brown or white, or often a combination of all three. And above the lowing herds, flights of storks flapped slowly in the direction of the lake. We drove in silence, as if the better to absorb such splendours.

And then, by the roadside, a rusting metal carcass tilted at an angle and half concealed in long and graceful grass. 'One of Amin's tanks,' Joseph said with a slight smile in his friendly eyes.

More evidence of the Tanzanian counter-invasion in Masaka, an untidy scattered town hardly 90 kilometres from the border. Destroyed buildings still lay in heaps of concrete rubble all softened with the growth of weeds.

'Here, for a while, Amin's soldiers resisted. Then they ran away. Some were caught, but others got rid of their uniforms and mixed with the civilians.

'But it was not a good time for the people here,' Joseph went on, his patient eyes gazing out into the thriving streets. 'People got caught in the cross-fire. Amin's soldiers were looting and raping as they ran. People could get killed at any moment. The Tanzanian soldiers also looted to get food, and, in Kampala, they liked to have the watches. Many Tanzanian soldiers were wearing Uganda watches. With the Tanzanians came Uganda exiles, including Museveni. Yes, the people were happy when they came. You see, they were fed-up with Amin. I was in Kampala when the soldiers came, but Amin had long ago escaped.'

The streets of Masaka were choked with buses. Many were going to Kampala. A few were marked for Kisumu and Nairobi in the east; others headed to Kigali or Bukoba in the south. The roof-racks were piled high with bundles and boxes, baskets and bags; and the buses bounced on the rough ground where they stopped to set down and pick up new passengers. Vendors cried their wares while the smoke of cooking fires faintly smudged the scene. I saw a young man with a T-shirt bearing the slogan, Africa in the Year 1994.

'People have long ago forgotten the past, the war, and are looking forward now,' Joseph said. 'That is the way for human beings. But we have learned from the past so that we try not to make the same mistakes again. One thing I have seen. You can't dictate to people. If you try, then you are a dictator.'

On the road to Kampala now, close to the lake but with the water unseen, the country had flattened to broad plains, and the stalls at the roadside sold smoked fish. But it was not at these temptations where Joseph soon stopped. He chose instead young men holding aloft tethered chickens. The young men clustered around him, and I heard the chatter of their bargaining above the squawks of the upside-down chickens. Joseph made his choice and placed the chicken, bound but still living, into the boot with the bunch of bananas.

'For the family,' he explained. 'When I go away, I must always buy for them to eat.'

We passed women by the roadside, walking in single file; and men walking with hoes towards the fields. The women, Joseph pointed out, carried small bundles of banana fibre, to be used later to tie the bundles of fire-wood which they were going to collect. Big trucks trundled south, belching black smoke. We went into a patch of high natural forest with hornbills flapping and gliding across the road. The earth and undergrowth beneath the trees showed wet and dark. We came to an accident: a small lorry with crooked wheels standing sideways off the road and green bananas strewn everywhere about the tarmac. A few armed soldiers lolled at the scene.

Joseph stopped momentarily as the road crossed the equator, its position marked by two concrete circles facing each other across the road. Beyond, on either side, stood a few houses surrounded by banana trees and the sheen of young beans studding the surface of freshly turned earth. 'So you were born right in the middle of the world,' I said. Joseph smiled as he replied: 'Yes, this is the middle.'

He sauntered among roadside stalls to buy some vegetables, no doubt to go with the chicken which still lay in the boot of the car. I watched as he selected onions, avocados, tomatoes and large purple egg-plants. Women in long skirts sat in the shade of the stalls and the trees beyond. Children played languidly as the heat of the day increased. The shade seemed almost black, the sunlight brilliant on the green of the vegetation. Chickens scratched through the pumpkins and blackjacks growing under the ever-present banana trees. Some of the stalls had been ornamented with sprays of crimson bougainvillaea flowers.

The road to Kampala seemed to ascend as we continued along it. Joseph turned on the radio in the car, and we listened to the end of a choral work, at first a soprano solo, and then the fuller sounds of an entire choir. The houses stood close together by the roadside now, and the muddy verges carried a growing stream of pedestrians, carts, bicycles, goats and small children kicking through the puddles. Shops stood in long and untidy rows, some of them with a date inscribed at the apex of their simple stepped façades. Most had been built in the early 1990s.

Advertising hoardings began to litter the horizon as we entered the city. On one of them, in gigantic letters, was emblazoned this message: Get Rich From Scrap. Joseph said incongruously, as if articulating the outcome of a succession of thoughts: 'Planning for survival: that's life. And if you can survive, anything can come your way. There's always that chance.'

A keen consciousness of the past, both colonial and African, pervaded Kampala. The publicity brochures referred to a 'beautiful city set on seven hills', like Rome. It was also described as the capital of a country known as 'the pearl of Africa' or 'the cradle of the Nile'. The Speke Hotel, named after the explorer John Hanning Speke, reminded modern travellers of the great European obsession regarding the source of the Nile. The bars in Kampala served Nile special beer, and many of the eating places Nile perch. The great river's source lay 80 kilometres to the east of Kampala where rapids, first seen by Speke in 1862, drew water from the inexhaustible supply of Lake Victoria. In those pre-colonial days, the present land within Uganda's borders had been divided among several independent kingdoms, the largest and most powerful being Buganda, which had been centred on the hills now occupied by Kampala.

The evenings in the city, lying just north of the equator but at a high altitude, were invariably cool, conducive to going out. In one restaurant I tried, two black pianists played soft jazz while people dined by candle-light. Beyond the glass of one of the restaurant walls, light played on neat lawns and in the intricate foliage of shrubs and flowers breathing slightly in a night breeze. Only once in Kampala I saw bullet holes sprayed across the mosaic façade of a building. 'That's from long ago,' my taxi driver told me when I pointed out the disfigurement. 'It's peaceful here now. There are many police. People can walk freely anywhere at night. Except at the market. There they snatch your bag.'

On one of Kampala's graceful hills the British had established a fort in 1890. On another, called Kasubi, lay buried the Buganda kings. Such diverse histories had settled like a web across the city. All through the 19th century the Buganda kings had resisted domination by an increasing European presence. Protestant and Catholic missionaries had in turn found favour and been persecuted. I visited a church outside Kampala which had been built to commemorate twenty-two Catholics who were killed by a Buganda king named Mwanga in 1886. These Ugandan martyrs had been canonised in 1967; and their church, built inside a structure of twenty-two interlocking steel supports, had been named The Minor Basilica during a visit of Pope John Paul II in 1993. The martyrs were depicted in stained-glass windows ranged around the walls of the circular church. Inside stood a life-size wood carving of their leader, a young man of twenty-five, baptising the youngest, a frightened boy of thirteen. An earlier Pope had travelled to Uganda in 1967 to hold a mass for the Church's then newest saints. I asked the young woman who showed me the church and told me these things if she had met the Pope in 1993. 'I met him,' she said in a gentle voice, her eyes filled with quiet joy.

Yet such details served largely to enmesh the mind with doubt. Was it not in 1967 that Idi Amin had led the Ugandan army into the Buganda palace to smash the power of the kings? He had been acting on Obote's orders, true enough, but such a deed had helped to pave the way for his own autocracy as well. The British had engineered an independence which made Obote prime minister and the Buganda king president of Uganda. But such arrangements could not last in the presence of those almost demented appetites for absolute power. Amin's house still stood near the summit of another of Kampala's hills. It had welded gates of black metal, but I glimpsed the house itself, suburban more than imposing, yet commanding sweeping views of the city. Journalists had found pictures of aeroplanes and tanks stuck to Amin's bedroom walls, and empty beer bottles had littered the cupboards.

I thought of these things as I sat without shoes in the large grass building on Kasubi Hill where the Buganda kings were buried. I sat with other tourists on mats on the floor. The dome of the structure was supported by a score of stout timber poles, all dressed in bark cloth. Cutting off one side of the interior, a fence of gleaming spears and skin shields demarcated the area where the kings were buried. Along the fence had been affixed framed pictures of this line of proud and illustrious African kings. My attention settled on Mwanga, the king who had provided the Catholic Church with twenty-two martyrs and saints, the king also who had reigned through the coming of colonialism. Uganda saw no settlers, yet the transformations caused by Europe's demands were often brutal. Coffee, coffee, coffee, shouted the English administrators to the Ugandan farmers, the ancestors of those whom I had seen working in their contoured fields in the hills and mountains so close to the gorillas.

The Irishman, Gordon, had told me when I saw him briefly during my few days in Kampala, that the local word for coffee and the local word for whip had been the same.

So here was King Mwanga, staring out at me from the spears and shields in front of his grave: a youngish face, big-lipped and broad-nosed. He sat with his hands clasped together in his lap. Was that confusion in those sullen eyes of his, or only anger? No answers here, in the twilight of the grass-built mausoleum. Only a sense of the old being overtaken, yet asserting itself again. I listened to the twittering of the tourists and the soft voices of the African guides. To one side sat elderly women, working silently with their hands. I saw that they were making mats. They were the descendants of the widows of the various Buganda kings, still keeping vigil as they had done through all the change and turmoil that had battered this once proud African kingdom. The air in the gloom of the mausoleum smelled rich with a mouldering past.

Yet how quickly fortunes changed. On another hill in Kampala stood an unfinished mosque, half-built concrete domes still caged in scaffolding, and a soaring minaret which changed direction halfway up, a fault in the building, a kink which glared like a failed joke across half the city. 'Amin commissioned this,' Gordon said in his lilting accent as we drove beneath it one afternoon. 'We call it Amin's folly. It's probably the only monument Kampala will ever want of that disgusting rascal.'

One of the dominating landmarks in downtown Kampala, with its streets choked with traffic and pedestrians, was the pale and complex structure of the Hindu temple. Strange that this symbol of the Asian presence should have remained intact in a city where thousands of Asian shops and homes had been so eagerly expropriated. The walls were filled with horizontal ledges, and lower down with reliefs of sacred Hindu figures. In the concrete yard stood the statue of a white cow, and coloured lights had been strung about the various porticoes. I found a way, one afternoon, through the security fence which surrounded the temple. Ablution facilities stood to one side, an entrance to the actual building to the other. A white-haired old man with thick spectacles welcomed me inside. I sat down on a chair and looked around.

The interior was characterised by columns holding up ornate arches which resembled the inside of cog wheels painted in pastel pinks, blues and mauve. The columns themselves resembled painted cotton reels placed one on top of the other. Around the edges of the interior space smaller archways gave access to individual shrines, containing images and bowls of fruit and lighted candles sometimes. The windows of the temple stood wide open and the clatter of the city tumbled in.

'The real beauty,' the old Indian with white hair and thick-lensed spectacles said, 'is that there was no metal used in the building. It was built by Indian architects who specialise in temples.'

I asked when.

The old man looked at me with shrewd eyes slightly magnified behind the lenses of his spectacles. 'It was started in 1954 and we opened it in 1962.'

'The year of independence,' I remarked.

'Yes,' the old Indian replied with a smile, 'the year of independence. And it has never closed since then. Always we have worshipped here.'

'Even through the Amin years?'

'There were not many of us, but we never closed the temple.'

I asked him why he had not gone with the rest of the ejected Asians in 1972. His enlarged eyes glinted in amusement. He told me that he had made himself indispensable to the Amin regime. He had been a supplier of laboratory and scientific equipment, including chemicals. He had been one of several, but the others had fled, and Amin had asked him finally to stay on.

'But they suspected me of loading the prices,' he said. 'They even sent spies to Nairobi to check on the prices there. But they found I was even cheaper than Nairobi.'

'How did you manage that?'

The old Indian laughed. He looked at me with his bright and magnified eyes. 'I had a blood brother somewhere,' he said evasively. 'He supplied me at less than cost. In that way, he helped me to survive. And in return I looked after the temple.

'All those years we would worship here,' he went on. 'Other temples were destroyed. All the statues destroyed. Amin made some of the temples into mosques. Others became night-clubs. But this temple was not touched. Every week we worshipped here, and then we would sit outside on the steps and talk about the day-to-day events. It was not easy to find out what was going on. But some of us had short-wave radios: we listened to BBC, and also to German and Indian radio to keep us in touch with reality.'

I asked if the remaining Indians had been harassed. He shook his head. 'There was one man, but he was not quite right — ' he tapped at his own forehead to indicate the nature of the problem. 'The army wanted to take his car, but he hesitated to give over the keys. They killed him on the spot. That was a bad thing. But this was the soldiers, not the ordinary Africans. The ordinary Africans helped us a lot with food and water when times got hard.

'But the soldiers were very bad. They smashed the statues,' he repeated, his enlarged eyes glinting. 'And the torture. They would cut off hands and arms in stages. Little bit little bit,' he added, showing the stages on his own thin forearm. 'We heard that even Amin didn't like it. The trouble with Amin was that he had no education. He had a weak mind for decisions. And when everything collapsed — the roads, the hospitals, the clinics, the water supply and electricity, even the sewerage — he did nothing.'

But there was no rancour in his eyes. Indeed, there seemed to be a simple gratefulness as he added: 'It is only by God's grace that we are still here.'

Often, as my time in Kampala (and in central Africa generally) came to an end, I sensed the sceptre of Amin not far beneath the surface of the noisy city. His reign had scarred the city's psyche, bringing brutal specifics to a place where all Africa seemed embedded: a place so beautiful, yet so filled with disappointments and general memories of tyranny and want.

'He ate the flesh of his enemies,' Joseph said to me on my last evening in Kampala. In Joseph's eyes, for a second, his habitual expressions of friendliness and patience were clouded by rebuke.

He had come to see me at my hotel. He had driven me to his small house on the outskirts of the city. I had sat in an easy chair in a diminutive living-room without a ceiling and watched him unpack an obviously prized possession: a machine for playing video cassettes and a remote controller. After he had plugged this apparatus into his small television set, he inserted the film he wanted to share with me. It was on a plain cassette in a plain slipcase, obviously pirated. But the title soon enough appeared on the small screen before us: The Rise and Fall of Idi Amin.

The opening scenes appeared to take place in an operating theatre. 'This is how it always starts,' Joseph said, sitting on the edge of his chair. Some of his children had gathered about him. I could hear his wife at the cooking fire outside. Then Joseph pressed a button on the remote control and the images burst into absurd rapidity. 'Wait,' he said, 'I want to show you.'

Suddenly we were confronted by a swaggering Amin, his chest emblazoned with ribbons and medals. Tanks and marching soldiers lumbered past. Joseph pressed the button again, engrossed in the images flickering before him. The picture steadied once more; and here were some severed heads in a refrigerator, and a voice saying: In Africa, power always means that a few heads must roll. 'Do you see that?' Joseph said in excited indignation. 'But sometimes I saw him riding a bicycle, just like any other man.'

He pressed the button again and released it just in time to see figures slump before a firing squad, then pressed it again and released it, again and again, thereby providing snippets of horror: Amin cutting a strip of flesh off the murdered body of Uganda's chief justice; Amin's chewing jaws; screaming Indian women and children pressing towards an aircraft; people being beaten to the ground. 'This was day to day,' Joseph said, his eyes seeming slightly inflamed as I had seen them when we had first spoken about this film on the road from Kisoro to Mbarara.

And the images became more brutal: clubbings, the cutting off of hands and ears, smashed faces in close-up, lancing blades, eyes in agony or terror, blood streaming from mouths and nostrils.

One of Joseph's children began to whimper. I could see how she had begun to rock her body rapidly to and fro in distress. Joseph placed a hand on her head, a consoling gesture which she accepted. But Joseph himself was hardly consoled. He sat forward, the remote controller gripped in tense hands. His patient eyes were transfixed with a sort of muted fear. This was his history here on the flickering screen before him. He could never forget that history — and in this way he mirrored the sense which I had caught in Kampala generally — nor could he free his spirit of its manifold horror.

In the early morning a fierceness of wind, and of thunder and lightning, descended on the quietened city. Then the rain came down in a deluge. I awoke to find the curtain of my room sodden, and the view from the window was of trees bent back and a darkness whitened somewhat by the spray from the driven torrent.

The day came as a low grey presence, and on the way to the airport, in the lower parts of town, brown water still churned along gutters and galloped round traffic circles, or lay in wide sheets where there was no escape. Thousands of people waded through, and occasionally an umbrella lent a dash of colour to the sodden scene. On the Entebbe road, water had engulfed a hundred shops and houses. Cars had sunk into a lake. Belongings and merchandise lay strewn on higher ground. Women with skirts hitched up stood with arms akimbo as if in defiance. Others with stiff brooms stooped forward in purposeful salvage.

Rain as excess, I thought, looking at traffic up to its axles in the flood. Rain as symbol of unrestraint. But now I wondered — and the process brought a chill — how close to such immoderation innocence lay.

I remembered then Kampala's independence statue. Every African capital had one. But I had found Kampala's to be the most surprising, offering more ambiguity than many of the others.

A slender sculpture stood on a white-washed plinth, flanked by two palm trees and a few unkempt flower beds. The sculpture depicted a woman, bound from the feet to the chest in broad flat bands of bronze. But her arms were free, and she held them crooked at the elbows as if in prayer, except that her hands had parted to release into the air above her head a small boy child with his own arms outstretched. The woman still held him by the legs as he prepared to soar upwards.

The key elements of the sculpture's broad intent were positioned high above the gaze of ordinary viewers. The woman's face, for example, could only be seen by a deliberate effort; and then the reward was mixed. No suffering here, in the face of Mother Africa, no extravagant pains of birth. Rather, the woman's eyelids drooped in an expression of patience and some slight satisfaction perhaps. The boy child's face seemed equally uncharacteristic. Here was no cliché of triumphant freedom. Here was something else entirely.

All at once, as the impact of these images coalesced, it looked as if the child's arms had been deliberately outstretched for crucifixion. I searched his expression again: and there it was, high up, the mouth open in a sort of transfigured delirium, or perhaps simply in stoical expectation of the nails and cross.

From the terminal building, I could see the old airport where the Israelis had raided, a few roofs, and the tall white walls and continuous windows of the control tower just visible from that distance. But I turned from such memories, lured away by the haunting vision of Kampala's independence sculpture and the equally haunting connection I had found between innocence and excess.

In the airport bookshop I found a volume of speeches by Yoweri Museveni, the Ugandan president. In one of the speeches, as I paged through the book, he asked: 'So why is Africa backward?' He then proceeded to isolate three main reasons. The first was geographical, he said, a topography of deserts and mountains and tropical forests which had 'prevented the easy spread of ideas and commerce'. The second related to a climate that was too comfortable to generate struggle which in turn would have engendered development, as a bad climate in Europe had done. The third reason was 'the intrusion of foreign forces into the affairs of Africa'. In short, slavery and colonialism. But such reasons gave rise to another question: why had independence not changed anything? Museveni did not mince his words. He pointed squarely to the first generation of independence politicians, the ruling élite who grew rich on the spoils of perpetuating a neo-colonialism under which ordinary Africans 'were crushed with a sense of impotence'. But Museveni rejected such impotence and the dejection and complacency it had inspired.

At this point I was obliged to put the book back on the shelf. I had heard a woman's voice on the loudspeakers, and I hurried out to catch my aircraft. But my thoughts continued. It seemed to me that what Museveni implied was this: Africa should believe in its own resources now, and no longer so stoically hold out its arms for crucifixion.

I sat in the aircraft, looking out at wet buildings and a wet corner of the concrete apron upon which the aircraft stood. I heard the doors close and felt the pressure change in my ears. While I waited for the aircraft to move, I had a sudden remembrance of myself lying in the wet leaves and volcanic ash high up on Africa's spine. I remembered the slight breathlessness of expectation as I had looked into a face of unutterable innocence then.

The aircraft charged down the runway and lifted clear. For a moment I saw the rippled waters of the lake beneath the wing. Then we went into clouds. When we emerged I could see that the clouds lay softly, like wool, to cosset the lake and all the lands surrounding it. We were in an unreality of sky. Yet the sense of innocence, and its chilling juxtaposition with excess, did not fade. We flew on into a rushing emptiness and into the brilliant sunshine of an African morning which sat high up, waiting for the clouds to clear.